The Edge of Chaos

2

THE EDGE OF CHAOS

Financial Booms, Bubbles, Crashes and Chaos

BERNICE COHEN

John Wiley & Sons

Chichester · New York · Brisbane · Toronto · Singapore

Copyright © Bernice Cohen 1997

Published by John Wiley & Sons Ltd,
Baffins Lane, Chichester
West Sussex PO19 1UD, England

National 01243 779777
International (+44) 1243 779777
e-mail (for orders and customer service enquiries): cs-books@wiley.co.uk
Visit our Home Page on http://www.wiley.co.uk
or http://www.wiley.com

Other Wiley Editorial Offices

John Wiley & Sons, Inc., 605 Third Avenue,
New York, NY 10158–0012, USA

Jacaranda Wiley Ltd, 33 Park Road, Milton,
Queensland 4064, Australia

John Wiley & Sons (Canada) Ltd, 22 Worcester Road,
Rexdale, Ontario M9W 1LI, Canada

John Wiley & Sons (Asia) Pte Ltd, 2 Clementi Loop #02–01,
Jin Xing Distripark, Singapore 129809

Library of Congress Cataloging-in-Publication Data

Cohen, Bernice.
    The edge of chaos : Financial booms, bubbles, crashes, and chaos /
Bernice Cohen.
        p.   cm.
    Includes bibliographical references and index.
    ISBN 0-471-97237-1 (cloth)   ISBN 0-471-96907-9 (pbk)
        1. Financial crises—History.   2. Stock exchanges—History.
3. Speculation—History.   4. Chaotic behavior in systems.
I. Title.
HB3722.C64   1996
338.5'42—dc20   96–34241
                                                              CIP

British Library Cataloguing in Publication Data

A catalogue record for this book is available from the British Library

ISBN 0-471-97237-1 (cased)   ISBN 0-471-96907-9 (paperback)

Typeset in 10/12pt Palatino from the author's disks by Dorwyn Ltd, Rowlands Castle, Hants
Printed and bound in Great Britain by Biddles Ltd, Guildford and Kings' Lynn
This book is printed on acid-free paper responsibly manufactured from sustainable forestation,
for which at least two trees are planted for each one used for paper production.

This book is dedicated to the memory of my dear father,
Abraham Jacob Deitsch,
still a source of great inspiration for all my endeavours.

CONTENTS

Consistent patterns of behaviour in crashes. The purpose of this book. Study the past. An era of rapid financial and monetary freedom.

Evocative terminology for crashes. A model for stock market extremes. Do rational markets boom? Chaos in our universe. After the boom, the crash. Anatomy of a crash. A brief historical overview of some major crashes. Dutch Tulipomania, the 1720 bubbles in the Mississippi and South Sea Companies. Twentieth-century crashes; 1929, 1987 and tempestuous weather. The chain reaction crash. The Japanese bubble (1982–92). A Chinese footnote. The global bond market bubble of 1993–4. The crash mentality.

Investor types. Introducing the irrational investor. Jekyll and Hyde investors. They got it right: they got it wrong. The basis for rational behaviour. The real stress factor. People don't change, but circumstances do.

The speculation mania. Imaginative new trading ideas. Fraudsters galore. The pinnacle in sight. The world economy at the peak. The technical view at the peak. Nagging doubts. The flood of selling. The aftermath.

ACKNOWLEDGEMENTS

Because the booms and crashes described in this book range over two centuries and across three different continents, Europe, America and Asia, a great deal of the detailed events and analysis has been taken primarily from a wide collection of historical accounts specific to each separate episode. The research that made this book possible rests squarely on a number of books which I want here to acknowledge.

The model for stock market booms and slumps that formed the starting point for my analysis was taken from *Manics, Panics and Crashes* by Charles P. Kindleberger.

For information on the Dutch Tulipomania I am indebted to *Crashes* by Robert Beckman and Peter M. Gerber's chapter, "Who put the mania in the Tulipomania?" in *Crashes and Panics*, edited by Eugene N. White. My main sources of reference for the Mississippi Bubble were *Cantillon, Entrepreneur and Economist* by A.E. Murphy, *John Law*, by Montgomery Hyde and John Carswell's *The South Sea Bubble*. I also obtained much valuable detail from these three books on the course and ramifications of the South Sea bubble itself, as the two great eighteenth century bubbles were so closely aligned.

For the Great Wall Street Crash of 1929, J.K. Galbraith's masterpiece *The Great Crash* is the undisputed reference work and I have included many important statistics from this account. In addition, I have included material from F.K. Allen's *Only Yesterday* and *The Day the Bubble Burst*, by G. Thomas and M. Morgan-Witts.

Information on the background to the long 1980s boom was provided from G. Blakey's *The Post-War History of the London Stock Exchange 1945 to 1992*. For information on the build-up to the October 1987 crash I have included the analysis provided by Brian Reading in *Japan, the Coming Collapse*, which was also a central source for the Japanese bubble of 1985 to 1989.

On the theory of chaos, much valuable information was found in James Gleick's *Chaos*, Ian Stewart's *Does God Play Dice?* and *The New Scientist Guide to Chaos*, edited by N. Hall. My reliance on graphic representations of stock market action, as evidence of chaos at work, has encouraged me to draw endless lines on my charts. So a hearty thank you goes to Reuters Holdings for producing all the charts, complete with my copious annotations, for Chapters 3, 4 and 5.

I should like to take this opportunity of expressing my grateful appreciation to Jim Slater for all his helpful comments on the manuscript and to the whole enthusiastic team of people at John Wiley, spearheaded by the publishing editor, Nick Wallwork who have laboured tirelessly to transform my manuscript into a book. Finally, a huge thank you goes, as ever, to my wonderful husband, Alan. I have a nagging suspicion that I may be highjacking his retirement, but he proves time and again that he is, without question, my better half.

PREFACE

This book has had a very long gestation. In 1984 my life-long interest in archaeology and history launched me onto a line of original research based on Professor Colin Renfrew's idea that civilisation is a "system". Having recently completed a Systems Analysis course I decided to investigate this interesting concept by treating civilisation as if it were a huge business concern about to have all its manual systems computerised. During the 1980s Systems Research was much in vogue and my research culminated in a trilogy of books, *The Cultural Science of Man*, which I published in 1987–88. Volumes I and II covered the structure and function of the "system", with Volume III devoted to the emergence of the modern world.

To promote my ideas, I embarked upon a lecture tour. During a 12-hour flight to Los Angeles, where I was due to speak at a conference, I read most of *Chaos* by James Gleick, and suddenly discovered that my Systems Research on civilisation and learned human behaviour was all about chaos in human behaviour. *The Edge of Chaos* is my first attempt to bring this notion into the public arena, as it focuses on one particular, highly mathematical aspect of human behaviour.

I have to admit that I have now become rather fixated on chaos, especially as it seemed to me that if it is the driving force that governs the markets, chaos should leave its imprint on all aspects of stock market behaviour. If so, then one should find a chaos explanation for almost everything that happens in the markets. After all, one cannot be only a little bit pregnant. As the reader will shortly see, this approach produces some rather unexpected and controversial explanations, which may sometimes seem rather contrived.

To build my case I have resorted extensively to a technique much used by researchers into the relatively young disciplines of chaos and complexity – namely, borrowing ideas freely from both these fields.

Adopting well-tried notions from other areas to probe into the complicated and poorly understood realm of the capital markets seemed an appropriate route to pursue. My confidence in this method was boosted by knowledge that Professor Robert May had shown that animal population cycles are governed by chaos. It may be a leap of faith, or simply lateral thinking, to suggest that populations of stocks should also be governed by chaos, but I have used this as a valid starting point.

No one has yet conclusively determined the mathematical underpinnings for chaos in the markets. *The Edge of Chaos* is really a journey into the unknown to try to discover whether chaos theory can offer any profound insights into how the markets work. Many people have begun to address this area and it is a fertile field for experimentation by fund managers hoping to benefit their clients financially from the use of chaos-based mathematics in their search for enhanced fund performance. I do not know if many of their attempts have yet proved fruitful, but intuitively, as the mathematical basis for chaos in the markets has not yet emerged, it seems logical to suppose that it would be difficult to profit from efforts to exploit mathematical chaos at the moment. That does not mean, however, that knowledgeable investors cannot benefit financially by using chaos concepts in their investment decisions, as I shall show in this book.

To date, although the mathematics remains unknown, this is also the case for some other highly complex examples of physical systems that are widely suspected to be driven by chaos. Turbulence in fluids is one of the best-known and most frustrating illustrations of this knowledge hiatus. As efforts to resolve the impasse continue unabated, it is to be hoped that ultimately, a satisfactory answer will emerge. So perhaps this will be true of chaos in stock markets. I believe a model of chaos-based markets, built by comparing similarities of features found in other examples where chaos has now generally been accepted as operating, offers a constructive way forward. Chaos in the social sciences is still in its infancy and this book, however incomplete, is an attempt to progress the issues.

Professor Ian Stewart of Warwick University suggests, "The essence of scientific observation is to be systematic". By examining the historical evidence for five of the most important and best-documented bubbles and crashes in the record of industrial capitalism, I hope to have adopted a systematic approach that relies on the use of a model and extensive comparisons to stimulate a lively and productive debate.

Bernice Cohen
London

CRASHES IN CONTEXT

Whole communities suddenly fix their minds upon one object, and go mad in its pursuit; millions of people become simultaneously impressed with one delusion, and run after it. . . .

Charles Mackay
Extraordinary Popular Delusions and the Madness of Crowds

Attitudes to stock market crashes seem strangely ambivalent. Viewed impartially, accounts of these spectacular incidents make riveting reading. Books about them are peppered with amusing anecdotes describing absurd investor behaviour. Their appeal no doubt, rests partly on our secret yearnings to effortlessly acquire fabulous wealth; or maybe we feel smug satisfaction when speculators emerge as greater fools, making and then losing colossal fortunes in double-quick time. Crashes hold a morbid fascination when we read of the ordeals and misfortunes to which their victims were swiftly and somehow inexplicably exposed, but there is surely more to our interest than that. For even as these dramas rouse our curiosity, so they prompt us to wonder why they should keep recurring.

On a personal level, since the global stock market crash of October 1987, many investors must harbour a nagging doubt that another horrendous collapse could be lurking in the future. However, not knowing why they happen or how to decide if one is looming leaves us floundering in an ignorant haze. Every autumn, especially when confidence is low, financial commentators and journalists dust down the hoary old crash nightmare scenario to add some spice to their reporting. It can be difficult to stay unruffled, as no one can be sure there will never be another shocking financial meltdown. On the contrary, the frequency with which they have occurred in the past means the chances must be high that another great crash could occur at some future date. Since that ill-fated week in October 1987, the dread that one's capital could disappear over-night, in an uncontrollable global sell-off, remains a secret fear for most investors.

The purpose of this book is to shed some light on this mystifying process. With the benefit of hindsight, we can study in detail stock market crashes to discover what went wrong and to learn from these past traumatic episodes. We will find that they conform to a clear pattern, based on the young science of chaos. Analysis of stock market behaviour is sometimes disparagingly called a voodoo science, unrelated to anything so regular and disciplined as the pure physical sciences. Yet recent research has shown that even precise disciplines, such as mathematics and astronomy, although governed by classical science, can sometimes harbour previously unsuspected chaotic elements.

Once the deeper chaos-basis of market behaviour is understood the fundamental structure of a crash stands revealed. The ability to recognise the symptoms leading up to such an event can then be grasped. As the global investment scene becomes ever more closely integrated, with huge volumes of currencies and securities flowing in massive international tides, the spectre of a crash is ever present.

Understanding how and why crashes develop is the first essential step to protecting one's capital from exposure to serious loss. Then, if the circumstances leading to another crash should begin to emerge, the knowledgeable investor can quickly liquidate his position and watch the mayhem unfolding with his own cash safely out of harm's way.

Consistency in Crashes

Just as the cliché, "the poor are always with us", suggests poverty and civilisation are inseparable, so crashes and bubbles seem to be an inherent part of industrial capitalism. More often than not, one group of people, the entrepreneurs, have great ideas for exciting new products but they have no cash, and the people with the money are forever seeking new opportunities for putting it to work. While keen to plough capital into ventures they hope will prove exceedingly profitable, they are often anxious to avoid the necessary physical commitments involved in bringing risky projects to successful fruition. A financier class of bankers, brokers and jobbers were quick to emerge in Holland, France and England during the early eighteenth century, bringing these two groups into direct contact.

However, even if crashes and the evolution of capitalism do go hand in hand, the history of over 450 major crashes in the last 360 years contains some unexpected surprises. As we shall discover, many speculative bubbles share a cluster of common features, even when they are separated by centuries and occur on different continents. Superficially, it seems logical to think that crashes are totally random and unpredictable. So how do we reconcile this common-sense view with the idea that they are linked together by uniformly recognisable behaviour patterns?

Not surprisingly, perhaps, the greatest thread of uniformity stems from the manic behaviour of the investing crowd. We cannot look at the history of crashes without being struck by the amazing irrationality of many investors caught up in these episodes. Greed and absurd expectations, fanned by cheap money or easy credit, seem to fuel an unsustainable boom. Abruptly, perhaps due to some unexpected event, a spreading fear takes hold, triggering the crash. Although in each boom and bust situation the economic, political, historical, financial and social structures are uniquely different, there is an underlying similarity in the way events unfold that belies the disorderly antics of a frenzied crowd of get-rich-quick speculators.

How are we to explain evidence of numerous unexpected similarities in the widely differing crashes that we shall explore in this book? We might simply conclude that even if the actual circumstances vary hugely in each case, human nature never changes. That is patently true, but I believe that although the psychology of investor behaviour may indeed be constant, on its own it does not give a comprehensive explanation for the recurring pattern of crashes. Investor psychology provides an observable effect, but the cause of crashes is chaos. This is the underlying force of nature fuelling these crazed events.

Chaos is Everywhere

Colloquially, chaos signifies a total breakdown, utter confusion; in the young mathematical science of chaos, however, it has a more precise meaning. Chaologists study the behaviour of complex dynamical systems: complex because they frequently consist of a multitude of interacting elements; and dynamical because they are in a constant state of flux, forever changing. Scientifically speaking, chaos describes unpredictable behaviour that is governed by rules. For this reason it is known as deterministic chaos; the determinism implies there are rules and a definite order, despite the conspicuous unpredictability. The definition sounds contradictory, but although the events seem random, scientists have been convincingly able to reveal an existing underlying order that accords with strict mathematical laws.

In this book, I shall show how chaos governs the collective behaviour of investors in financial markets. These deeper chaos forces are operating because the securities markets are typical examples of chaotic systems. Therefore, although they are complex, inherently unstable and subject to continuous, often unpredictable, change, they behave in a remarkably similar way to other examples of complex dynamical systems that are found everywhere in nature and also in the earth sciences. One school of advocates who espouse the Efficient Market Hypothesis claim the markets are random and structureless, but I believe this observable randomness is **an outcome, a visible effect in the markets** – it is not an explanation; for that we must turn to the young science of chaos.

Moreover, I believe share price and index charts give us a graphic depiction of investor psychology expressing the presence of chaos in the financial markets. Charts are financial fractals, where fractals are the graphic representations of the intricate geometry of chaotic systems. For the markets, the chaos should ultimately prove to be the same deterministic chaos governed by simple mathematical rules, that predominates in nature. Although I can show many similarities between financial markets and chaotic systems, I have not yet found the underlying mathematical rules that I believe must be operating. However, the search is seriously underway and in time, I am confident they will be uncovered.

To date, most of the chaotic scenarios researchers study are physical, as opposed to the human or social systems concerned primarily with man. If we, however, place man in the context of the evolution of biological life on earth, the human sciences are a sophisticated extension of other life sciences and it therefore seems plausible that they too should be governed by chaos. Researchers have probed the disorderly behaviour of turbulent fluids and gases, including tumbling waterfalls, viscous liquids churning through pipes and the complex weather systems circulating the planet. They have successfully examined animal populations for evidence of chaos, but studies in the human, or social, sciences have not been widely tackled as yet.

I shall describe a group of chaos features which fit with recognisable patterns of human behaviour in financial situations. This is fortunate because it means we need not concern ourselves with those highly mathematical aspects of chaos which apply mainly to natural physical systems. Although chaos theory is complicated the concepts that I have studied, which closely apply to financial markets, are non-mathematical, descriptive and fairly straightforward. I shall discuss the strong similarities between typical financial markets and the crashes themselves on the one hand, and classical chaotic systems on the other. The evidence suggests that financial crashes are indeed examples of chaos and, accordingly, they can be fully described by chaos concepts.

I shall explore a small group of past stock market manias to demonstrate the consistent features of chaos they reveal. Only six will be considered out of hundreds of historical examples which have occurred in currencies, bonds, money inflation, railroad manias, runs on banks and stock market panics. In each case, the prevailing background conditions are introduced, followed by an account of the chief chronological events. These are then considered in the context of the underlying chaos features which, I believe, enabled them to thrive under their own inherent momentum.

The Layout of the Book

The chapters are organised into three parts; the five chapters in Part I set the scene. In Chapter 1 we consider a typical crash scenario using it as a model for crashes. (There is a brief historical resumé of the crashes we shall be examining in Part II.) Chapter 2 introduces the active participants in crashes: the rational and irrational investors. In Chapter 3 we consider the features of chaos which will be relevant to our study of these historical crashes. Chapters 4 and 5 discuss the direct relevance of chaos concepts to the activities of financial markets, using the stock market as the prime example.

Part II explores the two major crashes of 1720, known to posterity as the Mississippi and South Sea Bubbles. Because they were moderately self-contained and are well documented historically, they are almost perfect case studies for evidence of chaos in financial crashes. Part III examines three major twentieth-century examples: the Great Crash of October 1929, the global crash of 1987 and the recent Japanese financial bubble of 1986–95. The final illustration takes the form of a short footnote; it covers the 1993–4 speculative bubble in the global bond markets. The inevitable decline associated with this bubble is discussed in terms of the chaos characteristics that have featured consistently throughout the book. These are the undercurrents of forces that drive financial markets.

Chapter 14 outlines a strategy for surviving the next great crash. How to recognise its approach, how to take avoiding action or, better still, how to exploit the coming collapse. And finally, how to benefit financially in the aftermath, ready for the next great upswing.

I hope the book proves as entertaining to read as it has been to write. There is undoubtedly a fascination in exploring the bizarre behaviour of investors exhibiting all the symptoms of the madness of crowds. However, there is also a serious purpose.

Learning from Past Errors

What we need to know is whether a study of the past assists us in our never-ending quest for a better knowledge of ourselves. If we are to benefit from the lessons of history we must study the past in an attempt to understand the major forces at work. Those who think crashes and bubbles are entirely random happenings, of course, will hotly dispute that such forces are operating. History, however, is not on their side and I hope this book will help to dispel this serious misconception.

Historical accounts of crashes have been amply covered by other books. In the main, these books highlight the folly of the masses who, time and again, get whisked up into these traumatic events by the lure of unimaginable wealth. Sadly, many people, in countless generations, including our own, have suffered severe social and monetary hardships in the fall-out from these financial fiascos.

I hope to expose the behaviour of speculative manias in financial markets as examples of typical chaotic systems so that we can draw the appropriate lessons. If we do not analyse the past objectively we shall surely repeat previous errors through ignorance, since at present we do not have any systematic ground rules for avoiding them.

Moreover, we now live in an era of rapid financial and monetary liberalisation. On a global scale, with virtually instantaneous communications, massive capital flows chase elusive short-term profits around the 24-hour trading clock. In recent years, the emergence of enormous speculative hedge funds in America with numerous innovative derivative instruments at their disposal, has brought much closer the possibility of a major market destabilisation. Instability is an essential forerunner to chaos, so the markets could be evolving towards the next global crash. With the unprecedented levels of financial freedom and innovation now available, any future crash could be colossally devastating and millions of unfortunates will be caught in the slipstream. As far back as 1936, before the post-Second World War mega-explosion of global markets that has brought them to their present enormous size, John Maynard Keynes, the world-renowned British economist, was cautioning on the dangers of economic instability from rampant market activities, when he said, "Speculators may do no harm as bubbles on the steady stream of enterprise. But the position is serious when enterprise becomes the bubble on a whirl-pool of speculation."*

As a recipe for avoiding such a disaster, every investor needs to personally understand how crashes develop and how to recognise the signs that a crash event may be building. The need to protect one's capital from any forthcoming financial calamity is a priority concern for every serious investor. In the pages that follow, the patterns of each evolving crash will clearly reveal what avoiding action is needed, and how to diagnose the right time to implement it.

* From The General Theory of Employment, Interest and Money, p. 159, London: Macmillan, 1936.

PART I

Setting the Scene

CHAPTER ONE

A CASCADE OF CRASHES

> The first message is that there is disorder. Physicists and mathematicians want to discover regularities. People say, what use is disorder? But people have to know about disorder if they are going to deal with it.
>
> James Yorke, *Period Three Implies Chaos*

The sensationalism surrounding bubbles, crashes and panics may be due to the way in which they thrust themselves, abruptly, into public awareness. They become notorious because, by their very nature, they entice a majority of unsuspecting but gullible neophytes into their cruel snare right at the very peak, just when the crash is imminent. From the sidelines, the watching public become increasingly fascinated by the emergence of seemingly effortless wealth, but they are naturally appalled when it evaporates before their gaze, apparently without warning, casting thousands into a sudden black despair.

The legendary US investor, Benjamin Graham compared the behaviour of the stock market to that of a manic depressive. "Mr Market" is forever ready both to buy and sell, but his views on prices veer from the ridiculously high to the absurdly low as his excessive optimism gives way to an equally extreme gloom. Psychology teaches that the exaggerated highs and lows of depressives generate phases of unsustainable expansion, exuberance and euphoria, interspersed with phases of contraction, decline and depression. In this book I shall show that a deeper explanation links extreme investor behaviour and human psychology. This cardinal link is the young science of chaos.

Evocative Terminology

Initially, it is helpful to clarify the colourful language used to describe the boom/bust incidents we shall be discussing. A speculative excess called a "mania", implies an underlying insanity or irrationality is gripping investors, while the term "bubble" forewarns of the inevitable bursting. It describes the entire event: the rush to an unsustainable peak, followed by the equally dramatic collapse. A bubble implies the price of an asset, or an entire market, is no longer in balance consistent with the underlying fundamental value. A crash deals only with the sudden collapse, the disintegration in the prices of assets. It usually entails a fall of 10 per cent or more, over a matter of a few days, sometimes just one or two. It can start with the failure of a major firm or bank or some other triggering event, but if it seems to occur spontaneously, even in the absence of any key information, it may then be termed a panic, from the name of the Greek god Pan, when there is a sudden fright without obvious cause. When this arises in asset markets, there is a frenzied stampede out of illiquid stocks or bonds and into cash. A financial crisis often involves a mania, a bubble, a panic and a crash, but not necessarily in that order. How all these terms fit together is best illustrated from a model for crashes in financial assets.

A Model for Stock Market Extremes

Every crash clearly has a unique, individual profile, so the idea that they all follow a typical path contradicts the suggestion that they are random, haphazard dramas of an unpredictable nature driven by the psychological human weaknesses of hope, fear and greed. On the other hand, the very fact that psychological disorders can be medically classified, analysed and treated systematically, lends weight to the view that crashes should be amenable to a similar scientific analysis. Like other forms of extreme human behaviour, detectable patterns can be found in most of these abruptly occurring incidents.

In an earlier analysis, Kindleberger, in his book *Manias, Panics and Crashes*, expanded on a model developed by Minsky for stock market booms and busts, outlining an ordered sequence of eight phases. First comes a triggering shock which lights the fuse of the boom, and in the second stage the flames are fuelled by expanding bank credit and money supply. Thirdly, an inflationary demand for goods spills over into rising prices for financial assets, leading to phase four, the onset of overtrading. In this phase, the pace of events often speeds up. Pure speculation, exaggerated expectations and mass borrowing to participate, send the investing community into a buying frenzy. Stage five arrives when the gullible mass public plunge in. The buying develops its own inner self-feeding momentum, but knowledgeable insiders sell to the newcomers thereby banking their outsized profits. A sudden event or the realisation that near-term prospects are less rosy than assumed, marks phase six, implanting the first niggling doubts. This sparks a trickle of selling, and the prices of the favoured assets begin to drift gently down from the peak, but this gradual slide is soon overtaken by the onset of phase seven, the selling flood. Banks call in loans and sell off collateral assets, thus adding to the selling pressure and the widespread distress of phase seven. Finally, phase eight ushers in the collapse, sometimes accompanied by raw panic. Now a massive sell-off gets underway, again increasing in strength under its own self-feeding momentum. This is a rerun in reverse of the previous huge buying surge. To match the upthrust of the exorbitant rising prices that occurred, there is now a phenomenal selling climax and the market collapses amid a growing clamour of despair, exhaustion and recriminations.

Do Rational Stock Markets Boom?

This model, implying gross irrationality, was introduced by Minsky and refined by Kindleberger from an analysis of several historical cases where unbridled booms lead to crashes. I have used this model as a starting point for my analysis, but the pattern that marks out these mystifying events consists of other strongly repeating themes. I have added several features which occur with a surprising regularity in the bubbles and crashes we shall examine. If, however, as theorists suppose, markets are rational in the long-term, how can these periodic bouts of mass hysteria arise? My explanations to this puzzle rely on chaos theory, which is discussed in Chapters 3, 4 and 5, but a brief answer rests on two prongs: first, irrational phases are possible because any complex chaotic system, such as the weather or a financial market, is inherently unstable and dynamic (that is, conditions are forever changing). This is readily seen in the way a fierce storm or hurricane abruptly originates and then dies, while in the markets, similarly, the mood of the majority of its participants, investors, speculators and traders, can flip almost instantaneously from one state to another. The switch from a relatively placid, orderly phase may repeatedly dissolve into chaos and then tip back to a more ordered state. Sudden market gyrations are accompanied by huge swings of volatility and abrupt mood changes. The behaviour of the US stock market in June and July 1996 was a typical example.

The second explanation concerns the make-up of the market itself. In total, it reflects the collective behaviour of many thousands of individual participants, but this entity, "the market" can sometimes acquire different properties (and hence, behave differently) to the properties of its individual participating members. On such occasions the long-term behaviour of the whole market can differ from the short-term behaviour of the investors who comprise it. Even under the stress of a surging boom, thousands of investors will manage to stay rational, but at its peak, when there is mass participation by outsiders, the majority should, by definition, be acting irrationally, for if they were not, the speculative upthrust of the climax, followed by the crash, could never emerge. Stock markets, like other complex dynamic systems, are holistic: sometimes their global conduct will be different to that of their component units, the individual investors. Occasionally, the global action differs from the behaviour of individual members. Hence, occasional deviations from rational behaviour are perfectly feasible if the markets are governed by chaos, especially since chaos and order repeatedly intermix in these complex unstable systems.

Chaos Within Our Universe

However, the central concept to grasp is that chaos as a scientific process is itself part of the fundamental behaviour of our universe. On our planet, scientists have shown that chaos pervades the natural world of the earth and life sciences. As we owe our origins to evolution from primate (ape) precursors, by extension, chaos concepts should apply therefore to the human sciences. If human behaviour dovetails into physical and biological chaos science, again, by extension, all aspects of human behaviour in the financial markets will be governed by chaos principles. From this reasoning the stark fact emerges that all financial behaviour should be explicable in terms of chaos precepts. It is an all or nothing explanation; either everything fits into the chaos theory of markets or nothing does.

This stark approach seems overtly all-embracing, but on two counts we need to know whether chaos is the driving force underpinning market action or not. First, in globally operating markets, it is vital that government officials understand how markets function. Secondly, for investors themselves, it is indisputably true that by following a proper system they can achieve substantial profits without knowing the chaos-basis of markets. However, for both groups, the same logic applies: if you do not understand why things happen, you may be playing poker with your country's (or your own) precious capital, and at some stage, as the records confirm, you may hold the losing hand.

The Link Between Crashes and Capitalism

Before the birth of industrial capitalism manufacturing was mainly financed by and run for the benefit of autocratic rulers. The early porcelain factories of Sèvres and Limoges, for example, were exclusively within the patronage of the French King. The dominant philosophy of the period was mercantilism, with trade and industry organised and run exclusively by ruling Kings and Emperors.

By contrast, at this early stage, budding entrepreneurs had to find their finance from money-lenders, interested "shareholders" or with bank loans, as they still do today. Private enterprise, run by commercially-minded individuals, was a rough and rudimentary affair. It was first stirring into life as modest cottage industries, in the small city-states of northern Italy during the Italian Renaissance of the fourteenth and fifteenth centuries. As it began to gain ground, it spread through northern Europe, with the growth of private industry and activity in Holland during the early decades of the seventeenth century. Here, better manufacturing methods along the lines of mass production for ship-building were being introduced.

A little later, private enterprise began emerging in England where the Industrial Revolution was slowly crystallising during the last two decades of the eighteenth century. Machinery for new inventions, like the steam engine and spinning jenny, helped English cottage industries to flourish and expand into mass production factories during the early nineteenth century. Industrialisation then radiated out to France, Germany and other European countries, and crossed the Atlantic, with a flood of emigrating European pioneers, to America during the early decades of the nineteenth century. Primarily, industrialisation was the brain-child of private entrepreneurs.

France was an authoritarian state, remaining an absolute monarchy until the French Revolution in 1789. There was no national institution with the right to prevent the King from doing whatever he wanted. This was in direct contrast to a country like Great Britain, where royal power was beginning to be curbed by Parliament. There was a long tradition of state-directed interference in all walks of life in France. In England, however, the "invisible hand" of free enterprise was so well established by 1776, Adam Smith immortalised it in *The Wealth of Nations*. He wrote of the profound changes he observed, recognising the potential for economic growth and expansion inherent in the changing industrial scene he saw materialising all around him. The idea of "shares" was an ingenious British invention, originating over 400 years ago during the Tudor era of voyages for trade and discovery. The Crown stood to benefit greatly from these ventures, but English sovereigns were notoriously mean when financing risky projects. In 1553, Sebastian Cabot solved the problem of financing his seafaring adventures by creating the first "company". London merchants paid up £6,000, split into shares of £25 each to limit their individual risk.

The growth of banking and financial markets was closely linked to the slow emergence of industrial capitalism. State-run factories had limitless access to funds; they rarely went bankrupt from competition or inefficiency, but men with novel ideas on how to turn clay into porcelain, or how to build new machinery to weave raw wool and cotton into cloth, had to find their own sources of finance. This meant stimulating the interest either of bankers, in the newly forming banks which were arising to cater for their needs, or of the lay public.

In 1694, the Bank of England was founded by a group of Whig merchants to lend money to William III to pay for the wars with France and to tidy up the mess of unfunded debt after three Anglo-Dutch wars. The organised financial markets were very rudimentary and restricted to government debt and the paper of a few chartered companies, like the East India Company. Stock-jobbers, financiers and bankers emerged as intermediaries as the great stock market booms of Holland, France and Britain took hold during the first decades of the eighteenth century.

Similarly, the huge rise in share prices in these early booms created a new class of shareholder, from princes to the middle classes, and a new word, millionaire, came into the French and English languages. Originally, the Bank of England was not a state-run enterprise; it was finally nationalised by the first post-war Labour Government in 1946. A unique feature of the Bank at inception was that it was the only public bank in Europe with the power to issue notes. The wheel has now come full circle, for central banks today have a monopoly over note issue and play an influential role in money supply control.

As a corollary to the rise and growth of capitalism, there have been hundreds of booms, panics and crashes. Kindleberger suggests crashes are linked to peaks in business cycles which follow the uneven expansion and contraction of normal economic affairs, although not every cycle will culminate in a crash. However, the historical records of irrational speculative manias suggest their sporadic occurrence makes a nonsense of claims that markets are unfailingly rational.

After the Boom, the Crash

The evidence shows booms constantly recur. They have resulted from colonisation and the discovery of gold, silver and other valuable resources. They have followed the emergence of some new innovations and the growth of major new products, like the railways, automobiles and computers. Booms have frequently emerged as a war is ending. Panics and crashes occur in an endless stream. Because banking is so notoriously difficult to regulate, there have been innumerable serious runs on banks, often culminating in a mass banking collapse. Many eminent private commercial empires have collapsed into worthless hulks during booms. Panics have also arisen from spectacular bouts of European and Latin American hyper-inflation.

This book will not discuss or analyse the numerous mini-crashes linked to the business cycle, or the major crashes tied to corporate collapses, bank-runs or hyper-inflation, although I feel sure the same chaos principles apply. We shall focus on six representative stock market events which have surprisingly strong links with chaos theory.

Anatomy of a Crash

The long record of major financial crashes reveals that collectively, investors can behave quite irrationally. We shall meet some of them in Chapter 2. Their conduct seems to support the claims of Random Walkers (a group of market theorists who consider markets are random and unpredictable), as frenzied crowds imply complete randomness. Yet offsetting the randomness claim is evidence that during extreme booms, many investors, living on different continents and separated by centuries, exhibit strikingly similar forms of irrational behaviour. Anecdotal records show collective behaviour can be absurdly illogical as investors lose sight of fair value. In a crash, greed and wild expectations, fanned by cheap money or easy credit, fuel a zealous boom. Abruptly, at the peak, however, a spreading fear simultaneously grips thousands of investors, triggering a massive sell-off.

Phase One – The Initial Trigger

In this chapter we shall look briefly at six of the most notorious stock market crashes to illustrate that they share a set of common features. In addition to the outline structure of eight sequential phases, there is a group of 12 extra supporting features which together produce an impressive profile of a bubble/crash scenario. The eight-phased sequence provides the underlying time-dominated anatomy of the crash, as it proceeds remorselessly towards a grim denouement.

So we begin with a brief explanatory comment on each phase. It can, with some justification, be argued that in the financial markets, there are numerous incidents that could be interpreted as an initial triggering shock. Some might usher in a period of boom, followed by bust, but others may not. How are we to decide which of several external shocks has set the eight-phased movement in motion? When trying to assess whether any particular boom will become chaotic, however, the actual triggering incident is not in itself, of major importance. What matters is the identifiable unfolding sequence of eight phases, moving relentlessly towards the finale of the collapse.

Evidence from other chaotic systems suggests that when they have entered a state of extreme instability (termed a far-from-equilibrium state), they are more susceptible to sudden random shocks than quiescent systems. This effect offers a meaningful explanation of how, as the eight-phase sequence begins to unfold, each, or any, succeeding phase can be swiftly ushered in by an unexpected triggering event. The impact of such triggers may be modest in themselves, or extremely significant, because the market in question is already seriously destabilised by the slow build-up of a boom which is driving it into a truly chaotic state. Even at the outset, because the market can flip so rapidly from an orderly to a disorderly state, a minor triggering event can set the whole system careering off in an unstable direction. The chaos name for this dramatic occurrence is the Butterfly Effect, which we will examine in detail in Chapter 3.

Phase Two – Easy Credit and an Increasing Money Supply

The second phase, when easy credit or a growing money supply fans the boom, looks equally problematic. Evidence suggests that during the height of the 1630s Dutch Tulipomania, in 1929 and in the autumn of 1987, interest rates were rising and a credit squeeze may have begun to bite. How can markets be rising frantically, if the money supply is being tightened? Again, chaos offers an explanation. A lusty boom, initially fuelled by lax monetary policy, develops its own inner self-feeding expansion. So it continues along its ballooning course, even after some official attempt has been made to dampen it. Although economists and central bankers may not realise this chaos explanation, they have now accepted as a well-recognised fact that a lag occurs between implementing interest rate changes and producing an impact on events. Unfortunately, the timing for changes is so crude it often amounts to slamming on the brakes too late to avoid the collision.

Phases Three & Four – Inflationary Rises, Overtrading at the Edge of Chaos

During phases three and four, when the inflationary rise in prices leads to rampant overtrading and pure speculation, the emergence of greatly exaggerated expectations often plays a dominant part in robbing investors of their sense of "fair value". In many cases, the object of greatest favour is a novelty, a new industry or product, which might bring untold wealth at some future date. This treasure was rare tulip bulbs in 1636, trading potentials in the New World for 1720 investors, new prosperity through major new industries, like radio, electricity, movies and motor cars during the 1920s, and computer technology and new mega-leisure industries during the 1980s. Calculating the future benefits of these unprecedented new outlets may be so difficult that other perceptions, like the direction of the price movement itself, can become more central to investors' views. During phases three and four, the system can move towards the edge of chaos. This is the critical point where it is hovering, perhaps only momentarily, in an unstable hiatus between order and chaos.

Phase Five – Mass Participation at the Peak

The late arrival of the gullible public onto the scene often creates the most extravagant stories of irrationality and greed. Not surprisingly, this rush of small, mainly ignorant, neophytes has received a prominent bad press in several bubbles. They appear simply as walk-on bit players, fulfilling their expected role as irrational unsophisticates seeking a quick profit and buying from knowledgeable insiders eager to bank their outsized gains. Their antics, while amusing, are really a side-show.

Astonishingly, the true culprits are to be found elsewhere, in the strange behaviour of two other groups. First, the elites and opinion-formers in society who suddenly display surprising degrees of speculative mania and avarice, in company with the second group, the big professional players: the bankers, brokers, fund managers and company directors. Despite their reputation for caution and ability, these high profile "experts" demonstrate far greater levels of speculative fervour and outright irrationality than the mass public. Moreover, some of the biggest scams, frauds and scandals emanate from their ranks. This striking fact occurs in each example we discuss.

Phase Six – Early Nagging Doubts

It seems odd that the peak in each case is followed by a halting pause of early nagging doubts, marked by a gentle downward drift in prices from the all-time highs. This is a breathing space as people await events. However, if almost everyone has been a buyer, resulting in an enormous imbalance of buys over sells, it seems reasonable to wonder where the next buying surge can come from. Periodically, on the route to the top, there will be volatile bouts of heavy profit-taking, but these are followed by a renewed upthrust, as new buyers emerge. Phase six is different. Its arrival clearly identifies the top. No new buying occurs. The downward slide marks the early profit-taking by insiders, before the selling onslaughts begin.

Phases Seven and Eight – Massive Selling

Analysts trying to understand why these peculiar bubble incidents recur, stress the tautology in the argument that the massive boom creates a situation that can only end in bust. They do not accept the reasoning that **without the excessive energy built up during the boom there would be no cause for the collapse.** This problem has a chaos explanation. During the extreme examples, **the intense instability of the boom is an over-reaction, generating an untenable peak**. The decline is inevitable because balance can only be restored by unwinding the previous buying surge. Abrupt mood swings by investors or speculators are often responsible for the dramatic over-optimism followed by an equally exaggerated over-pessimism.

There are occasions, however, when a market may fall remorselessly but without a dramatic rout. The world-wide decline in stock markets from May 1972 to January 1975 illustrates an extended downturn that reduced share prices by 60–75 per cent of their spring 1972 values, without a whiff of a real panic or a crash. More often, the falls can be frighteningly abrupt, as the desire to sell becomes so universal that bargain hunters wanting to buy will be swept aside by the sheer weight of selling. At a certain stage, termed the critical point, the bubble scenario becomes predictable. It will always end in collapse: the deep-seated chaos-induced forces ensure this result.

And what we find with all the major incidents that progress to this unpleasant conclusion is the surprisingly invariant shape of the boom/bust scenario. It is seen in the way these phases unfold with a startling regularity, almost as if each episode were following a pre-ordained path. Despite the uniqueness of the detail, we shall see this effect in all the six cases we discuss in Parts II and III. This regularity means a certain amount of repetition occurs in the six examples to be discussed, especially since they are all chaos-induced events.

Perhaps we should not be surprised at this amazing consistency. Like baking soufflés, if all the ingredients are correctly in place, this artificial concoction will puff up to a breath-takingly unstable size, only to collapse again when withdrawn from a piping hot oven. The soufflé, and the crashes, although both man-made inventions, are still obliged to follow nature's laws. When the evidence to support this idea for bubbles is presented, as we shall see in later chapters, the randomness argument looks as flat as yesterday's soufflé.

Seven Additional Common Features

Moreover, there is additional evidence we can muster to support the notion that underlying rules govern bubbles and crashes. For within the eight-phased crashes outline are many extra features which portray how the essential **structure** is supported through the unfolding drama. These features appear repeatedly in the crashes we shall discuss. They include at least seven major elements which gradually destabilise the market in the build-up to the crash.

First is a growing supply of new securities to feed the rising demand. There is a sudden avalanche of new issues which are consistently over-subscribed, sometimes to ridiculous proportions; new investment trusts emerge, to draw additional cash into the market and numerous dis-counted rights issues are produced, which are equally well supported. Secondly is the introduction of imaginative new financial instruments which become instantly popular. These include options, futures con-tracts, foreign exchange futures, other derivatives, short selling and mar-gin trading, junk bonds, leveraged buy-outs, program trading, index arbitraging and portfolio insurance. Every bubble has its very own spe-cial invention, often a variation on an old theme, perhaps not fully real-ised by the later "innovators", but the welcoming reaction of investors to whatever the new craze happens to be is incredibly consistent.

The third common factor is the arrival of the irrational investor. He materialises like the genie in Aladdin's lamp at the first whiff of rampant speculation. Fourthly is the clumsy mismanagement of affairs by the presiding financial authorities. This exacerbates the fifth common ele-ment, namely, the fatal lure of easy money which excites a wide recourse to leverage or gearing. However, not every period of easy money creates a bubble scenario. All the many factors involved in the anatomy of the boom need to be present before it can take off. Like the pieces in a complex jig-saw puzzle, the complete picture remains elusive until the last few pieces are slotted into place.

The sixth common feature is the emergence of frauds and tricksters, sometimes on a massive scale. Although such scandals can obviously occur without a bubble forming, in most crashes the mega-fraudsters reappear. This same proviso applies to the seventh factor, namely the sudden demise of a vast corporate empire or financial institution. It might be a bank or a major deposit-taking firm; alternatively, it could be a huge commercial or property corporation, which suddenly faces immense problems and goes into liquidation or bankruptcy. Due to its size, this occurs in a blaze of national publicity. In some instances, the frauds and company failures are closely linked.

The Bubble Effect

In addition to these extra key features, a further two are of special interest in bubbles and crashes, and are briefly mentioned here. First, is the intriguing way most examples retrace around 80 to 99 per cent of their previous rise, with a minimum 75 per cent retracement as the norm. This persistent effect has given rise to the "bubble" term; the sudden complete crash emphasises the bursting aspect of the previous unsustainable rise. Numerous examples of retracement can be cited. It occurred in the 1630s Dutch Tulipomania (which suffered a 93 per cent fall), and in the 1720 bubbles in the French Mississippi (a 99 per cent fall) and British South Sea Companies. In the last case, there was a rapid 84 per cent fall, with the boom and crash complete within just eight months. More recent examples include the 1929 Wall Street crash with a four-year 87 per cent fall and the silver bubble of 1976 which showed a 90 per cent retracement.

Although there is an old stock market adage that the boom precedes the crash, it might not seem clear as to why the mass hysteria of a boom should often end in a 70–99 per cent retracement to create the bubble profile. Again, there is a chaos explanation. The self-feeding mechanism that activates the boom goes into abrupt reverse at the peak. Now, the self-same effect takes hold again in a repeat performance, but this time, driving the action right back to where it began by a process of an almost complete "unwinding". We shall see this in operation in the great 1993 global bond bubble, described in Chapter 13.

Pictures Tell the Story

The second interesting feature is equally strange. Many crashes show the surprising recurrence of classic chart patterns. These identifiable formations are well-established in the repertoire of a group of market followers called technical analysts or chartists. They study various technical factors relating to the market or to individual company shares and record the actual movement of share prices or indices on charts, to interpret the movements and hopefully to predict the future behaviour of those prices. In chaos terminology, they are searching for structure, as this indicates more predictable trading phases, where above average returns involve below average risks.

Technical analysts ignore factual data on national economies or companies. They think the chart patterns and technical market details so completely mirror mass investor behaviour that the charts themselves provide sufficient information on investors' aggregate behaviour to enable chartists to make profitable investment decisions. In contrast to technical analysts, fundamentalists concentrate on the detailed performance of companies and national economies to arrive at their investment decisions. They may ignore or pay scant attention to erratic share price movements, preferring to make judgements and forecasts only on the copious evidence of the fundamental data itself. Many fundamental analysts are sceptical of chart patterns and the arcane jargon chartists use to describe them. However, what these sceptics have failed to realise is that chaos science is steeped in graphics. Hence, interestingly, we can see that during explosive booms or crashes, over a long time span and wide geographical range, some classic chart patterns do recur. In the jargon of technical analysis, among the most prevalent formations that repeatedly occur are two patterns known descriptively as a head and shoulders and a double top formation. These patterns are discussed in Chapter 5, where the puzzle of their recurrence is explained in the context of chaos theory.

Headache Time – After the Party

The awesome fall-out from bubbles and crashes should really be a footnote. However, the severity of the hype which sends markets soaring to untenable heights often brings enormous suffering and despair in the wake of the ultimate collapse. So consistently does this unrelenting depression follow in the footsteps of the frothy rise that gave it birth, its appearance invariably becomes another major aspect of the crashes scenario. This shock-horror story has acquired a respectable name. In economic circles it is termed a debt deflation.

The financial meltdown of the crash eliminates the wild speculative excesses, almost overnight. Apart from the ghastly knock to confidence administered by the crash, everyone feels savagely impoverished. Some speculators will be completely wiped out, especially if they have been speculating on borrowed money. Their numbers can include many respectable bankers, professors, company directors and government officials. A downward spiral of financial distress grips the afflicted country. Once this credit vortex evolves, the underlying value of an asset, such as a house or shareholding, reduces faster than the value of its associated loan. New vocabulary sprouts like poisoned mushrooms; negative equity for over-stretched home owners, non-performing loans or discounted-debt bonds for reckless bankers. Inappropriate phrases by politicians predicting a quick recovery are met with a hollow laugh. In 1929, Herbert Hoover's unshaken confidence in the value of stocks on Wall Street ranks with Irving Fisher's "plateau of prosperity" enthusiasm.

Again, the debt deflation takes a predictable form. The massive inflation of the boom is followed by the crisis of the crash and demands for cash become overwhelming. This triggers the liquidation: a massive sell-off in financial and other assets to convert everything as quickly as possible into cash. This phase follows hard on the heels of the crash crisis because, no matter how inadequate, borrowers and lenders must agree on the reckoning. Every debt must be settled. Loans will either be repaid and the borrower suffers, or the borrower will default and the lender bears the loss. In the scramble to repay debt, property, commodities, precious metals, antiques, art objects, all will be sold, even at rock bottom prices, to eliminate debt.

New in-words take centre stage; restructuring and refinancing. In chaos theory, this phase is termed self-organisation. It represents scattered islands of order emerging within the chaos of the collapse. At this stage, thousands of careworn speculators and investors now develop a new revulsion; they become debt-averse. As confidence in the credit system reaches an all time low, the recession tightens its grip, accompanied by a drop in interest rates and commodity prices. As this gruelling phase unfolds, the wily investors, who sold out in good time, may slowly begin to reinvest their hoarded cash-piles. Base-building phases on charts mirror this recuperation process. With a glacial slowness, confidence returns and the depression lifts.

No matter how harrowing the crisis and liquidation, the onset of the deep depression actually marks the dawning of a new credit cycle and the turning point for a new upwave. This usually requires months of painful base-building. The economy shows intermittent signs of revival amongst the gloom. Prices of shares or a national index, begin to form a floor, or base level. The human urge to rebuild takes hold.

Structure of the Crash

The twenty recurring features in Table 1 describe the entire bubble profile. Collectively, they comprise an eight-phased time-dominated outline, seven additional elements often found, two bubble features seen on the

Table 1 The structure of the crash scenario

Phase	Description	Added Feature	Description
1	Trigger event	1	New securities emerge
2	Cheap credit	2	New financial innovations
3	Inflation in asset prices	3	The irrational investor arrives
4	Overtrading and speculation	4	Inadequate financial authorities
5	Gullible public joins in	5	Leverage increases
6	Nagging doubts form	6	Frauds and tricksters appear
7	The selling flood	7	Major firms or institutions fail
8	The panic sell-off	8	Consistent chart patterns occur
9	Onset of debt deflation	9	Massive retracements in bubbles
10	Base-building in recovery	10	Base-building in prices/indices appears on the charts

charts, plus the ensuing debt deflation and rebuilding phase. They form a full structure which is readily observable in almost every case. This structure is an essential undercurrent that belies the superficial appearance of bubbles and crashes as random, haphazard events.

Structure is the crucial essence illuminating the order within the chaos. As such it is the equivalent of the Holy Grail for analysis of the capital markets. For the appearance of structure separates the predictable from the unpredictable phases in market conditions. When structure emerges it fulfils the two central purposes of this book: it elucidates the complete rationale for the chaos-basis of crashes and bubbles, and it illustrates those attributes necessary for cautious investors to make super profits with below average risk. We shall identify structure in the six examples to be covered in detail. Its formative elements, revealing the consistency of crashes should be borne in mind now as we take a short walk through history, forward from the 1630s, to review some of the most famous crash scenarios.

The Dutch Disease

We begin with the first notable European crash, Tulipomania, or Tulip Madness. It is introduced here as it is replete with fascinating glimpses of bizarre investor antics and because it is the first of its kind. All the elements of the crash structure are detectable as the drama unfolds, but the historical accounts are short on detail and the finale of the crash occurred with an astonishing speed, which telescoped the final phases of the crash into one flowing catastrophe. Rich in anecdote but poor in hard facts, this crisis decimated the Dutch economy in the 1630s. At this time Holland already had a thriving enterprise culture. While aristocrats had ample funds to fritter away on such exotic rarities, as the virus-ridden tulip bulbs fashion took hold, there was also a large and affluent bourgeoisie keen to possess this novel status symbol. At the peak of the boom, family fortunes were squandered to buy a single bulb. Lesser folk eagerly traded vital possessions (e.g. homes, clothes and livestock) to acquire this highly prized object, the simple tulip bulb. The most highly valued bulbs had a rare virus infection which produced the fabulous, often unique streaking patterns on their petals. This made each bloom totally exclusive, and fuelled the craze to possess them.

In 1594, on their first introduction from Turkey into Germany and the Netherlands, tulips were no more valuable than other rare plants. Yet early in the seventeenth century, they became the focus of a remarkable collecting craze. By the 1630s, although they were cultivated by a growing group of specialists, they also were desired, not as a source of pleasure or as collectors' items, but purely for speculation – buying to sell on quickly at a profit. And what evidence there is suggests that the inexperienced middle classes and monied workers were attracted to the rich opportunities possessing rare bulbs seemed to offer. They flocked into the market almost at the peak.

To cope with the burgeoning demand, an army of travelling salesmen spread the buying frenzy to remote hamlets and villages. In the provincial towns "colleges" were established in taverns, so that people could attend evening auctions, where frantic bidding for tulips took place. Innovative trading concepts were soon introduced to satisfy the clamour to own bulbs: futures contracts to buy or sell were introduced, so bulbs could change hands even before they had been planted to produce the following year's crop. And later, options were used, to obviate the need to handle the actual bulbs.

Between 1634 and 1636, rising tulip prices fuelled one of the most stunning bubbles ever recorded. By 1634, a bulb "of no intrinsic value", it is said, could be exchanged for a new carriage, two grey horses and a complete harness. One story relates how a tulip breeder–grower committed suicide, after being driven into bankruptcy when his entire stock was eaten by a cow! Another tells of a merchant who traded about four tons of wheat, eight tons of rye, four oxen, eight swine, twelve sheep, two hogshead of wine, four tuns of beer, two tuns of butter, 1000lb of cheese, a complete bed, one slightly used suit of clothes and a tarnished silver drinking cup – for one Viceroy bulb as he thought this rare variety would appreciate greatly over time.

Tulipomania at the Peak

At the height of the mania in January 1637, prices were almost doubling every day. Tulip growing became a national obsession; each new variety was over-subscribed and completely sold out months before coming to market. There is some recorded evidence of daily price movements, and it is known that at the peak, a Semper Augustus bulb, of incredible rarity fetched a colossal 6,000 florins, equivalent to £500,000 in today's money. One story tells of a shoemaker in The Hague, who like many of his fellow artisans, grew tulips on a smallholding for profit. He made a lucky strike when he produced a great rarity, a black tulip. News of this event brought him a visit by two important Haarlem tulip traders. They bought his rarity for 1,500 florins and immediately destroyed it, to safeguard the uniqueness and value of the black tulip they already possessed.

Grotesque details of Tulipomania at the peak have secured it a central place in the annals of irrational investor behaviour. How could a bulb that sold for over 5,000 guilders in 1637 be worth only one-tenth of a guilder in 1639, and still be rationally priced? This type of pricing behaviour seems impossible to explain if we assume market fundamentals are driving the price. However, there is another side to this story. A rare tulip bulb is not the same kind of asset as a common stock or even a unique Rembrandt painting. It has to be compared to the pricing of any similar self-reproducing asset with a premier breeding tag. Prize bulls, thoroughbred horses, pedigree dog breeds and growers of quality plants all belong in this same category.

The possession of one highly prized rare tulip bulb, may, over the course of a 100-year growing period, produce a million equally highly rated bulbs. Although each bulb in this million will be worth a fraction of the initial bulb price, the rational case for the astronomical price of the original bulb is built around the enormous future potential of its propagating ability. In the financial markets, anticipation of future worth invariably operates as a powerful influence on current pricing and valuations. This special pricing phenomenon of valuable assets with the ability to reproduce themselves a million times over must be part of the explanation for the unprecedented tulip craze. However, by January 1637, the pricing behaviour had clearly lost touch with fundamentals by most normal rational standards. The bubble had been driven to unsustainable levels and its bursting had become inevitable.

By January 1637, the authorities became concerned that tulip-hysteria was out of control. On 2 February, fearing it might destabilise the local economy, officials in Haarlem attempted to dampen the wildest speculation. This triggered a crash. Within two days it had spread throughout the country. Because prices had long since failed to reflect demand from genuine tulip-lovers, when confidence disappeared there was nothing to support the absurd heights which prices had reached. As the boom broke, an anguished reckoning began. Almost overnight, bulbs became unsaleable; thousands of people across the whole spectrum of society faced instant ruin. In Amsterdam, even the world-renowned merchant banking houses were crippled by the financial repercussions. Lawsuits clogged up the courts, but, interestingly, in view of their enormous importance in today's financial markets, the judges decreed debts on futures and options contracts fell into the category of gambling, and were not recoverable in law. Holland, the centre of a powerful trading empire, slid into a fearsome depression as the debt deflation took hold. Financial credibility, previously so high, declined greatly. In outline summary, the structure of the boom and collapse, shown in Table 2, is easily identified.

Table 2   The structure of Tulipomania

Phase	Description	Added Features	Description
1	Viruses emerge on tulips	1	New varieties of tulip bulbs
2	Holland had access to credit	2	Futures and options
3	Inflation (silver from Baltic trade financed Dutch trading)	3	Irrational investors
4	Overtrading and speculation	4	Inept authority intervention
5	Most adults joined in	5	Leverage – options and futures
6	Nagging doubts in Haarlem	6	98% retracement in the crash
7 and 8	instant panic sell-off		
9	Onset of debt deflation	7	Tulips become almost worthless

French Bubbles

The Mississippi System was the brain-child of the Scottish economist, John Law. He had a trail-blazing new idea. He wanted to expand economic growth by introducing a national paper currency not backed by gold. In the spring of 1717, after unsuccessfully presenting his innovative monetary ideas to most of the crowned heads of Europe, he finally persuaded the French Regent, Philippe Duke of Orléans, to allow him to start implementing his plans in France. In the style later adopted by aggressive twentieth-century entrepreneurs, within two years of his first venture – setting up his private bank – Banque Générale, Law had built up a huge "conglomerate". In Law's case, it was fully backed by the State. This "nationalised" monopolistic trading conglomerate, later renamed the Compagnie des Indes, is known to posterity as the Mississippi Company.

The breakneck expansion of his enterprises, culminating in the enlarged Compagnie des Indes, required further fund raising measures. This set Law on the path of a succession of rights issues accompanied by increased paper money issues which released an unbridled currency inflation upon the French economy and a monumental boom exploded into life.

"It is inconceivable what immense wealth there is in France now," wrote the perplexed Dowager Duchess of Orléans, mother of the Regent, in December 1719. "Everybody speaks in millions. I do not understand it at all, but I see clearly that the God Mammon reigns as an absolute monarch in Paris."

In September 1719, Lord Stair, the British Ambassador observed in a letter to James Craggs, "Everybody in this town is so much taken up with Mississippi that they seem to mind nothing else. Mr Law tells them that their first returns from the East Indies will bring them fifty millions profit." On one estimate, over 30,000 visitors descended upon Paris, eager to invest. Among the prominent foreigners flocking into town and keen to buy were several from Britain: Hutcheson, the economist MP, Lambert, a South Sea director, and a whole family of Campbells, including the Earl of Islay, who being on friendly terms with Law, gained instant access through the crowds forever waiting in the projector's outer room. According to Antoin Murphy's account, Thomas Crawford, the British envoy to France, wrote to his superiors, "The reason for the sudden rise of the stock here is the great number of people come from the Provinces who arrived all at once in the rue de Quincampoix on Saturday last – miracles are revived."

In cafés, restaurants and at street corners around the narrow rue Quincampoix, the operators set themselves up as traders in the Compagnie des Indes shares. The brokers' booths (very few had offices) were crowded from eight o'clock each morning until dusk. Local artisans earned more by renting out their stalls and benches than by plying their usual trade. The daily rental for a park bench to a stock-jobber was 200 livres, while a stall fetched 300 livres. Property in the narrow street near the Hotel de Ville was rented out for 800 livres a month, where formerly it had been let at 40 livres a month. Stories of the fortunes being made circulated freely adding to the air of expectancy and excitement. Anecdotal tales recount a chimney sweep netting 40 million livres and a waiter who amassed 30 million livres in six weeks.

Stories circulated of vast fortunes made almost overnight. One servant, sent by his master to sell shares at 8,000 livres was quickly able to find a purchaser for 10,000 livres and proceeded to speculate with the profit he had made on this deal. Within a few days he was reputed to be worth a million. Another story relates how a man used money, given to him to repay a debt, to buy shares. He then went to dine at a restaurant near the rue Quincampoix. After his meal, he discovered the share price had advanced by 11 per cent; he sold out at a profit of 40,000 livres, discharged the debt and kept the surplus.

The clamour for shares was so intense, it was now a commonplace for servants to become as rich, if not even richer than their employers. In his biography of John Law, Montgomery Hyde tells the story of Law's coachman who made such a fortune from his visits to rue Quincampoix that he arrived at Law's residence one morning, accompanied by two possible successors for his job. "But I only require one of them," protested Law. "Of course," replied the coachman, now resplendent in a nobleman's outfit. "The other I shall engage myself." The tale of one small rational investor bears repeating. In 1717, a poor widow, Madame Chaumont, came to Paris from the Provinces, to collect a debt. Her debtor could only offer her state bonds, standing then at a heavy discount to their face value. In desperation, she took this offer, immediately exchanging them for Mississippi stock. When she sold out her holding three years later she was worth 100 millions, with which she purchased a chateau at Ivery and enjoyed a life of perpetual luxury.

In December 1719, Law reached the pinnacle of his financial success. But it was very short-lived. Sadly, the speculation took on a life of its own when Law began to act like a modern central banker. And the rickety structure he had forged was sprouting irreparable cracks, even as its two main planks were being amalgamated. Doubts surfaced when rumours spread that the Prince of Conti sought cash payment in silver and gold for a huge block of many thousand shares. The clamour for payment in hard currency gathered pace and the Banque Royale was steadily drained of its coin. Drastic measures were enacted to halt the haemorrhage. A decree in May 1720 to gradually reduce the value of shares and bank notes in circulation by around one-half, literally, a devaluation of almost 50 per cent, precipitated a panic. A week later the bank suspended payment. Law was removed from office and his grandiose scheme was destroyed by his numerous enemies.

British Bubbles

The tale of British investors who bought shares in the South Sea Company in the second decade of the eighteenth century is similarly eccentric. In the first few years of its existence, nothing untoward happened and the price of South Sea stock stood below its initial issue price of £100 for years. The Company's respectability grew when King George I became its Governor in 1718. The boom was generated by a dubious scheme initiated early in 1720, by some of its dishonest directors. They planned to take over almost the whole of the national debt, to be purchased from the Government for £3.5 million. The share price stood at £128.5 in January 1720, reached £330 in March, £550 in May and £890 in June. It hit the round number peak of £1,000 on June 24.

In the spring, when demand for the the shares was flagging slightly, the directors hit upon the brilliant ruse of lending money at an interest rate of 5 per cent against issues of new shares held as collateral.

Investors unable to purchase South Sea Company shares were consoled by offers of shares in many other ventures, most of them highly dubious. They sprang up almost instantly to take advantage of the public thirst for new issues. As the wave of inflated expectations spread, some truly peculiar ventures appeared as "bubble" companies. One was formed with capital of £31 million, for a "wheel of perpetual motion". Another stated in its prospectus that it was formed "for carrying on an undertaking of great advantage, but nobody to know what it is." The promoter claimed that every subscriber "who deposits £2 per share is to be entitled to £100 per annum". Within five hours he had attracted £2,000 to his make-shift office in London, whereupon he shut up shop and instantly disappeared. Yet others sold stock in companies "To Make Salt Water Fresh – For Building of Ships Against Pirates – For importing a Number of Jack Asses from Spain". It has been estimated that these various speculative schemes hoped to raise about £300 million, a vast sum of money in 1720.

Viscount Erleigh, in his colourful account of proceedings entitled *The South Sea Bubble*, noted, "Statesmen forgot their Politics, Lawyers the Bar, Tradesmen their shops, Debtors of Quality their Creditors, Divines the pulpit, and even the Women themselves, their Pride and Vanity!" Such scenes conjure up the crush of expectant crowds, similarly fixated on the happy pursuit of effortless enrichment in rue Quincampoix in Paris. In April 1720, with the manic hysteria rising daily, the cynical Dutch banker, Crellius observed, that Exchange Alley resembled "nothing so much as if all the Lunatics had escaped out of the Madhouse at once". For the many unfortunates who bought and held onto their holdings, it was the proclamation declaring the plethora of "bubble" companies illegal, without quite specifying which were legal and which not, that punctured the expectation for extravagant hopes in the summer of 1720. South Sea shares began a precipitous slide, falling from £1000 in June to £400 by mid-September and to £124 by December, the same price they had been in January of that year before the great conversion scheme was launched. The South Sea saga therefore illustrates the bubble to perfection, with the entire giddy rise and fall encapsulated within the brief space of only eight months. It is also a stunning example of fraud associated with a bubble scenario. Some commentators suggest it was the biggest fraud ever perpetrated on a gullible British public.

Twentieth-century Crashes

Accounts of crazy investor antics make amusing reading. Rationality seems to have been a scarce commodity. What, however, are we to make of twentieth-century bubbles, when surely, we should be wiser now? The parallels are salutary. These recent crashes highlight with a surprising clarity the consistent format of the model crash profile with eight phases and twelve added features. Moreover, the irrational investor seems to have a season ticket for every event. His invariant appearance is quite astonishing.

The 1929 Crash was BIG

The Great Crash had a very long genesis; an unsustainable post-war boom began in 1918, followed by a short, sharp slump from 1920–2. But by 1922 a new mood was abroad, with a strong sense in America that the nation had finally come of age. With the mounting feel-good factor came rising output, economic growth and personal wealth. Many thought prosperity was now assured and would spiral up uninterruptedly in an ever upwards trend. This sense of optimism and well-being spread around the world.

In Britain, share prices had almost trebled between 1922 and 1929. A flood of new issues with varying degrees of ingenuity were rushed to market, and a torrent of British money crossed the Atlantic drawn by the magnet of ever soaring stock prices on Wall Street. Encouraged by the lure of cheap credit, after a reduction in dollar interest rates in 1927, to help ease the monetary problems of post-war Europe, this sense of national well-being gave rise, over the the next two years, to the speculative ferment of 1928 and 1929 centred on New York.

The upward surge was boosted periodically by comments from influential notables. In September 1928, Roger W. Babson claimed the election of a Republican Congress would ensure continued prosperity in 1929. Andrew W. Mellon, President Hoover's Treasury Secretary, was equally convinced "the high tide of prosperity will continue".

The market peaked on 3 September 1929, and in the nagging doubts phase, the collapse of Clarence Hatry's empire on 20 September had a sobering effect on investors. Throughout the 1920s his industrial and financial enterprise grew massively. Built up initially on coin-in-the-slot vending and automatic photograph machines, he expanded into the ubiquitous investment trusts and the lucrative arena of high finance. The expansion included forging stock certificates. His fall surely planted a seed of doubt in the minds of cautious investors.

The end, when it came, was horrendously alarming in both the scale and magnitude of its impact. On 24 October 1929 a wave of selling sent prices spiralling down. To check the decline bankers and politicians stepped in amid high publicity to steady prices, but on 29 October the selling pressure returned and prices plummeted. The ensuing debt deflation became the infamous Great Depression.

But the 1987 Crash was BIGGER

So we come to the recent history of 1987 and its resilient aftermath. Do you recall what you were doing on the evening of Thursday 15 October 1987? Britons who heard the weather forecast that evening might have been alarmed to learn that a hurricane out in the Atlantic was rapidly approaching the south-western coast. A hurricane? Surely not in Britain? Listeners, however, were instantly reassured by weather forecasters who confidently predicted that the full force of the impending storm would miss the mainland and wear itself out at sea. Quite so.

Tempestuous Weather

There has recently been a vastly increased success rate for short-term weather forecasts. Over the last decade, computer simulations and satellite transmissions from space have greatly enhanced forecasting performance. Sadly, however, the reality on that fateful autumn night was totally adrift from the comforting assurances of the forecasters. When inhabitants of the sleepy, leafy southern counties awoke on the morning of Friday 16 October, assuming they had slept through the howling fury of the gales, they might easily have thought themselves transported in some freak Wizard of Oz nightmare to the hurricane-prone islands of the Caribbean. After all, as the refrain sung by Eliza Dolittle, in My Fair Lady reminds us, "In Hertford, Hereford and Hampshire, hurricanes hardly happen".

The scale of destruction was immense. It was the worst storm this century, causing hundreds of millions of pounds worth of damage. Whole swathes of mature forest lay ruined, with trees blown over, like tossed-up piles of matchsticks fractured by the unrelenting force of the winds. Uprooted trees crashed across roads and railway lines, crushed cars or fell through the roofs of houses. Across the southern counties, damaged cables disrupted electricity supplies and severed telephone links. At the Royal Botanical Gardens at Kew over one thousand rare trees were lost, including the valuable nineteenth-century cluster of mulberries, planted in the reign of Queen Victoria. Estimates suggested it would be over one hundred years before the Gardens were fully restored. Roads were impassable; trains could not run on tree-strewn rails; and, almost uniquely, even the London Stock Exchange was unable to function on that epic Friday.

Tempestuous Stock Markets

Unpredictable tempestuous weather over southern England – and later over Europe – was not the only record-breaking turbulence to hit the headlines during that eventful week. The New York Stock Exchange was buffeted by a series of knocks that culminated in the global panic now known as Bloody Monday. The background to this event was the exuberant boom in stock markets around the world during 1986 and the first nine months of 1987. *The Sunday Times* of 25 October gave a graphic account of the events surrounding the global crash of 1987, summarised here.

After the crash, President Reagan asked Nicholas Brady to study its causes: he concluded that massive sales of Treasury Bonds by Japanese investors had acted as an initial trigger. However, the slow-burning fuse that ultimately sparked the stock market crash was America's huge twin deficits – the trade deficit with the rest of the world, and the Government's domestic budget deficit. Although they had been an almost continuous source of worry to economists and analysts for over five years, it only needed one sudden, severe jolt to shake the confidence of nervous investors; now that jolt had arrived.

On Wednesday 14 October the market reacted badly to the announcement of a $15.7 billion gap between American imports and exports. The gap was larger than analysts had been predicting and Wall Street closed with a record-setting fall of 95 points on the Dow Jones Industrial Average (DJIA) which monitors the performance of 30 representative blue-chip American Companies. Meanwhile, on the same day, in Frankfurt the West German Central Bank, the Bundesbank, had raised interest rates. The second blow to confidence struck on Thursday, when James Baker, the US Treasury Secretary, told a White House briefing to reporters that the sickly dollar might have to fall further. He was responding to the German Bundesbank interest rate move, which he felt went against the spirit of intent that had been reached in Paris earlier in the year, at the Louvre Accord. There, the seven major industrial nations agreed on active co-operation to steady exchange and interest rates. The briefing was called to warn Germany that American policy-makers were annoyed with its deflationary stance which they thought threatened global growth prospects.

For investors, however, Baker's warning carried a different message. A decline in the value of the dollar might prompt a rise in US interest rates to arrest its fall, and interest rate rises spell bad news for share prices because higher rates mean larger outlays on bank interest and other loans, thereby reducing company profits. Moreover, as interest rates rise company dividends become less attractive compared to income returns on fixed interest bonds. Wall Street, nervous after the 95 point plunge of the previous session, responded to the Baker briefing with a further fall of 57 points. On Friday 16 October, while southern England was reeling with the aftershock of the hurricane, America awoke to the alarming news that at dawn in the Persian Gulf, an Iranian Silkworm missile had struck a US-flagged tanker. Later that day, rumours spread that America would retaliate for this attack. In New York, on that crisis-ridden Friday, the DJIA fell another 108 points setting, yet again, a new record fall. With so many besetting worries, in hindsight, we can clearly see that the stage was being set for a massive adverse reaction; the beautiful '86–7 boom was fast unravelling. That weekend, unwittingly, the actions of the Reagan administration were to unintentionally sow the seeds for the impending crash. Wall Street's collapse made headline news over the weekend, although many market professionals were reportedly quite sanguine about the decline. However, some analysts and investors, to judge from their subsequent behaviour, had grown more restive. Their mounting concerns may have been heightened by James Baker's Saturday interview with CNN, the cable news network. He repeated his warning that America would respond to interest rate rises in West Germany by allowing the dollar to fall. On Sunday, his remarks were reinforced by a senior Treasury official who briefed the *New York Times* that America had already begun to implement its policy of letting the dollar fall. To the Reagan administration this approach was an appropriate leak intended to alarm the West Germans. Whether it would ever have achieved this objective will never be known, for its immediate impact was to strike sickening fears into the hearts and minds of investors, almost *en bloc*.

The Chain Reaction Crash

The build-up to the crash was therefore a chain reaction of related events. Now, with the miracles of computer technology and international satellite telephone networks, stock markets operate in a global marketplace, working on a 24-hour clock (on British Standard Time – BST). The selling panic of Bloody Monday, 19 October unfolded like a giant chain reaction, igniting first in the Far East (01.00 BST), before rolling on to London (08.00 BST), from where it leapt across the Atlantic to hit America, when the exchanges opened there (14.30 BST), and so back again to Japan, Hong Kong and Australia for Tuesday, ready for the start of yet another panic-ridden cycle.

When, on that epic-making Monday morning, London dealers arrived at their desks, the Far East had almost completed its frenzied opening trading session for the week. Tokyo's 225 Nikkei Dow market average had fallen 620 points by the close, its sixth worst ever fall. The Hong Kong market had experienced its biggest ever one day fall, losing 420 points, to wipe $HK65 billion (£5.2 bn)* off share values. Australia also recorded its biggest single day loss, taking $Aus10 billion (£4.4 bn) off total capitalisation. Harassed British investors knew of this frantic selling cascade right across the Far Eastern markets at the outset of trading in London, but for them, in addition, there was a pent-up urgency to sell left over from the tail end of the previous week: with the closure of the London exchange on the preceding Friday due to the hurricane, they had been forced to take the role of impotent bystanders, unable to react, while the New York market had suffered two days of severe falls – Thursday (57 points) and Friday (108 points). At the opening, prices were marked down savagely to discourage sellers but this tactic was completely ineffective. Sellers ignored the initial 150 point drop and dumped their stocks at such a rate that the FT-SE index continued falling, to a maximum drop of 300 points before recovering to close 250 points down on the day, with a total loss of £50 billion on British share values. Meanwhile, across Europe the falls on the main exchanges of Frankfurt, Paris, Amsterdam and Rome were equally dramatic and record-setting. The maximum drop of 300 points in London coincided with the 14.30 BST opening for Wall Street. By lunch-time, Wall Street had lost 100 points, but during the afternoon, there was a full-blown rout. At the close, the DJIA had shed a horrifying 508 points, a loss of 22.6 per cent. This was the largest ever one day fall on Wall Street, and twice the size of the collapse seen on Black Thursday in the 1929 crash. On Tuesday, Tokyo (01.00 BST) saw a mass panic sell-off as the epidemic of fright was escalating. By the close Tokyo's Nikkei index was down almost 15 per cent, losing 3,836 points. Expectations of a 1,000 point fall for Hong Kong so alarmed officials they closed the exchange for a week.

---

* All figures relate to October 1987 currency conversion rates and valuations as reported in *The Sunday Times*, 25 October, 1987.

The global financial community was in the grip of an uncontrollable contagion with the frenzy still raging when London opened for trading on Tuesday. The British Treasury found itself in the embarrassing position of offering partly-paid shares in BP, the nationalised oil company (then in the process of being privatised), at a suddenly unattractive price. This threatened to jeopardise the Government's whole privatisation programme. Chancellor of the Exchequer, Nigel Lawson, urged investors to stay calm, but prices had retreated by another 300 points at lunch-time. In its biggest fall in history, the London market had lost a staggering £100 billion in value in two days. At the opening on Tuesday (at 14.30 BST), Wall Street managed a short explosive rally, before another frantic sell-off ensued. Although the Reagan administration sought anxiously to stem the panic throughout the two principal days of the crash, their efforts appeared unsuccessful. However, around lunch-time on that turbulent Tuesday several major companies announced they were buying back large blocks of their undervalued shares. Slowly, during the afternoon, the mood of the market began to turn in a more positive direction. A steady recovery set in and the DJIA closed up 176 points on the day.

A Question of Chaos

Like the horrific mess left after the English hurricane, it took a considerable time for millions of investors around the world to recover from this traumatic débâcle. What, however, apart from that aftermath reaction, did these two apparently unrelated episodes have in common? In a book which hopes to reveal the imprint of chaos in the markets, the simultaneous occurrence of these two extraordinary incidents provides an appropriate and dramatic illustration for this topic. The link between them is wholly fortuitous – a matter of pure chance! Yet in common parlance, even without any scientific knowledge of the subject, we observe the notion of chaos in the hectic unfolding of both events. And, more to the point, the weather is one of the most famous examples of a classic physical chaotic system in nature.

The inability of experienced forecasters to predict the timing of hurricanes or global stock market crashes seems to imply it is a waste of time to study such events with a view to improving prediction potential the next time around, but as I shall show in this book, that conclusion would be a serious misjudgement. We may never be able to predict exactly the outcome of any individual event, but a proper understanding of the true nature of chaotic motion allows a more penetrating insight into the operation of financial markets, just as this knowledge is now improving the reliability of weather forecasting. And a deeper knowledge of the mechanics of market behaviour is a vital first step for achieving superior investment returns. And this is doubly so because a study of chaos in financial markets reveals the hidden structure within, on which one can build above average profits.

The Unpredictability Factor

Sadly however, with chaotic systems, nothing can ever be taken for granted. Although the weather forecasters had predicted that the hurricane would skirt the southern coast of Britain, the depression skittishly refused to follow the computer prediction. For it slowed and stopped briefly off south-west Cornwall. This allowed time for it to deepen and for the winds to gather additional force. Dr John Howton, director general of the Meteorological Office was emphatic in his defence of the television weathermen and women who assured viewers on Thursday night that there would be no hurricane. "There was no hurricane," he insisted. "A hurricane can last for hours. These were intense gusts of short duration." Whatever the definition of a hurricane, this freak storm produced exceptionally severe results among communities where people had been led to believe it would not happen. Yet one unexpected pause in the progress of the tempest off Cornwall generated a huge amount of devastating damage right across the southern area of England. This is an illustration of the powerful chaos concept known as the Butterfly Effect. One tiny change in one part of a complex unstable system can trigger a chain reaction of unforeseen events which culminates in huge overall changes.

Similarly, while some canny investors had always suspected the Great Crash of 1929 would not prove to be a unique event, in the main they never expected its successor would reverberate around the global market place as rapidly and catastrophically as it did 58 years later, almost to the day, in that disastrous week in October. And during November, once the reality of this huge financial calamity was squarely faced, many investors predicted, wrongly, as it turned out, that the world-wide plunge in share prices was foretelling the imminent arrival of another period of severe depression to mirror the three tragic years (from 1929–32) of an unrelieved contraction or slump in the real economy which had followed the October 1929 crash. The authorities in America and Europe were only too aware of the implications for a rerun of the 1930s depression, following the immensity of the global crash. To counteract the sudden massive loss of capital suffered world-wide, they reduced interest rates shortly after the crash.

Although there appeared to be an obvious parallel between the two Wall Street crashes of October 1929 and October 1987, the details reveal astonishing similarities together with some surprising differences. First, for the similarities: the behaviour of share prices as depicted by the closing levels of the DJIA on the last day of each month show some striking parallels. Both bull markets began in the second quarter; each lasted about 21 quarters; each hit its peak in the third quarter, with the timing of each separated by only a few days (3 September 1929 and 25 August 1987); in each case the nagging doubts phase lasted for 54 days – this was the period which elapsed between the peak and the crash. And, lastly, both crashes wiped more than 20 per cent off the stock market averages.

The main difference in these two events was the market reactions after the collapse, taking stock market performance as an indicator. Over the past nine years since the 1987 crash, the DJIA has risen steadily, to reach impressive new highs. This performance contrasts starkly with its moves between the September 1929 high and its ultimate low, nearly three years later, during which time the DJIA lost 89 per cent of its value. Many commentators have recently suggested that with the growth focus of the world economy shifting remorselessly towards Asia, the true comparison between events in America some 60 years ago is not with America today but with modern Japan. The collapse in the Tokyo stock market from 1990–5 has been less steep and more orderly than the dramatic collapse on Wall Street during October 1929, perhaps because there is more intervention in Japan by government officials. Nevertheless, since December 1989, when it hit an all-time high, the Japanese Nikkei Dow had lost 60 per cent of its value by July 1995.

Japanese Have Bubbles Too

This loss stems from Japan's financial bubble of 1986–95. Following the 1987 crash, the Americans and Europeans (excluding the reckless British) soon realised no recession would ensue. Early in 1988 they tightened monetary policy by raising interest rates, although Nigel Lawson chose this inopportune moment to introduce drastic tax cuts. However, despite a number of adverse factors then operating, the Americans persuaded the Japanese to retain their lax monetary policy. Japan's authorities held interest rates at a record post-war low until May 1989.

As the Japanese asset bubble sprang into being, their great penchant as remarkable copyists came into its own. One cannot know how much European history they had read, but like the Dutch, they invented marvellous new investment instruments. They issued convertible and warrant bonds. The detail of how these operate to give geared gains, or losses, is covered in Chapter 12. Like John Law and the directors of the 1920s investment trusts, they discovered the miracle of incestuously reinvesting in each others' shares. Like the directors of the South Sea and English Bubble Companies and Dutch tulip growers, they enjoyed the wonders of exciting new issue finances. As the bubble grew, the world watched, transfixed by the sheer scale of the numbers. Analysts thought the Japanese, with their inherent skills to succeed, were different. Sad to tell, they trod the well-worn path millions of irrational investors have trodden before them.

The Cheap Money Lure

The continued lax monetary policy of the Japanese Government after the 1987 crash fuelled rising share and property prices. Cheap money triggered a massive domestic buying spree as personal savings fell and personal wealth rose. Money was cheap enough to cease being a relevant criterion for evaluating new business projects. The strong yen impeded company prospects, so the government kept credit cheap and plentiful. Rather than borrow cheap funds for capital investments, Japanese companies began to speculate in the financial and property markets. The name given to their financial operations was "zaitech". It began quite modestly, as a way of cutting costs when profits fell, but in true bubble fashion, it rapidly acquired an inner momentum of its own, and had reached truly staggering proportions by 1989.

Too Good to Last

Ignoring any lessons posed by the October 1987 crash, Tokyo's stock market shot passed its 1987 peak in March 1988. Share prices rose by 120 per cent in the two years after the October 1987 crash. The Nikkei index rose from the post-crash low of 17,387 to a peak of 38,915 by late December 1989. And then the speculative bubble burst. The stock market ended 1990 with share prices 40 per cent lower. The 1990 low point on 1 October, saw the Nikkei index down to 20,221, almost half its December 1989 peak. However, during 1991 the slide continued so that prices reached a six-year low of 14,309 in August 1992 on the eve of a government announcement of measures to reflate the economy. This produced an eight-day rebound of 25.6 per cent. Meanwhile, the debt hangover is astronomical. Bad debts are guessed to be at least Y50,000 billion (£55bn). The world may have been spared the horrific consequences of a global debt deflation after the October 1987 crash, but the Japanese have been less fortunate. They have suffered a full-blown debt deflation, since the stock market slump began in December 1989.

A Chinese Footnote

From around the world, foreign investment is pouring into China as it opens its doors to Western technology and capital. The slumbering Asian giant is stirring. By the year 2000, China's economy may be three times its 1989 size. The potential for this vast untapped market of over 1.2 billion inhabitants is unimaginable. As part of the sweeping economic and financial reforms, begun in 1978, two stock markets were opened in Shanghai and Shenzen in the early 1990s. The Chinese have over £100 billion in underutilised savings; the stock markets have a mere 40 quoted companies; and demand is overwhelming. Share mania is gripping China.

In May 1992 two people were stabbed to death outside a stockbroker's office, while queuing for share application forms. In August, around 1 million people from all over China descended upon Shenzen, where the usual population is 2 million, to queue for share applications. They rioted in the streets for three days, smashing windows and cars, attacking each other and the police who fired shots and wielded wooden clubs.

The Global Bond Market Bubble of 1993–4

So we come finally to the great bond market bubble of 1993–4. On the seismic scale of crashes and bubbles, this comparatively recent incident rates very lowly; it is little more than a pimple on the long upward march of the global markets. The detailed account of this bubble is given in Chapter 13. At that stage, after we have more fully discussed the two 1720 bubbles and the three major twentieth-century examples, the reader will be more conversant with the way I believe chaos drives the markets. It will then be easier to see how replete with chaos features the '93–94 bond market bubble was. To avoid undue repetition we will therefore leave further consideration of this event until Chapter 13.

The Crash Mentality

This brief review of the crashes we will examine reveals the chequered persistence of the elements we have identified in the typical model. Many themes recur: the perennial attraction of new issues, the draw of leverage and margin trading, the circular loop of highly valued paper notes or profits chasing prices in a never-ending spiral, innovative financial instruments, the ingenuity of investment trusts building mighty pyramids of profits or losses, a swift convergence of new initiates as "investors" to where the main action lies, a mesmerising infatuation with rapidly rising prices, the arrival of crooks and tricksters, merger mania and silly sayings.

All these facets conspire to encourage more new entrants, until the top arrives in an explosive final climax, whereupon everyone is abruptly faced with a dramatic turnabout from the peak to the imminent plunge and the slump.

Participants, including the authorities, see each event as unique, but this is a tragic misinterpretation. Every example is a slight variant on a central theme – this is a key message of this book. History is a stern teacher. If we do not know where we have been in the past, how shall we ever understand where the future is leading us? The other vital message in the book is the role structure plays in separating profitable phases from unprofitable phases in market activity. And structure, as we shall repeatedly see, occurs everywhere in the markets, making prospects for profits all the more enticing. Yet one of the most absorbing themes that runs through all the speculative manias is the behaviour of the irrational investor, and our search for this intriguing character begins in the next chapter.

CHAPTER TWO

THE SEARCH FOR THE IRRATIONAL INVESTOR

Men, it has been well said, think in herds; it will be seen that they go mad in herds while they only recover their senses slowly and one by one.
Charles Mackay, *Extraordinary Popular Delusions and the Madness of Crowds*

Theorists talk at length about the rational investor, but in this chapter I want to find his opposite number, the irrational investor. He is the enigmatic anti-hero of every crash. If he exists, he surely will leave clear historical traces of his presence in the explosive booms and busts which are the stuff of most stock market crashes. We want, if possible, to identify some real and famous characters within the existing records, to fill this rather unglamorous role.

Apart from the obvious contradiction of irrational investors operating in a rational market, as suggested by orthodox market theory, there is also a contradiction linked to chaos theory to consider. If financial markets obey strict but simple mathematical rules, because they are governed by chaos, how does this match with the image of illogical investors acting out their dreams of unbridled wealth through impulsive emotional responses of hope, greed and fear? As we have seen, investor behaviour in bubbles is remarkably constant, and I believe the answer to this puzzle is that the behaviour of the markets is reflecting investor psychology which is governed by the presence of chaos in the financial markets. And this behaviour is not confined to gullible members of the public arriving almost at the peak. As we shall see, a throng of "experts" and professionals are just as likely to swing from a sober rational to a rampantly irrational investment frame of mind.

Common sense suggests that essentially the majority of investors should be a rational group. However, something specific is needed to flip investors *en masse*, including their professional advisers, from a rational to an irrational mental state. It requires a triggering act. And it is only possible for this peculiar switch to occur because the markets are driven by chaos. As we shall see, we cannot roundly lump all irrational investors into one bunch, comprising porters, lift attendants, shoe-shine boys and chamber maids. Some of the most worthy people in society can be smitten by the irrational investor bug. Professors, academics, bankers, company directors, politicians, ministers of the crown, all can make this curious leap from rational to irrational in the arena of investment moods. The evidence we shall discuss shows that they can become enthralled by certain wonderful enticements operating in the markets. Occasionally, facing these alluring inducements, and acting under the influence of the forces of chaos, ordinary investors develop Jekyll and Hyde personalities.

Investor Types

It is not easy to categorise types of investor/speculator. Definitions of both, whether rational or not, are rather vague. And because order can flip into chaos, we shall find, in later chapters, that people seem able almost effortlessly, to slip between the different categories. Sometimes even the most orthodox and cautious people switch from a rational to a hopelessly irrational mood, influenced, I believe by prevailing conditions in the markets. We do need some working definitions, however. Patently, the irrational investor is not the same as a speculator, who can be an extremely rational person, carefully evaluating his or her chances for making short-term gains. The Oxford dictionary defines "rational" as able to reason, sensible, sane, moderate, not foolish, absurd or extreme; it defines "irrational" as unreasonable, illogical, not endowed with reason. In any documented speculative boom and subsequent bust, the irrational investor, no matter how exorbitant his views, will clearly be in the majority, for this is what the plain statistics of escalating price performance towards the height of the boom is impassively recording.

An investor usually searches for long-term financial security, mainly through a stream of regular and rising income from his assets. He buys only what he sees as "safe" securities which can be held for a considerable time. The speculator is the person who buys any security purely to achieve a short-term gain. He buys solely in the expectation of being able to sell on quickly at a fine profit. He pays scant regard to either the pleasure of possession or the income prospects of the assets he buys. However, Jesse Livermore, the renowned 1920s speculator, claimed that the true speculator is the "long-term investor" who buys an investment at what he thinks is "fair value" and holds on faithfully, even while watching it fall until it has lost one- or two-thirds, or more, of the price he originally paid. Livermore saw the usual definition of a speculator as ill-suited, since speculators study the market closely to judge most shrewdly when to sell for a small loss and when to hold for a long-term gain. Such individuals may personify successful investors or speculators but are not by any definition, irrational investors.

Balancing Risk and Reward

Most rational investors apply some test to balance the level of risk against the possible rewards for any potential investment they plan to make. Methods for gauging risk can be rather *ad hoc*, especially among small private investors. Yet the complicated risk-control equations used by the professionals do not seem to prevent them succumbing periodically to the herd instinct approach when tempting new investment crazes come to light.

The enormous growth of interest in emerging markets during the early 1990s was fostered on the assumption, quite falsely, as it turned out, that diversifying into underdeveloped regions of the globe would spread the risks always associated with purchasing equities. By placing a small percentage of capital in the emerging regions of Latin America, China, India and Eastern Europe, investors sought to diversify their risks. This idea, attractive in theory, suddenly came to grief when the Mexican financial crisis over the peso erupted in December 1994, fuelling a stampede of investors exiting all the emerging markets *en masse*.

The authors of *The Beardstown Ladies Common Sense Investment Guide*, offer a better method of balancing risk and reward. Their hugely successful small investment club, run for 12 years by 16 ladies in middle America, had notched up an average gain of over 23 per cent annually in that time. Their recipe for measuring risk should be worth copying as they use an intriguing concept termed "the upside-down ratio". This evaluates the relative odds of potential gain versus the risk of loss for any given price of share. They suggest a 3 : 1 potential upside in the forecast appreciation of the stock is the safest ratio. The calculation works like this: first, you deduct the present cost of a share (say 150p) from its projected high, (perhaps 400p). This gives a figure of 250p. Then you subtract the forecast low (say 100p) from the present price, which gives a figure of 50p. By dividing the downside potential of 50p into the upside potential of 250p, you arrive at an upside-down ratio of 5 : 1. Using this formula, the share at this price of 150p would be viewed as a very attractive, low risk investment.

Chasing Fair Value

John Maynard Keynes, who made a fortune from his equity investments in the 1930s, had clear views on the way people gauged their investments. He argued that "professionals and speculators are not primarily concerned with making superior long-term forecasts but with foreseeing changes in the conventional basis of valuation a short time ahead of the general public". This activity he quaintly compared to a beauty contest; rather than selecting the contestant he thought the most beautiful, each judge would attempt to choose the contestant who was likely to be judged most beautiful by others.

The Efficient Market Hypothesis is the prevailing academic explanation of financial market behaviour. It currently ignores the idea of irrational investors, judging rationality by reference to investors' collective ability to calculate "fair value". This majority view of value is reflected directly in share price movements at all times so that, over the long term, no one can make exceptional profits in the markets except by the statistical law of averages, or by taking proportionally above average risks. It suggests that detailed analysis of the market, either through examining the fundamentals or by using technical analysis and charts, is a waste of time. In aggregate, share prices represent investors' current views of what is "fair value", whatever the state of the market.

This idea seems rather odd, since it implies that, collectively, at certain times, most investors may have a totally inaccurate view of "fair value". For how else are we to explain the sudden crashes that undoubtedly do happen? Although this "fair value" view of prices may be valid when markets are experiencing one of their frequent quiet or damped, phases, I do not think it applies in boom and bust scenarios. These latter are chaos-driven events when "fair value" will no longer be a relevant yardstick for the majority.

As noted in Chapter 1, bubbles sometimes develop in association with an emerging new product, industry or sector. Markets anticipate a future stream of earnings and dividends. When something entirely new arrives, it can be difficult to calculate its future potential by any of the usual financial yardsticks. At such times ideas of "fair value" are so fuzzy, they might play only a secondary role in investors' views. Instead, their focus centres on the immense potential returns a novelty may open up. This may be years into the future, but buying shares now is relatively easy. Hence, a band-wagon effect ensues; a boom mentality grips the investment community and overblown prospects help to fuel price rises even more. We shall see that this is a common theme in several of the stock market bubbles and crashes we will investigate in later chapters.

Yet even if the markets are governed by chaos, they can easily be rational in the long-run but liable to outbreaks of irrationality under extreme circumstances, as we know that order and chaos are forever intermixed in complex unstable systems. Milton Friedman, the Nobel prize-winning economist, has claimed that there is no such person as a destabilising speculator, since it implies he would be buying as prices rose and selling as they fell, thereby losing money. However, history reveals that this is precisely what the mass untutored public do at the height of every major boom, as the figures for purchases and sales of unit trusts in Britain and mutual funds in America confirm. Friedman suggests such people would fail to survive, in a Darwinian sense, thereby negating the idea that a destabilising speculation can occur.

I think that his analysis confuses financial distress with a terminal demise. Even in severe crashes, very few ruined investors commit suicide. Most simply struggle helplessly along, experiencing varying degrees of hardship and deprivation, as the 1930s Great Depression shows. A few determined characters may even rebuild their fortunes. Moreover, time after time, the authorities, as we shall see in later chapters, intervene in the calamitous aftermath to relieve the plight of the worst-off victims and re-establish some form of order. Finally, since history is on the side of the irrational speculator, confirming his presence time and again with a ruthless consistency, it contradicts Friedman's analysis. The species is clearly very much alive. I believe we must look for a better explanation; and we will find it in applying chaos concepts to these unstable markets, since the irrational investor is a product of chaos-induced market events.

Introducing the Irrational Investor

In our search for the irrational investor, we will find ourselves constantly comparing him to our ideal of the rational investor. This intuitive sage will recognise that the market has temporarily lost its senses and will retreat from the action, carrying off to safety a substantial booty. Rational investors, who may include among their number the hard-nosed speculators who ruthlessly calculate every risk, will be recognisable because they make and keep super-profits which they bank. Irrational investors, both novices and experts alike, either plunge in near the peak, or stay in to the bitter end, losing all their gains and often facing ruin. In some mysterious way, irrational investors have temporarily lost their sense of true values. Together with our yardsticks for profits or losses, these are the benchmarks we can apply to review some historical evidence for irrational investors as we take a time trip forward from 1720 to the present day, in our quest for these intriguing characters.

Anecdotal evidence for the existence of the irrational investor abounds in several books describing the most famous crashes, so this account will be brief. It is intended only to set the scene for a detailed examination of crash situations explained in terms of chaos concepts which follows in later pages. The records give us occasional glimpses of real participants in many of these dramatic incidents, but in addition price movements will sometimes have to serve as a vicarious indicator of mass investor behaviour since it is impossible to divorce the performance of share prices or relevant index movements from the behaviour of investors as a group. For it is these people themselves who give each crash scenario the kiss of life. This reliance on share price and index performance is especially important in both the Japanese and global bonds bubbles which are short of anecdotal stories.

I believe that crashes are pure chaos events and that irrational investors not only exist, but it is they, in fact, who become the raving majority, driving unstable booms and crashes to their ultimate extremes. What the chaos analysis will show is that investors are willing dupes, or in polite language, victims. They do, however, have Jekyll and Hyde personalities. Time and again, the evidence shows misguided people in authority create conditions for chaos to emerge. This prompts investors by the thousand to abandon their rational views in favour of an abrupt irrational "get-rich-quick" dream. And social standing, even academic brilliance, will be no protection from this cloak of avarice which suddenly descends, engulfing a personality entirely and separating him completely from his faculty of reason.

Silly Season Quotes

One warning sign that a bull market is nearing a dangerous peak is when some sectors of the press turn from their usual interests to examine prospects for future gains in the market. Philip Coggan noted this cautionary signal on 18 March 1996, a week after the Dow Jones Industrial Average (DJIA) had lost 171 points on Friday 8 March, only to rebound by 110 points on the following Monday. In a *Financial Times* article on 18 March 1996, he commented:

> Collectors of stock market omens need look no further. The cover of April's *Playboy* magazine highlights an article on picking successful mutual funds. When Joe Sixpack stops looking at naked ladies long enough to phone his broker, that is probably a sign that the top of a bull market is near.

Another clear signal that investors are veering towards chaos is the sudden rush of public pronouncements extolling the cheapness of shares, the limitless opportunities for gains and the equable climate for future prosperity. The more expensive a market becomes, with meteoric price rises, the more financial analysts, commentators and notable public figures argue it is cheaper than it looks. The higher prices rise, the more explanations will be forthcoming to justify the rises; and everyone becomes convinced that **this time it really is different**. Every raging bull market brings its cluster of arresting silly season quotes by influential people who are thought to be more knowledgeable than the rest of us.

In *The Great Crash*, J. K. Galbraith quotes the distinction between an investor and a gambler offered by Will Payne, in the January 1929 issue of *World's Work*. He concluded a gambler wins only because someone else loses, but with investment, all gain. "One investor," he observed, "buys General Motors at $100, sells it to another at $150, who sells it to a third at $200. Everyone makes money." Even President Coolidge, on leaving office in 1929 considered the economy was absolutely sound, and stocks were "cheap at current prices". Such ill-judged observations reveal quite starkly what a muddle intelligent people can land themselves in when discussing this tricky topic.

In July 1995, when Wall Street was blasting up to new highs on a daily basis, Professor Merton Miller, a Nobel economics prize-winner, argued in a speech at Manila that derivatives horrors are just wealth transfers. There is no net social cost to ordinary people or nations. This view of derivatives as a zero sum game because sellers match buyers every time these innovative instruments change hands, sounds superficially appealing. However, this analysis ignores the definition of a derivative. As their name suggests, derivatives are based on (that is, "derived" from) the underlying value of more conventional forms of investment. In a crisis, therefore, there will be a crucial link between extreme price movements of derivatives and the underlying real assets from which they are derived. They will be based on shares, bonds, currencies or commodities, but a wipe-out of derivatives in a future crash might create a chain reaction of losses in real assets, with a massive tangible reduction in wealth. This link explains the nasty knock-on effect after the collapse of the British Barings Bank in March 1995, due to unauthorised futures trading by one high-flying trader in the Far East. The bank's collapse caused large personal and business losses for its innocent depositors, whose capital was swallowed up in the fall-out from this mammoth trading disaster.

An author in a *New York Times* article early in 1995, lampooned the kind of thinking which carries people away as the boom rages on. A strong economy is good for earnings, which is good for stocks; a weaker economy lowers interest rates, which is good for stocks. Again, we have a win-win situation. Another common belief is that everyone will know when to sell, and there will be willing buyers at that time. While this atmosphere of persuasive delusion spreads, any notion of "fair value" becomes almost irrelevant as a boom peaks. Very few investors can recognise a peak, or even the warning signs of price extremes. Initial declines tempt in those who watched impatiently from the sidelines, as prices were rising before they had bought their investments. They are waiting for prices to drop, so that they can join in the next upsurge in prices. This is precisely what Lord Carnavon hoped to do.

Where is the Market Heading?

In a revealing biography of Richard Cantillon, an Irish banker living in France during the Mississippi Bubble, Antoin Murphy documents share purchases by Cantillon, Lord Carnavon, Joseph Gage and Lady Mary Herbert, some of the biggest speculators in Mississippi shares. Cantillon was associated with John Law at an early stage of the Mississippi System. The correspondences which Murphy quotes highlight the attitudes which shaped their investment decisions. Although these cover only a few of the thousands of speculators operating in Mississippi shares at the time, the letters do not offer much insight into "fair value" considerations. Rather, they tend to show that for these people, at least, their **views of future market direction** was an over-riding perception and a prime motivator of their actions.

A letter from Lord Carnavon (originally plain James Brydges and later, the Duke of Chandos) reveals his thoughts on missing out on the first big rise in Mississippi shares. "It was by great ill fortune I missed having my share of good luck in your Company," he wrote to Richard Cantillon, his protégé, on 3 August 1719. He goes on to ask if Cantillon will enquire of John Law "whether he judges the harvest be over or if there is room still left to be a gainer in my own affairs". Lord Carnavon was considering investing £20,000 in Mississippi shares in August 1719 assuming he received favourable inside information from John Law via Cantillon. During September, when the ultra-cautious Cantillon had already banked his hefty Mississippi gains, Carnavon placed £40,000 at the disposal of Drummond's Bank, to be invested under the personal supervision of Law himself. His letter suggests his primary concern for judging whether to buy centred on the possibility of further rises, since he had missed out on the early gains.

For Joseph Gage, a letter from Daniel Pulteney, working at the British embassy in Paris, sheds light on his immediate ambitions. "Mr Gage reckons himself already worth 50,000 l.t. a year [livres tournois were the French unit of account equivalent to the pound sterling in Britain, neither of which existed as a coin at this time] and says he will not be satisfied till he has got 100,000." Although in his early dealings Gage did amass a fortune in Mississippi shares, he was wiped out by the collapse of the French stock market in 1720.

The tale of Lady Mary Herbert, his long-term partner and mistress, is equally enlightening, for correspondence on her investment activities reveals her to have been a speculator extraordinary. She was so optimistic about the prospects of profiting from Law's paper credit schemes, she entered into a large series of speculative positions in the three financial centres of London, Paris and Amsterdam. She made dealings through among others, William Law, brother and agent of John, Lord Londonderry, the Bank of England, Richard Cantillon and Samuel Edwin, a wealthy trader. The range of financial instruments she used included buying and selling shares, options and foreign currencies. Through these activities Murphy calculates that her debts notched up to an amazing total of £94,938.12s.8d in the South Sea and Mississippi booms, indicating the extent of her outstanding expectations.

The idea of "fair value" is only obliquely alluded to by Cantillon, who was clearly a rational investor. He retained his fortune by selling out well before the peak. As a result of his caution he joined the ranks of those successful 1720 investors who were dubbed "millionaires", a term introduced to the financial vocabulary to mark those who made seven-figure fortunes and sold out before the collapse.

Robert Schiller, in a questionnaire survey of 1987 individual and institutional investors, found that what was chiefly on peoples' minds on the morning of the crash, 19 October, was the drop in prices that morning. And the second most important news story on their minds was the price drops of the previous week. This again suggests that in a time of rapidly changing prices, what preoccupies investors is nothing more complicated than the future direction of the market. This point is endorsed by a study of peoples' attitudes to the 44 per cent plunge in the DJIA on 3 September 1946. The American Securities and Exchange Commission held detailed interviews with most large participants and a sample of smaller public customers who bought or sold securities on that day. The reason most frequently mentioned for selling was that prices were falling and other people were selling exactly what Robert Schiller found 41 years later in his questionnaire on the 1987 crash.

Jekyll and Hyde Investors/Speculators

Booms are presumed to be driven by speculators, while rational investors stand sagely on the sidelines, having sold out to incoming gamblers.

Examples of investors with a timely talent for retaining their gains include, Thomas Guy (the South Sea Bubble), Richard Cantillon and Madame Chaumont (Mississippi Bubble), Joseph P. Kennedy (the Wall Street crash of 1929), Warren Buffett (the major decline of 1972–4) and Sir James Goldsmith (the October 1987 crash). However, just as it is thought that a fragile thread separates sanity from madness, so perhaps only a delicate strand separates the rational from the irrational investor. Moreover, I think that the one can metamorphose swiftly into the other, when the conditions are right.

Shop assistants, waiters, doctors and lawyers might be speculators or simply irrational investors, as they plunge indiscriminately into the market at a major top, determined purely on making instant gains, but what are we to make of the thousands caught up in the Great Crash of 1929, or the tens of thousands involved in the débâcle of 1987? The definitions, like life itself, are complex and offer multiple choices while we prefer clear-cut explanations and tidy answers. Rather than ponder on the definitions, let us turn now to meet some of the investors themselves.

Shrewd South Sea Investors

Consider some who bought shares in the South Sea Company. Amid all the frenzy of the Company's rising fortunes, the behaviour of a few prominent investors stands out. The shrewd Thomas Guy is notable as a beacon of financial prudence. He was a bachelor with a reputation for meanness, publishing and distributing English translation Bibles from his premises in St Thomas Street, beside London Bridge. In the early years of the Company's existence, Guy bought several blocks of shares, keeping detailed records of his purchases in a ledger. In April 1720, he had total holdings of £54,000, worth well over £150,000 on the open market. As the price began to rise, he slowly fed his entire holding into the strongly rising market over a period of six weeks between April and June. He was careful never to sell in parcels exceeding 1,000 at a time, to obtain the best prices, accepting only cash. He amassed an immense fortune of £234,000, with which he built and endowed the famous Guy's Hospital on the site of his book publishing premises. This was the largest honest profit achieved in South Sea shares, and was reckoned by Carswell in *The South Sea Bubble*, as "the best memorial of the Bubble".

Or compare the rational Madame Chaumont, whose bumper Mississippi millions allowed her to join the ranks of the nouveau rich, with Sarah, Duchess of Marlborough, another shrewd South Sea investor. Sir Winston Churchill, her famous descendant, whom we shall shortly meet caught up in the Great Crash of 1929, praised what he termed her "almost repellent common sense" in creaming off £100,000 before the bubble burst. In his biography of the Duchess, David Green recounts how in early June she sold out all her holdings and put the money into bank and insurance shares. When James Craggs Senior subsequently suggested the Duke should buy South Sea stock, the redoubtable Sarah replied, "I had persuaded him to sell out of the South Sea and I would do all that I could to oppose him buying again." She was greatly shocked by the whole sordid affair and boldly said so.

And their Irrational Counterparts

Those who lost a fortune heavily outweighed the gainers in the bubble; the Duke of Chandos admitted to having lost £700,000 of his profits from other speculations in the collapse, but this was clearly extreme. His penchant for speculation was captured by the 1st Earl of Onslow's quip, "a bubble to every project". Lord Londonderry had lost over £50,000, while the Dukes of Bolton and Wharton were facing ruin.

Then, again, consider the behaviour of the Master of the Mint, Sir Isaac Newton. As one of the most remarkable scientists who ever lived he surely ranks as an exceptionally rational man, yet his actions over South Sea shares illustrate the fatal magnetic attraction posed by a spectacular bull market. When asked early in 1720 for his views on the stock's prospects, he is said to have replied that he could calculate the motions of the heavenly bodies, but not the madness of crowds. Acting promptly on this sensible view, he joined the band of the few known rational investors by signing a power of attorney on 20 April to dispose of his £7,000 holdings in the shares for a 100 per cent profit. Unfortunately, in the early summer, he was seized by a compelling impulse to re-enter the market, reinvested a larger amount right at the top and finally showed a loss of £20,000. The story goes that he could never afterwards bear to hear the name, "South Sea", without experiencing a shudder, and who, alas, could blame him?

The share dealings of another prominent investor, King George I, Governor of the South Sea Company, repeat Newton's miserable experience, endorsing how easy it is to slip from being a rational to an irrational investor. Despite his immense wealth as King of England and Elector of Hanover establishing him as one of the wealthiest men in the realm, George's incongruous behaviour casts him in the role of thousands of his own humble subjects, anxious not to miss out on prospects for future enrichment. He was an initial subscriber for £20,000 in the First Money Subscription on 14 April 1720. The royal archives at Windsor confirm he paid this amount as a first instalment on £100,000. He was therefore not party to the massive fraud tied to the directors' launch of the conversion scheme.

Early in June, at the high tide for South Sea finance, the Chancellor of the Exchequer, Aislabie, persuaded the King to cash in his sizeable profit of £86,000. With his "insider" knowledge of the fraudulent scheme, the Minister was growing daily more worried about looming hazards. With the King about to depart for his customary summer trip to Hanover, imagine Aislabie's misgivings when His Majesty demanded his entire profit plus his original investment should immediately be reinvested in the ludicrously over-generous Third Money Subscription. In what must have been a most unpleasant interview, Aislabie cautioned that "the stock was carried up to an Exorbitant height by the madness of people, and that it was impossible it should stand". After much wrangling the King finally agreed to place £40,000 in the safety of tallies (a form of government debt) but insisted that £66,000 should be returned to South Sea stock in which he had total confidence. By November this investment had fallen to below £10,000. The final total estimated loss on his holdings, according to Aislabie, was £35,704. In 1721, after the Parliamentary inquiry into the South Sea débâcle, Aislabie quietly reinstated most of the King's lost paper profits.

We can complete this trio of tribulation now by citing the harrowing experiences of Sir Robert Walpole, arguably the most celebrated British Prime Minister who ever served the crown. He still holds the record as the longest serving first minister in British history. Moreover, his career took a vaulting upwards leap when he was appointed, by public demand, to resolve the awesome financial and political crisis thrown up by the collapse of the Company in December 1720. His unsullied reputation rested on two supposedly brilliant insights: first, his bitter opposition to the passage of the South Sea Bill through Parliament where he was reputedly warning of the speculative dangers involved, and secondly, his timely retreat at the end of July to his Norfolk estate which effectively dissociated him from the imminently unfolding scandal.

In 1956, a carefully researched biography of Walpole by J. H. Plumb reported the details of the debate on the South Sea Bill written by Thomas Broderick MP. Plumb exploded the idea that Walpole was vehemently against the scheme. In fact, his dealings in South Sea shares reveal him to be yet another major loser, on a par with Newton and King George. Walpole's account book with Messrs Gibson, Jacob and Jacombe of Lothbury Street, Scriveners and Bankers, recounts his dealings. In June 1719 Walpole owned £18,760 7s in South Sea stock. By 1 January 1720 he had reduced this to £9,760 7s, but on 25 January he sold £18,000 of nominal stock for £24,383 15s. On 15 February he received £9,000 in South Sea stock from a Mr Soper, paying him £8,770. Plumb assumes this curious transaction provided the stock Walpole had earlier sold. Having finally disposed of his remaining £760 7s on 18 March, he had divested himself of all his holdings just a matter of a few weeks before the passage of the Bill. His timing was excruciatingly poor, for if he had held his stock, he would have made a fortune. Instead, he did not reinvest in the Company until June 1720, just when the shares were peaking. Plumb reckons his personal loss was in the order of £50,000.

The common thread uniting the pragmatic King George, the scientific genius, Newton, and the greatest British Prime Minister of all time, which tossed them all into the irrational investors' camp, was the announcement of the unbelievably generous Third Money Subscription. Its terms were so absurdly generous, it proved exceedingly difficult, even for sober-minded people, to avoid temptation.

Irrational Investors – 1929 Style

Accounts of two of the many thousands who suffered substantial losses in the Great Crash are mentioned here because their significant contributions to twentieth-century history mark them out as exceptionally rational men. Treading in the footsteps of the genius Sir Isaac Newton who was lured into irrationality by South Sea Company propaganda, each succumbed to the beguiling influence of 1920s prosperity blooming all around them. First, is the famous theoretical economist, Professor Irving Fisher. We met him briefly, waxing lyrical on the eve of the crash, about encouraging prospects for the American stock market to remain on a permanently high plateau. This slender academic, with a patrician manner and an immaculately trimmed beard, is known to posterity for his brilliant insight in formulating a simple equation to illustrate the circulation of money in a modern economy. This was his major contribution to the "dismal science" of economics. He had the reputation in the 1920s as perhaps the greatest economist America had yet produced.

Even after the 1929 crash, Fisher remained convinced the rise of stock prices was justified by the fundamentals. He based his assessment on the evidence of the exceptional economic growth occurring during the 1920s and the transformations wrought by new financial innovations. In a book published two months after the crash (but mainly written before it had occurred), he presented his carefully reasoned arguments to show the market was not overpriced. His genius as a theorist was offset by his pathetic performance as a speculator. During the late 1920s, he made a series of disastrous stock market investments, losing between $8 and $10 million.

Winston Churchill was another celebrated crash victim. He earned his place in history as one of the greatest twentieth-century statesmen, master-minding the Allied efforts to destroy Adolf Hitler in the Second World War. He was also a great historian and wrote several major works. With such a pedigree, it seems odd that he succumbed to the rampant speculative urge. Ironically, destiny had brought him to New York in October 1929 while on a lecture tour of Canada and America with his son, Randolph. They were guests of Bernard Baruch, one of the most acclaimed speculators of the age. Randolph described Baruch in his diary as "the greatest speculator there has ever been. He actually bought a seat on the New York Stock Exchange costing one hundred thousand pounds solely in order to transact his own business."

Churchill purchased a large block of shares, investing his past literary earnings. On royalties for future and past books and articles he had made £8,700. "I am trying to keep £20,000 fluid for investment and speculation," he wrote to his wife, Clementine, on 29 September. He put up a total of £20,000 for his purchases with money earned during his American visit. "This vast sum," he explained in a letter to her, "must not be frittered away." His prospects for gain, however, were completely illusory with the market poised for its great collapse even as he was putting his hard earned income into it. He lost £40,000 in the crash, equivalent to more than half a million pounds in 1981 money. He could ill afford this savage loss, which necessitated some painful "belt tightening" over the next few years.

Rational 1929 Investors

Anecdotal evidence for rational 1929 investors, who made a fortune and hung on to it, make equally fascinating reading. Bernard Baruch became legendary for his ability to build a massive fortune during the great bull run, selling in good time to conserve it through the 1930s. One light-hearted story features the world-famous song composer of the age, Irving Berlin. He found himself crossing the Atlantic in an ocean liner which had newly installed telegraphic links with the land, for the convenience of stock-watching passengers. On the luxury liner, Ile de France, his was one of the first transactions effected on the opening day of 17 August. Berlin sold 1,000 shares of Paramount-Famous-Lasky at 72. By this sale, he joined the ranks of the rational investors. The stock later fell to almost nothing and the company subsequently went into bankruptcy.

Joseph P. Kennedy, father of President, John F. Kennedy, who had built a fortune of around $300 million by 1961, was one of the most successful speculators-turned-investors of the age. During a three-year stay in Hollywood, he had accumulated between $6–$8 million, returning to New York in the spring of 1929 as a multi-millionaire. Although he had been a great speculator during the early 1920s, his assessment of the market in 1929 shows he had suddenly become rather conservative, anxious to preserve his new-found fortune. To the surprise of all his friends, he refused to be drawn into the market to reinvest the huge cash proceeds from his Hollywood shares. When asked why he had become so bearish, holding mainly cash, he replied that when shoe-shine boys were handing out tips and calling the turns in the market, as he saw now, it was time to get out. His pet saying was "Only a fool holds out for the top dollar". During that summer, while most big Wall Street traders were buying, Joe Kennedy was steadily selling out of all his holdings.

Other big-time operators who avoided being swept along by the growing hysteria included William Crapo Durant. This big-time pool schemer was the founder of General Motors. He sold out in May. John D. Rockefeller, Jnr. began moving into cash during June. And Michael C. Bouvier, head of his old established and influential family which would witness the marriage of Jacqueline to Jack F. Kennedy in 1953, had unloaded almost all his common stock by September, thereby keeping at least $3.8 million of his $7 million fortune intact. Aged 82, he was one of the most senior members of the exchange. He sold his rights to a second seat on the New York Stock Exchange for $125,000, nine days before the first panic in prices. John V. Bouvier, Jnr, Jaqueline's grandfather kept a diary of the crash. On Tuesday 29 October, the worst day in the history of Wall Street, he wrote, "XXXX Blackest Panic Day of All. Record 16,410,000 shares traded. No bids at last prices. No bids – no bids." On 13 November, the day on which the lowest prices of 1929 were reached, his diary recorded, "no bids in many stocks". By this time the *New York Times* index had slumped 249 points from its 3 September high of 452, and more than $30 billion worth of securities values had disappeared. John V. Bouvier, Jnr, principal heir to his uncle M. C. Bouvier, lost at least half of his $250,000 inheritance from his parents.

His son, John V. Bouvier III, shorted the market during the early November falls and made substantial profits, only to see them disappear on 6 November, a day that was quickly dubbed "the crash after the crash". His father, John V. Bouvier, Jnr, wrote of this day in his diary, "Market opened with a severe decline. Steel went to a new low at 166. Exchange closed at 1.00 pm. Jack's $100,000 profits (off short sales) swept away."

Joseph Kennedy was brilliant at making money. Not only did he emerge unscathed through the Great Crash, he actually grew richer. He made profits of about one million dollars from the collapse; as the market fell, he sold stocks short (selling stocks he had borrowed, hoping to buy them back and return them, after the market had fallen). Working from a desk at the Madison Avenue branch of the brokerage firm of Halle and Steiglitz, Kennedy became the leader of the fraternity of "bears" who rode the market down towards Black Thursday. His reputation spread so widely, it was known even to his young children. Within a few weeks, his short selling strategy had produced amazing profits, reputedly of $15 million, mainly by selling Anaconda and Paramount. It has been said that by 1930 he was worth $100 million.

Other Wall Street bears who came out winning handsomely included the legendary Jesse Livermore and William Danforth. During the week before the crash, 14–18 October, they became very active. Joseph Kennedy had a social conscience that was possibly keener than other Wall Street bears, however, for he later described his fears at this critical juncture in America's evolution: "I felt and said I would be willing to part with half of what I had if I could be sure of keeping, under law and order, the other half."

1987 Investors

People aged under 70 were too young in 1987 to remember the suffering caused by the 1929 crash and the Great Depression that followed in its wake. Most leaders of the Western world, excluding the octogenarian President Reagan, learned of the crash in books, history lessons, or by hearsay. Perhaps that is why people seem to repeat the same mistakes at long-term intervals. The cycle of errors misses one generation, so that people tend to repeat the mistakes of their grandparents. In investment circles, one reason for this is that the market has only a limited long-term memory, and history book lessons are not as potent and unforgettable as bitter first-hand experiences. People are by nature invariably optimistic, always imagining that this time it will be different. Yet even if the circumstances differ slightly each time around, people's behaviour is uncannily constant.

The irrational investor has survived, almost unscathed, the great and awesome panics of past generations, and he hovers, like a dispossessed spectre over today's location-less financial markets. His manic behaviour recurs with outstanding regularity, but his persistence springs from the provocation offered by cheap money, limitless credit, imaginative new trading facilities or techniques and a boundless optimism, born from the dying embers of each preceding slump. Only when all these elements conspire together does the irrational investor re-surface, charged with a new vigour, to stalk yet again his old familiar haunts.

In our search for 1987 rational and irrational investors, we will look at the behaviour of some of the key American players in the drama, including four short accounts from interviews given by top traders to expound on their guiding rules for achieving investment success and avoiding failures. The stories of Paul Tudor Jones, Bruce Kovner, Marty Schwarz and Michael Steinhardt appear in Jack D. Schwager's best seller, *Market Wizards*. This was first published in 1989, so his interviews naturally included questions about traders' activities in the run up to and aftermath of the crash. All four were active market participants, keen to make profits in any market conditions; as such, the terms rational and irrational are hardly applicable. However, although they are professional fund managers or traders for their own account, it is interesting to compare their thoughts and actions with those of Mississippi speculators, described earlier in the chapter.

Although the age and circumstances were entirely different, and admittedly, only four opinions are quoted, once again, their comments indicate their chief considerations centred mainly on market direction, rather than "fair value". Perhaps the message of their actions is that when rational investors face turbulent market conditions, short-term market direction becomes the critical indicator for capital preservation rather than "fair value" itself.

They Got it Right

In the month of October 1987, when most investors were nursing unbelievable losses, the Tudor Futures Fund, managed by Paul Tudor Jones, registered an incredible 62 per cent return. He described the week of the crash as one of the most exciting periods of his life. He had been expecting a major stock market crash since mid-1986 and had drawn up contingency plans because he foresaw a "financial meltdown".

He noted that the Friday before 19 October saw a record volume on the selling side. This same occurrence had happened two days before the 1929 crash. He reckoned the weekend comments by Treasury Secretary Baker on disagreements with West Germany's interest rate policy were the kiss of death for the markets. Not only did he correctly guess the direction of the stock market, he also made huge profits on bonds.

> I kept on thinking: What is the Fed reaction going to be? I thought they would have to add massive amounts of liquidity to create a very rosy environment, instantaneously. However, since bonds had been acting poorly all day, I couldn't bring myself to pull the trigger on a long bond position (meaning to buy bonds). During the last half hour of trading, bonds suddenly started to turn up, and it clicked in my mind that the Fed was going to take actions that would create a tremendous upsurge in bond prices. As soon as I saw the bond market act right for a moment, I went wild.

He expected interest rates to fall, which would cause a drop in the yield on bonds and the price of the bonds would therefore rise, giving him bumper profits, which was precisely what subsequently happened.

Bruce Kovner was one of the world's largest traders in interbank currency and futures markets in the 1980s. In 1987 he made profits in excess of $300 million for himself and the clients in his funds. He spoke of the tussles in his mind during the week following the 19 October collapse, to find a convincing scenario of what would happen to the dollar. By the end of the week his confusion was resolved.

> It was then that it all coalesced in my mind. It became absolutely clear to me that given the combination of a need for stimulative action, dictated by the tremendous world-wide financial panic, . . . someone had to play the stimulative role, and that someone would be the United States. As a result, the dollar would drop and it would not be in the interest of the other central banks to defend it.

This action to bolster shaken confidence was based on the inflationary impact of a falling currency, equivalent to a drop in interest rates, to give the markets a boost. This response by the authorities was completely different to the deflationary attitudes of the American central bank in 1929 and the attitude of the Japanese authorities from 1990–5, when facing an intractable 1990s debt deflation in Japan. In 1987, the actions on the dollar, as a boost to help in restoring the confidence of global investors demonstrates, in this instance, the readiness of the authorities to learn the grim lessons of deflation that had plagued the tragic history of the 1930s.

In *Billionaire*, Ivan Fallon records the superb timing skills of Sir James Goldsmith. This phenomenal sense of timing, enabled him to keep his massive fortune intact during the October crash. Not only did he accurately forecast the impending crash, he had the foresight to act upon his instincts. He sold almost everything he owned, including his house on 80th Street, just before the October calamity struck. In late July, he astonished his business colleagues by selling 95 per cent of his French flagship company, Generale Occidentale. In September, he and John Aspinall sold the London Casino to Brent Walker for £90 million, of which Goldsmith's share was £34 million on an original investment of less than £800,000. He also sold his French publishing interests, L'Express and Les Prèsses de la Cité.

Rumours of his massive sell-off began to circulate among the business community. Share and asset prices world-wide were streaking up, the economic boom was in full swing and political stability seemed well-assured. With scarcely a serious problem looming, this seemed like the worst possible moment to abandon the market, but his perceptive talents had warned him in good time on several previous occasions. He spotted the 1971–2 boom, the mid-1970s collapse and the early 1980s boom. How did his finely tuned antennae alert him to the imminent demise of the 1987 boom? He was later to say, "It wasn't any one sign. Everything was pointing to it. Prices were much too high, and the bills coming out of the Congress were as bad as anything produced by the socialists in Britain in the early 1970s." For this exquisite piece of market timing, he became the most talked-of person in the investment fraternity of America. He now had almost 1 billion in cash, as he prepared for the financial meltdown he expected would soon materialise. Having managed his exit from the market almost to perfection, *Time Magazine* compared him with Joseph P. Kennedy, who as we noted earlier, had escaped unscathed in 1929.

Another celebrated financier of the decade was Donald Trump. His charmed escape from the market was also a brilliant stroke of timing, as he liquidated all his holdings with just a few days to spare. This larger-than-life property developer, hotel and casino owner tycoon was so enthralled by his dealing achievements, he co-authored a book *Trump: the art of the Deal* explaining how he had made himself into a billionaire. Unfortunately, his property empire disintegrated under a mountain of debt during the late 1980s property crash, so his excellent market timing on Wall Street soon began to look rather superficial.

They Got it Wrong

In *Market Wizards*, Marty Schwarz described his bad experiences in the week of the crash.

> I came in long. [He was a buyer]. I have thought about it, and I would do the same thing again. Why? Because on October 16 the market fell 108 points, which, at the time, was the biggest one-day point decline in the history of the stock exchange. It looked climactic to me, and I thought that was a buying opportunity.

On the Monday, he liquidated his position and lost $315,000. Another top trader, Michael Steinhardt, was also heavily exposed, 80–90 per cent, on the buying side. He recalls how he increased his position during the day of 19 October, strictly because he always takes the contrarian trade.

> When the markets have an enormous move, most of the time, it is right to take the view that there is a lot of emotionalism and extremism in that move. If you can maintain a bit of a distance from the emotionalism, you tend to do well.

Although this is a good philosophy for removing the emotionalism from market trading, in this instance, it was mistimed as the market continued to fall even lower.

Some of the most sophisticated and experienced financiers of the age were completely wiped out, including the Australian entrepreneur, Robert Holmes à Court. Rupert Murdoch, the newspaper tycoon, saw his fortune collapse by $700 million in one day, mainly in a single hour. Many of the famed Wall Street traders got caught, including Carl Icahn, who was left holding the bankrupt TWA airline when the crash struck, and Ron Perelman, who had built his empire on junk bonds. He had to sell his Revlon holdings, to reduce his enormous borrowings.

Finally, there is the tale of George Soros and the October crash. His account was not included in Market Wizards, but it became known that his hugely successful fund, the Quantum Fund, was estimated to have lost up to $800 million in the crash, although it still managed to boost investment returns by 14 per cent for the year as a whole, because the markets had risen so strongly prior to the crash. Soros had warned for months that the Japanese market was wildly overpriced. He was expecting a crash, but had predicted that it would mainly affect Japan. He had not expected it to be in America.

Japanese Irrational Investors

During the late 1980s, as the Japanese asset bubble bloomed, the metamorphosis of investors from rational to irrational spread like a contagion through the entire investing community. With a wondrous predictability that can only be savoured with the benefit of hindsight they trod the paths taken by previous bubble players as if they knew the script by heart. Indeed, part of the miracle of Japan's post-war economic success has been based on their brilliant ability to copy from others what they perceive to be winning formulae. Their uncanny knack of imitating the pivotal features of all the preceding bubbles we have mentioned is a truly exceptional irony of fate.

The South Sea Bubble – Japanese Style

It is hard to think of a greater cultural or social contrast between pre-industrial, aristocratic Britain in 1720 and the mass democracy of post-industrial modern Japan, but the chequered histories of the South Sea Company and Japan's largest telecommunications company, NTT, seem effortlessly to bridge this huge cultural divide. As Brian Reading relates, in *Japan: The Coming Collapse*, mid-way through 1987 the Japanese Government announced the sale of the second tranche of NTT shares in the on-going privatisation of the company. The first tranche of NTT shares had been issued in February at a mind-numbing price of Y1.197 million, valuing it at nearly 100 times more than the average company quoted on the Tokyo stock market. Yet despite this startling overvaluation, 8 million Japanese investors applied for the second tranche, clearly anticipating that the future direction of NTT shares would continue to be upwards.

For surely, if they had thought the shares were overvalued, they would not have expected to make additional gains from their new NTT holdings. This collective vote of confidence in the future performance of the privatised NTT rested on a widely-held view among investors that the issuing authorities would want the privatisation programme to be successful so that they could subsequently launch further issues. To achieve this it was presumed they would do everything possible to ensure the shares reached a satisfying opening premium on the launch. To judge purely from their actions, it seems an unavoidable conclusion that, like other irrational investors we have discussed, the main preoccupation of Japanese investors with the imminent flotation was the expected upwards direction in which the shares would move rather than any notion of "fair value", since the shares were already standing at a colossal premium to the market. The expectation of further rises was among their foremost reasons for buying more NTT shares.

Japanese Investors Search for "Fair Value"

However, due to the astronomical price of NTT shares, the second tranche, planned for 9 November 1987, required the massive sum of Y5.7 trillion, ($35 bn) from the Japanese investing public to fully finance it. *En masse*, Japanese investors now faced the problem of raising this amount of cash to fund their additional purchases, a problem which unavoidably involved a search for "relative fair value" within their portfolios of financial assets. During the early autumn, in an aggregate "search" exercise, they had to evaluate which of their current assets to liquidate to raise the cash to take up the forthcoming NTT issue. The statistics tell the story.

Virtually in unison, under the pressure to raise cash, they decided that the US dollar looked weak and they began selling their huge holdings of US bonds to repatriate funds to Japan. From January to August 1987, purchases of US Treasury bonds had averaged $8 billion a month. These slumped to $1 billion in September. In October, Japanese investors sold vast amounts of these US government bonds. Their concerted selling actions depressed the bond prices and drove the yield on a 30-year Treasury bond up through 10 per cent, since bond prices and the yield on them always move in opposite directions.

American Investors Search for 'Fair Value'

The role of thousands of Japanese investors in forcing the yield on the 30-year Treasury bond up through 10 per cent was not known until months after the October crash, when Nicholas Brady submitted his report on the causes of the crash to President Reagan. Yet, even in their ignorance of what had caused the huge bond sell-off, it was now the turn of US investors to respond to the rise in the yield of the Treasury bonds. Did they face the dilemmas of "fair value"? Their actions suggest the answer was "yes", but what were their possible motives for a massed panic flight out of equities that now began?

The great sell-off of US bonds by Japanese investors forced US investors to confront a domestic investment puzzle. What were the implications of a yield of 10 per cent on a long-term US Treasury bond? At this level it offered a return that was four times the return on equities, standing then at a historical low of 2.5 per cent. For some US investors, this yield gap between equities and bonds might seem an ominous signal that equities were alarmingly overvalued compared to bonds. Others would think inflation was set to rise as bond yields always rise when investors suspect inflation is about to increase. Yet others might simply decide to take instant advantage of the higher yield, switching from equities into bonds. Whatever the reason for action, very few, presumably, until the inquest into what went wrong was finally published, would have guessed that the major reason for plunging bond values was the proposed November sale of NTT shares in Japan, about 6,700 miles away. Yet this tenuous link caused huge capital flows across the world's financial markets and contributed to the worst catastrophic sell-off in global securities for 58 years. As the bond price sank, the flight from equities accelerated, first on Wall Street (in the week before 19 October), then on the Far Eastern markets of Japan, Australia and Asia, and on to London and Europe. The entire world was gripped by the horror of the largest securities selling crescendo ever known.

The Voice of Japan's Rational/Irrational Investors

And what of the share price for the fabled NTT? From its original flotation price of Y1.197 million in February 1987, and its rapid ascent to a peak of Y3.18 million in the spring, it closed on 7 August 1992, at an all time low to date of Y509,000 (£2,100), with a fall of Y42,000 on that day. In true bubble tradition, this is a fall of 84 per cent from the high. The company has 1.6 million individual shareholders, mostly owning only one share because of its high initial cost. The *Financial Times* quoted Mrs

Nobuko Otake, a metropolitan housewife and one of NTT's army of small private shareholders. "The price right now is below half the price I paid. I can't see it ever getting back to the original price, because a second release of shares is on the way." Is this the voice of the rational or irrational Japanese investor?

Three years later, in August 1995, The *Financial Times* interviewed another Japanese housewife who had invested Y10 million during the stock market boom. She said she still tuned in to day-time television stock market programmes, but only to be alert for a good opportunity to sell the rest of her holdings. The evidence strongly suggests that an army of small private investors, whose fingers were badly burned during the collapse of the bubble have been driven away from the market by the scale of their losses, and still heartily distrust it.

The Basis for Rational Behaviour

Our brief search for the irrational investor in these different crash events poses an odd question. How and why do normally rational investors suddenly become irrational? Within all the frenetic activity of a booming market, there must be a point where the normal stability of the usual market environment is irreparably changed. At this moment, I believe, it switches into the turbulent onset of a chaotic phase. We can assume that wily investors will now leave the centre stage, taking with them their bulging cash profits. They become passive observers, patiently biding their time until the storm has blown over. However, the sheer extent of participation in the crashes we have examined suggests that either there must be a vast army of hidden irrational speculators lurking in the background, waiting for their moment of mass madness to arrive; or if that explanation seems unsatisfactory, then the majority of rational investors must have suddenly become transformed into crass irrationality. The bizarre antics of many staid, upright professionals is added food for thought. By the very abruptness of their appearances, we should remember that as these enormous sell-offs take hold, there is hardly time for investors to indulge in a process of rationalisation, especially when monumental losses are staring them in the face. It is possible, of course, that the onset of a rampant boom coincides with the temporary take-over of the market by non-investors. They will be generally ignorant of market techniques, seeking only a rapid gain. Lars Tvede in *The Psychology of Finance* comes down heavily on the side of Jekyll and Hyde investors, with this pithy observation: "The truth is that human decisions are rarely made on the basis of logical reasoning. Instead they arise as a consequence of more or less irrational changes in what psychologists call 'attitudes'."

Investor Attitudes

We can look briefly at some of his evidence for this sweeping generalisation. Psychologists say attitudes are the hidden needs and wishes which influence human behaviour, although we may not be aware of them. They function like psychological crash helmets, keeping us calm, well-adjusted and socially flexible. Empirical evidence has shown that people take up attitudes to virtually everything. It has been suggested that these attitudes are responsible for four vital categories of functions in the human mind; these are known as adaptive, self-realising, knowledge and ego-defensive.

Attitudes in Human Behaviour

Adaptive attitudes arise because, unconsciously, we are influenced by our surroundings. Many tests confirm the surprising reality of this extra-suggestive response. In one experiment, groups of people in a darkened room were asked to watch a luminous spot from a metal box. They were told the spot would move, and their task was to decide the distance it had moved. Each group quickly agreed on a distance, and all the groups had different answers, but not one had the right answer. The spot did not move at all. The experiment clearly revealed this direct effect of human psychology. When someone whom we respect makes a decisive comment, we are more likely to believe it than not. This effect is visible in modern financial markets. Respected analysts and forecasters can have a formidable impact on prices. In general, of course, this reaction pattern is particularly important for a social animal, like man, since it allows rapid communal adjustments.

Clearly, this adaptive attitude is significant for pending boom conditions. If a massive trend becomes evident, everyone will be influenced by the rising prices. By mutual agreement as they witness each other's positive reactions, concurring attitudes emerge. Hence, as everyone expects the trend to continue, more people will concur than will disagree. For this reason contrarian investors are very rare. As the trend becomes well established it is reinforced by a powerful effect; investors' adaptive attitudes.

The second attitude, self-realisation, concerns actions we take to help us feel important. Surveys by the New York Stock Exchange indicated the public's estimation of the Stock Exchange and brokers fluctuates with share prices. It improves when prices rise and falls when they fall. This was evident during the late 1920s boom on Wall Street. Before the crash everyone loved Wall Street.

The third significant attitude applies to information management. Since we are continuously bombarded by far more information than we can possibly handle, information gets bundled up into blocks for swifter handling in the mind. Every information bundle then acquires a snappy heading, to facilitate the mental filing of continuous new data. "The market is oversold", or "stocks are cheap" are examples of the information compression which bombards us daily.

Once an attitude has formed, the knowledge on which it was based can be quickly forgotten, like jottings on a memo-pad before the final report is filed. Over time, however, the attitude itself will tend to lose force. On the stock market, when this knowledge attitude weakens sufficiently, the investor may experience an awakening, described as the "riot point". Knowledge attitudes are relevant to some trend indicators. For example, moving averages reflect the underlying trend, but the average always lags behind the price. Although this occurs because of the way the averages are calculated, the time lag also corresponds to the adaptation time required by market participants. This is the time it takes for people to adjust to new prices. Inevitably, it takes time for the psychology of a primary trend to undergo a reversal. The market metaphorically catches its breath until the sellers move in and the trend is decisively broken. This pause corresponds to the early nagging doubts phase in the crash. Even then, only the most agile operators will act quickly. For everyone else it can take much longer before the change in direction registers the need for a change in attitudes. Perhaps this long pause also explains why most investors, even the brilliant stock-pickers, can occasionally get stuck with a losing share they are reluctant to sell, until the losses ultimately become too large to carry.

Finally, consider human attitudes as ego-defensive mechanisms. These arise from the tortuous disparity between what people know and believe and what they say and do – an inconsistency that provokes ego-defensive attitudes. Many investors who purchase shares, will easily recognise this mechanism. The purchase may have been made with an expectation of short-term gains. Unfortunately, within hours or days, the price falls. There is now no longer a harmony between what has actually happened and what was believed. An attitude change has become essential. Either the deal was wrong and the share must be sold, or the time frame was wrong and the expected gains have a long- rather than short-term horizon. Assuming the investor decides to continue holding, another conflict arises if the price falls further. Two separate defence mechanisms, "selective exposure" and "selective perception" are now forced into play.

Through selective exposure, the investor ignores negative news, attending only to the positive items that support his or her view. If these are scarce, an active search for reinforcement is the normal response. Selective perception is more subtle; the investor distorts the facts to support the current view, making it more tenable. Psychologists describe this as "assimilation error". Finally, before abandoning the position because the losses are insupportable, the investor undergoes one last attitude change; "you win some, you lose some, it's all in the game", sums up this final thought shift. Making light of the error helps to take the sting out of being utterly wrong. We become victims of our own unconscious egos, and make what is known in the jargon as "transaction slip rationalisations". Investors often buy at the price they mistakenly sold, or *vice versa*, on an unconscious wish to exonerate a previous transaction error. Such ego-defensive attitudes contribute to identifiable support and resistance levels seen on charts which show share price activity. We shall discuss these chart patterns in Chapters 4 and 5.

One final aspect of this ego-defence device is the frequency with which investors are willing to close out good positions for a small gain, while holding on to the big losses indefinitely. For a majority of investors, an unrealised loss exists only on paper, while a small profit can be seen as money in the bank. This commonly seen behaviour towards profits and losses helps to explain why turnover is lower in a bear than in a bull market. In the bear market, more people hold on, hoping for a recovery. It also explains why the bottom is often signalled by a massive sell-off. Holding the unrealised losses ultimately becomes absolutely untenable when the investor is finally forced to make a last ego-defensive attitude change.

Number Drunk Investors

Can we use this knowledge of investor psychology to explain the emergence of a boom? As share price rises continue at an amazing rate, it must be assumed that rational investors will sell into the rising market as concepts of "fair value" become increasingly swamped by the sheer exuberance of the price gains. Yet it demands a granite disposition to sell into strength in a rising trend that looks capable of scaling ever greater heights. We saw this strength of character in the actions of Richard Cantillan, Madame Chaumont, Thomas Guy and Sarah Churchill, Joseph Kennedy and Sir James Goldsmith.

As canny investors take profits, the market becomes increasingly dominated by speculators, arbitragers and the ill-informed lay public. For all these opportunists, the newcomers and those holding in the expectation of even greater gains, history shows people may become number drunk. When the rate of daily price changes is too rapid, the mind cannot cope. Panic situations can create a sense of disorientation.

Robert Beckman in *Crashes*, describes events during the 1920s German hyper-inflation. Many people were admitted to psychiatric hospitals suffering a kind of temporary madness, unable to cope with the vast numbers in the escalating inflation of the German mark. In the three years prior to 1922, notes in circulation increased nearly six times to 200 milliards (thousand million) and the value of the mark on the foreign exchanges plummeted. After 1922, money supply continued to grow by 10 per cent every 10 days, until employees had to be paid twice a day because money was losing its value so rapidly. Notes were carried about in mail sacks, or so the tradition said, in wheelbarrows.

By March 1923, Dr Rudolf Havenstein, Chairman of the Bundesbank, was proud to announce that note production was keeping 30 paper mills, 150 print works and 2,000 presses working three shifts a day. With this prodigious effort, the amount of money circulating rose by two-thirds in just a few days. By 1924, the entire money stock in Germany was doubling every few weeks, inflation was rampant and the mark worthless. To assess their degree of disorientation, the doctors asked simple questions: "How old are you? How many children do you have?" People who had lost contact with numerical reality would answer, "I am 25 million years old, I have 1,000 or 15,000 children."

The Real Stress Factor

Another feature of ultra-fast moving share prices is the actual metabolic effects which people experience, induced by rapid market movements. When facing an acute threat, the body releases adrenalin to prime the senses and assist a quick escape from danger. At the same time, the tendency to behavioural attitude changes is greatly increased. Changes that normally take days or weeks can occur in hours, minutes or even seconds. In an acute crisis, rapid improvisation can mean the difference between survival and death. Robert Schiller's 1987 survey, previously mentioned, revealed this effect. During the week of the crash, he sent questionnaires to 2,000 private and 1,000 institutional investors. Although he received a less than 30 per cent reply rate, the results from 889 replies showed that on 19 October, when Wall Street fell 508 points, 20.3 per cent of private and 43.1 per cent of professional investors suffered panic symptoms: sweaty palms, irritability, poor concentration, chest pains and a high pulse.

People Don't Change . . . but Circumstances Do

This search for the irrational investor, albeit highly abridged, shows how he is drawn out of hibernation by timeless recurrent themes that delineate financial crashes and bubbles. Together, they conspire to turn many professional sober-suited 'experts' into get-very-rich-very-quick enthusiasts, while encouraging mass participation and a raging mania, until the peak arrives with meteoric finality. Now everyone, amateur and professional alike, is abruptly confronted by the onset of a precipitous decline, and the selling stampede begins.

For me, personally, two impressions stand out: first, the sheer scale of active involvement, even back in the 1630s, when Dutch Tulipomania was raging. And secondly, the striking consistency of extreme behaviour patterns in the boom. I think this frenetic activity is explainable in terms of chaos theory, to which we now turn.

CHAPTER THREE

CHAOS RULES

It is remarkable that a science which began with the consideration of games of
chance should have become the most important object of human knowledge.

Marquis de Laplace

Exploring chaos in the financial markets suggests a boring dust-dry academic world, but contrary to all expectations, chaos is weird, eccentric
and full of curious happenings. It comes dramatically to life when seen in
the context of stock market crashes and today's global bond and equity
markets. This chapter will introduce some basic features of typical chaotic systems to illustrate how closely they resemble the features of financial markets. Later chapters will use these classic chaos concepts to
explain the progression of a boom/crash cycle in terms of chaos theory.
By exposing the structure beneath the overt mayhem, profitable situations emerge which knowledgeable investors can exploit.

Why Bother to Understand Chaos Theory?

To the ill-informed, stock market gyrations are disparagingly compared
to the antics of a casino. Keynes himself is said to have observed that if
investment is the by-product of a casino, the job is unlikely to be well
done. So it probably seems most damning to admit that the laws of
chance and probability play a central role in chaos theory, lending
weight to the gambling charge on markets! On a philosophical level,
however, life itself often seems a bit of a gamble, no doubt because we
live on a planet dominated by chaos principles.

Because we know financial markets are highly excitable and unpredictable, it seems a waste of time to study crash events with a view to
improving prediction potential in the future, but as I hope to show, I

believe that conclusion is misplaced. We may never be able to predict the exact outcome of any single event, but a better understanding of chaos allows more penetrating insights into how financial markets function, just as this knowledge is improving the reliability of weather forecasting. And a fuller knowledge of the mechanics of market behaviour is an indispensable aid to government officials wrestling with the awesome complexities of fiscal and monetary policy. For investors, there is the added bonus of new knowledge in the search for superior investment returns.

As we shall see, the operation of derivatives, options, margin trading and buying on credit depends on a leverage tenet – nonlinearity – that is fundamental to chaotic systems. Investors from the seventeenth century on have profited (or suffered) from that enduring principle, probably without knowing that chaos theory even existed. Since everyone knows that geared investments can produce greatly magnified gains or losses, why do we need to realise that this entire concept rests on chaos? On a profound level I think the answer must lie in the unending quest for new knowledge which is such a deeply enmeshed quality of being human. Additional knowledge emanates from new knowledge in unimaginable flows. More parochially, however, for investors there is the abiding maxim that something you really understand gives you a better investment edge.

So What is Chaos?

Although chaos encapsulates conditions of unending instability, those who study it have revealed that simple rules underpin this seeming turbulence. In his book, *Does God Play Dice?*, Ian Stewart defines deterministic chaos as unpredictable behaviour that is governed by rules. Research has shown that, in many cases, it is underpinned by a mathematical precision that astonishes as it informs. And while mathematics itself has been defined as "the great instrument of exact statement and mental manipulation", advances in chaos thinking have challenged even that conclusion. By extension, if chaos is applicable to financial markets the inference is starkly apparent. Chaos in the markets implies the fundamental operation of a definable set of rules governed by a mathematical core. Attempts to discover those rules have so far been unsuccessful, because intrinsically it involves boiling down the whole complex financial world into just those few seminal variables which are driving the markets. To discover what those key variables are has, to date, proved an elusive quest.

Paradoxically, however, by ignoring the presence of chaos as the basis for market behaviour, most investors are denying themselves access to the fundamental principles that I believe govern market movements. I hope to show that the **imprint** of rules governing chaos, if not the rules themselves, is visible with market analysis, and can be used to improve the skills of traders and long-term investors, especially when making buy or sell decisions. In essence, the market reflects the underlying psychology of its main participants. Events repeatedly reveal that markets express an ever changing but potent brew of raw emotions: excesses of euphoria, greed, fear and uncertainty predominate in turn. Awareness of this does not advance us very far, however, for it is difficult to profit from a knowledge of investor psychology without first unveiling the intrinsic forces responsible for its outward expressions.

The Science of Complexity

Chaos theory is part of a new scientific philosophy, the study of complexity itself. This multi-disciplinary research endeavour suddenly came alive during the 1980s when several researchers, exploring a wide range of vastly different topics, found themselves united in their thinking by one common theme. This idea was eloquently captured by George Cowan as "a unified science". Cowan is the founder of the Santa Fe Institute, a think-tank formed in 1984 for studying the central issues of complexity. This new science embraced numerous areas, including physics, chemistry, biology and the human sciences; it encompasses, in Cowan's descriptive phrase, "the sciences of the twenty-first century".

At the inaugural workshops, held in the autumn of 1984, Professor Murray Gell-Mann of Caltech, an eminent particle physicist, distilled the essence of their insights:

> We had **fantastic** amounts of similarities. There were huge numbers of common features in the things that were presented among various fields. You had to look carefully, but once you got past the jargon of all these things, it was there.

On pooling their experiences, the unifying feature this group of disparate scientists discovered was that all these diverse topics – archaeology, mathematics, economics, molecular biology, cosmology and many more – comprise complex dynamical systems that are continually evolving. Coveney and Highfield, in *Frontiers of Complexity*, suggest the two indispensable elements that allow complexity to occur are the irreversible medium of time, in which events are unidirectional and can evolve or change, and nonlinearity, which produces complex, essentially unpredictable results.

According to Stephen Wolfram, who established a Centre for Complex Systems Research at the University of Illinois,

> Whenever you look at very complicated systems in physics and biology, you generally find the basic components and the basic laws are quite simple; the complexity arises because you have a great many of these simple components interacting simultaneously. The complexity is actually in the organisation – the myriad possible ways that the components of a system can interact.

Peter Carruthers, head of the Los Alamos centre where chaos research came to play a prominent role, described the interdisciplinary emphasis that the study of complexity engendered:

> Here was a collection of many of the most creative people in the whole world, in many fields. And they turned out to have a lot to say to each other. They basically had the same world view, in the sense that they all seemed to feel that "emerging syntheses" really meant a restructuring of science – that the overlapping themes of different parts of science would be put together in a new way.

Complex systems consist of numerous elements which constantly interact with each other in hundreds, thousands and often millions of varying ways: a living cell comprises unnumbered chemically reacting proteins, lipids and nucleic acids; the brain is composed of billions of interconnected neurons; while a modern society consists of hundreds of thousands, even millions of unique individual participants, who constantly interact with each other in countless different associations and groupings. Coveney and Highfield suggest it is these vastly differing examples that indicate complexity must be intrinsic to nature; it is not simply the result of combinations of simpler processes that occur at a more fundamental level. In short, complexity is holistic.

It is the very richness of these myriad connections which allows complex systems to undergo spontaneous self-organisation, a process that often produces elaborate hierarchies of new arrangements at higher levels of organisation possessing entirely new properties, regardless of what the constituent agents may be. This is seen in living species; they can be organised into millions of genera of animals and plants through the stages of biological evolution moving from the very simplest to more complicated forms. It is seen in the arrangement of nation states – through villages, towns, cities and counties. Again, at the core of the universe, hierarchies form the essential building blocks of nature; elementary particles build up into atoms, molecules, elements and compounds. And on the cosmic scale, gas clouds condense to form stars which cluster into galaxies, which group themselves into clusters of galaxies, to form the massive structures of the observable universe.

Emerging Properties

When hierarchies form, groups of free units coalesce into larger entities and in the process they evolve properties that transcend the separate features of those individual entities from which they have formed. By grouping into larger units, collectively, they acquire new traits, unique to these complex, larger systems; they become "emergent" systems. Their ability to recreate themselves in new ways springs from their success in adapting to changing conditions, through constant self-organisation, a process extensively studied by the Nobel prize-winning scientist, Ilya Prigogine. The study of this process of self-organisational change, this "emergence" is termed anti-chaos.

Philip Anderson of Princeton, awarded a Nobel Prize in 1977 for his work in condensed-matter physics, cites the weather as an emergent property. He describes the energetic processes involved:

> Take your water vapour out over the Gulf of Mexico and let it interact with sunlight and wind, and it can organise itself into an emergent structure known as a hurricane. Life is an emergent property, the product of DNA molecules and protein molecules and a myriad other kind of molecules all obeying the laws of chemistry. The mind is an emergent property, the product of several billion neurons obeying the biological laws of the living cell.

Complex systems that recreate themselves display a vitality or dynamism that separates them from static complicated structures such as computers, aeroplanes and other advanced machines which are relatively rigid in design and activity by comparison. Whatever the complication in their design, these latter are examples of closed systems, operating within fixed boundaries. They can only undergo specific changes that have been built into their fundamental structures. In contrast, complex nonlinear dynamical systems are open. Forever fluctuating, they exist in a highly unstable, "far-from-equilibrium" state. They often dwell in that shadowy zone, the edge of chaos, where unpredictability is at its highest. These open self-organising systems draw on the environment for energy, information and other resources to expand their fields of operation. Their openness enables them to constantly adapt, to grow and to recreate themselves in a multitude of varying, often unexpected, ways.

We can see from this description of complex self-organising adaptive systems, that the evolution of the financial markets over the past 200 years has created vast open financial systems that share many of these features. From descriptions presented in Chapter 1, it is clear that in Holland, during the 1630s, the rapidly expanding market for tulips was an emergent system. Again, in the late seventeenth and early eighteenth century, several emergent systems arose simultaneously: the rise of industrial capitalism, the appearance of the first joint stock companies and a new breed of financial intermediaries – the bankers, jobbers and stockbrokers. Even the two notorious 1720 bubbles demonstrated features typical of an emergent system. In all these cases, I think these complex financial markets showed evidence of anti-chaos, that is, "emergent properties". Yet this idea must be contrasted with evidence presented later, in Parts II and III, where the six great financial bubbles/crashes are explored. Once the reality of a dynamic financial market had emerged, I was surprised to note how sophisticated were the innovations of seventeenth-century Tulipomania and the two eighteenth-century European bubbles. Essentially, they simply pre-date the twentieth-century crashes, where modest variations of their practices reappeared, but on a vastly greater scale.

However, it is possible that the evolution of financial markets has now reached a crucial stage in globalisation development, so that new "emergent properties" could more easily be created. The pace of growth, expansion and development is so incredibly fast, it is reasonable to suppose that unknown global forces could be unleashed in response to an important unforeseen event with serious implications for the worldwide investment community *en masse*. Of course, by definition, what these new "emergent properties" would be cannot be known in advance, but this idea has a bearing on the recently much discussed concept of a seminal "crash of crashes", which could, even now, be moving towards a climactic denouement. This "crash of crashes" idea is discussed in Chapter 14.

At the Edge of Chaos

Closely linked to the emergence of the "crash of crashes" scenario is another intriguing feature shared by most complex adaptive systems. Their abiding dynamism creates a restless animation as they pulse through spontaneous adaptations and upheavals. In Philip Anderson's words, "emergent properties often produce emergent behaviour". This idea is explored in greater depth in Chapter 5, but essentially, it rests on the inherent instabilities that reside at "the edge of chaos". This evocative phrase was first used by Christopher Langton of the Sante Fe Institute during his research on cellular automaton rule tables. It is the fluctuating zone where a tenuous balance prevails and a complex system somehow acquires the ability to bring order and chaos into a transient kind of equilibrium. This balancing point is the border area where odd, maverick elements in a system never quite get locked into a fixed position, but yet never quite disintegrate into outright chaos. **At the edge of chaos, the boundaries of change are forever shifting between a stagnant status quo and the anarchy of perpetual disruption**.

As we shall discover, the edge of chaos can be a realm of huge volatility, but it often has only a fleeting duration. Complex systems can flip, with a sudden alacrity, between states of order and disorder. Sometimes they act chaotically, at other times they are more orderly and predictable. They may slip into a precarious state at the edge of chaos, where long lasting fluctuations occur across a wide range of time scales and magnitudes. According to Tonis Vaga, in *Profiting From Chaos*, the fluctuations follow a power law similar to the distributions that govern earthquake measurements of different magnitudes on the Richter scale. These scales are exponential, growing geometrically rather than arithmetically; a feature which explains the large-scale fluctuations to which they are prone.

The new science of complexity studies emergent structures, with new properties arising from abrupt transformations of earlier systems, existing in the ever fluctuating zone that lies on the edge of chaos. And within this complicated framework, chaos theory plays a central part in the continuing research efforts to explain the detailed behaviour of all complex nonlinear dynamical systems.

Confronting the Chaos World

The chaos world is awash with amazing notions. Conventional ideas have sometimes been turned upside down by insights chaos has revealed. Many orthodox opinions held by the scientific, astronomic and mathematics community have been substantially revised following new revelations. We shall grapple with some of these remarkable new ideas in the next three chapters, but, by way of introduction, let us briefly consider some of the bizarre features chaos produces.

Among its unexpected findings are such oddities as the fact that under the right conditions, simple, classical systems, like the ubiquitous pendulum or a roulette wheel, can behave chaotically; and chaos is now known to exist in many inherently stable systems, like number theory, the Solar System and electronic circuits. Moreover, it appears that a nonchaotic system can settle into either one of two separate equilibria or stable states. Of all the arresting insights evinced by chaos theory, the idea that disorder creates order, so vividly related in the biblical Genesis, seems closer to theology than scientific fact. Then again, the thought that simplicity breeds complexity is equally odd, even though biologists have shown convincingly that the history of life on earth confirms precisely that progression, from extremely simple to more complicated life forms, through evolution by natural selection. But the idea that disorder obeys simple rules seems strange beyond belief. And as extraordinary as it sounds, it is known that in many chaotic systems **the order descends into disorder at an orderly rate**, obeying a universal rule that covers all examples of chaotic motion, from tumbling fluids to tumbling bodies in the Solar System. Finally, in this fantasy-like catalogue, we now know that in our planetary home we are totally immersed in deterministic chaos. It is the enduring hallmark of the everyday world in which we live.

In Chaos, Events are Not as They Seem

Parochially, we all talk about chaos, but it is not a subject we might willingly study for its new scientific disclosures. Yet this short introduction provides the essential explanation of why we should bother to look more closely at this intriguing new science. If financial markets are classical examples of chaos, we need to explore those aspects of chaos theory which will give us greater insight into the complex nature of the capital markets. The first lesson to emerge from such a study is that nothing is actually what it appears to be on the surface. In fact, in a financial setting, first impressions are often an unwary trap for the unsuspecting investor. This means, unfortunately, that to thoroughly understand chaos, we have to grasp its medusa-like tentacles and wrestle with some of its mind-bending notions. Lack of understanding might be an expensive handicap when trying to anticipate a future crash scenario.

For as we know, the financial world is a hornet's nest of sudden surprises. Expect the unexpected and you may still be hopelessly wrong-footed by the turn events do take. Economic happenings are a minefield of false starts and U-turns. They rarely develop as anticipated. So we might wonder, "How can market order be generated from disorder?" or more specifically, "If panic is an irrational investor behaviour, can we benefit while others panic?" Watching a favourite share or currency price gyrating violently, we might well reject, in total disbelief, the notion that discord obeys simple rules. But if the secret to market behaviour is encapsulated in the chaos theory of markets, we cannot become proficient investors unless we learn in a little more detail, precisely what that entails.

Unfortunately, it is not possible as yet to present a rigorous mathematical proof to show that the financial markets are categorically chaotic. Such a proof has not yet emerged because of the inordinately complex nature of these markets. In general, chaos theory applies to systems which have only a small number of important interacting variables. Although it would appear that this cannot apply to the huge networks of inter-related global financial systems, other examples in chaos research suggest it is too soon to make dogmatic refutations. Chaos is still a pioneering discipline and its wider ramifications are constantly being explored. The situation for turbulence in fluids is an example. Researchers suspect that it is a chaos-induced phenomenon, but a rigorous proof remains elusive. As Ian Stewart writes: "Turbulence is immensely important in many branches of science, from astronomy to meteorology. . . . But its true inner nature remains a problem of the highest order." Yet we can lift the veil of mystery to some extent on the behaviour of financial markets by exploring a large range of similarities with classic chaos concepts and by setting them in the framework of our "cluster of 20-features" model. In 1984, when the Sante Fe Institute for the study of complexity sciences was being formed, Louis Branscomb, chief scientist at IBM, said, "It's important to have people who *steal* ideas." This is the most fruitful way in which an interdisciplinary study topic can advance.

Chaos is Discovered

Chaos theory is complicated. It tackles the irregular, capricious side of nature that was ignored for centuries by orthodox science because it seemed incoherent and not amenable to serious study. The messy, highly unpredictable nature of many complex physical systems had put them out of the research domain of most classical physicists. Traditional science developed from the precise mathematical laws of nature discovered by Newton over 300 years ago. Yes, this is the same brilliant Sir Isaac Newton who lost a fortune in the South Sea Bubble. Through centuries of usage and a comfortable familiarity, Newton's laws had become almost sacrosanct in scientific circles, as an all-embracing and comprehensive explanation of natural phenomena. Using Newton's mathematical laws, astronomers have predicted the motion of the Solar System over 200 million years into the future, confident in the knowledge that their detailed calculations are reliable. In the majestic sweep of the vast universe, the triumph of classical physics has reduced its enormity to a handful of governing principles – the fundamental laws of motion, gravity, light and electro-magnetism. These laws seem permanent and incontrovertible. Describing the message of Newton's laws that have been absorbed into the very foundations of our culture, Ian Stewart writes, "That message is: *Nature has laws, and we can find them*. . . . Simple. Elegant. Elusive."

Yet here on earth, we live in a truly chaotic world. Once we recognise this unshakeable reality and start to search for it, we discover that almost everything in our daily experience of the natural world is built around chaos. It confronts us in the tumbling waters of rivers and waterfalls, in the streaking flashes of lightning strikes, in our unpredictable weather and in the unceasing patterns of ocean waves. To date, the main thrust of chaos theory centres on the natural physical sciences on earth, where chaos occurs in the behaviour of turbulent liquids and gases; it is most evident in the volatile gaseous atmosphere surrounding the planet, where it creates the infinite variety of weather conditions. But chaos occurs also in viscous fluids within pipes, in smoke twirls associated with fire, in stalactite and stalacmite formations, on the convoluted floors of underground caves and a multiplicity of other natural phenomena.

In our Solar System, chaos is far more prevalent than was assumed even 20 years ago. We now know chaos controls irregular movements in several astronomical bodies: in Jupiter's Red Spot, asteroids circling in the Ort cloud and the peculiar tumbling motions of Hyperion, one of Saturn's many moons. Moreover, astronomers analysing information from the solar heliospheric observatory (Soho) launched in December 1995 have realised the internal workings of the sun itself are far more chaotic and complex than was previously thought. Even the convoluted shapes of mountains and coastlines defy Newton's laws. The delicate shapes of snowflakes and swirling tufts of smoke do not conform to his orderly, uniform laws that still dominate the school science curriculum. All these irregular systems throw up contradictions that fly in the face of conventional science.

Today we know the simple linear systems, so thoroughly studied by Newtonian science, are the exception rather than the rule for we live on a planet dominated by chaos. Its complex processes govern the science of living forms: changes in animal population life cycles, cell metabolism, the propagation of nerve impulses, heart beat irregularities and the growth of plant and animal structures. The magnificent branching networks that create structure in trees, veining on leaves, or the typical cauliflower shape, also occur in branching growth patterns in many animal organs – the lungs, kidneys, nerve and blood vessel networks. These organs grow according to repeating chaotic patterns which halt at maturity. In this, they differ from other, usually physical dynamical chaotic systems, which are open and forever evolving or becoming.

Generations of researchers, confronting the messier side of nature, had brushed these contradictions aside as aberrations with no material bearing on the profound natural laws which have dominated their philosophical approach throughout decades of professional careers. Paul Davies at Newcastle University suggests the discovery of Newton's laws inspired belief in a clockwork universe, with the future precisely determined by the past. This firm bedrock imbued the thoughts and attitudes of the scientific world so thoroughly, it could not be jettisoned without a struggle. However, in the 1950s and 1960s, scientific research was finally confronted by an unpalatable truth: the classical view of nature was incomplete. Its comfortable assumptions were shown to be manifestly inadequate when researchers discovered that although these laws are highly reliable, they are, none the less, only close approximations.

Yet more shattering still was the realisation that many widespread natural phenomena – weather patterns, strange astronomical phenomena, population dynamics and turbulent fluids – while seeming to be random and inherently unpredictable, are actually governed by simple mathematical rules. Gradually, this research led to the formalisation of a new science: chaos. What an incredible irony the physical sciences have thrown up; for just when it is finally conceded that the immutable laws of classical physics are nothing more than reliable estimations, complex chaotic systems, which seem so haphazard and capricious, have been found to rest upon an underlying order, governed by simple mathematical rules.

On the topic of the capital markets, a comparison of typical chaotic and market systems reveals many close similarities. To examine them, we must know exactly what scientists mean by chaos, and introduce some of the basic concepts underpinning this young science.

Colloquially, chaos signifies a total breakdown, utter confusion and pandemonium. In *The New Scientist Guide To Chaos*, Ian Percival sees chaos as "a science of the computer age. And some of the elegant mathematics used to model chaos has important applications in many fields." But he cautions that we cannot use the theory of chaos everywhere:

> Science takes words and shapes their meanings to its own ends, and "chaos" is no exception. The state of Lebanese politics and British education may look chaotic, but you cannot study them using chaos theory. There are many other situations that are chaotic in the ordinary sense, but not in the scientific sense of chaos.

Clearly, applications of chaos theory to the social sciences are, at present, firmly in the camp of "chaotic in the ordinary sense" in Ian Percival's terminology. Increasingly, however, researchers recognise how aptly the science of complexity applies to many aspects of the social sciences, especially in economics. Can complexity exist without chaos? I think not, as the process of emergence is axiomatic on randomness that seethes at the edge of chaos. I think it is too early in the history of complexity sciences to rule the social sciences completely out of court. By "borrowing" classic chaos ideas to describe stock market behaviour, which is patently dominated by mathematical concepts, I hope that chaos in the capital markets might ultimately work like a Trojan Horse for subsequently exploring chaos in the wider fields of the social sciences.

In the young mathematical science of chaos which studies behaviour in complex, physical (as opposed to human and social) systems undergoing continuous change, the term "chaos" has a very precise meaning. Ian Stewart defines deterministic chaos scientifically as random behaviour occurring in a regulated system, where an inner order exists in accordance with strict mathematical laws. It is the paradoxical coupling of order and disorder in the definition which produces the term "deterministic chaos". The intermixing implies many apparently random processes are governed by simple rules.

The Weird World of Chaos

In chaos, truth is undoubtedly stranger than fiction. We discover a topsy-turvy world where incredible notions have to be taken seriously. Indeed, all the monumental complexity stems from the operation of extremely simple rules. Other disturbing ideas suggest that tiny causes bring monster effects and irregular patterns and shapes repeat themselves almost identically at ever smaller scales, like a set of Russian dolls, one inside the other. Or again, consider the bewildering way chaos and order mix intricately together like currants in a fruit cake. Yet more unbelievable is the idea that order disintegrates into disorder at a regular rate and chaotic systems contain within themselves the self-organisational spark to reimpose a new order from amidst the prevailing chaos.

And finally, what are we to make of the eccentric idea of chains of actions, one following on from another, to create totally unexpected results later on? Yet one thing leading on to another turns out to be the very essence of chaos. As Winston Churchill said, "History is one damn thing after another." He could just as easily have said, "Chaos is just one damn thing after another." The bizarre flavour of possibilities is captured in the sorry saga of the missing horseshoe nail. Folklore suggests it relates the outcome of the battle of Bosworth in 1485, when Richard III lost his throne to the Tudor successor, Henry VII.

> For want of a nail, the shoe was lost;
> For want of a shoe, the horse was lost;
> For want of a horse, the rider was lost;
> For want of a rider, the battle was lost;
> For want of the battle, the Kingdom was lost.
> And all for the want of a horseshoe nail!

This list of oddities covers only a few of those we face when probing the typical features of chaos. We will focus on those most applicable to behaviour in financial markets.

The Logic of Applying Chaos Theory to Crashes

One obvious question is whether we can benefit from understanding booming stock markets as typical chaotic systems. As noted earlier, a study of over 450 historical booms and crashes in the past 360 years reveals several strikingly consistent patterns. The self-propelling momentum of the boom followed by the seeming inevitability of a crash suggests an underlying force is operating. If that force is mathematically based chaos, the intriguing possibility arises that financial market behaviour can be better exploited, just as weather forecasting performance has improved markedly over the past two decades once its chaos basis was eventually understood. As we shall see, successful investment decisions can be made once the hidden nature of the forces driving the market are better appreciated.

In academic circles, capital market theorists, quaintly called Random Walkers (because of their views), suggest that markets are random as they are visibly haphazard and unpredictable. The antics of crazy investors caught up in a manic boom/bust drama seem to support their case, as it is logical to link randomness with frenzied speculation. Our task, then, is to explain why the actions of a crowd of illogical investors, seized by a powerful gambling urge, produces recognisable, oft-repeated crash scenarios which can be systematically analysed. The strange contradiction of speculators of different nationalities and ages, under various investment conditions, recurrently acting out fantasies of boundless wealth in identifiable behaviour patterns implies that mayhem can be studied by method and disorder by systematic analysis. This is the logic for applying the science of chaos to financial markets. But is it valid?

The Randomness Red Herring

We answer this question with a second question. What precisely is meant by random behaviour? Heinz Pagels, in his eminently readable book, *The Cosmic Code*, provides a good explanation. He suggests randomness implies there is absolutely no relationship between units in a set of events or a sequence of numbers. Each event is unique and unpredictable and unrelated to all past, present and future events. However, the possibility exists that although there is an underlying rule in a set of "random" events, we have failed to spot it. In the future, if this rule is found, that particular set or sequence will cease to be random. Pagels concludes that all we can say with any certainty about randomness is that it reflects a present state of ignorance; a sequence now considered random may later be shown to obey a simple rule we have currently overlooked.

Applying Ian Stewart's definition, we can enter the eccentric world of chaos through a door marked "random". Chaos is "stochastic behaviour occurring in a deterministic system". Stochastic means "random" and deterministic implies order and regularity, obeying strict mathematical laws. The definition is a paradox. It suggests that random behaviour obeys rules. Ian Stewart highlights the evident contradictions:

> Deterministic behaviour is ruled by exact and unbreakable laws. Stochastic behaviour is the opposite: lawless and irregular, ruled by chance. So chaos is "lawless behaviour governed entirely by law."

He illustrates this weird notion by iterating numbers on a simple calculator. Depending on which number you choose, different results emerge; by repeatedly hitting one number, the iteration may settle down to a single value, **converging** to a steady state, or it may swing between two values, producing a **periodic** iteration with period two. If you iterate $x^2 - 1$ (by hitting the x^2 button and then $-1 =$), the result leads to a cycling between 0 and -1. However, if you start with a value between 0 and 1 and iterate $2x^2 - 1$ the results look patternless or random. Experimenting with numbers on the calculator, therefore, reveals, as Ian Stewart suggests, "the ability of even simple equations (in this case $2x^2 -1$) to generate motion that is so complex, so sensitive to measurement, that it **appears** random". I've added the bold type to emphasise the curious mystery that emerges when we start to explore the phenomenon of chaos, even in such an exacting example as mathematics.

To explain the paradox of lawless behaviour governed by laws, Ian Stewart supplies this summary: "Out of chaos emerges pattern. The two are inextricably related." In essence, order and disorder coexist everywhere in nature. Sometimes the chaos dominates but at other times, order is more prevalent. Again, our experience of the weather offers an understandable example: sometimes a high pressure zone emerges with endless days or weeks of glorious sunshine, at other times persistent clouds and rain occur, but there are also occasions when the weather is so variable we cannot know from day to day how it will turn out.

The strange paradox at the centre of the definition of deterministic chaos is highly significant; it is telling us a profound truth about nature which scientists have only reluctantly come to accept in the last 30 years. A great deal of the prolific disorder we see about us has a strict mathematical basis.

Although this suggestion appears to defy common sense, once we are tuned in to this possibility, we begin to recognise that our everyday world is overwhelmingly built up from constantly repeated chaotic patterns. Mountains, shorelines, rivers, oceans, leaves, trees, clouds, snowflakes and waves continuously beat out the intricate rhythms of chaos to produce all the marvellous patterning of nature. The remarkable rich mixture of chaos and order produces an infinity of patterns. And patterns – inner structure – are the essence of chaos. Back in the 1960s, when the formless shapes of nature were studied more closely through the eyes of pioneering researchers in chaos, what emerged was an extraordinary new insight. Lawlessness is a shallow veneer. Rather than being a deeply rooted principle of nature, it is only apparent, not real. However bizarre it seems, order and structure exist within nature's abundant upheavals and disorder.

With no known rules for chaos in the social sciences at present, the randomness argument seems strongly persuasive. It convinces us that human affairs are eternally capricious and hence random, especially in financial markets. Lacking a more convincing explanation, there is comfort in grasping something feasible, and randomness neatly fits that empty slot. Of course, there are numerous times when the markets do exhibit short-term randomness, but predominantly, the occurrence of randomness is a visible effect in the markets – **it is not an explanation**. For that we have to turn to the young enigmatic science of chaos. I think randomness is a red herring, thrown up to deflect us from the real quest, namely to establish the rules governing deterministic chaos in human affairs. Ironically, the source of the randomness is almost certainly due to chaos. This has not been recognised because chaos is still a young, poorly understood science. It has yet to enter into full public awareness in the way that Newton's precise mathematical laws of gravity and motion have done.

Why Randomness is Due to Chaos

The Random Walkers claim share prices are random so that there are absolutely no connections between one day's price movements and the next. This means that in any sequence of share price data, each day's price is unique and isolated. I think this idea simply reflects our present poor understanding of the deeper forces governing financial markets. The unrecognised links between chaos and outright randomness arise from the preliminary state of conditions that exist in any complex dynamical system. If these initial conditions are not completely known at the outset, or if they are quite uncontrollable – clearly the most probable state of affairs in extremely complex cases like weather systems or financial markets – precise and reliable predictions will never be possible.

For financial markets, this imprecision is called randomness. However, it is simply a form of unpredictability totally consistent with the behaviour of most complex dynamical systems; never at rest, they change from minute to minute, through the constant interplay of their constituent multitude of interactive elements. This generates their complexity. Chaotic systems readily flip from order to disorder, from stability to extreme instability. Such behaviour is senseless, unless it relates to a formal set of rules. The randomness sounds plausible; with intricate mixing, endless patterns emerge and re-emerge, but, like pieces in a kaleidoscope, endlessly shaken, they have the exasperating habit of never precisely repeating themselves – a description that clearly applies to financial markets.

Impossible Timing

Within the paradox of lawless behaviour governed by laws, there is yet another paradox. For even though these ever-changing systems are not precisely predictable, reliable forecasts can sometimes be made about their future behaviour because they are governed by chaos rules. Look, for example, at the earth's turbulent atmosphere; it is chaotic, like any other turbulent gas. Some weather systems have such a high variability with a profusion of many competing elements, reliable forecasts cannot be made; but at other times, such as with an approaching hurricane, more reliable predictions are possible.

The unexpected events in chaotic systems arise because it is impossible to predict exactly when and where they will occur. However, financial crashes follow a familiar pattern because, like the emerging hurricane, they have structure and, like the hurricane, they may indeed be emergent systems. Forecasting the onset of a crash when certain phases of crash behaviour appear may not be an impossible task. Timing it accurately will be tricky, but if the conditions look right, prediction should be feasible without being exact on the timing. As we saw in Chapter 2, at least two experienced Wall Street traders expected a crash during 1986 or 1987, although its exact timing remained elusive. When the crash finally arrived, they were swiftly able to gauge its probable outcome for personal gains, by rationally thinking through the short-term consequences, as the drama of 19 October unfolded.

Nature's Rule Book

Both Newtonian and chaos science study the physical world of nature, replete with ordered patterns and disorderly processes. Classical physics offers mathematical predictability. Paul Davies captures the essence of

Newton's impressive endowments to scientific understanding through the idea of the mathematical formulae he championed:

> A law of nature not only implies simplicity and universality, but also tractability. It meant that it was no longer necessary to observe the world to ascertain how it would behave: you could also compute it with a pencil and paper. Using mathematics to model the laws, a scientist could predict the future behaviour of the world, and retrodict how it behaved in the remote past.

This reliability is a powerful tool in the hands of scientists and researchers. But Newton's laws chiefly describe simple, linear systems, which are directly (that is, arithmetically) proportional. The motion of planets or comets in the Solar System is the classic example. Astronomical systems are so vast, we naturally expect them to be inordinately complex. They are, however, surprisingly simple to fathom once the basic governing laws are known. Such unexpected simplicity is one reason why the laws were discovered over 300 years ago. Astronomical systems have remarkably regular behaviour and their mathematical formulations are constant. Because they give repeatable, predictable results they are called "deterministic". Although Newton's laws are mainly close approximations, the results are relatively error-free and so are acceptable to scientists, engineers and technicians who rely on them. For example, in practice, the trajectories of a space craft must be modified very slightly during flight to allow for tiny computational errors which arise because the laws of motion are not precise enough for the required course to be charted from the outset of its journey.

Yet numerous problems defy exact analysis: Coveney and Highfield, in *Frontiers of Complexity*, discuss the inability of traditional physics to describe the long-term behaviour of three billiard balls on a snooker table, even though the equations of motion that describe the relationship of **any two bodies in space** are precisely known. The French mathematician, Henry Poincaré, as early as 1889, proved that it is impossible to describe the behaviour of nonlinear systems, such as the motion of three related bodies – say, the sun, earth and moon – because complex behaviour emerges. Attempts to study the motion of these three relative to each other with analytical methods does not produce exact solutions. Moreover, during the 1980s Gregory Chaitin, while working at the IBM Thomas J. Watson Research Laboratory in New York, discovered that even the simplest version of arithmetic, using whole numbers, contains intrinsic randomness. He concluded: "I have found an extreme where you have no pattern, indeed complete chaos." Such experimental oddities should caution us not to put science into neat packages, labelled "classical" or "chaotic", but in many respects chaotic systems contrast directly with classical linear systems, as Table 3 shows. It illustrates the distinguishing features of classical Newtonian and chaos sciences.

Table 3 Features of Newtonian and chaos science compared

Newtonian science	Chaos
Order and regularity	Disorder and irregularity
Predictable results, therefore deterministic	Unpredictable results, therefore probabilistic
Ruled by law	Ruled by chance and simple rules
A clockwork universe	Irregularity dominates
The future is precisely determined by the past	The future cannot be determined by the past
Simple, modular systems, linear, i.e. directly proportional	Complex, non-linear systems
Very simple to calculate	Not proportional therefore difficult to calculate
Discovered 300 years ago, e.g. the Solar System	Only discovered 30 years ago, e.g. population growth cycles
Orderly motion, e.g. the tides – a fluid under the daily influence of sea and moon	Disorderly motion, e.g. the weather – a turbulent fluid, unpredictable, with numerous unquantifiable influences
Reductionist approach	Holistic, global approach

Chaotic systems are messy and unreliable, ruled by chance with unpredictable results, so the future is not determined by the past. They are profoundly nonlinear – the results are not proportional to the forces acting upon them. Small events can produce enormous consequences. This property of nonlinearity makes chaotic systems difficult to understand and calculate. Chaotic systems are in process of becoming, while the simple systems predominantly studied by classical science are more static. Chaos pioneers dubbed it deterministic on discovering these complex systems are governed by simple mathematical rules. They provide the certainty which engenders the determinism. Intriguingly, this strange conjunction of hugely complex behaviour produced by the stark simplicity of hidden rules marks yet another curious feature of chaotic systems. They appear to be grossly complicated, but in effect, all this complexity stems from a set of simple rules, endlessly repeated or iterated.

However, as befits the bewildering world of chaos, complication is not a strict requirement for chaotic behaviour. Under the right conditions, even simple, highly regulated systems can act chaotically. The swing in a simple pendulum, a gradual change in the rate at which a tap drips, a rise in the speed of a spinning roulette wheel, a change in an animal's heart beat – all are examples where slightly modified conditions can suddenly trigger chaos. The ability of regular systems to become chaotic forms a tantalising bridge between regularity and disorder. Although chaos and classical physics differ markedly, only one set of laws governs nature and in the real world, especially here on earth, systems flow endlessly from ordered to chaotic and back again. Unexpectedly, classical physics is not exactly precise – it has fuzzy edges; while chaos is not purely random – it obeys simple rules. And this extraordinary blurring between the two scientific disciplines has drawn them closer together as our knowledge and understanding of chaos continues to enlarge.

Linear and Nonlinear Systems

For generations, scientists naturally preferred to study topics of pure physics which embody analytical simplicity and mathematical elegance, far removed from the messiness of the everyday world. Problems on classical linear systems are enticing. They can be solved because the whole is precisely the sum of its parts. Each unit can act independently, regardless of other influences. The mathematics of such systems can be reduced down to a few equations offering workable solutions. These equations, plotted on a graph, produce a straight line, hence their name – "linear". As Ian Stewart explains, "An equation is linear if the sum of two solutions is again a solution." Linear growth is arithmetic. The special feature of linear systems derives from the way each unit acts separately, even when they intermingle. Many natural processes work like this. With sound waves, the melody from a flute is clearly audible above its piano accompaniment. Light is similarly linear. Various light waves operate independently, passing right through each other, as if no other waves were there. Light waves bouncing off a pub sign can still be seen, even on a very sunny day, because all the rays of light retain their own identities.

This contrasts with nonlinear systems, where all units can interact and interfere with each other. Hence their equations are exceedingly complicated. There are no neat or precise results, so it is difficult to calculate or even predict the outcome. Multiple results are equally possible. The tides are a good illustration of a linear process. They are relatively straightforward, directly influenced by the sun and moon and can be quantified. The earth's atmosphere, by contrast, is nonlinear. It is a fiercely agitated gaseous fluid, prone to wild, capricious motions and subject to a multiplicity of unquantifiable influences. Weather systems are typically chaotic, capable of a vast range of behaviour, much of which cannot be accurately forecast.

Nonlinearity in Chaos – Little Actions, Big Results

Chaos predominates in nature, and is mainly nonlinear: its effects are not proportional to the cause. A linear change is arithmetic, like adding tins of beans to a grocery shelf. Nonlinear growth is not directly proportional: a baby grows most rapidly in its first two years of life; or consider the proverbial last straw that broke the camel's back, implying just one straw can be too many, producing a major change; or the case of one small step at the edge of a cliff, resulting in a tremendous fall. All are examples of a massive effect quite disproportional to its cause. Another surprising aspect of nonlinearity is the way tiny changes can generate any one of multiple outcomes. In advance, it is impossible to know which will be the final outcome. This peculiarity, the nub of their inherent unpredictability, explains the special attribute of the Butterfly Effect (see page 88).

A description of nonlinear weather systems instantly illuminates the nonlinearity of financial markets. Disproportionately large results can spring from modest events. They litter the record of bubbles and crashes. One example, described in Chapter 13, was the tiny quarter percentage point interest rate rise introduced by the American Federal Reserve Board on 4 February 1994. It produced a dramatic, almost instantaneous response in all the major international markets of the world, triggering a sharp decline in global bond markets within days. An unexpected news item on any topic of import can produce a disproportionately large market reaction, purely because it was unforeseen. The 1990 Iraqi invasion of Kuwait was one example; the unexpected Tory general election win in April 1992 was another.

Nonlinearity in Gearing

Today, the entire philosophy of a wide range of sophisticated financial instruments is based on nonlinearity. While they may not understand the chaos implications, speculators rely on it in their careful assessment of risk versus return. Exaggeratedly large gains or losses can arise from a modest cash outlay. All the get-rich-quick and portfolio protection ideas – gearing, margin trading, futures and options – rely on this effect. This central theme in bubbles and crashes goes way back to Tulipomania and the 1720s. Make a very small down-payment, and watch huge gains or losses emerge.

International speculators, lead by notorious American hedge funds, institutional fund managers and even small private investors, have grown to rely increasingly on slick derivative instruments. However, they are not a recent novelty. Their origins lie in the 1630s, perhaps even earlier. Essentially, derivatives are artificial investments, "deriving" from a real underlying asset, to which the price relates. Derivatives now exist for shares, bonds, commodities and even for the major indices of the main financial markets. In true chaos tradition, once conjured up into existence, derivatives acquire a life of their own; they have all the features of emergent properties, but their inherent nonlinearity means they can end up as the tail wagging the dog. They introduce extremes of volatility and can lead the underlying cash market, either up or down, with ever increasingly wild swings. In short, the entire panoply of derivative instruments is ideally tailored to exploit the underlying nonlinearity of the markets.

Nonlinearity and gearing play a crucial role in certain markets, where small movements in one factor generate large movements in another. One illustration is the way in which small rises in sales figures for specialised software companies produce substantial rises in earnings, because of the high return earned on their capital employed. A similar effect occurs in the gold market. When, in early January 1996, the price of gold bullion rose a modest 6 per cent, the FT Gold Mines index soared 25 per cent over the same period. A rise in the bullion price usually translates into a similar rise for a gold company's earnings. For an average company in the FT Gold Mines index, total costs including depreciation are about $315 an ounce. On 2 January 1996, with gold at $389, this company would make a profit of $74 an ounce. As the gold price rapidly rose 6 per cent, to $412, the company's operating profit rose to $97 an ounce – over 30 per cent.

More generally, the intrinsic nonlinearity of stock markets is often seen when trading volumes are low, as in the month of August or during the period between Christmas and the New Year holidays. At such times, market makers try to keep neutral positions. If there is an unexpected bout of buying or selling, due perhaps to a surprise news item, the market makers are forced into a rapid response and the market suddenly ignites with a nonlinear leap. August 1996 was a classic illustration; in thin trading the FT-SE 100 index hit a new all-time high of 3,871, after two months of declines.

Holism in Stock Markets

Although the market reflects the collective behaviour of many thousands of individual participants, in its totality, it can develop new properties not possessed by individual investors themselves. Sometimes, the whole market behaves differently to its constituent members; its global and local behaviours will differ. This may happen when the market crashes. Although normally, the market is dominated by rational people and events, occasionally in an intensely active boom, the majority of investors may begin to act irrationally, for in their absence, the manic crash would not occur.

When the whole (that is, the long-term behaviour of the market) behaves differently to the sum of its parts (individual investors), the system is holistic. Chaotic systems are invariably holistic. Consider the behaviour of Jupiter's Red Spot: from astronomical observations on earth, the spot looks constant and stable, but if we could float within Jupiter's storm-tossed atmosphere, we would observe its gassy contents changing continuously around us, in totally unpredictable ways. Globally, the spot appears stable, but its detailed turbulence is quite unpredictable. The red spot is a holistic chaotic phenomenon. Or listen to the glorious sounds of Beethoven's "Ode to Joy". Although sound waves are linear, when dozens of musicians combine their efforts to play one complex score, the end result will be a symphony in which the global sound is a fusion, creating a tremendous experience that transcends what they could achieve by performing individually or in a small group of six or ten players. A symphony orchestra produces holistic music: the choir of voices plus the strings, brass, woodwind and percussion may all play from slightly different score sheets, but the notes of Beethoven's choral masterpiece intermingle to create one magnificent overall harmony. It is only rarely possible to distinguish the separate individual performances involved, unless the composer specifically includes a solo section.

Such examples contrast with the reductionism of pure physical sciences; here the parts sum neatly together to reflect the behaviour of the whole. Reductionism is modular. Scientists spent 300 years on productive research dissecting systems down into the smallest, simplest units – elements, molecules, atoms – to discover how nature works. Her mysteries yielded to their probings to show how tiny units build up into bigger ones, all acting in the same repeatable way. The scientist breaks complicated systems apart to examine their components one by one, confident that the behaviour of the parts mirrors that of the whole. The scientist looks for a solution to an idealised set of problems, far divorced from the messy, everyday world. By confining the problem within a narrow context, reasonable solutions can be found.

Reductionism Versus Holism

Newton's discovery of the nature of light is a good example. He split apart a beam of white light with a prism to discover its basic units. He realised the pure colours created from the beam were the elementary parts that add together to produce white light. Many aspects of nature were so successfully studied by reductionist techniques, classical science uncovered some of nature's deepest secrets at an early date. As in many contrasts between classical and chaos science, holism and reductionism are opposites. The reductionist takes a modular dissecting approach; holism explores the global scenario.

George Cowan paints the contrasts:

> The royal road to a Nobel prize has generally been through the reductionist approach. You can look for the solution of some more or less idealized set of problems, somewhat divorced from the real world, and constrained sufficiently so that you can find a solution. And that leads to more and more fragmentation of science. Whereas the real world demands – though I hate the word – a more holistic approach.

In the real world, everything affects everything else, and it is difficult to know what is happening if you do not recognise the whole intricate web of connections.

The separate specialist functions of individual organs in a living animal illustrate a holistic system, where the parts do not simply sum together to produce the whole. It is impossible to take a living animal apart and examine all its myriad working parts in the confident expectation that the secret of what makes it alive will be discovered by understanding how its various organs function. And on a smaller scale, the incredible complexity of a living cell cannot be understood simply by examining the workings of its numerous constituent bits. Each cell is a centre of intense manufacturing activity functioning in an abundant variety of ways. The incredible mystery of life is enshrined in its holistic totality.

Even if the stock market displays rational long-term behaviour, at times it will differ from the separate investors', just as Jupiter's Red Spot appears stable when viewed from earth while close-up it shows erratic gaseous turbulence. The chaotic behaviour of individual gas molecules differs from the spot's global behaviour. Likewise, some deviations from rational behaviour are possible, even if markets are governed by chaos. Just as extreme conditions flip a simple pendulum or dripping tap from order into turbulence, so I think, under extreme conditions, a becalmed market can erupt into a typical bubble or crash event. Financial markets become chaotic during a boom/bust episode. The early phases of the eight-stage crashes model produce conditions that presage this abrupt transition. With no internal or external shock the transition from order to chaos perhaps might not develop. Usually, a trigger or background setting acts as the spark.

The Order/Disorder Mixture

The ease with which complex systems pitch from order to instability is a strong characteristic of such systems. Unstable states are an essential precursor to the onset of chaos. As the system veers away from a stable equilibrium, the conditions to trigger chaos emerge. Yet astonishingly, as Ilya Prigogine has shown, systems in a far-from-equilibrium state are adept at self-organisation. Open and adaptive, they display a striking ability to evolve and change through time. Like a set of tiny pieces in a kaleidoscope, a simple twist of the tube creates innumerable pattern possibilities – in M. Mitchell Waldrop's memorable phrase, "A handful of pieces and an infinity of possible patterns." This aspect of chaos merges with the new science of complexity. It studies the enigma of emergent properties that spring into being within the formless state of a chaotic system from which a new order will ultimately synthesise.

In human affairs, history is replete with examples of the adaptive, self-organising skills of human societies. Repeatedly, even the most anarchic collapse will finally burn itself out by the faltering reimposition of order, sometimes associated with truly emergent phenomena. Consider the events in the crashes we examined briefly in Chapter 1. Amid acrimonious recriminations, as law and order was haltingly reimposed, the mayhem and confusion subsided. A collapse, through extreme instability followed by a new self-organisation to recreate order, so typical of chaos, has occurred in all the great stock market crashes.

Positive Feedback in Chaos

The dynamics of chaotic systems embodies a profound complexity; the rich diversity of recurring patterns are elusively similar but rarely identical. Coveney and Highfield suggest their instability, the nonlinearity, creates the concomitant effect of feedback. Nonlinearity is inextricably linked to the positive feedback that dominates these systems; the outcome of one effect triggers more change in the same direction. Positive feedback, so central to surging bull markets, is the main chaos mechanism that first fuels a speculative boom to an unstable peak and similarly powers the subsequent collapse as shown in Figure 1.

A good account of feedback is given by Peter Marsh in his book *The Robot Age*. Feedback involves monitoring future behaviour by actual rather than expected performance. It occurs widely in animal and human behaviour, enabling animals (or people) to respond rapidly to life threatening events to ensure survival. Marsh reminds us that during the nineteenth century engineers freely copied feedback principles that occur in nature as these are ideally suited to machine design. They incorporated the fundamental operation of biological feedback in their blueprint designs for control systems in machinery.

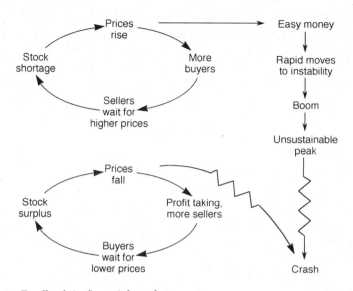

Figure 1 Feedback in financial markets

Both types of feedback: positive (which is change amplifying) and negative (which is change reducing) coexist in chaotic systems. Negative feedback is dampening: it returns the system to rest; positive feedback is additive: the loops can swiftly create run-away instability through a chain reaction effect. It is this repetitive positive loop that creates the far-from-equilibrium states chaotic systems are frequently prone to.

This is clearly seen during a bull market. As it gets established, a rush of new issues or rights issues emerges to take advantage of the buying optimism, but paradoxically, the main response to a rising share price is a further rise. When everyone wants to buy an asset, the price rises. Additional buying stimulates even more buying, building a trend, while prospective sellers hold back hoping to sell later at even higher prices. More buying and less selling creates a stock shortage, with another price rise to reflect the scarcity and yet another turn around the positive feedback loop. Additional fuel comes from investors who sold short (selling stock they do not own in the hope of buying it back more cheaply after it has fallen further). They soon realise they misjudged the intensity of the new uptrend, as it becomes self-sustaining. As the market rises, so do their potential losses. They now buy stock, closing out their losing short positions and adding a further turn to the positive feedback spiral. Step by step, a strong uptrend gets established. Viewed as investor psychology, discussed in Chapter 1, the onset of a strong buying surge fuels a herd instinct of further buying through the adaptive attitude for consensus actions; in terms of a chaos effect, the buying urge fuels further buying to create a self-perpetuating feedback loop, as shown in Figure 1.

At its height, almost everyone is beguiled into hoping the rise can be sustained for longer. But prices are now so excessive, they may have overshot rational levels. In extreme cases, this has been triggered by chaos-inducing factors such as those discussed below. It becomes the peak of an unsustainable boom, preparatory to a calamitous decline.

Positive Feedback in the Crash

Paradoxically, this same positive feedback loop operates when prices drop in a crash. However, in a selling frenzy price falls can be more rapid than during the rise when bargain hunters will be waiting on the sidelines, watching the action. They come into the market to buy cheaply whenever profit-takers pull the price down. This buying pushes the price higher again, thereby prolonging the uptrend. During a major collapse, when naked terror grips thousands, most will be trying to dump their stocks in a synchronised rout. The collective selling accelerates alarmingly; any bargain hunters will be overwhelmed by the stampede of sellers. The uptrend reverses and the downtrend dominates, as shown in Figure 1. But the outcome is the same; during the decline a positive feedback loop of intensifying selling develops, gathering momentum as it grows.

At both the extremes of a rise or a fall, the feedback loop ultimately triggers chaos, with self-fulfilling, unsustainable booms when buyers monopolise the market, and self-destructive panics when selling becomes a contagious cascade of further selling during the crash. Strong trends, both up and down, result from positive feedback loops; a good example was the massive sell-off, built up in response to a string of bad news items over three days in America during the 1987 October crash. The panic spread to other financial centres, triggering a global chain reaction selling surge of amazing proportions. Endless hours were subsequently spent analysing the causes. Perhaps it is a futile exercise to blame the messenger if the underlying conditions to trigger a chaos-type crash have unwittingly been previously slotted into place by the misguided actions of the regulatory authorities.

The Butterfly Effect

So we come to the exotic Butterfly Effect – first, to fit it into chaos theory and then to suggest its relevance to stock markets. Constantly fluctuating complex systems, like the weather and financial markets, are extremely sensitive to their initial state. In practice, since they are never at rest, an arbitrary moment must serve as a starting point. From there, as they evolve through time, minute changes amplify rapidly throughout the system through the effects of positive feedback. Two systems, under only slightly different conditions (the stock markets of America and Japan immediately after the October 1987 crash, for example), may swiftly diverge from one another. Edward Lorenz was the chaos pioneer way back in 1963, who grasped that an inherent nonlinearity in the weather means tiny changes spawn huge changes and one of many possible outcomes can arise from quite a modest change. So there is a strict limitation on future predictability, as it depends on how accurately, if at all, the initial conditions can be measured.

It was Lorenz, a meteorologist exploring the onset of convection in weather systems, who first identified and evocatively labelled this decisive chaos phenomenon as the "Butterfly Effect". While researching the weather he stumbled, quite accidentally, upon this pivotal insight: the chaos credentials of complex weather patterns could be lucidly exposed by computer-generated mathematical modelling. His trail-blazing discovery is covered more fully in Chapter 5, but his findings led him directly to this description of the Butterfly Effect, as Ian Stewart relates:

> The flapping of a single butterfly's wing today produces a tiny change in the state of the atmosphere. Over a period of time, what the atmosphere actually does diverges from what it would have done. So, in a month's time, a tornado that would have devastated the Indonesian coast doesn't happen. Or maybe one that wasn't going to happen, does.

Lorenz was interviewed by science writer, James Gleick, whose enthralling book, *Chaos*, brought this challenging new science into the popular domain. Gleick recalls how Lorenz reasoned the Butterfly Effect was necessary; it was no accident.

> Suppose small perturbations remained small, instead of cascading upwards through the system. Then when the weather came arbitrarily close to a state it had passed through before, it would stay arbitrarily close to the patterns that followed. For practical purposes, the cycles would be predictable – and eventually uninteresting. To produce the rich repertoire of real earthly weather, the beautiful multiplicity of it, you could hardly wish for anything better than a Butterfly Effect.

Substitute "financial markets" for "weather" in this quotation for a stunning explanation of why it is so difficult to make profits in unpredictable stock markets, unless you have a discipline to allow you to hold the winners and cut the losses. As we discuss classic chaos features, we repeatedly see interesting similarities between the weather and stock market behaviour.

In both cases, one minute change in the initial conditions sparks a rapid chain reaction to produce a totally new outcome. But as it is only one of many possible outcomes, the end result is unpredictable. Minute initial differences, after many repetitions around the feedback loops, create enormous subsequent differences. Although this is officially called sensitive dependence upon initial conditions, it is more popularly called the Butterfly Effect. It takes us back to the chain reaction impact of history and folklore, with King Richard III, who lost his life and the English throne when his horse went lame on Bosworth field. This was a seminal turning point in English history, as he was the last Plantagenet king whose rule passed at Bosworth to Henry VII, founder of the notoriously celebrated Tudor dynasty. James Gleick quoted this rhyme to highlight the truism that "In science as in life, it is well known that a chain of events can have a point of crisis that could magnify small changes. But chaos meant that such points were everywhere."

Financial Butterflies

Since there are many similarities between the weather and financial markets, it should come as no surprise to find financial butterflies are almost as commonplace as bulls and bears. In fact, they keep cropping up in all the booms, bubbles and crashes we shall examine. One recent case occurred in summer 1992, when a slender majority of Danes voted "no" to the Maastricht Treaty on 2 June. A "no" vote by a mere 50,000 Danes led, during August and September, to massive currency turbulence affecting 340 million people in the European Community and around 20 million Scandinavian citizens. The ultimate drama in this astonishing chain of events was the abrupt, totally unforeseen 15 September expulsion of the Italian lira and the British pound from the Exchange Rate Mechanism (ERM). Another financial Butterfly Effect, discussed in Chapter 2, was the simultaneous decision of thousands of Japanese investors to sell US Treasury bonds in the autumn of 1987 to fund applications for shares in the second privatisation tranche of NTT to be issued by the government in November. This was later highlighted as a critical factor in sparking off the monumental October global stock market crash.

Creating the Financial Butterfly Effect

In numerous ways, investors create Butterfly Effects. Consider the technique of "short covering". Pessimists who hope to profit from a falling market or share price borrow stocks and immediately sell them, on the expectation that when they have to return the borrowed shares they will be able to buy them back in the market at a lower price. Short selling is a minority activity but it can produce useful profits if traders get the timing and direction of the price movement right. However, it carries obvious risks because they are selling shares they do not personally own. The risks increase if prices unexpectedly start to rise, throwing the whole strategy in jeopardy.

When short sellers are suddenly faced with the prospect of lost profits or big losses, they must buy back their borrowed stocks at a higher price. Dithering can be catastrophic. The only way to rescue the position is to rapidly accept the situation has changed. Sensible traders act swiftly to cover their exposure, buying back the necessary shares before the price rises too far against them. A hasty rush to buy adds to pressure building in the market, accentuating the buying demand even more. This activity may involve relatively few investors, but often triggers greatly exaggerated price movements – a Butterfly Effect. Long-term investors, watching prices rise, see a buying opportunity. They pile in, fearing to miss an expected market surge, thereby adding to the momentum caused by the short selling. In this way the positive feedback loop gains strength, adding to rising prices. A strong uptrend takes hold.

A real example of the Butterfly Effect on short selling occurred on 24 August 1994. The Dow Jones Industrial Average (DJIA) rose 70.9 points; analysts were quick to note that activity in the derivatives market had given share prices a significant boost. Widespread "short covering" was thought to have occurred late in the session when a sudden unexpected rise in share prices prompted traders, who were expecting the Dow to weaken, to rush into the market to close out their short positions. These speculators had bought a particular derivative product (a short-term stock index option) from Loomis, Sayles & Co, a Wall Street firm. It sold the option as a hedge, convinced share prices would fall during the week. However, as prices rose above a certain trigger level during that afternoon (when the option was "in-the-money" and therefore had a real value), anyone who had bought the index option started to make money. These investors now came into the market to buy, because the higher prices rose, the more money they would make on their options. This sudden late buying surge panicked the short sellers into buying. The end result was a gain of 71 points on the Dow with at least 20 points of it attributable to this late afternoon activity. Two days later, on 26 August, further short covering may again have helped prices to rise, although by then the rise had gained a strong internal momentum. Accordingly, from Wednesday to the close on Friday, the Dow added a total of 105 points to stand at 3,881.05.

Irregular Cycles

The chaos characteristic of sensitive dependence on initial conditions triggers the Butterfly Effect. James Gleick's earlier quote on the weather (see page 89) applies equally to the markets; if small perturbations did not ripple through the entire system to magnify small changes, the markets, like the weather, would eventually become wholly predictable. And contrary to one's initial instincts, the scope for profitability would be dire, as the markets would be superefficient. Instead, as we know, business, financial and economic cycles are frustratingly irregular in timing and duration. They experience quasiperiodic motion, a feature common to chaotic systems. Ian Stewart describes quasiperiodic motion in *The New Scientist Guide to Chaos* as "a more complicated type of motion" where "two (or more) distinct periodic motions, of unrelated periods, are combined. The result is a motion that almost repeats, but never quite gets back to the exact starting state."

We are fully conversant with this idea from climatic seasons; they illustrate this irregularity to perfection. The cycles will only repeat exactly if their motion is resonant, that is, there is some time period operating which is an exact whole number of each of the separate periods combined. This is a rarity in the weather, just as it is in stock market situations. Accordingly, each business and economic cycle will be tantalisingly similar yet uniquely different.

The sensitivity arising in dependence upon initial conditions stems from stretching, as points close together in a system get stretched apart, and folding, as points that were far apart move closer. This insight stemmed from the work of Stephen Smale of the University of California at Berkeley. He was a mathematician who applied topology (the study of properties that remain unchanged when shapes are deformed by twisting, stretching or squeezing) to dynamical systems. He used "shape" to help visualise the whole range of behaviours which they are capable of displaying. His topological transformations of shapes revealed the new geometrical essence they enshrine.

The mix of stretch and fold creates the gross irregularity of chaos. We see it unfold when chocolate syrup is blended into a cake-mix to make a marble cake. The final cake has irregular streaks of chocolate woven throughout the vanilla-coloured mix, illustrating holism: every slice will be uniquely individual in its amount and arrangement of chocolate and vanilla, but each is quintessentially recognisable as marble cake, revealing how global and local behaviours differ.

Numerous financial examples show topological transformations similar to those Smale identified. Points on an index or share price chart often show stretching and folding. Such outcomes are endemic in financial and economic markets, where almost every variable, from inflation to interest rates, from exchange rates to unemployment, can be drawn as a point on a chart. In the financial press, charts show points converging, diverging or alternating between the two.

It is the rich mixture of positive and negative feedback loops inherent in chaotic systems that generates the fluidity of patterns endlessly forming and re-forming. But perhaps one of the most important roles of feedback in creating an unsustainable stock market boom is the antagonism that exists between negative (dampening) and positive (amplifying) feedback in every chaotic system. This antagonism produces what chaologists refer to as a damped, driven system. We shall explore this interesting phenomenon and its relevance to financial markets in the next chapter.

CHAPTER FOUR

PROFITABLE CHAOS

Just for the sake of argument, let's say you could predict the next economic boom with absolute certainty, and you wanted to profit from your foresight by picking a few high-flying shares. You still have to pick the right stocks, just the same as if you had no foresight.

Peter Lynch, *One Up On Wall Street*

In the stock market, mathematical chaos may still be tantalisingly elusive, but the heavy hand of chaos is visible everywhere for those who can decode its messages. This chapter will introduce more classic chaos features – fractals, pumps and damped, driven systems – to explore the existing copious visual evidence. Assiduous investors can profit from insights into how chaos drives the markets, even without number-crunching computers to formulate successful mathematics-based investment strategies.

As we saw, Ian Stewart defines chaos as lawless behaviour governed entirely by law. This weird paradox can be explained because the observable lawlessness is only a superficial veneer. However, unpredictable events sometimes intrude when we least expect them, so the disorder attracts attention and we ignore the possibility that an underlying order may exist. Chaotic systems are like a magician's practised skill. While we stare at the complicated antics performed by his left hand, we miss the subtle right-hand moves which may pluck a coin, a handkerchief or a card from up his sleeve, right before our eyes. The magician's deception is convincing because we were looking in the wrong place. By concentrating on the left hand, we failed to spot the right-hand movements which achieved the trick.

Secret Structures

If there are hidden rules, there should be a coherent structure within the restless mêlée. First, we must reveal this inner structure; and secondly, we must understand what it is telling us, so we can benefit from our new-found knowledge. The presence of structure in the markets is the financial equivalent of the magician's secret tricks. Structure is our passport to profitable situations; it is literally everywhere in the markets, but to exploit the best opportunities, we must recognise it and decipher the signals. This chapter focuses on evidence for structure in financial markets to enhance our ability to profit from market movements.

Obviously, not every situation will be rewarding. We want to know which have the best and worst potential. In between lie ambiguous periods with unreliable signals which may or may not prove fruitful. And surprisingly, as Richard Cantillon's investment successes show, we can profit from bubble and crash events, in addition to many other situations, once we are alert to the right signals. Essentially, profiting from chaos means identifying the intrinsic structure in any market phase, and knowing which configurations produce above average returns with minimum risk and which are best avoided. Many brilliant investors and speculators have mastered this skill because they have grasped the core practicalities of successful investment without knowing the chaos-based reasons why their strategies work. But the chaos foundations build a credible framework making this result more attainable for informed investors who want to understand and profit from their greater insights.

Fractals Tell the Story

The many similarities between complex physical systems and financial markets are clearly seen in the close links between share price charts and fractals. These provide prolific evidence for an underlying structure in the capital markets and are doubly important because fractals play such a dominant role in the fledgeling science of chaos.

The ultimate emergence of chaos as a scientific theory owes a huge debt to the rapid development of computers. During the 1960s, chaos theory progressed in tandem with the growing sophistication of high speed computing power, evolving from a synthesis of readily accessible computers and a new approach to mathematics. By following millions of separate paths over countless steps, the computer reveals in simple, direct graphics the abstract, geometrical nature of chaotic systems. One surprising result was the discovery that intricate, convoluted graphics are generated from quite uncomplicated equations. The computer is the modern equivalent of a mathematical slave. Designed to remove the drudgery of elaborate manual calculations from the work load of the human operator, it will loyally perform endless streams of arduous calculations within a fraction of a second. It is most adept at iterating (constantly repeating) brief programs of simple-step formulae. Iteration works on algorithms, which are short sets of rules, continuously repeated. Iteration is the algorithmic equivalent of positive feedback: repeating the same sequence around a given loop. This is the link with chaos, which emerges when strong positive feedback acts within a far-from-equilibrium system.

The marriage of computing power and chaos theory created a wonderful, new geometry – the visual mathematics of irregularity. It was the brain-child of a maverick French mathematician, Benoit Mandelbrot, working in the 1950s at the giant IBM research centre in Yorktown Heights, New York. Gleick quotes his appended statement to his entry in *Who's Who*:

> Science would be ruined if (like sport) it were to put competition above everything else, and if it were to clarify the rules of competition by withdrawing entirely into narrowly defined specialities. The rare scholars who are nomads-by-choice are essential to the intellectual welfare of settled disciplines.

Mandelbrot's seminal contribution to the infant science of chaos was to literally make it visible. He invented a means of depicting it – through geometry. By creating a geometry of nature, he could map its roughness and irregularities. Confronted with natural shapes that were, in Mandelbrot's words, "monstrous and pathological", his new revolutionary mathematics was born by conceiving an intuition from scratch. "Intuition is not something that is given. I've trained myself to accept as obvious shapes which were initially rejected as absurd, and I find everyone else can do the same."

Today, Mandelbrot's revolutionary view of nature is generally accepted as epitomising the chaos at its core. Fractals, the name he himself chose to evince all the jaggedness, derives from the latin adjective *fractus*, meaning broken. Computer printouts of chaotic systems as fractals are constantly used to represent natural phenomena in graphic form. They provide a unifying framework to study them in depth. Geometry is a visual mathematics dealing with relationships in space, exploring the properties and measurements of points, angles, planes, etc. The two types of geometry, Euclidean and fractal, are distinctly different. Their key features are compared in Table 4.

Table 4 Two systems of geometry

Euclidean (Newtonian) geometry	Fractal (chaos) geometry
1. Classic Greek, *c.* 300 BC	Fractals, Mandelbrot *c.* 1950s
2. Smoothness	Roughness
3. Regularity, e.g. circles, spheres, cones, triangles, planes	Irregularity, e.g. clouds, waves, coastlines, frost, lightning
4. Expressed by formulae, which can be solved	Expressed by algorithms, which may not be solvable
5. Static, in a state of being	Evolving, in a state of becoming
6. Lose structure when magnified; a circle becomes a featureless straight line at high magnitudes, e.g. flat earth on a far horizon	Retain complete structure at all levels of magnification; self-similar, e.g. a surface ripple is similar to a giant wave

Just as fractals give a graphic mathematical representation of chaos, so Euclidean geometry shows the graphic mathematics of classical or traditional physics. Mandelbrot's fractals describe the geometry of nature's vast variety of irregular objects – clouds, smoke, lightning, snowflakes, mountains, coastal shorelines and waves. Euclidean geometry describes the artificial world of smoothness and regularity. Circles, squares, triangles, cones and the other shapes of classical physics are rarely found in naturally occurring objects on earth, which have a characteristic roughness.

The Technical Route

Fractals map irregularity in chaotic systems. They result from an algorithm repeated thousands of times. Fractal geometry graphically reveals jaggedness as an evolving process, reflecting how complex dynamical systems exist in a perpetual state of flux. Euclidean geometry depicts regularity: it is static, in a fixed state of being. Chaologists rely on fractals, saying geometry is helpful in their study of chaotic phenomena because they can use one picture to reveal information that is almost inaccessible within a welter of tabulated data. James Gleick writes, "Graphics are the key. 'It's masochism for a mathematician to do without pictures,' one chaos specialist would say." This is precisely the rationale claimed by technical analysts for their use of charts to depict the time series of share price movements or market indices.

Technical analysts claim price movements on charts represent investors' collective behaviour – the sum total thinking of everyone involved with one market or a particular financial asset. This includes the market movers – politicians, central bankers, analysts, strategists and brokers –

as well as investors. From this information analysts search for repeating patterns, hoping to predict future price movements. Brokers and investors who are suspicious of charts doubt the logic behind the repeating patterns idea. They deride the bizarre names to depict these patterns: head and shoulders, double tops, triple tops, double bottoms, wedges, flags. Technical analysts think repeating patterns depict the human psychology of investors' hopes, fears and greed. I believe this is a partial explanation. Charts are financial fractals: they reveal the face of chaos in the markets.

Besides charts, technical analysis covers many facets of investment information. It spans a systematic study of financial market behaviour itself, using charts, special indicators and statistical calculations. This cluster of indirect information is used to dissect and interpret past activities and motives of all market operators: traders, speculators and investors alike. Yet active participants are responding to the actions of innumerable background market movers, so in aggregate, all this information is utilised to spot when profitable patterns are re-emerging.

No one analytical tool is conclusive. Charts alone rarely give decisive signals and interpretations vary from one analyst to another; this itself contributes to an active market. When several indicators together give confirmatory signals, they are infinitely more reliable. At present, few technical analysts fully understand the powerful chaotic force driving the markets, but on two counts they already benefit from its influence. First, they rely heavily on charts; these are financial fractals, exposing the inherent structure. By searching for recurring patterns, they seek out the perennial patterning so characteristic of all complex chaotic systems: the hidden structure. Secondly, when promising patterns appear, they hunt for confirmatory signals in other indicators. This caution stems from sensitive dependence on initial conditions, where two similar patterns can evolve completely differently; even if one produced a profitable outcome, another may not. Confirmatory signs reduce the importance of diverging outcomes, as only those occasions with the greatest chance of success will be acted upon.

The Fundamental Route

The other main form of financial analysis, termed "fundamental", relies exclusively on essential data relating to current and future performance of a company (which affects its share price) or of a national economy (which will affect the indices representing its stock market). Fundamentalists look at current asset prices or indices levels to assess good value. Despite insistence by advocates of the Efficient Market Hypothesis that no one can make exceptional profits without assuming higher risk, these investors use a set of rules to weigh the stock-picking risks. Applying rules is patently a method of risk reduction. Rules will be individualistic, but they secure the discipline to maximise profits and minimise losses. Rules have helped some super-investors achieve outstanding results, successes which leave me sceptical about academic claims that spectacularly wealthy investors, some of whom we met in Chapter 2, are simply thrown up by the laws of averages. But if the theorists are right, knowledge of how the markets operate can only help to give an edge to methodical investors, so they can join the band of happy winners with above average returns.

Financial Fractals

Use of fractal geometry is directly relevant to financial markets as it is ideally suited to analysis of time series, such as a sequence of share price data collected over time, and fractals, like capital markets, are prone to trends and cycles. A considerable amount of key economic and financial data driving the markets is clustered and repeated monthly or yearly. This generates the underlying iteration of a financial time series, as depicted by the charts. The repetition contributes to creating structure, since many prime statistics – GNP, the rate of inflation, government borrowing, the trade figures, unemployment statistics, bank and building society lending, etc. – are routinely reported each month.

Government policies are closely tied to a political timetable geared to elections, generating four- or five-yearly patterns of cyclical data. Taxation and spending plans may be generous before an election, bribing voters with their own money. Later, some tightening might be needed. Unpopular measures are taken early in the political cycle to allow overt generosity to be repeated three or four years later. These swings become reflected in indices and share price data and are mirrored in the charts. Although the record gets peppered with major unforeseen events, sufficient routine, repetitive information reaches the markets to validate the obvious clustering. It appears as recurrent chart patterns, furnishing the fundamentals that mirror the consensus view of anticipated prospects.

The Scaling Effect of Fractals

Fractals show self-similarity; they retain complete structure at all levels of magnification and across different scales. James Gleick gives this description: "Self-similarity is symmetry across scale. It implies recursion, pattern inside of pattern." Self-similarity surrounds us everywhere: in a child's building blocks, one inside the other in ever decreasing size; when you stand between two mirrors and spot your endless reflections thrown back at you in an infinity of reproductions. Mandelbrot quoted Jonathan Swift to catch the self-similarity flavour:

> So Nat'ralists observe, a Flea
> Hath smaller Fleas that on him prey,
> And these have smaller Fleas to bite 'em,
> And so proceed ad infinitum.

Computer-generated fractals are identically self-similar, as they are pro-duced by an algorithm, **the exact iteration of a simple set of steps**. Financial charts, like most naturally-occurring fractals, are statistically, not identically, self-similar. **While they are fundamentally similar, they are not identical at every scale of magnification**. They resemble waves, where a surface ripple has roughly the same shape as a giant wave; or a coastal outline, where small indentations are never exactly identical to the larger shoreline shapes. Fractals retain their structure even down to the tiniest level of magnification. Euclidean shapes always lose structure when magnified. The arc of a circle becomes a straight line at very high magnifications. On extremely large circles this is recognisable in our experience of a flat horizon at sea because we are too close to observe the earth's curvature. To view the roundness of the planet we have to fly miles above the surface, in an orbiting satellite.

Financial Examples of Self-Similarity

During the 1920s and 1930s Ralph Nelson Elliott was the first researcher to note that financial charts are intrinsically irregular all over, with the same degree of irregularity at every scale. Chaos theory made its great forward leap in the 1960s after his death, so he did not live to realise charts are typical fractals. He formulated his Wave Principle by the scientific method of direct observations and analysis of American stock market data. His Wave Principle is based, like the earlier Dow Theory, on wave theory; but waves are fractals. Self-similarity for waves occurs across the full range of seven scales – from the massive seventh to the most minute surface ripple. From observations of Dow Jones Industrial Averages, Elliott compiled an idealised scheme of wavelike motions for share prices through time: cycles within cycles. Each wave is subdivided into subwaves of the next lower order of magnitude, right down to the tiniest possible degree. Beginning with the greatest wave, the Grand

Supercycle, they progress down through the Supercycle, Cycle, Primary, Intermediate, Minor, Minute, Minuette and Subminuette. His conclusions lead Elliott to the view that Dow Jones Industrial Averages waves – Elliott Waves – apply to all financial waves, being approximately self-similar across nine degrees of magnitude. A Minor wave magnified up four times has a similar shape to a Supercycle wave.

The idealised waves (shown in Figure 2) are fractals, with symmetry across every scale. Every wave consists broadly of three up, impulse waves and two down, corrective waves. They are statistically self-similar

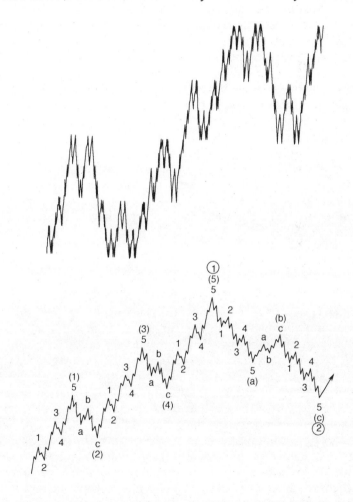

Figure 2 (a) Idealised Elliott Wave showing its fractal nature; (b) Idealised Elliott Wave showing three up (impulse) waves and two down (corrective) waves.
Source: R. R. Prechter, Jnr. and A. J. Frost, *Elliott Wave Principles*

with roughly the same structure at all levels, independent of scale. In practice, financial charts are intensely irregular and convoluted, like coastlines, another natural self-similar fractal form.

The Triple Links in the Crash Scenario

Elliott Waves, with three impulse waves up and two corrective waves down, mirror established psychological patterns of human behaviour. Each upwave reflects expansion, exuberance and the euphoria of rising optimism, leading to the downwave of correction when decline, depression and despair set in. Both well recognised psychological phases are reflected in the patterns of Elliott Waves, but Elliott Waves are fractals, depicting the graphics of chaos. Psychology, Elliott Waves, Chaos – the three fundamentals which forge the elements of every bubble and crash profile. The predominant human emotions expressed by investors are hope, greed and fear – behaviour patterns visible in the charts; the charts are fractals, mapping manifestations of chaos in financial markets. So charts are vital tools for in-depth market analysis; they are a defining feature of chaos in the markets, exposing the intrinsic structure. This triple link unites the psychology of investor behaviour, rational and irrational, with the graphic evidence in charts and with the emerging science of chaos.

Moving Averages as Fractals

One facet of fractals widely used by technical analysts is the application of moving averages to charts. These are lagging indicators; they follow rather than lead the price. While they do not predict movements, they do help to confirm them. The calculation is made by averaging a price over a set number of days. On each successive day, the latest figure is added and the earliest figure in the previous day's calculation drops out. Moving averages work best when used in clusters of short-, medium- and long-term duration. Technicians choose from a wide range of time scales. A short-term moving average might cover 5, 10 or 20 days, a medium-term average would involve 30, 40 or 50 days, while a long-term average covers 90, 100 or 200 days. Moving averages are fractals having self-similarity across all scales, which explains why clusters with differing numbers of days work best in unison. As statistical smoothing aids, they isolate an underlying trend formation. Trends, discussed below, are another key source of structure in the markets.

Strong Buy Signals

Being statistically self-similar fractals, all moving averages are inter-related and depend on the intrinsic movements of the underlying price line. Used in clusters of three – short, medium and long – they help with buy and sell decisions. A positive signal occurs when a rising short-term average cuts up through a rising medium-term average; this is termed a "golden cross". It is endorsed if the long-term average is also just turning up, after falling or being flat for some time. In conjunction, the three averages are now indicating a bullish turning point as the best buy signals occur when three averages of different time scales are all moving up in line, one behind the other, under the rising share price. Two buy signals appear on Figure 4.

We can illustrate the importance of the basic trend with the behaviour of moving averages; many charts show the price movement of an index or share dropping back periodically to make contact with its 20-day, 50-day or 200-day moving average. Alternatively, the price hovers for a time, allowing the moving averages to meet up with the price action. For a share or index in a rising trend, a dip or catch-up pause is a good buy signal; a price often bounces up after touching, or briefly dipping below, an average. It indicates a bullish mood. New buyers enter the market after a bout of profit-taking. Watching the price relative to its moving averages offers better buy signals. The optimum signal occurs when the price starts to bounce up from the-average, shown in Figure 3. Here, the Nasdaq composite is seen closely

Figure 3 Nasdaq Composite Index 1994–5, hugging the 20-day moving average
© Reuters

hugging its 20-day moving average during 1994–95. It dropped back to meet the average several times, and then bounced up again.

Strong Sell Signals

Conversely a warning signal is given when a share or an index stands way above all the moving averages. In a manic boom, this may herald an unstable peak. An adverse triggering incident at such a time may spark a sudden plunge with some technical indicators turning negative. Among such confirmatory signals moving average movements are helpful. As the market drops, the falling shorter, 20-day moving average will cut down below either the falling price or a medium-term average (the 50-day), or both. When two falling moving averages cross, a dead cross results; the opposite to the bullish golden cross defined above. These effects are marked on Figure 4 for the UK FT-SE 100 index.

Identifying Major Turning Points

Traders complain that markets persist in frustrating "do-nothing" phases. They spend 75 per cent of the time drifting aimlessly and only

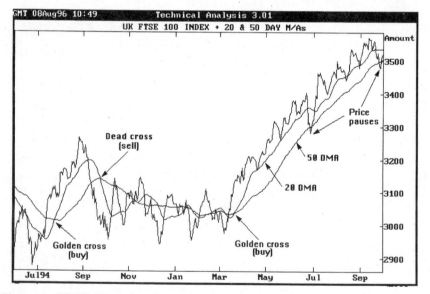

Figure 4 FT-SE 100 index showing two golden crosses, a dead cross and price pauses as the moving averages meet up with the price line
© Reuters

25 per cent moving energetically up or down. It is tricky making money in drifting markets. Therefore, recognising when the market is about to switch from sluggish to active helps to separate out profitable from ambiguous phases. Searching for major turning points is important, as they signify a reversal in the market's mood and hence in chart patterns. Spotting reversal signals allows an early withdrawal from deteriorating situations or entry to a newly emerging favourable one.

In the search for major turning points, understanding how chaos drives the markets helps to pin-point when the market will become active and throw up potentially profitable phases. The central chaos feature here is known as a damped, driven system. It is yet another manifestation of definite structure in what appear to be randomly drifting markets.

Financial Markets as Damped, Driven Systems

Tussles arising between buyers and sellers in the markets are an example of this typical, widely observed chaos feature. A damped, driven effect is created in complex systems when positive and negative feedback operate simultaneously. It can even arise in elementary simple cases, like a playground swing, as James Gleick explains:

> The swing accelerates on its way down, decelerates on its way up, all the while losing a bit of speed to friction. It gets a regular push – say, from some clockwork machine. All our intuition tells us that, no matter where the swing might start, the motion will eventually settle down to a regular back and forth pattern, with the swing coming to the same height each time.

This result is certainly possible, but the swing's motion can also turn erratic. It may fail to settle down into a steady state and never repeat the pattern of earlier swings. Gleick describes how the swing acts as a damped, driven system:

> The surprising, erratic behaviour comes from a nonlinear twist in the flow of energy in and out of this simple oscillator. The swing is damped and it is driven: damped because friction is trying to bring it to a halt, driven because it is getting a periodic push. Even when a damped, driven system is at equilibrium, it is not at equilibrium, and the world is full of such systems, beginning with the weather.

We saw, in Chapter 3, that negative feedback invokes a dampening, while positive feedback exerts a driven impulse. James Gleick takes the weather as an excellent illustration of the core antagonisms within a damped, driven system. The weather is damped by negative feedback when heat rises from the earth, dissipating into space; it is driven by steady exposure to the sun's energy. The earth cools as hot air rises and friction from cloud formation increases the heat loss; this is the dampening effect. But the sun beams out a constant heat to earth, creating a fiery positive feedback. At any time, the outcome of these two opposing forces depends on their relative strength and intensity. As shown in Figure 5, this governs the prevailing state of the weather. Three principal states arise: first, phases dominated by dampening factors; secondly, phases ruled by the sun's fierce output in cloudless skies; thirdly, unsettled conditions when the outcome is essentially unpredictable.

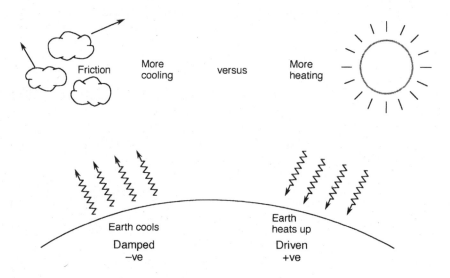

Figure 5 A damped, driven system: the weather

Damped Market Action

Financial markets are among numerous examples of damped, driven chaotic systems in nature. They are damped by the antagonism of buyers and sellers, simultaneously adopting opposite views. Together, buyers and sellers unwittingly act in concert neutralising extreme movements; the strong negative feedback dampens price movements. The *Financial Times* market report of Thursday 14 September 1995 indicates how this struggle unfolds:

> The UK equity market was stranded in midstream yesterday. The market bears maintained the view that share prices had run ahead too far, too fast. And the

bulls were pointing to the latest excellent company reports from Legal & General and British Aerospace. There was further ammunition for the bulls in the latest batch of economic news in Europe and the US.

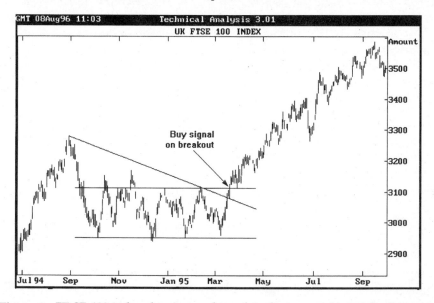

Figure 6 FT-SE 100 index showing prolonged trading range (rectangle chart pattern) and a breakout
© Reuters

Directionless phases stem from this dampening; they create the endless drift to which markets are prone. Drifting markets are the most uncertain for generating profits. Several chart patterns reveal the long delay before either buyers or sellers finally take control; examples include defined trading ranges as rectangles (see Figure 6 for the FT-SE 100 index) and base-building phases, where no decisive movements occur for months.

If they last for some time, base-building phases also create structure, as the moving averages slowly converge, until they all bunch together, in contact or close to the price line. Now, the inner structure distils out. All the randomness has visibly disappeared. The next move is often decisive, up or down, because convergence of the moving averages with the price line creates a broad band, temporarily eliminating random movements. There is nothing random about a straight line – it is an expression of order and structure.

The rectangle is an ambiguous pattern. It is impossible to predict the outcome, but once a clear rectangle trading range develops, structure appears. The box pattern has a lower support level where buyers enter the market and an upper resistance level when profit-taking occurs. If the trading range is wide enough, profits can be made by buying as the price ticks up from the lower support level and selling at the top of the range. The rectangle pattern represents areas of trading where two stable prices exist, one at each end of the range. Such situations with two equilibria are another common feature in chaotic systems, as discussed by Edgar Peters in *Chaos and Order in the Capital Markets*.

Even without a rectangle formation, support and resistance lines are further evidence of structure, indicating the strength of buying or selling pressures. When the line is finally broken by a decisive move up or down, it indicates the resolution of the battle, giving another good clue to the likely turn of events, as the move will usually be strong enough to continue for some time.

Driven Markets

When buyers triumph over sellers, the index (or share price) breaks out from its trading range. If this occurs on high volume (plenty of buyers) it is a strongly bullish buy signal. The breakout points are marked on the charts. Cautious investors wait until a price is 2 per cent above the old high, for confirmation. Conversely, a breakdown gives a sell signal, especially after a lengthy trading phase. Selling short, or taking out a put option or futures contract, might be profitable as the lower level of the trading range now becomes a firm resistance to an upthrust of the movement once the breakdown occurs. After a prolonged trading range, the breakout or breakdown marks a turning point, a switch from damped to driven. Active markets are news-driven. They respond to a constant flow of information, mainly unexpected. The news may be economic, political, corporate, national or international. Active markets create strong positive feedback loops, so a breakout on high volume is a powerful buy signal. The fabled speculator, Jesse Livermore, made a fortune with his breakout system on Wall Street early in this century. His best gains accrued from exercising a strict discipline; waiting for the breakout to be confirmed. Acting ahead of the signal gives unpredictable results.

As with the weather, the state of the market at any time is ruled by the competing strengths of the two opposing forces. The exact outcome of the damped and driven forces is unknowable, and the result rarely predictable, but markets constantly throw up useful clues for those with the right antennae to receive them. The markets anticipate or discount most news items, so a clash exists between reality and expectations. If good news is expected and it duly arrives, there may be no reaction; if bad news is expected and the news is good, market reaction can be swift and excessive. A dominant positive feedback loop quickly arises, as optimism surges.

Beneficial Trends

Prices begin moving predominantly in one direction. The final outcome may produce an extreme overshoot, but if the fundamental view is good, a new bull trend emerges. This is one of the most profitable formations markets produce. An established trend can last for weeks, months, years or decades. The duration depends upon the time-frame used. It can link with the four-year political cycle, the eight-year business cycle, or the 40 to 50 year prolonged cycle of rising prosperity seen in the West since the end of the Second World War. Whether a trend lasts one, four or eight years, it offers the prospect of superb profits with lower risk, at least until it is decisively broken.

The emergence of a trend is one of the strongest market structures. It acquires a ratchet shape, often with two spurts up followed by one down. The jagged pattern is a fractal, with a series of highs and lows. The lows mark the point where the bulls return to dominate the action. A good trend has a series of rising highs and lows. It is confirmed if its accompanying relative strength chart also shows an uptrend. The relative strength line records the movement of the price relative to the whole market. A weakening in the relative strength warns of a possible change in the trend. A line joining the tops and bottoms of the chart creates the up- or downward channel in which the trend travels. The number of points making contact with the lines measures the strength of the trend. Only a few contact points give a weaker signal than on a trend with many contacts.

Super Grandcycle Trends

As noted in Chapter 1, the long six-year bull trends of the 1920s and 1980s both ended in crashes. Japan's surging bull market survived through almost two decades. The astonishing world economic growth of the post-Second World War era, with more democracy, international trade and rising wealth, generated phenomenal long-term growth in all the stock markets of the Western industrial nations. On the long-term charts, even the global crash of October 1987 is merely a blip.

This long-term growth epitomises Elliott's Grand Supercycle, predicted in the 1930s. It is chronicled in George Blakey's *The Post-War History of The London Stock Market, 1945 to 1992*, which records the long-run growth of many giant multi-national British companies – Hanson, Racal, BTR among others. The UK FT Industrial Ordinary 30 Share index rose from 105.9 at the start of August 1945 to a staggering 2,772.4 on 2 August 1996. The Dow Jones Industrial Average shows an even more prodigious rise, from 125 on 1 August 1945 to a monumental 5,763 by the end of May 1996 when the Dow Jones index celebrated its centenary.

Secular Bull Trends

Some US investors have become billionaire super-stars, profiting over decades from the astronomical rise in the US economy, reflected by incredible leaps on the stock market over this prolonged period. The legendary Warren Buffett, America's second wealthiest man (after Bill Gates of Microsoft), spearheads this advance. In his holding company, worth $29 billion, he and his wife own 44 per cent. Anyone clever enough to buy 40 shares at $20 dollars each in 1965 for an investment of $800 would now be a millionaire. Or consider the rise of Fidelity's Magellan Fund under Peter Lynch's stewardship. He became fund manager in 1977. An investment of $1,000 in Magellan when Lynch arrived, had grown to $28,000 by the time he retired in 1990.

Brian Reading in Weekend Money of the *Financial Times*, 11 August 1996, suggests Wall Street has experienced three great secular market phases:

> From 1948 to 1968, the Standard and Poor's index rose 8 per cent a year in real terms (that is, after adjusting for inflation). During the following 14 inflationary years, it fell 7 per cent a year on average in real terms. Now, since 1982, it has risen by 10 per cent a year on average.

An article in August 1995, by Canada's RBC Dominion Securities in their *Strategic Review* – US Market section, highlights the notion of secular bull trends over extended periods in market sectors that are enjoying exceptional growth. Historically, secular leadership appears in all major bull cycles, within a strongly rising trend. The article suggests secular leadership extends beyond one normal business cycle as it reflects the fundamental growth potentials of the leading edge sector. In the 1970s this was energy, and the uptrend lasted from 1961 to 1985; in the 1980s it was consumer goods with the trend in place from 1970 to 1985; we currently may be at the start of a new extended secular trend in technology: computers, software, semiconductors, bio-technology, communications equipment and pharmaceutical products. The secular trend can be volatile, mirroring investors' psychological reactions of fear and greed. Periodic declines of 15 to 25 per cent with recoveries reaching new highs depict its development. An early scepticism finally yields to a stronger upthrust when each recovery reaches a new high, increasing investors' confidence. On this analysis recent bubble-like technology sectors may enjoy strong recoveries after periodic short-term correction phases.

West Versus East on Economic Growth

The West's astonishing explosive economic growth contrasts sharply with progress in the communist world of Eastern Europe. It reveals how an active, open, constantly adapting system can grow exponentially by absorbing more energy, resources and information from its environment. This compares with the inefficient use of resources through central planning, a form of closed system, that gripped communist thinking for 40 years. Over 25 per cent of Gross National Product in the now extinct Soviet Union went on military and space projects, while the domestic economy stagnated, like a Third World state, with acute shortages of consumer goods, perennial rationing, unimaginable levels of industrial pollution and waste, and widespread corruption among bureaucrats and officials. The failure of the communist experiment has left Eastern Europe struggling, decades behind the West.

Profiting from Structure

Responding to good news, a strong trend can form. Positive feedback loops are mainly news-led because buyers (or conversely, sellers) react to new information on the assets they follow. While the performance of all positive feedback loops is the same, leading to a vigorous bull (or bear) trend, the news-led loop is more localised and often far less ebullient than positive feedback created by too much money liquidity. As we shall shortly see, a liquidity driven positive feedback loop creates a financial pump.

When a positive loop becomes the dominant market force, prices are driven up in several spurts punctuated by profit-taking or short-run recession driven pauses. It creates the most prominent market structure, producing cycles: Grand Cycles, Super Cycles and Grand Supercycles of Elliott Wave patterns. The history of markets is packed with examples of trend formation in action. The post-war expansion of western democracies fuelled the growth of the corporate sector to produce the industrial, commercial and consumer goods people were demanding. And this growth and corporate expansion ignited the phenomenal long-term rises of national stock markets. It generated market structure and gave numerous buy signals for sharing in this trail-blazing progress. Aggressive entrepreneurs of the 1960s have ridden this Grand Supercycle all the way, becoming multi-millionaires in the process.

Figure 7 Technical features on a Glaxo chart between 1984 and 1991

Befriend the Trend

Short-term trends are further manifestations of market structure. Alert investors can benefit as they emerge (see Glaxo chart in Figure 7) by examining clues that suggest the onset of phase two in the eight-phase crashes model, even if the boom ends before it reaches a state of gross instability. George Soros explains why the trend creates super profits. "Short-term volatility [i.e. instability] is greatest at turning points and diminishes as a trend is established." Hence, the old market adage, "The trend is your friend." In chaos terms, turning points are zones where buyers match sellers. But the battle to swing the market decisively up or down can involve huge gyrations. The final outcome is often uncertain in advance.

The young stages of a new trend are usually the most lucrative, since the earlier you invest, the more investors will follow you. They help to bid share prices way above the levels you paid. Young trends offer the best prospects because once established, a trend feeds on itself with a chaos-induced momentum, thereby acquiring a useful longevity.

British Euphoria

In the British market an unpremeditated trend formed twice during 1992. The first occasion was in April, when to the astonishment of all informed commentators the Tory Government, led by John Major, scraped back into office for a third term, albeit with a reduced majority. The markets had confidently expected a Labour victory, with doom-laden misgivings for higher taxes, public spending and government intervention. With the Tories triumphantly returned to power, the markets rejoiced. The index rose over 100 points in a day, marking the start of a good three-month trend.

The second 1992 occasion when an unexpected outcome secured a huge driven response was the fiasco on 16 September, of sterling's forced expulsion from the Exchange Rate Mechanism (ERM) of the European Monetary System. By releasing Britain from the deflationary impact of high German interest rates, this jubilant day was promptly dubbed White Wednesday. It heralded reflation for Britain, to reduce unemployment and increase activity in the economy through lower interest rates. Investors greeted it with a rousing response which launched a strong 16-month bull market.

Without any major news or random events, buyers and sellers can easily balance each other out, creating lethargic markets. Prices stay locked in a narrow trading range. While random events disturb the markets, a vast amount of incoming data is clustered, or non-random. For companies, there are interim and annual results and general meetings. Routine national news items cover a wide range of government statistics: monthly Gross Domestic Product, trade figures, money supply, government borrowing, inflation, unemployment, etc. A regular diet of data induces the driven effect. The response to sudden adverse or favourable data clusters is a massive surge generating huge positive loops, with a lively rush of selling or buying.

Gains on the Edge of Chaos

A forming trend is easily spotted on a chart. Moving average signals, (golden crosses for buy, dead crosses for sell) help identify when to take decisions. This, in conjunction with the checklist discussed in Chapter 14, gives useful guidance for judging when profitable trends emerge, get established, over-reach themselves, and look ready for a set-back or a sharp collapse. The overshoot in a driven phase can incline the market towards the edge of chaos. Yet even in a roaring boom, one can still make super-profits. Knowing when to withdraw with them intact is the clever trick that separates rational from irrational investors. Spotting tell-tale signs at the edge of chaos is not impossible, as in every case the warning signals are uncannily similar. When a chaos-induced instability erupts, it may be extreme enough to create a bubble. This produces the eight-phase model that we will see unfolding in the bubbles examined in later chapters.

Volume Indicators

Before we examine the driven side of market behaviour we will look at another two technical indicators related to trend behaviour: first, volume and secondly, the emergence of gaps. The significance of a price movement is strengthened if it is accompanied by high volume (i.e market turnover). Volume follows the direction of the trend and a high volume in a rising market, or conversely, a low volume when the market drops, indicates a further market move. The rule is that volume must confirm the trend. A high volume on rises indicates buying strength, working through the force of a positive feedback loop. A strong rise in volume often follows a breakout from an earlier congestion area. High volume occurring **after** the breakout is a reinforcing signal. Paradoxically, breakouts in thin volume can be very good signals for a further price upthrust due to the market's inherent nonlinearity. Excellent trading days can occur in the thin markets of public holidays, such as between Christmas and the New Year.

Understanding Gaps

A gap is a price interval in which no trading occurs. There is a vacuum of buyers or sellers and the price leaps either up or down on absolutely no turnover (volume). In a rising market the gap is extremely bullish. It means the buyers have overwhelmed sellers. A very strong surge often results, shooting the price rapidly higher. Jesse Livermore, in the 1920s, was adept at spotting profitable gapping moves, as the gap indicates an area of no resistance. Not only is it a strong psychological sign, but it signals the defeat of the bears in the damped, driven system. The feedback loop of rising prices quickly becomes dominant and very large profits can swiftly emerge.

One powerful combination is a gap arising on a breakout from a congestion area. The gap indicates thin or no resistance, and therefore confirms that the breakout is genuine and an upward trend can rapidly develop. Just such a combination occurred in the UK market in April 1992, following the surprise Tory election result, (see Figure 8). If buying momentum remains strong, more continuation gaps may appear, signalling the move may continue for as long as it has previously run. The exhaustion gap, as its name implies, emerges as a trend is about to break down. It stems from a vigorous acceleration in a large preceding rise and is confirmed if it is soon closed by a falling price. Exhaustion gaps are more common in bull than bear markets. They come at the end of a long trend, with one final push of a strong feedback loop, before it goes into reverse.

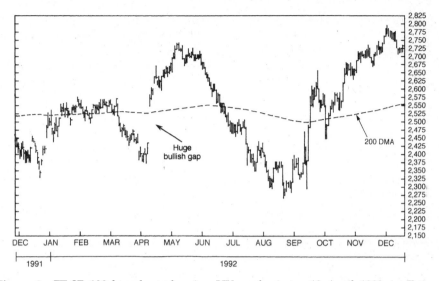

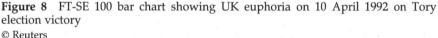

Figure 8 FT-SE 100 bar chart showing UK euphoria on 10 April 1992 on Tory election victory

© Reuters

Profiting from Breakouts

A breakout is a price movement out of a defined congestion area. It takes the share price up into new territory, or away from an earlier declining trend. A strong breakout, confirmed by high volume, is a most profitable investment profile. It works equally for a market index, a major company or a tiny, illiquid company. It signals the triumph of bulls over vanquished bears. The breakout is a driven system. Rising momentum rapidly carries the price higher. A pull back to the previous congestion area can occur, as stale bulls who have been nursing losses for months rush to sell finally with a profit. The next upthrust can be yet more profitable, as resistance has disappeared and the upthrust gains new momentum as it rises. Figure 9 shows gaps and breakouts marked on the Nasdaq Composite index.

Exaggerated Expectations

Small 'blue sky' shares with huge future expectations but non-existent current profits can show spectacular rises as the price/earnings (P/E) ratio explodes to the 30s, 40s, even 50s, anticipating a profitable story soon coming to fruition. These are bubble-creating tales – first, as they

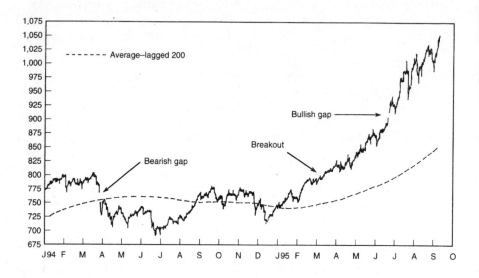

Figure 9 Nasdaq Composite index showing gaps and a breakout

are primarily news-driven, they can respond excessively to news items on their progress or lack of it, and secondly, because it is hard to estimate "fair value" on a stream of future profits in companies making start-up losses. The whole investment plan may go horribly wrong, ending in disaster. But understanding how such stories unfold from their chaos origins means, in the early stages, it is possible to make superb profits by watching the technical indicators for evidence of an unfavourable turning point. The two 1720s bubbles were in this category, as was Radio Corporation of America in 1929.

Fantastic Flags

One of the most exciting chart formations with huge profit potential is a flag. It is a short-term counter-reaction in an aggressive trend and it is yet another stunning display of market structure. A sudden rapid run-up on large volume in response to exceptionally good news is often followed by a profit-taking pause of two to three weeks. Profit-taking creates a dip on the chart, allowing the moving averages to catch up with the great share price spurt. When the price rises back to the first high point, the chances are good that it may continue rushing up to duplicate the initial

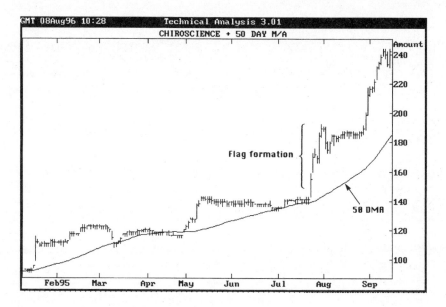

Figure 10 Chart of Chiroscience showing a flag formation
© Reuters

rise. Measuring from the breakout to the first high point as a percentage gives an indication of where the second great leap up will peak. The flag formation is visible on the chart of Chiroscience in Figure 10 and on the Glaxo chart (Figure 7 on page 112), where it occurred in February/March 1987, coinciding with Glaxo's final results. Conversely, as for all the structures we have discussed, a flag in a falling asset price is a strong sell signal.

A flag formation is another example of a driven phase in a rising price. The first upward leap is accompanied by heavy volume perhaps with a gap up. After a short profit-taking pause, another rapid rush up occurs. It may arise from institutional buying or an important news item, or some other key fundamental event. However, it seems amazing that the second rise often mirrors the first in percentage terms. Why does the price often so neatly double? Is it perhaps a strange attractor, an enigma we will discuss in Chapter 5?

Candlesticks Light the Route to Profits

Several books describe candlestick chart analysis, and it is included here only to display its technical links with chaos. Charting by candlesticks originated in Japan and was associated mainly with rice futures trading by farmers. Although first introduced centuries ago, like modern-day charting, candlestick analysis was devised to identify repeating price patterns in similar trading situations. Today, their use is more widespread among Western investors as candlesticks give good signals on an imminent change in a long-term trend and highlight notable short-term movements. In addition to providing these crucial insights, one interesting chaos aspect of candlestick charting is the way it reveals the interplays of a damped, driven market.

The candle is constructed from four readings per day: the session's open, high, low and close. The four readings are marked as one candle to represent the highlights of the day's activity. The wick runs from the day's high down to the low and a wider "candle" or "body" goes from the open to the close prices. If the open is higher than the closing price, the body is shaded black. But if the closing price is higher than the opening, the body is white (red in the original Japanese charts). The basic candle form is shown in Figure 11. Clusters of predominantly white bodies form recurring patterns that indicate a bullish mood – the predominance of buyers over sellers (a driven system); while groups of black bodies suggest a bearish trend, when sellers are ascendant (again a driven system). When neither buyers or sellers can prevail, the market is damped.

The candlesticks expose this chaos-induced battle in the market. They show the endless struggle by bulls and bears for outright supremacy. A long white body marks the triumph of the bulls, a long black body sees them in retreat as the bears advance. A small body at the base of the day's trading range with a very long upper wick or shadow shows the buyers' attempt to control the action has failed. They bid up prices, but were ultimately forced back by the bears. The long upper wick signals their assault could not hold. A body at the top of the day's trading with a long lower shadow below shows the opposite. Sellers pushing prices down

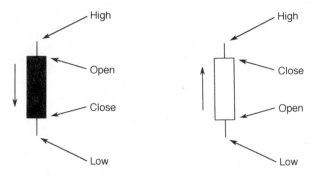

Figure 11 Diagram of candlestick formation

were overwhelmed by enthusiastic buyers, leaving the price back around its opening level for the struggle to resume on the next working day.

Another major clue from candlesticks concerns gaps. By charting the opening price it is easier to monitor their occurrence. As we saw, gaps give vital clues linked to volume levels and market momentum. A group of three black candles separated by gaps is an exhaustion sign; it indicates a reversal to a bullish mood. Similarly, three white candles with intervening gaps are bearish; the bulls are flagging. Examples are shown in Figures 12 and 13. Candlesticks are an excellent tool for spotting market tops and bottoms, because they give a visual display of the chaos clash of buyers versus sellers every day in the market. The tops and bottoms indicate moments when buyers or sellers suffer their greatest anxiety or their strongest aggression.

Financial Pumps

Unexpected news is one of the primary driving forces when a market operates as a damped, driven system. Overall, the effect is manageable although a totally unexpected, major news item, like the 1992 British eviction from the ERM or the August 1990 invasion of Kuwait by

Figure 12 FT-SE 100 index showing three black candles with gaps (indicates a turning point after the third black candle)
© Reuters

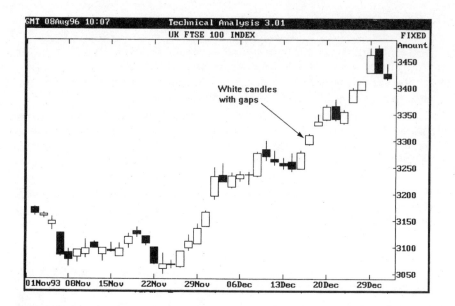

Figure 13 FT-SE 100 index showing three white candles with gaps (indicates the market may be reaching a top)
© Reuters

Saddam Hussein, can produce an excessive result, driving the market rapidly for several months in one extreme direction. Another important driving force stems from high liquidity, especially when a bout of take-overs, mergers or company share buy-backs hands plenty of cash to shareholders who promptly reinvest it. However, analysts frequently note the link between cheap money, as an excess of credit, and a strongly rising market. Popularly, this is called the "weight of money" explanation for the boom. Experts accept that a wall of money can drive the market, forcing up asset prices, but I believe chaos theory and the damped, driven system idea offer a more meaningful explanation of how cheap credit fuels the boom. In chaos, the responsible mechanism is graphically described as a "pump".

Chaotic pumps arise whenever a continuous source of energy is fed into an unstable system to create a self-sustaining positive feedback loop which **drives the system into chaos**. We saw earlier in the chapter how it operates for a simple playground swing. In Chapter 5 we will consider how a laser beam is created under the force of an energy-directing pump. The intriguing Belousov-Zhabatinskii, or B-Z, chemical reaction, which is described in several books on chaos, not only shows dazzling oscillations, but can display chaos under some conditions. A cocktail of chemicals –

sulphuric acid, potassium bromate, cerium sulphate and malonic acid – produce dramatic oscillations in both composition and colour, from blue to red and back again. Hypobromus acid, formed during the reaction, acts as an autocatalyst, resulting in positive feedback. Autocatalysis occurs when **any product of the process**, in this case hypobromus acid, enables further reactions to continue, often in a self-perpetuating loop. In the *New Scientist Guide To Chaos*, Stephen Scott explains how the reaction can be prolonged, in order to study its amazing dynamics in detail, by maintaining it far from equilibrium. To achieve this, he writes, "We drive the reaction by continually pumping in fresh reactants, into what is called a continuous flow reactor (with a corresponding outflow of products to maintain a constant volume). Flow reactors are ideal for studying autocatalytic reactions." Pumps are a device for maintaining an unstable system in a far-from-equilibrium state.

Closer to home, another pump-effect driving a system to turbulence can be demonstrated with the simple domestic tap. It is created, as Ian Stewart describes, "when the rate of flow is **slowly** increased". Turning the tap through a series of very tiny steps gives more energy to the water falling into the sink, first as individual drips and finally as a violent stream. A very slow-motion action is needed to see the many separate transitions involved, quite close together, before the dripping tap emits a frothy flow. With the first tiny turn, the steady drip-drip-drip changes in rhythm: the drips are different but remain regular. Next, the drip pattern becomes irregular, and then with another tiny turn, a steady stream emerges. Ian Stewart writes, "Fluid dynamicists call this **laminar** flow: the fluid moves in thin layers (**laminae**) sliding smoothly over each other like a pack of cards being spread out on a table." On turning the tap to a normal flow rate, the water remains laminar, but it may show evidence of splitting or even spiralling. When the tap is turned fully on, the smooth laminar flow breaks up, a forceful jet of water is produced, the flow is frothy and irregular; it has become turbulent, although whether it is chaotic has yet to be confirmed.

I believe turbulence in the capital markets can be produced by the introduction of a financial pump. Again, whether this is chaotic still awaits further proof, but another link between the dripping tap and financial markets is that they can both be shown to descend into turbulence under the influence of a "pump" of increased energy through a progression of four steps or phases.

When a financial pump is operating, a powerful positive feedback loop can rapidly destabilise the market as a damped, driven system. It occurs with the sudden presence of one of two main activating forces. A significant unexpected news item hitting the market is the first force. Its impact will clearly depend on the type of news involved. Most will have only a limited influence, although it might drive the market to gross extremes of despair or exuberance. The second, far more destabilising force, is an immense increase in the availability of money.

A sudden flood of cheap money is a far more potent and prolonged source of a financial "pump". Expressed in terms of chaos, therefore, the boom effect of a "wall of money" is actually creating a financial "pump". It can arise from a lengthy period of low interest rates, or an excessive issue of paper money. In the 1920s and 1980s examples, important financial innovations and industrial restructuring added to the action of the pump following reductions in interest rates. The pump triggers enormous positive feedback loops in the prices of financial assets, fuelling mercurial price rises. As they soar to stratospheric levels, the markets temporarily lose touch with reality. Once they are destabilised by a financial pump, asset markets are much more susceptible to making exaggerated responses to any random shock. This is a characteristic of complex, unstable systems as they move into an edge of chaos far-from-equilibrium state. Such shocks can then become the abrupt triggering event which sends the market careering into the next phase of the eight-phase crashes model.

Numerous examples of this financial "pump" effect have occurred in the volatile history of the capital markets. We shall observe its potent effects as it fuelled the ballooning note issue inflation of the 1720 French Mississippi Bubble. It generated the massive 1720 boom and bust in the South Sea Company's share price, with a chain letter effect of new share issues followed by attractive loan facilities to power the boom. It was a major destabilising feature of the burgeoning American stock market from 1927 to 1929 and again from 1986 to 1987. It ran absolutely rampant in the destructive bubble in Japan's economy from 1985 to 1990. Details of these events (in Parts II and III) will illustrate how this potent mechanism, the "financial pump", works.

The historical record reveals the birth pangs of a boom, with the financial pump as midwife, just as the early phases of the eight-stage crashes model unfold. It invariably rests on the abrupt input of cheap, abundant credit, plus attractive, new financial instruments – share issues, bank notes, margin trading, futures, options or financial innovations. Once a vigorous financial pump is set in motion, a boom/bust becomes more predictable. The timing and specific details of every case will vary, due to sensitive dependence on initial conditions. In the detail, they remain essentially unpredictable, but the determinism of the long-run behaviour of such events is evident from the historical record. Asset prices, most notably in stocks, bonds and property, begin to rise. Runaway positive feedback loops destabilise the market; prices soar to untenable heights. A cluster of confirmatory warning signs emerge. The market reaches the fragile edge of chaos; a dramatic collapse becomes inevitable.

Patterns that Fail

No one indicator is infallible, because the market is complex, capricious and prone to periods of chaos. The indicators work best when used in conjunction with each other. The most reliable buy and sell signals occur with confirmatory indications from more than one area of technical analysis: chart patterns, moving averages, volumes, trend formations, gaps. Indeed, on many occasions, chart patterns fail. They do not proceed to their expected completion. Their chaos nature provides the reason. As with the weather, because the initial conditions can never be completely known, precise predictions are impossible. Yet again, as with the weather, some situations will be easier to predict than others, depending upon the degree of chaotic behaviour present. When a multitude of factors interact, events are so confused, a chart cannot trace out the full identifiable pattern.

To benefit from the defining structures beneath random shock events which disturb the markets, we should focus on situations that offer the best potential rewards with the lowest level of risk. As we have seen, technical tools can help us to reveal and study market structure to identify super profitable phases. While this represents a small part of the market's overall dynamics, in the most predictable phases we can make a lot of money. Chart patterns, moving averages, trends, financial pumps are examples of structure-illuminating features which distil out strong movements from the lengthy periods of idle drift – the damped phases, when it is far more risky and unprofitable to be heavily invested. When a trend develops, the market has become orderly, more predictable, more highly structured.

Coppock's "Bereavement" Indicator

Although we do not yet know which simple rules govern chaos in financial markets, I believe the charts reveal the profound human psychology expressing the presence of chaos in the markets. Consider the technical signal known, after its originator, as the Coppock indicator. Edwin Coppock, a 1930s economist, was asked by American clergy to devise a long-term, low-risk buying strategy for church funds. Coppock thought the best time to buy shares was after a crash, when investors have gone through a "financial bereavement", mourning their lost wealth. He asked some clerical clients how long people need to adjust to the death of a close loved-one. They estimated 11 to 14 months, so Coppock devised an indicator relating share prices to their values 11 to 14 months previously. The sums are complicated but it gives a buy signal when the monthly calculations turn positive having previously been negative. The Coppock buy signal has proved a reliable buying tool for the British market: since 1962 there have been 10 buy signals with rises from 8 to 46 per cent, and an average rise of 30.5 per cent. Apart from its use as a buy signal, the fact that the Coppock indicator was devised from the sense of bereavement after a crash highlights the potent psychological and chaos links that are revealed by the charts.

Using the Charts

Technical analysts claim charts are indispensable for detecting important turning points in a market, but from the chaos viewpoint, their importance rests on three key issues. First, charts help to establish the close links with chaos theory. If this was more firmly rooted, the scientific underpinnings of financial markets would rest on a formal base, namely chaos science. This is crucially important for financial regulation, monitoring and policy making by the central bankers who supervise these markets. If they have an imperfect grasp of how the markets operate, they will continue to treat every crisis incompetently. In this unsatisfactory scenario, we may all be losers.

Secondly, the charts reveal the consistent fractal patterns that emerge in many financial booms and crashes. These are the esoteric patterns, like head and shoulders and double tops, eagerly sought by technical analysts. As we shall see, these patterns commonly occur in crash events, suggesting that when certain conditions prevail, a crash may be a predictable outcome.

Thirdly, charts provide a graphic representation of the long-run behaviour of a share price or index. This, as we will now see, ties in well with strange attractors, one of the most outstanding features of chaos theory, which, as with the financial markets, is also studied extensively by graphic representations.

Ian Stewart offers a descriptive summary:

> The great discovery of chaotic dynamics is that apparently patternless behaviour may become simple and comprehensible if you look at the right picture. Thus visual imagination, one of the most powerful attributes of the human mind, is brought to bear. Not only are the portraits of chaos strikingly beautiful: they encapsulate an enormous quantity of information in a single coherent structure. In the world of chaos, a picture is worth a million numbers.

In a crash, a picture of chaos might well be worth a million dollars.

CHAPTER FIVE

THE CHAOS ROUTE TO PROFITS

The usual bull market successfully weathers a number of tests until it is considered invulnerable, whereupon it is ripe for a bust.

George Soros

To exploit and profit from our knowledge of chaos, we must first identify the hidden structure underpinning the superficial randomness. Every day there will be random noise; it is the most obvious feature confronting participants and observers alike. So obvious, indeed, one can easily be persuaded that markets are entirely unstructured and fickle. Believers in the Efficient Market Hypothesis, faced by this incessant volatility, claim that profiting from market mayhem is simply due to the luck of averages; no one can make exceptional profits unless they are willing to take exceptional risks.

I think these theorists have failed to recognise the abundant order beneath the evident disorder. Uncover the bedrock structure and the prospects for making above average gains at below average levels of risk are dramatically improved. The structure we are searching for is the invisible buttress on which knowledgeable investors can build super profits. Many tremendously successful investors have done this for decades, without knowing the chaos fundamentals of the market. Instead, they have relied on an exacting discipline. Whatever strategy is employed, every successful investor or speculator uses a carefully thought out overall plan and an appropriate set of rules to minimise losses and maximise the gains.

Although it is possible to make superb profits without understanding chaos, I still believe this knowledge is of outstanding use to both investors and market regulators. In this chapter we shall explore two of the most intriguing forms of structure deriving from chaos which I believe occur in the markets: the first is a peculiar, most distinctive event, known as the phase transition; the second is equally elusive – the all-mysterious strange attractor phenomenon.

Phase Transitions in Chaos

Because islands of order are forever regrouping within the disorderly matrix of complex nonlinear systems, such systems are exceedingly vulnerable to chaotic motion. And one of the most impenetrable effects thrown up by this vulnerability occurs at the nebulous boundary zone where order disintegrates into disorder. As we have seen, this area is known by the evocative term, "the edge of chaos".

The rapid onset of turbulence in liquids and gases illustrates the abrupt collapse of relative stability into extremes of instability. The **precise** nature of this sudden conversion still eludes the scientists, making this an unsatisfactory example to use. However, several others, more clearly understood, are thought to undergo this shift through the process known as a phase transition, defined by Ian Stewart in *Does God Play Dice?* as "a macroscopic change of state due to reorganisation at a molecular level". James Gleick pin-points the abiding mystery: "Like so much of chaos itself, phase transitions involve a kind of macroscopic behaviour that seems hard to predict by looking at the microscopic details."

Listing some cases reveals a kind of medieval alchemy: solid metals melt, liquids transform into vapours or solids; magnets reverse their direction of magnetism; ordinary conductors become super-conductors; course sand metamorphoses into brilliant, fragile glass and common clay assumes the delicate appearance of translucent porcelain, a strong but dainty material of stunning clarity.

These are all examples of physical phase transitions; no chemical change takes place in the physical structures of the materials themselves. The phase transition can occur instantaneously but may involve only a gradual process. A pot of boiling water can take some time to fully evaporate into the air as steam, and similarly, a thin sheet of ice often forms on a surface, before it deepens to solidify the whole body of water. Many examples of phase transitions appear to occur like this, as a gradual rather than an abrupt change.

What appears to happen is that the molecules become realigned. The chemical structure itself stays unchanged but a rearrangement of the molecules gives the same substance a whole range of entirely different properties. While, in every case, the transformed substance retains essentially the same chemical material, it has acquired a new set of properties during the phase transition process which can dramatically alter the entire behaviour of the substance. Some of these cryptic phase transitions, like the emergence of porcelain, are irreversible; others, for example, in liquids, magnets and conductors, can flip between two different states of being, depending upon the prevailing conditions. As a liquid, water can freeze into solid ice when the temperature reaches 0°C, but on heating it to 100°C, water boils off as a vapour. Temperature changes, through decreasing or increasing the amount of heat, alter the physical state of water in never ending phases, but throughout all these transformations, it remains essentially the same chemical molecule, namely H_2O.

Early researchers realised that scaling could be a clue to unravel the mystery. Gleick recounts physicist Leo Kadanoff's insight that phase transitions involved scaling; "The best way to think of the metal is in terms of a fractal-like model, with boxes of all different sizes." Copious mathematical analysis and experimentation gradually put flesh on the scaling idea, as Gleick relates:

> Part of the beauty lay in its universality. Kadanoff's idea gave a backbone to the most striking fact about critical phenomena, namely that these seemingly unrelated transitions – the boiling of liquids, the magnetizing of metals – all follow the same rules.

Landslides in Sand Piles

Recent work has examined the phase transition phenomenon in such unlikely examples as sand piles and lasers, to shed more light on what may actually occur at the focal point of the transition – a moment termed the critical point, where order descends into chaos. An inherent, non-linear instability exists at this critical threshold. When it is reached, even small forces can trigger massive fluctuations across a wide range of magnitudes and time scales.

Per Bak, a physicist at Brookhaven National Laboratory, studied the behaviour of sand piles as they approach the critical point. Adding more grains of sand to a flat layer on a table gradually builds up a cone-shaped sand structure. The slope of the pile slowly evolves towards criticality, marked by the point where one further grain dropped onto the pile triggers a landslide. The landslides vary in size; there may be several small ones or a single really large one. At criticality, the size of the landslide does not depend on the size or the number of new grains added. It depends on the holistic behaviour of all the grains acting together. The global behaviour of the total pile transcends the behaviour of the individual grains within it. At criticality, every grain is interacting in complex ways with all its neighbours. The motion of one grain on the slope can induce motion in thousands of others, producing the landslide. Because every pile will have a unique formation, it is almost impossible to say what any one impact will produce, or whether there will be numerous little landslides or just one enormous slide.

Per Bak and his colleagues have also investigated the behaviour of earthquakes, reporting their findings in an article entitled "Self-Organised Criticality", in *Scientific American*, January 1991. They suggest the size of the fluctuations is related to the relative frequency according to a power law of distribution, where there will be many small avalanches and just a few larger ones. The power law principle is very common in nature; it governs the frequency of earthquakes of a given size on the Richter scale; it occurs in the chemical table on hardness for minerals. Benoit Mandelbrot showed how it also operates for financial fluctuations.

Tonis Vaga, in his book *Profiting From Chaos*, notes

Both sand pile avalanches and earthquake models evolve to a critical state at which point the power law characterizes the relative frequency of events of a particular magnitude. Other examples in which the distribution of objects (or events) [are] of a given magnitude include the size of mountains, clouds and stock market fluctuations. When the number of objects of a given size, r, follows a power law, r^D, where D is a constant, the distribution is called a **fractal**.

As we saw in Chapter 4, fractal structures are prevalent throughout nature. Their widespread appearance can, according to Per Bak and Kan Chen, "be viewed as snapshots of self-organized critical processes. Fractal structures and flicker noise are the spatial and temporal fingerprints, respectively, of self-organized criticality."

Recently, Bak and Chen co-operated with economists Jose Scheinkman and Michael Woodford to devise a simple model of economic activity. They suggest a power law does govern the size of economic fluctuations. Their findings confirm Mandelbrot's earlier claim that the Random Walk model of financial and commodity markets does not explain the relative frequency of major fluctuations occurring in those markets.

Sand Piles and Chaos in Human Societies

The notion of a link between sand piles and chaos in human societies sounds extreme. However, investors in a manic boom do appear to have herd instincts, which suggests their behaviour can become holistic in triggering massive price changes. Moreover, fears of chaos and the need for unity has been a recurring theme in Chinese politics. Earlier in this century, Sun Yat Sen, the nationalist leader, cautioned on the dangers for a nation if it were reduced to "a heap of loose sand". In July 1993 China's President and party chief, Jiang Zemin, issued a similar warning: "We will become a heap of loose sand and be unable to begin to talk about cohesion, fighting capacity and creativity, and there will be no bright future." The idea of landslides in a sand pile triggering chaos which reduces the pile to a heap of loose sand is a good metaphor for chaos in the financial markets when a bubble bursts, but it may be more than simply a metaphor; it may be describing a similar descent into chaos as can be seen to occur in a collapsing pile of sand.

A Phase Transition in Light

In *Chaos*, James Gleick relates how physicist, Leo Kadanoff, explored the opaque problem of phase transitions as an "intellectual puzzle", back in the 1960s:

> Think of a block of metal being magnetized. As it goes into an ordered state, it must make a decision. The magnet can be oriented one way or the other. It is free to choose. But each tiny piece of the metal must make the same choice. How? Somehow, in the process of choosing, the atoms of the metal must communicate information to one another.

To illuminate the puzzle, James Gleick invests the metal with the very human qualities of "decision" and "choice". This is helpful for the analogy I am about to draw between human behaviour and lasers, but I prefer to turn the argument on its head: instead of metals behaving like humans, we will consider investors behaving like metals. Then we eliminate human "choice" and "decision" from stock market behaviour. At the phase transition I believe an unavoidable imperative comes into effect. **Part of the explanation for this mysterious event must lie in the forces that operate on the material, even when that "material" is human**. When those forces exceed a critical level, both the metal and investors are "coerced" into the change; the elements of "decision" and "choice" have been overwhelmed by the imperative of the acting force.

The behaviour of light in a laser illustrates the principle; it is another intriguing example of a far-from-equilibrium system that displays criticality. The discovery of lasers led to numerous practical applications for telecommunications and transmission over fibre optic media. They are now also increasingly used in other fields, especially in medical surgery for eliminating small cancer growths, warts or polyps and for removing cataracts.

A laser consists of a collection of energised atoms or molecules confined within an optical cavity. Energy pumped into the cavity energises the electrons associated with the atoms in it. The excited electrons give up energy in the form of light which is emitted into the optical cavity. If the power pumped into the cavity is below a critical level, the laser emits normal light because each electron emits light independently and the waves from adjacent atoms will be out of phase with each other. **However, under the right physical conditions, which include the mixture of gas, alignment of mirrors and the prevailing pressure, if sufficient power is pumped into the laser cavity, at a certain critical threshold all the atoms begin to emit light in phase with their neighbours. The system has undergone a phase transition**.

Above this critical level, an orderly beam of light emerges within the optical cavity, even though the energy transfer from the external pump into the cavity is random. The light from each energised atom is now coupled or emitted in phase with that generated by its neighbours. Above the critical point, the light has become orderly on a macroscopic level. In his account of the laser phenomenon, Tonis Vaga observes, "The laser can be viewed as a nonlinear, positive feedback system."

However, the crucial point I want to highlight for producing this laser beam at criticality is its dependence upon a pumped source of energy. The criticality requires a driven system, created by the force of the power pumped into the optical cavity.

In addition, central to the laser production is its applicability to other physical examples. According to Vaga,

> At the critical transition the laser undergoes large, long-lasting fluctuations which are analogous to the avalanches in a sand pile. Such **critical fluctuations** are a characteristic common to state transitions in a wide variety of complex systems.

The laser transition is a fascinating illustration of an open system, far-from-equilibrium, which undergoes an abrupt shift from a macroscopic state of disorder to order. The laser transition is especially worthy of note in the context of financial pumps, discussed in Chapter 4, since it depends upon the amount of power pumping through the system. A critical threshold exists, below which the laser emits ordinary independent light rays. Above the threshold, a strange transformation occurs; the light from each atom is emitted in harmony with that of its neighbours. This unity gives the laser its concentrated energised transmitting or cutting ability. Under the potent force of the pump, the behaviour of the light beam is transformed although it is still essentially a beam of light. **Its structure has not altered; yet its central characteristics have changed significantly**. Its changed, orderly state is only upheld by pumping energy into the system.

Phase Transitions for Investors

The behaviour of the laser undergoing a phase transition is characteristic of other physical systems, although the laser shift goes from outright disorder to a highly ordered state. In other cases, the transition moves the other way, from order into chaos. In water, the shift to steam is to disorder, while the shift to ice is a transition to a greater degree of order as the molecules get locked into a rigid framework. I believe this phase transition concept, especially as applicable to lasers and reversible processes such as water switching from liquids to gases and solids, shares strong affinities with volatile investor behaviour.

Although this may sound a bizarre comparison, the behaviour of crowds suggests they **do** acquire a "crowd mentality". If this comparison is valid, when we examine financial markets at the moment of what would effectively be a phase transition, we shall expect to find that similar conditions apply. Investors will retain their physical bodily structures and remain essentially the same human beings as they were before the transition occurred. But to be consistent with the conditions of a physical phase transition, we will expect to find something equivalent to a change of molecular arrangement which would manifest itself by the demonstration of a set of entirely new **behavioural characteristics** by these self-same people. Essentially they have undergone a change in their mental state.

Not every situation in a financial market will necessarily evolve towards the critical point, because markets are damped and driven. When the damped influences are strong, the system stays near to equilibrium; but if the driven influences are excessive, the system quickly becomes acutely volatile. It can reach the boundary zone where its structural characteristics may change: the edge of chaos, the critical point. Criticality is a universal phenomenon; when it emerges, as we saw, small triggers set off massive disruptions.

Fascinating books have been written on the madness of crowds. In the intensely physical drama of a food riot or a nation-wide revolution on the scale of that in eighteenth-century France or twentieth-century Russia, the fury of pent-up emotions engendered horrendous acts of violence, bordering on insanity. Until recent times capital markets have always depended upon a physical market place, with buyers directly confronting sellers. Such close contact is patently helpful in propagating a contagion of irrational behaviour. Today, however, even when investors are physically separated by thousands of miles, such is the miracle of modern technology, the harmony generated by the global economy and the integration of the main financial centres, that telephones and ticker-tapes in the 1920s and satellite links with computerised networks for the 1980s provide close enough contacts to bring the interested parties into direct association.

The great historian, Braudel, observed that during the eighteenth and early nineteenth century, with capitalism still in a formative stage, there was an understandable blurring of activities. Investors were often speculators and both were frequently compulsive gamblers. The divisions between all three activities were rarely clear cut. I think this blurring of roles is still very evident. As we have seen, numerous accounts relate the improbable antics of investors whisked into a hysteria of unbelievable intensity by compulsively rising or falling markets. However, history undeniably reveals it is a fallacy to imagine that the only irrational investors are small "punters" who enter the market at the peak. The records are awash with company directors, bankers, investment trust managers, politicians and academics all equally likely to undergo a sudden phase transition that sends them frantic in their search for short-term gains and renders them panic-stricken when they fear their exposure to loss. This was graphically evident when pandemonium gripped the entire world's financial community during that fateful week of October 1987. The early selling cascade generated a yet more massive selling avalanche, until it finally burnt itself out, like a spent hurricane.

Writing of the great Wall Street Crash of October 1929, J. K. Galbraith described investor behaviour picturesquely as a "luminous insanity". It may sound ridiculous to compare changes in complex human behaviour with the strange phenomenon of a phase transition in an inorganic substance, like water, porcelain or light, but nature works with only one set of rules. For generations we have thought we are above the rude forces of nature. However, if deterministic chaos is the mighty all-embracing force that underpins stock market behaviour, it seems logical to suppose that humans can be driven to the absurdity of madness by experiencing the equivalent of a phase transition, temporarily rendering them outrageously irrational.

Phase Transitions for Investors at Criticality

How then do investors, caught up in a grossly unstable boom, undergo the equivalent of a phase transition transformation? Perhaps the contagion of greed spreads through the absurdly over-extended market, taking it to the edge of chaos as it surges on towards the peak. Here, with prices rising daily to amazing levels, the emotional and rational balance of the majority of investors will be so disturbed, they are driven into a new collective role; they become the anti-heroes of the crash, displaying for a remote posterity the incomprehensible face of "the madness of crowds".

The enigmatic coherent behaviour of the laser beam above its critical threshold offers an insight into how independently acting units can suddenly act in unison under the driving force of an external pump. In the markets, when the authorities unleash a financial pump of cheap money or easy credit, a similar result might occur. Investors, traders, speculators and even sober-minded academics and professionals will undergo a phase transition, entering in unison a state of collective temporary insanity. The critical point at the edge of chaos can be pin-pointed in the eight-phase crashes model. The onset of phase two is triggered when the financial pump has been activated. While phase three would, in general, indicate the arrival of a healthy boom, the emergence of phase four, with overtrading, outright speculation and exaggerated expectations, is obviously the stage where we should expect the phase transition to occur for experienced investors who now increasingly become rampant speculators. Phase five arrives when the mass public join in; many of these neophytes enter the market as irrational get-rich-quick speculators, suggesting they have also undergone a phase transition. Accordingly, the edge of chaos change for most investors will occur during phases four and five of the crashes model. During this time, share prices undergo large and rapid daily increases, sudden bouts of profit-taking introduce extreme volatility in prices, investors display extremes of irrational behaviour and crowds throng to the bustling centres where the main trading actions are unfolding.

In chaos theory, scientists have shown that order descends into chaos at a regular rate – a phenomenon known as universality because it is the same rate for almost every type of chaotic system that has been studied. The idea of order descending into chaos at a regular rate may be seen with the phase transition in financial markets as there is substantial evidence to illustrate how this strange behaviour change grips many normally sane investors.

It is known that several physical systems undergo a phase shift by a gradual process. In the financial markets, as we shall see, there is clearly a progressive slide; some investors become irrational in phase four while the mass public mainly get involved when phase five emerges. This gradual tide towards widespread irrationality may, perhaps, be demonstrating an orderly descent into chaos.

Is There a Market Strange Attractor?

The phase transition is a subtle shift in structure, producing a startling change in the main characteristics of the system undergoing this bizarre event; disorderly states become more orderly and order disintegrates into chaos. But true to its chaos basis, it is undoubtedly an enigmatic phenomenon. Yet in chaos theory things can go from "curiouser to curiouser", as Alice said of Wonderland. The phase transition occurs at the edge of chaos, at criticality; **it alters the immediate state of the system**. But according to Stephen Smale, the most important property of a dynamical system is its long-term behaviour. Ian Stewart suggests, "This 'selects' a much simpler set of motions from among those of the entire system." Discussing this in terms of the close resemblances between chaos theory and financial markets brings us to the topic of chaotic strange attractors.

True to their name, these attractors certainly are most strange. They highlight a central enigma of chaos theory on two seminal accounts: first, because they imply a subtle but concealed **form of attraction** is operating within a chaotic system; but secondly, because the strange attractor is the hidden structure that underlies the apparent disorder. Chaos explores order within disorder – structure buried in randomness. Of all the types of structure we have discussed that are observable in the dynamics of financial markets, this is the deepest, most profound and most enduring. And when used to describe the behaviour of demented investors, it also seems the most inscrutable.

The Weather's Strange Attractor

The first, and still the most celebrated example of a chaotic strange attractor is that of the weather discovered in 1963 by Edward Lorenz (shown in Figure 14). As James Gleick writes,

> Lorenz took a set of equations for convection and stripped it to the bone, throwing out everything that could possibly be extraneous, making it unrealistically simple. Almost nothing remained of the original model, but he did leave the nonlinearity.

In fact, he fed his three boiled down equations into his primitive computer, a Royal McBee, and graphed the results. As we saw in Chapter 4, by a pure accident, mapping his results uncovered the existence of the Butterfly Effect.

However, Lorenz's most brilliant insight was yet to emerge, as Gleick records:

> Had he stopped with the Butterfly Effect, an image of predictability giving way to pure randomness, then Lorenz would have produced no more than a piece of very bad news. But *Lorenz saw more than randomness embedded in his weather model. He saw a fine geometrical structure, order masquerading as randomness.*

With his ultra-simplified convection model, Lorenz made the weather's strange attractor visible. It exposed the delicate structure concealed within his disorderly stream of data. An inspection of the trajectories in phase space (the area occupied by the strange attractor) for the Lorenz attractor shows that the system spends more time relatively at the extremes of its behaviour range than it spends near the middle.

Interestingly, a recent application of the Lorenz attractor has been made in the area of laser physics. It has been shown that the problem of

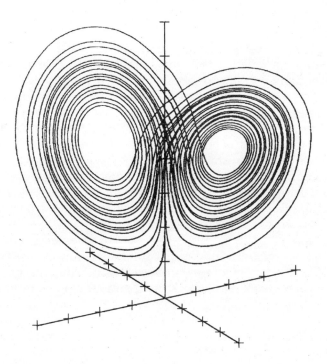

Figure 14 The Lorenz Attractor (a strange attractor for the weather)

the transition from ordinary light to a phased beam can be studied with a similar set of three nonlinear differential equations.

In a Glossary in *Chaos and Order in the Capital Markets*, Edgar Peters explains a strange attractor as

> an attractor in phase space [a graph that shows all possible states of a system], where the points never repeat themselves and the orbits never intersect, but both the points and the orbits stay within the same region of phase space. Unlike limit cycles or point attractors, strange attractors are nonperiodic and generally have a fractal dimension [this is a number, usually a fraction, that quantitatively describes how an object fills its phase space]. They are a configuration of a nonlinear chaotic system.

Eventually, no matter how turbulent a system becomes, **it will settle down around the attractor which depicts its long-run evolutionary path or stable position**. Over time, points near to the attractor are drawn progressively closer to it; this characteristic gives the attractor its name. Two mathematicians, Floris Takens and David Ruelle, invented the name to indicate "a structurally stable attractor that is not one of the two classical types: a point or a circle." Ian Stewart suggests, "The name is a declaration of ignorance, a euphemism for 'I don't understand this damned thing'."

For structurally stable systems, there are two main types of classic attractors: first, **a single point** as, for example, in the case of an ordinary pendulum coming to rest, and secondly, **a stable limit cycle**. This depicts a periodic motion, such as occurs in a hi-fi turntable or roulette wheel. As these examples cover regular motions, these two classic attractors are not relevant to financial markets. Any structurally stable attractor that is not one of these two types is termed a "strange attractor" and is usually associated with deterministic chaos.

If there is an attractor for the financial markets it must be presumed, by implication, that it will be a strange attractor. This implies, as Ian Stewart explains, in *The New Scientist Guide To Chaos*, "No matter from where you start, if you wait long enough, the system will follow this single trajectory to as high a degree of approximation as you wish." The system is attracted by a dominant form of long-run behaviour. Occasional deviations outside its confines will be short-lived. Errant excursions will quickly be pulled back into its sphere of influence. Beyond this area of influence is the out-of-bounds territory where the system can never exist. It is as if certain positions are off-limits and cannot be maintained. How this effect can occur is the enigma that is deeply enshrined in the concept of the strange attractor itself.

As with any chaotic system, in the financial markets the strange attractor, if it exists, would reveal the order buried deeply within the disorder. For it would be stable, because it represents the long-term behaviour of the market. Moreover, it would be stable even though from any initial condition each chaotic path is non-repeatable or unique. I try to picture this as a group of racing cars circuiting a track. For this group of cars, the track is the strange attractor. The drivers do everything within their ability to stay upon the track. The cars may occasionally veer off it, in an accident or a vigorous swerve, but if every car had a different coloured paint inside the tyres which trickled out as it roared around, the paint would mark out individual routes. This would show that every lap for every car would be completely unique; no two laps could ever be identical. But the track would still represent the total area of their long-run behaviour. So it is with the long-term behaviour of a chaotic system.

Strange Attractor Channels

In the midst of total disorder – the chaos – the strange attractor embodies a self-organising principle and is inherently stable. In theory, transient anomalies in market behaviour may arise, but in the long-term, the only possible behaviour of a chaotic financial system is the strange attractor itself. Indeed, if structure appears in a chaotic financial system as a strange attractor, the implication would be that the observed randomness does have a deterministic core. Finding the market strange attractor is therefore central to establishing its deterministic chaos credentials.

Ralph Nelson Elliott used channel analysis for his charts of the Dow Jones Industrial Average (DJIA), extrapolated back to the 1790s (a period which coincides with the earliest phases of the industrial revolution and the origins of the capitalist system of free markets) using British data for the earliest periods. The channel reveals a consistent upwardly sloping trading range for the DJIA extending over 200 years of data (Figure 15). This long-run chart, closely confined within its channel, is the closest approximation we have as yet for a strange attractor for this ever evolving market, although in recent years it appears to have broken out of the channel on the up-side. Will it get pulled back down into its long-term channel?

Over shorter periods, the existence of a trend confined within its channel may be another expression of the strange attractor. A major change, or turning point, is signalled if the trend breaks down below the lower level of its channel, as discussed in Chapter 4. The existence of long-run trends within their channels is a powerful example of a strange attractor that exhibits such a solid structure it is possible to make good profits,

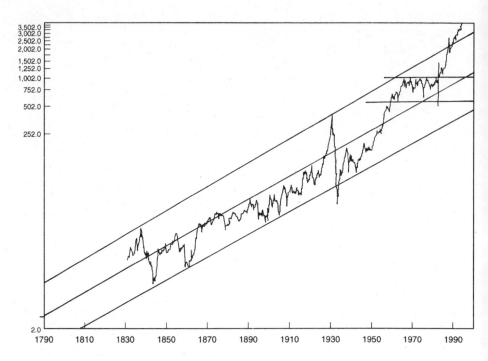

Figure 15 Channel analysis for the long-term Dow Jones Industrial Average (DJIA) from 1800 to 1990

Source: R. R. Prechter, Jnr. and A. J. Frost, *Elliott Wave Principles*

because the signals are so firm. As the trend emerges, it is confirmed by the appearance of the moving averages; as long as it stays inside its channel, it is safe to stay invested. When it breaks down out of the channel, it is giving a sell signal. And, finally, this will be confirmed by the downward crosses of the falling moving averages.

However, channel analysis is regularly used to evaluate the trading ranges of individual shares, bonds, commodities, currencies, etc., suggesting that a strange attractor can be operating at the level of any individual asset. It is often surmised that certain prices or index levels act as support or resistance areas, but if investors are being **attracted** to a certain price or index level, this could be the outward manifestation of the operation of the strange attractor in terms of a chaos explanation. I believe the operation of a strange attractor is evident in the peculiar case of the flags that sometimes occur when prices are rising dramatically, as noted in Chapter 4. The price movement is "attracted" to the patterns to create the flag. It sounds strange, as befits a "strange" attractor.

A Multitude of Strange Attractors

In Chapter 1 we discussed how many crash episodes appear on charts with the recurrence of certain distinct pattern formations. Among the most prevalent are the head and shoulders, the double or triple top formations. These patterns recur on charts over a wide chronological and geographical range. The repeated occurrence of a head and shoulders or double top followed by a steep collapse often depicts a classic crash or bubble event. Although such patterns **can occur at major market turning points even without a crash or bubble emerging,** I think in crash or bubble situations, these patterns may actually represent strange attractors for these specific stock market events. This idea is discussed in Part II in the context of the 1720 Mississippi and South Sea Company bubbles, for both companies were unproven enterprises with huge possible future prospects but absolutely no current earnings. Similarly, modern companies, which have "blue sky shares" with enormous potential and huge P/E ratios are, I believe, the most likely cases to show chaotic share price

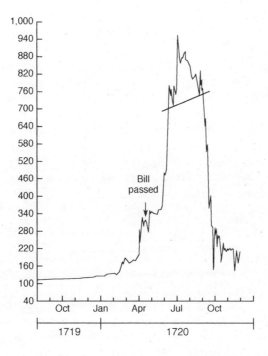

Figure 16 The South Sea Company share price 1719–20 showing a head and shoulders pattern

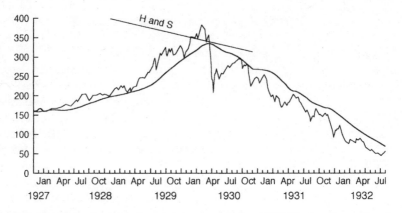

Figure 17 The Dow Jones Industrial Average index 1927–32 showing a head and shoulders pattern in 1929–30

behaviour. Here we will briefly introduce the main patterns that appear to act as strange attractors in a crash event.

A head and shoulders pattern has three clear peaks, with the larger "head" placed between the two lower "shoulders". At the base, the three peaks are linked by a "shoulder line". A classic example shown in Figure 16 occurs on a chart of the 1720 South Sea Company share price. It also occurs on the 1929 Dow Jones Industrial Average (see Figure 17) for the Great Wall Street crash.

Another recent case is the rise and fall over six years in Japan's Nikkei Dow Jones index (Figure 18). Double tops (like twin mountain peaks) formed at the 1987 highs for the US DJIA and the UK FT-SE 100 index, as shown in Figures 19 and 20. If financial markets are governed by deterministic chaos, consistent crash chart patterns might be expected to recur because some underlying rules must operate, even if we have not yet uncovered them. Indeed, their existence could explain why the madness of investor crowds can be studied by technical analysis.

Behavioural Changes in the Index

If channels, double tops and head and shoulders patterns are all examples of strange attractors, how is it possible to have more than one graphic depiction of a strange attractor? Classic chaos theory provides an explanation. In complex chaotic systems it is known that the onset of chaos is accompanied by two changes in the nature of the attractor. First, it undergoes a change in **quantity**, that is, a speeding up occurs in the

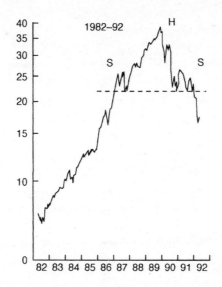

Figure 18 Japan's Nikkei Dow Jones index 1982–92 showing a head and shoulders pattern

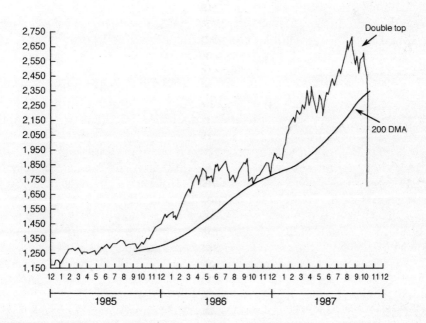

Figure 19 The Dow Jones Industrial Average for 1987 showing a double top formation from August to September 1987

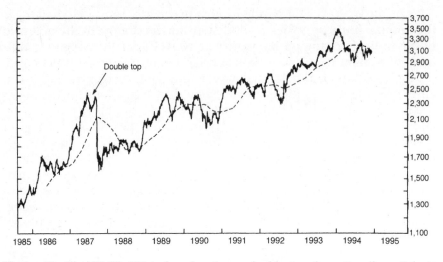

Figure 20 The FT-SE 100 index showing a double top formation from July to October 1987

rate of change within the system that is driving it rapidly into chaos. This would be equivalent to the rate of change occurring in strongly surging (or falling) prices. But secondly, there is a change in the **quality** of the strange attractor. Ian Stewart explains that "Any change in the qualitative nature of the attractor is called a bifurcation. . . . [It] provides a route from order to chaos." This quality change in the nature of a share price or index time series could be showing up on the charts during a crash as a change from a channel pattern to one of the classical "crash" patterns described above. As Ian Stewart points out, "if a fluid is pumped along at faster and faster speeds, it makes a sudden transition from smooth flow to turbulent flow."

Correspondingly, for the markets, rapid changes in the rate of growth (price changes) for a share or an index ultimately alter the **behaviour** of that share or index. As the share or index approaches the edge of chaos, it reaches the critical point. As the rate of growth rises, a trading range of two steady values can emerge. This is a bifurcation. It shows up on the charts as the boundaries of a normal trading range, as in a rectangle formation, or perhaps with a lower support and an upper resistance level. However, at even faster growth rates in changes to the index, price changes will come ever faster until the system becomes chaotic. At that stage, there will be an infinite number of different values which ultimately leads to chaos. Now, most investors have absolutely no idea or even any interest in what the "right" price of a share might be. Their overpowering urge is simply to make huge profits in the shortest possible time.

As in any typical chaotic system, what the charts seem to be showing is **the graphic route by which a sudden or drastic change in the quantity of the index is changing its quality as well.** Under the extreme conditions prevailing during an unsustainable boom followed by the crash, the typical channel attractor may be converted into a characteristic boom chart pattern, such as the head and shoulders formations for the South Sea Bubble and the 1929 Wall Street Crash, or the double top of both the DJIA and the FT-SE 100 in 1987. The chart depicts the invariant history of the boom and its inevitable crash. But the chart is also expressing the phase transition event that has pitched serious-minded investors into a neurotic state in which the acquisition of rapid gains has become their only obsession. The chart patterns of the bubbles and crashes are therefore showing us the psychological stress to which investors are being subjected as the system first passes through the edge of chaos on the way up, and then descends into a true state of chaos.

Can the appearance of sudden booms and crashes in the history of financial speculation be explained by an explosive cascade of price changes that interferes with investors' normal rational processes for judging future prices? At such times, price changes are so excessive in size and frequency, investors lose touch with reality. Exaggerated expectations cannot keep pace with the actual movements of an index or share price. Accordingly, investors suffer the human equivalent of a phase transition, driven to a temporary insanity by the exhilarating experience of phenomenally surging prices. Speculators rapidly lose control of their rational faculties and the destabilising boom proceeds erratically towards the irrevocable peak.

Anti-chaos After the Crash

Sadly, the boom is as unsustainable as the crash that inevitably follows it, because investors have been through the collective, herd experience of a financial phase transition. Irrational behaviour by the majority has overwhelmed all rational behaviour, in the same way that water blows off as steam at a temperature of 100°C. Conversely, we have seen how a laser transforms disorderly into orderly behaviour under forces produced by an external pump. This transition from a random or chaotic state to a state of order is as fascinating as the reverse process. In recent years it has been studied as the theory of emergence, or anti-chaos – the emergence of order out of chaos.

Unpredictable outcomes arise when complex systems experience a chaotic phase. Emergent properties appear when a system's components do not behave in the same way as the total system itself. The total system will have an irreducible type of global behaviour, completely different to the behaviour of the separate elements of which it is composed. This irreducibility is an emergent phenomenon. In the repercussions of highly traumatic bubble and crash situations, the affected societies will be suffering a psychological shock. But apart from introducing a few new rules and regulations, there is no evidence in the crashes discussed in later chapters for global emergent properties which would suggest a totally new system has been created, although clearly, when Tulipomania appeared in the 1630s, it was an example of a complex emergent system, being the first sophisticated boom of the early capitalist era. However, in a truly globalised financial market, such as that now evolving, a major crash of crashes could be a monumental event, affecting all markets on a world-wide scale. Under the impact of such a global "shock", new emergent properties, which are currently unknown, could begin to appear and the architecture of the global markets, as we understand them today, could be irreversibly changed.

Capitalise on Chaos

In this chapter we have looked at the two possibly most controversial aspects of my ideas on chaos in the financial markets: the concept of a phase transition that flips rational investors into an irrational state of mind, and the notion of market strange attractors. Whatever the theoretical basis for these concepts, they both provide striking evidence of structure in the markets. And structure, as we have noted, is the crucial evidence we need to identify periods of market activity where above average profits can be made with below average levels of risk. These are the safest, most rewarding profiles for investment decisions. The appearance of structure within the aimless noise of the financial markets alerts us to the possibility that the time is ripe for building super profits. So now we will turn to examine earlier crashes and bubbles, to identify the way profitable structures emerge.

PART II

The Bubbles of 1720

CHAPTER SIX

THE BUILD-UP TO THE BUBBLES

The India Company have for some time been granting lands in America on both sides of the Mississippi to persons concerned in the stock of that Company. . . . Mr Law himself has a square of 16 leagues on the west side of the Mississippi in the country of the Arkansa. It is pretended that a silver mine has been found within his grant.

Letter from Daniel Pulteney, January 1720

As the first and most spectacular of its kind, the great European stock market boom that swept through France, Britain and the Netherlands in 1718–20 soon became notorious, but the repercussions spread much further afield, igniting an intense speculative furore in northern Italy and Hamburg in Germany. The raging bull market produced two parallel manias, the Mississippi and South Sea Bubbles. Arguably, they epitomised the first major European capitalist crisis, and their legacy is immortalised in tales of the outrageous excesses generated. Antoin Murphy, in his biography of the Irish banker Richard Cantillon, suggests these popular images must be counterbalanced by the view that both schemes were serious attempts at financial innovation. This became an urgent necessity when an impasse arose in public finances in Britain and France, due to the exorbitant costs of servicing their war-induced national debts. As we have seen, new financial innovations are often a prerequisite in bubble formations.

Both bubbles occurred around the same time, with a similar origin, making them excellent case studies. Their research value is further enhanced as they were moderately self-contained, although the speculative ferment did ramify around northern Europe. Even so, unlike twentieth-century cases, they did not develop into all-engulfing global events that touched the lives of millions.

The Political Dimension

We set the scene with the political background which was vastly different in each country. France was ruled by an absolute monarch. He wielded autocratic power over everything pertaining to the State, including financial control; he was, in Nancy Mitford's colourful phrase, "Lord High Everything". Collective responsibility was unknown, both in doctrine and practice. Opposition to his government, in any form, never focused within one national institution, like the English Parliament, for in France no comparable institution existed. During the eighteenth century, the political paths of France and Britain began diverging dramatically as Britain moved further away from the concept of absolute monarchy, towards a constitutional monarchy.

Incipient Democracy

Britain was poised on the pioneering edge of a huge experiment with popular democracy; although the formative process was still unfolding it was further down the road than France, or indeed any other European nation, towards a modern democratic state. As events in Britain turned it ever closer towards a constitutional monarchy, power shifted irreversibly from the King to the elected House of Parliament, with the two great political parties, Whigs and Tories, endlessly manoeuvring for outright control. They increasingly made their opinions heard, by exerting more weight in running affairs of state. By 1720, amid a great deal of division and faction, the noisy, highly voluble Parliament had convincingly shown it no longer believed its monarchs had an unquestionable right to rule.

In 1688, England underwent an entirely peaceful transition, known for this reason as "The Glorious Revolution". By deposing the Catholic Stuart King, James II, and enthroning a Dutch Protestant in his place as William III, with no bloodshed, the English displayed a maturity of political purpose unique to the age. When Queen Anne's only surviving heir, the Duke of Gloucester, died in 1700, the king-making role of the English Parliament received another boost. By the Act of Succession in 1702, which secured the Hanoverian successors after the death of Queen Anne, Members of Parliament demonstrated that future rulers of England had been ordained not by the grace of God, but by the grace of Parliament. This Act and others to follow were serious checks on royal power. Parliament had finally won the long struggle with the crown. The "Divine Right of Kings" was obsolete and recognition was implicit that the power now lay with Parliament.

Although no longer omnipotent, day-to-day authority, however, remained at Court, centred on the person of the King. At this early date, Parliament had no grandiose pretensions to assume absolute power. Rather, it still saw its principal role as a counterbalance, to ensure that the King did not rule too autocratically. It wanted to uphold the rights of its own community, the propertied classes. A further major triumph won by the events of 1688 was the power Parliament abrogated to itself to control the annual army estimates through the Mutiny Act. The increase in Parliamentary authority over war policy forced both William III and then Queen Anne to maintain favourable Parliamentary majorities in both Houses of Parliament, to pursue their diplomatic goals which invariably deteriorated into ruinously expensive wars.

By 1715, on his accession, George I was still able to appoint his own circle of ministers, mostly from the Whig faction, although the Tories had a majority in the House of Commons. Increasingly, more key state decisions were made by his ministers, so under his regime, the reality of a Parliamentary monarchy slowly took shape. More tussles with Parliament still lay ahead and the selfish motives of the truculent Members of Parliament mainly dictated their behaviour. Added checks to royal power were imposed with the historic Act of Settlement, setting Britain firmly on the long and hard-fought road to a parliamentary democracy and political maturity. Britain was the trail-blazer for democracy, since the ancient system of absolute monarchy prevailed across most of Europe for another century.

Emergent Entrepreneurs

By 1720 England had a population of approximately six million with about 700,000 people living in London. However, the capital never dominated English life to the extent that Paris dominated in France. There was a greater political awareness in Britain among the general populace than elsewhere in Europe, and the average Englishman had achieved a higher degree of personal freedom than was evident in other European countries. By 1720, a sense of entrepreneurialship was also more highly developed in England than elsewhere on the continent, except of course, in Holland, which was equally dynamic economically, until the ruination of the prolonged wars of this age sapped her energies. A veritable boom in company promotions occurred in England during the last two decades of the seventeenth century. By 1695 there were 140 joint stock companies with a total capital of £4.5 million. Of these, no fewer than four-fifths had been founded after 1688. By 1717 total capitalisation had reached £21 million.

Prior to 1720 rising levels of activity in trading stocks and government securities through the institution of various government funds on offer, brought a new class of intermediary – bankers, brokers and jobbers – to prominence. Their activities were not covered by licenses and business was crudely enacted, lacking all proper organisation. Ceaseless complaints about noise and rowdy disturbance finally drove the stock-jobbers from their haunts in the Royal Exchange to Change Alley in 1698. In this minute territory, little more than the narrow passage between Cornhill and Lombard Street, where Jonathan's and Garraway's were two of the most notorious coffee-houses for trading in securities, the fledgeling stock-jobbing community firmly took root.

The free enterprise spirit was stronger in Britain than in France. By 1776, it was so flourishing, Adam Smith was inspired to immortalise the urge for private gain as "the invisible hand" in his epic masterpiece, *Wealth of Nations*. As the seventeenth century drew to a close, while Louis XIV ruled as an unapproachable despot in France, the English concept of the divine right of Kings had ceased to be the ruling philosophy of state. Parliament was growing ever stronger, and refusing to operate obsequiously at the call of its reigning monarch.

Special Conditions in France

The situation in France was starkly different. The King, with indisputable power, was free to do exactly as he pleased, no matter how extravagant or wasteful, although he had advisors, often including a Prime Minister. The 13 Parlements were completely different to the British format, as they were non-elected bodies with judicial rather than legislative powers. Unchanged since the fourteenth century, they sat in 13 major towns, with the most powerful in Paris, in the Palais de Justice.

The country was run by a royal bureaucracy of civil servants; but, with no checks on royal power, financial excesses of the court, the Government and the nobility were prodigious and had been so throughout the 60-year reign of the Sun King, Louis XIV. This had finally brought the State to its current ossified condition, with the King dominating production in industry and the manufacture of goods. The luxuries he favoured received state subsidies, especially for such goods as silk fabric, clothing, tapestries, carpets and items in precious metals or porcelain. There was unlimited financial support if the King patronised a factory, so matters of efficiency or the threat of bankruptcy were immaterial. During the War of Spanish Succession, the defeats of Blenheim, Ramillies and Oudenarde plus a severe frost in 1709 reduced the country to near starvation with the economy in ruins. As taxes rose and new levies were introduced, even the courtiers faced financial problems. In response to the King's appeal, many rich families sent their second-best silver to be melted down to replenish the empty state coffers, but hardship was relative; in its place, the fashion was for the court to "eat off china".

France Under the Regency

Amidst such blatant profligacy, on Louis X1V's death in 1715 the State was facing near bankruptcy. Philippe, Duke of Orléans, a nephew to the late King, master-minded a *coup d'état*, to gain effective control over France as Regent, with plenary powers to act for Louis's infant heir, his great-grandson, Louis XV. The Regent has acquired a salacious reputation in popular history for sexual licence and gastronomic excess, but this notoriety masks a serious side to his personality. He was a radical reforming minister, keen to restructure the French economy by pushing through a series of ambitious monetary reforms.

Philippe pursued a curious Walter Mitty life-style. During the day he assumed the role of an industrious administrator, working long hours, sometimes from eight in the morning until six in the evening, although there was much time-wasting in private and public activities. After six, he donned his libertine personality, idling the night away in an orgy of debauchery with favoured cronies. And once these reveries began, no affairs of state, however critical, could distract him from his riotous merry-making.

His mother wrote witheringly about his shameless ways.

> My son is no longer a youth of twenty, he is a man of forty-two years, so Paris cannot forgive him for running off to balls after women in such a hair-brained fashion when he has all the affairs of state on his shoulders. . . . He spends whole nights in that wicked society, [referring to Philippe's mistress Madame de Parabere], and stays at table until three or four o'clock in the morning, which is very bad for his health. I am terrified lest he get something worse with all these goings on.

There was rarely an evening during his scandalous supper parties when he was not besotted with wine and lust. Unsurprisingly, these schizophrenic habits, with an irksome work routine by day coupled with an untiring nightly round of depravity, brought his rule as Regent to a dramatic and unexpected end with his sudden death in 1723. At the relatively young age of 49, he expired abruptly at the feet of one of his numerous mistresses!

The Origins of the Two 1720 Bubbles

The direct cause of these two great stock market booms was financial instability – always a crucial element in triggering chaos – arising from the huge cost of the War of the Spanish Succession fought mainly between France and Britain, together with Britain's allies, Holland and the Austrian Empire. The war arose from the competing claims of Louis XIV of France and Leopold I of Austria for the crown of Spain. For several years the European situation had been intensely war-prone. Through a succession of wars, inaugurated under the Dutch William III, France and Britain had been almost continuously at war since 1693. The Spanish Succession problem simmered in the background, but became an acute international concern on the death of the sickly Charles II in November 1700. This war, yet another long drawn-out affair, convulsed Europe into prolonged hostilities between 1702 and 1711.

The Escalating Costs of Warfare

For several reasons, wars had gradually become hugely expensive. Some idea of the massive costs involved in this protracted war is gauged from the size of the combatant armies. By 1711 Queen Anne was probably employing 75,000 native-born troops with perhaps another 40,000 mercenaries, mainly from the smaller states of Europe. At the height of the wars, Louis XIV deployed 250,000 soldiers, Austria had 110,000 and the United Provinces engaged around 100,000 men. Another major expense sprang from new weapon technology. Regimental fire-power had been greatly improved by the issue of the flintlock musket to replace the less accurate, older matchlock musket. This advance had made battles far more expensive in human losses and casualties.

The opportunistic career of James Brydges (later, Lord Carnavon and then the Duke of Chandos), throws an interesting light on the colossal costs of the French wars. As we saw in Chapter 2, he was one of the keenest speculators of the era. His personal worth took a vaulting upwards leap, when, in 1705, through his connections with the Duke of Marlborough, he was appointed to the audaciously lucrative post of Paymaster General of the forces abroad. It was accepted practice in this high office to use army funds for private investment and to enter into contracts for army provisions which produced private profits. He availed himself enthusiastically of all the potential his post ensured, securing in the process a fortune of £600,000 by his retirement in 1716. He was under suspicion for excessive profiteering but no formal charges were brought. We can gauge his personal enrichment from office: it was equivalent to more than 1 per cent of the burgeoning national debt, standing then at £51 million. (By March 1996, the British national debt stood at £350 billion.)

Under the Duke of Marlborough's inspired leadership, the Allies had virtually forced Louis XIV into a humiliating submission by 1709, but their indecisive victory at Malplaquet and disputes over future strategy among the Allies, gave the French a useful respite, enabling them to return once more to the fray. Battles resumed during 1710 but hostilities between France and England effectively ended in 1711, when the Tory administration came to power committed to ending the war. Peace negotiations were accelerated by French victories against the Alliance and the sudden death of the Austrian Emperor Joseph I in April 1711. The Treaties of Utrecht, signed in March and April 1713, finally brought peace, but the monumental legacy of debts weighed heavily on both the French and British financial systems. Massive state indebtedness created a climate of gross financial instability in which innovative monetary policies could thrive. It provided the febrile backdrop against which the surreal bubbles of 1719 to 1720 were played out by the South Sea and Mississippi Companies.

The Gambling Bug

Other factors adding to the alacrity with which both bubbles took hold were the temperament and traditions of the typical European of the age. In their devotion to gambling, the French and English enjoyed a mutual passion that accentuated the booms. Gambling, one of England's foremost vices, had been banned during the austere period of Cromwell's Commonwealth, and was rapturously re-instated after the Restoration in 1660. Private card playing went to such unprecedented lengths it drew this remark in a report by the *Commentator* of 1720:

> This is one of those innocent diversions which is become criminal by the excess, and from an amusement to kill time and keep the faculties awake, is now the crying sin of the nation. There are few civil families in England which are not in some measure tainted with it and more or less impaired by it.

Lotteries, cards and dice were hugely popular. Cock-fighting, bull-baiting, horse-racing and bear-baiting were widely practised, mostly amongst the richest and poorest. The desire to invest in any project, no matter how extreme, or even whether it was genuine or bogus, reached manic proportions, as the *Commentator* again reported:

Tis plain, the Novelty of things at this time has its beginning in the new fashioned frenzy of men's minds, I mean in their hunting after money which is done now with such a rage in their avarice that suffers no restraint and that knows no bounds.

The French court of Louis XIV at Versailles was similarly infected by gambling addiction, allowing both populations to succumb when the chance to indulge in speculative ventures arose. Gambling and related vices were widespread during Louis XIV's reign, but Paris under the Regency of Philippe Duke of Orléans was notorious for depravity. In 1731, the libertine author, Abbé Prévost, in *Histoire du Chevalier des Grieux et de Manon Lescaut*, graphically portrayed Parisian society under the Regent as a period of unsurpassed and wanton dissipation. His residence – the Palais Royale – a focus for vice and drunkenness, set the tone for venal excesses of every kind. The currency became unstable, especially after the collapse of John Law's "System" and people of all ranks sought protection from fluctuating values and rampant inflation by gambling on a colossal scale.

Links Between the Two 1720 Bubbles

Expansion of the Mississippi and South Sea Companies progressed broadly in tandem, each in turn contributing to the development of the other by imitation. Their fortunes were strongly interlinked during their greatest growth period, 1718–20. Initially, the South Sea Company was the model, having been founded first, but once Law's System was established, it swiftly gained the initiative and South Sea events began to copy Mississippi ideas. The French scheme was already a bubble by late 1719, preceding the English scheme by a few months, and when the Mississippi collapse began around mid-May 1720, the avaricious directors of the South Sea scheme totally ignored its cautionary warning. Rather than fearing a repeat collapse of their own ingenious schemes, they welcomed the French failure, seeing it as a greater opportunity to advance their plans. They hoped disappointed Mississippi investors would swiftly turn their attention to the South Sea Company, eager for quick profits. Their assessment initially proved correct, as the thirst for grossly exaggerated returns switched from Paris to London. With the pace of the English bubble accelerating, foreign involvement helped propel it to the astronomical June peak, before the inevitable downfall began.

By early 1718, English investors were following events in the crowded rue Quincampoix in Paris, where Mississippi shares were traded. In May

1719, the British ambassador in Paris, Lord Stair, was receiving letters from relatives and friends pestering him to buy shares in the booming Compagnie des Indes. He was concerned by the capital outflow from Britain to Paris to pay for shares. By December, as Law's System peaked, speculative capital was pouring into France. Profits from the massive bull run began to move in the opposite direction, seeping back into Britain to inflate the domestic economy. As the British bought Mississippi stock in Paris, so Europeans bought South Sea shares in London. Subscribers were enlisted from Geneva, Paris, Amsterdam and the Hague, especially for the ludicrously over-generous Third Money Subscription of 18 June 1720. In June and July, 12-hourly relays of ships between England and Amsterdam allowed hoards of avid speculators to converge where the greatest action was unfolding. By mid-July, with South Sea fervour at its zenith, a group of 80 investment sophisticates of various nationalities, abandoned London's Exchange Alley to head hot foot for the next great bull run, speculation in insurance stocks in Amsterdam and Hamburg.

Sadly, by the autumn, all the centres which had been a focus for rampant speculation were united by the mutual anguish of disaster. That astute observer of human frailties, Leo Tolstoy, remarked, "All happy families resemble one another; each unhappy family is unhappy in its own way." As for families, so for investors. During the reconstruction following the collapse of Law's System, the French banker, Samuel Bernard, was sent to London to sell South Sea stock for gold, to be re-imported into France. Dutch banks recalled advances, refused further credit and indiscriminately sold the French, English and Dutch shares they held as collateral. The sterling exchange rate in Amsterdam, up at 36–1 (guilders to the pound) in April 1720 fell to 33–11 on 1 September, as "foreigners lost their taste for English securities". At the height of the panic it recovered to 35–2.

Similarities Between Mississippi and South Sea Schemes

Ostensibly, the English South Sea Company was established to develop trade in the Pacific region and exploit the mineral wealth of South America. The French Mississippi Company was founded somewhat later, to develop the vast agricultural and mineral potential of France's American possessions of Louisiana, primarily through building them up into a thriving colony. In England, the idea of acquiring special privileges by lending money to the Government was well established. It had been adopted in 1694 with the founding of the Bank of England, and again in 1698, for the East India Company. For both the Mississippi and South Sea

Companies, the initial intentions of the founders may have been a genuine desire to promote and expand colonial trade, but in practice, both were diverted from their original aims to follow a similar course, namely management of the ballooning national debt.

Although a copy-cat element was operating, both companies took on the function of national debt management by offering to convert part of the debt into their stock, at lower rates of interest. This was attractive to the cash-hungry governments, as it reduced public indebtedness. In return for accepting a lower rate of interest on the debt, the companies were granted exclusive overseas trading privileges.

Mississippi Trading Potentials

French Louisiana was a vast tract of land, covering over half of the country we now know as America (excepting Alaska). It included the present-day states of Illinois, Arkansas, Iowa, Louisiana, Minnesota, Mississippi, Missouri and Wisconsin.

Once explorers discovered the Mississippi flowed into the Gulf of Mexico, it was quickly realised that the territory was potentially valuable. In September 1712 the great financier Crozat was given the trading monopoly for 15 years, but in 1716, due to the stringent taxation Visa instigated under the Regent's draconian new regime to reduce the State's debts, he conceded his rights to Louisiana as part payment of his 6.6 million livres tax bill. John Law's newly formed Company of the West took over these trading rights in August 1717. The new company received a 25-year trading monopoly, in return for which it guaranteed to send 10,000 white and 6,000 black slaves to the territory over a 10-year period.

Glowing accounts of conditions in the new colony were published in the *Nouveau Mercure* in September 1717, shortly after the founding of the Company of the West. This deceptive information may have been propaganda spread by Law himself. In November 1718, he formed a company together with Richard Cantillon, the Irish banker–economist living in Paris and the Englishman, Joseph Gale, the Mississippi speculator. A sum of 50,000 livres (£2,080 sterling) was committed to financing a small expedition of colonists to Louisiana.

By midsummer 1719, with the price of Mississippi shares romping ahead every day, the French public began taking an interest in the colonising projects. And despite the strange early lack of enthusiasm for the colony's prospects, during the great bull run for the shares, the Company des Indes was popularly known as the Mississippi Company, as it still is to this day. Law himself may have been at the centre of rumours then circulating, which spoke of the exciting possibilities for mineral wealth in the new French territories. With the acquisition of several other trading companies, Law's Compagnie des Indes had grown mightily, controlling the markets of the world. With interests in Africa, America, Asia, India and China, the profitable commercial prospects seemed boundless.

Optimistic rumours fuelled the speculative hysteria then raging, but Law was cautious at the Annual General Meeting of the Compagnie des Indes, held on 30 December 1719, to play down the colony's short-term prospects. For at this time Louisiana was little more than an inhospitable desert. The delta was ravaged by yellow fever and unfriendly Indian tribes occupied the upper reaches. Colonisation in a virgin territory is no easy matter. New settlers have to contend with unfamiliar diseases, hostile natives, crop failures and difficult terrain among endless other hardships. Law's settlement did not prosper and its leader had returned to France by 1723. Even if conditions had been favourable, however, the new colony might possibly have taken decades to reach its full potential. When Napoleon lost patience and sold it as part of the Louisiana purchase in 1804, it was still largely under-exploited.

While Law must share responsibility for the failure of the Louisiana settlement, the founding of the great town, New Orleans stands to his credit. For years it was little more than a squalid cluster of wooden shacks in a malarial swamp, infested with snakes and alligators, but Law boldly predicted a great future for it and named it after his influential patron, the French Regent. The new town, straddling a wide bend of the Mississippi river, eventually prospered to become one of the foremost cities in America, thereby ironically serving as the sole tangible memorial to the Duke's indolent rule.

South Sea Trading Potentials

Trade with South America was thought to be one of the best commercial prizes following the lengthy War of the Spanish Succession. It was more highly regarded than India as it was more accessible and less civilised. Instead of being a drain on silver, like India, people assumed it would take traditional English products, such as wool and iron mongery and pay in bullion, dyestuffs or cochineal.

South America had an almost inexhaustible appetite for African slaves, one of Britain's foremost trades by this time. Daniel Defoe, a great literary figure of the age, set his classic account *Robinson Crusoe* against the backdrop of the lucrative Spanish American slave trade that it was hoped would be boosted by founding the South Sea Company. Defoe was a Tory supporter who helped to found the Company. When *Robinson Crusoe* was published in 1719, its huge success highlighted the attractions of slave trade possibilities and added to the excitement of purchasing the Company's shares during its fleeting boom.

Again in England, as in France, the power of propaganda was exploited, through journalism, then a newly rising star in the firmament of city life. The government press was only one of several sources extolling the many lucrative exports suitable for South America. Broadsheets and pamphlets proclaimed the strong demand for silk handkerchiefs, worsted hose, sealing wax, spices, clocks and watches, Cheshire cheese, pickles plus "scales and weights for gold and silver". The new Company would boost the slave trade, diverting to England the fabled profits which had enriched the pirates of Madagascar.

In 1711, South Sea stock was issued at a par of £100, and government debts to be incorporated stood at a sizeable discount of between 40 to 30 per cent against the par value of the stock. In the market £100 of South Sea stock was worth around £65, but the stocks involved in this first conversion quickly rose and the first quotations of South Sea shares were for between £73 and £76. The stock did not reach its par value of £100 until May 1715. Although the Company was severely circumscribed in its trading abilities, it was capitalised at the enormous sum of £10 million. This arose from the fortuitous fact that £9.5 million was the amount of unfunded government debt that was to become funded through this scheme. Even at this early date, the risk was recognised, in that there was a very large surplus of available credit which the directors might be tempted to employ in other directions. Nevertheless, this temptation was avoided for the first eight relatively quiet years of the Company's life.

The English Debt Problem

In France and England, the national exchequers were almost completely empty, taxation was discredited and grossly in arrears, trade was adversely affected, the economies were moribund and ministers were desperate to avoid resorting to the shameful stigma of national bankruptcy. This is a classic chaos description of a damped system, lying quiescent under the powerful drag of a negative feedback loop, slowly stifling all economic activity and initiative.

In England, state debts had escalated from a comparatively modest £664,000 in 1688, on William's accession, to £12.6 million by 1710. The inordinate cost of the Spanish War added hugely to the total; it shot up to £36 million by 1714, reaching £51 million by 1720. Government debts were a motley group of various schemes, only assuming the formality of the national debt in 1693, when Parliament first guaranteed state borrowings. The monetary crisis left an unprecedented burden for financing the navy at sea and the armies still stationed in the Low Countries. Trade was interrupted by the continuity of war, with hardly a pause, from 1693 to 1711. Public expenditure by this time had increased so dramatically that the revenues from taxes and duties still left a persistent deficit in the national accounts. The Talley system was a device that had been introduced to anticipate the collection of revenues, by which the public advanced money to the Exchequer in return for interest payments. By 1697, the system was so discredited, tallies stood at a discount of about 40 per cent.

Imaginative new methods were urgently needed to avoid insolvency. These included the Tontine Loan of 1693, followed in 1694 by the Lottery Loan, to raise £1 million, and a second in 1710, to raise £1.5 million. The Tontine and Lottery Loans were designed to appeal to the current gambling craze in an attempt to redirect cash frittered away on risky plays into the Government's empty coffers.

Robert Harley became Tory Chancellor of the Exchequer in 1710. His need for credit and loans was critical. The Treasury had no funds to pay the troops, Queen Anne's Civil List was £700,000 in debt, – state commitments not matched by specific assets – routine avenues for raising revenue were exhausted and a public debt of £9.5 million was unfunded (without provision of Parliament). The task of raising extra taxes was ruled out and government standing for raising credit was contemptuously low. Harley's solution was prompt and drastic. He proposed the founding of the South Sea Company, by issuing stock to the creditors comprising most of the £9.5 million of unfunded public debt, creating an incorporation of prominent Tory creditors intimately associated with the Exchequer, along the lines of the Whig-dominated Bank of England. It would have a charter granted by Parliament for a monopoly of trade to the South Seas.

Special Conditions in England

In England, as the national debt mounted, financial capitalism was emerging on which Harley could draw for inspiration for his scheme. The Bank of England, well established for 17 years, the East India Company, for 13 years, and the South Sea Company, soon to be founded, were all major holders of this debt. Joint stock companies had become a popular, flourishing vehicle for sharing the risks of private adventures. A series of these had been launched with varying success since Mary Tudor granted the first charter in 1553. The infamous Sword Blade Company, banker to the South Sea Company, was incorporated in 1689 for the manufacture of hollow sword blades but reconstructed itself into a finance corporation around 1714. We shall meet this notorious company in Chapter 8, when we delve into the extraordinary finances of the South Sea Company conversion schemes.

The French Debt Crisis

Ballooning French and English debts arose from similar causes, so it is interesting to compare the size of the problem and the different ways the two authorities tackled them. In 1693, the English had begun addressing the exploding war-induced debt crisis. In France, tackling the debts was delayed by the longevity of Louis XIV's reign. Frequent devaluations had made the currency unstable; it was finally stabilised in 1728, during the reign of Louis XV. At this time, the ratio of gold to silver and bank notes to coin was fixed, with the livre at 24 to the gold louis d'or (or six livres to the silver crown), a rate which survived until the Revolution in 1789. Together with the colossal burden of war-debt, the State faced onerous problems on Louis's death, from the unbridled extravagances of his court. Tax revolts, a virtual disintegration of the army and mass famine added to the spectre of imminent government bankruptcy. By 1714 the state debt reached 2.6 billion livres. Annual revenues of 145 million and government expenses of 142 million left only 3 million to pay the debt interest. By Louis's death, state indebtedness hit 3.5 billion livres (£233 million sterling). France's population, at an estimated 22 million, gave a debt per head of 159 livres (£10.6 sterling). For England's 6 million inhabitants, a national debt of £51 million created debt per head of £8.5 sterling.

In France, the annual budget deficit was about 80 million livres. The collection of taxes was iniquitously unjust and wasteful; future taxes had already been squandered to meet current expenses. Double entry book-keeping was not used by the finance ministry, so the exact scale and composition of the government debt was unknown. Bowed down by its monstrous weight, the Regency Council toyed at first with the extreme resort of declaring the State bankrupt, instantly wiping out all state liabilities. This drastic strategy was finally rejected but despite trawling a wide range of revenue sources, the State could not meet all its obligations and was technically insolvent. The Duke of Noailles, newly appointed Controller-General of Finance, wrote to the late King's mistress, Madame de Maintenon, "both the King and his subjects ruined, nothing paid for several years past, and confidence entirely gone". Noailles thought 11 years were needed to balance the state budget. The Regent was far too impatient to accept this time scale. He resorted quickly to draconian measures to reduce the debts.

Financial Reform in France

Correspondence from Lord Carnavon, later Duke of Chandos, to Richard Cantillon, newly resident as a banker in Paris, shows that by September 1715 the French economy was in such a parlous condition normal banking facilities with Britain had all but collapsed. To restore the State's finances, the Government introduced a series of crisis measures. Between 1715 and 1717 the main thrust was directed towards enforced reduction of debts, with a deliberate attack on the privileged financier class. Between 1717 and 1720, working with John Law, the Regent tried to reform the State's entire financial structure through Law's alternative System. Finally, with the collapse of Law's System, the Regent's prime financial policy goal from 1721 until his death in 1723, was to restore some semblance of normality through the old approach.

The First Stage of Reform

During the first stage of these financial reforms, the State's debts were forcibly curtailed by the compulsory conversion of all state securities, with a reduction from 7 per cent to 4 per cent in the interest rate paid on all long-term government debt. The bonds were linked to a tax revenue source, but after the interest rate reduction bond holders suffered extensive losses. The floating debt, not linked to a tax revenue source, was also drastically restructured. Two-thirds of it was wiped out, amounting to the sum of 400 million livres, while all the old debt was converted into a new uniform debt known as billets d'état (state notes). However, the 198 million livres of floating debt formed from the conversion was instantly increased to 250 million livres, for additional state revenues. After such drastic measures, the price of the new stock fell sharply on the money market, quoted at a discount of between 40 and 80 per cent of its face value.

These swingeing reforms had a horrendous deflationary effect on the national economy. Over 1,500 businesses failed, trade dwindled, money was extremely scarce as people hoarded cash, bills of exchange almost stopped circulating, for merchants feared ruin from sudden changes in coinage values. Government salaries and pensions were heavily cut and the coinage underwent a major devaluation, being reissued at nearly half its previous value. The harshest measure, however, was the setting up of a special tribunal to investigate and punish revenue and financial offences as far back as 1689. This so-called Chamber of Justice, the equivalent of a financial inquisition, provoked a period of terror throughout France. The Regent had succeeded in introducing an all-pervasive chaos damped system in France which solved nothing.

The Regent's Second Attempts at Reform

By 1719, faced with another acute crisis because his savage measures were throttling not expanding the nation's prosperity, the Regent turned in desperation to a different remedy. He took the first step towards adopting John Law's innovative financial solutions for national banking. The Scottish projector visualised the expansion of a national economy along banking principles, now almost universally in use. He sought state control of the money supply and a paper currency not backed by gold or any valuable, limited resource. Law achieved his goal to manage and eventually liquidate France's national debt in return for exclusive license to a newly created Bank of France (known as the Banque Royale). This was the first experiment in central banking, where the State alone controlled the issue and supply of money, managed the national debt and administered all government finances. At this date, no convenient paper currency had been introduced into Europe and note issues and their use were entirely unknown in France.

Law's experiments created a ferocious national currency inflation tied to the flotation of new share issues for his commercial company. The results were an ignominious and frantic monetary confusion, but this does not lessen the extent of his genius. Within four years, his achievements were impressive; he created a French "central bank" with authority to issue and manage the national currency. In this alone, he anticipated the fiduciary (i.e. based on trust) banking systems upon which all modern nation states depend exclusively for the conduct of commerce, trade, monetary stability and bank regulation. He sought to lubricate the wheels of finance and industry through state control, rather than through private enterprise. As France was run by a despotic monarch, Law's experiments fitted well with the authoritarian views of her absolute rulers. The Regent thought, "if five hundred millions of paper had been such an advantage, five hundred millions additional would be of still greater advantage". This approach would certainly not have succeeded in either eighteenth- or nineteenth-century Britain because Law's System was rigid and inflexible.

Despite the tragedy of the rapid demise of his System due to its speed of introduction and awesome excesses, in retrospect, seeing how the essence of his novel experiments have become the norm throughout the civilised world today, we should recognise the enduring spirit of Law's ideas. He was clearly a financial visionary, centuries ahead of his age. The history of subsequent financial excesses linked to the growth of industrial capitalism over the past 276 years, frequently dissolving in a bout of hyped-up boom followed by a devastating slump, are testament to the fact that very few monetary theorists have emerged with as decisive a command of their subject as John Law.

The Concepts Behind Law's System

However, the argument between expansionary deficit-financed policies and monetarism, or sound money, which assumed such a central place in economic debate since 1945, was equally a feature in this period of financial innovation. Cantillon probably formulated his economic views, of sound money and non-inflationary policies, as he watched Law's System unfold. His writings on these theoretical issues never mention either Law or the System, but they show he had fully grasped the economic and monetary factors that were shortly to overwhelm it.

According to Robert Neilson, later to become Law's private secretary, the great financier's achievements were "To recover the dispersed coin of a nation, to retrieve its sagging trade, to ease it of oppressive taxes, to introduce new manufactures and relieve the indigent in the most generous manner", His economic reforms of autumn 1719, when the boom was at its height, were designed to eliminate the bureaucratic rigidities burdening the economy. He hoped to abolish the clutter of arbitrary taxes, imposing one equitable tax, a 'royal tithe'. Numerous petty offices disappeared and prices fell dramatically. Retail prices for coal, wood, fish, corn, meat, poultry, eggs and other vital household goods fell by one-third. This was a welcome relief to millions of struggling poor peasants, but the enemies among the privileged classes that his schemes were attracting grew commensurately.

Law's Views on Money and Monetary Policy

John Law might properly be called a proto-Keynesian, for the guiding principal behind his monetary stance was the need for government intervention to galvanise the economy into greater activity. This approach was clearly in sympathy with the autocratic French method of running the State which may explain why he was finally able to effect his experiments there even though they had been emphatically rejected elsewhere in Europe. Although there is evidence that the Regent befriended Law during the reign of Louis XIV and was sympathetic to his financial ideas, the totally abject state of French government finances must surely have been the main deciding factor. Law's System was intended to improve the workings of the economy by revolutionising the existing financial structures of the State through the use of liberalised monetary, fiscal and exchange rate policies, but because the national economy which became the focus of his tests was France, special conditions prevailed. Strict dirigiste principles applied to virtually all aspects of communal life. The State was run as a despotic centrally controlled fiefdom of the monarch or his representative, the Regent. Therefore, Law's objective of expanding the sluggish French economy by increasing the levels of economic activity acquired many aspects of a centrally planned economy, with all the inherent faults such systems entail. These economies tend to be closed and insular, whereas democratically run economies are more open and expansive.

Law had firm views on financial themes and the role of money. He saw the monetary system and the real economy as deeply interwoven, believing that money has a unique identity of its own. It is not just an accounting unit for assessing real activity in the economy. Under appropriate conditions he thought money becomes implicit in the non-functioning failure of the entire economy. Under this interpretation however, failure can be a double-edged disaster. Lack of money in France had brought a severe depression with the Regent's failed early attempts at financial reform, but there can be a failure of excess, with a currency hyper-inflation, as Law would soon discover. In chaos terms, Law's approach to money was holistic.

From his concept of an inextricable linkage between money and the real economy, Law assumed that weak economic performance was associated with economies suffering from high levels of interest rates with excessive reliance on gold and silver as the two chief circulating media of exchange. He considered a metallic money system caused a shortage of cash because it suffered from inherent inadequacies. This view was widely prevalent in the 1930s; Keynes called gold "that barbaric metal", and campaigned to demonetise it to bring down high unemployment levels during the depression. Two centuries earlier, Law had sought to demonitise gold and silver, replacing them with a circulating paper currency and greater use of paper credit to oil the wheels of commerce. According to Murphy, the idea of centralising control of the money supply under the aegis of the Banque Royale was principally his chosen route to enable him to reduce interest rates to low levels and so stimulate economic activity, as this extract from Law's writings shows:

An abundance of money which would lower the interest rate to 2% would, in reducing the financing costs of the debts and public offices etc. relieve the King. It would lighten the burden of the indebted noble landowners. This latter group would be enriched because agricultural goods would be sold at higher prices. It would enrich traders who would then be able to borrow at a lower interest rate and give employment to the people.

His stress on low interest rates to increase employment is totally in keeping with Lord Keynes's attitude, over 200 years later. Moreover, in the sophisticated global markets of the 1990s the link between cheap money and booms and its converse, expensive money and recessions, is now almost axiomatic, endorsing Law's crucial early insight. To pursue his aims, he was forced to act on the massive overhang of public sector debt. His remedy was to convert all this debt into Company shares.

Cantillon Spots the Flaws

Cantillon became a close associate of Law in the early stages of his French experiment, but their paths separated in 1719, as Cantillon's misgivings grew on the viability of Law's System. Cantillon, one of the foremost economic thinkers of that age, has largely been ignored by later academics, but his great contribution to the development of economic theory was his lucid explanation of the circulation of money within an industrial economy. Murphy claims Cantillon's ideas were stimulated by close contacts with Law's System in operation. He took the opposite theoretical stance to Law. If Law was a forerunner of Keynes, hoping to expand the economy by massive government intervention, Cantillon was a proto-monetarist, keen on sound money and preventing excessive increases in the money supply. To his credit, and great personal gain, he saw the main weaknesses in Law's monetary stance and made two separate fortunes during the Mississippi boom, one in the shares and a second by speculating against the French currency. Cantillon's reputation as a savant on Mississippi shares was helped by the stance his lawyers took in the litigation that later arose between him and the Lady Mary Herbert/Joseph Gage faction.

> Unlike many others he was not taken in by the famous System which started to develop in 1719. On the contrary he believed it necessary to take shelter from the storm which he foresaw: this induced him to give up business in which he saw too many dangers.

And, we should note, he sold out of his Mississippi shares in August 1719, long before the January 1720 peak, thereby amassing the handsome sum of £50,000 sterling.

Unique Aspects of the South Sea Scheme

We have dwelt at some length on the French situation since it has a national dimension. By contrast, the South Sea Bubble was a far more localised episode. No profound theoretical issues were involved. Moreover, as the later parliamentary inquiry revealed, there was serious fraud and dishonest intent behind the South Sea scheme. John Law, for all his failings, died in poverty and scarcely benefited from the huge wealth, personal popularity and prestige that fleetingly attached itself to him at the height of the French mania. His writings reveal that he had a sincere and genuine desire to see the successful fruition of his economic experiments.

As with the Regent in France, the English Parliament was equally obsessed by the size and longevity of the national debt created by the French wars. By 1720, some directors of the South Sea Company foresaw the opportunity for personal enrichment by taking over the national debt and simultaneously eliminating their hated rival institution, the Bank of England. The Bank itself, although a major creditor to the King, and therefore the State, was still a private corporation and did not act as a proper central bank.

Differences Between the Mississippi and the South Sea Bubbles

In autocratic France, Law's commercial trading companies met no opposition. They were aggregated together into what amounted to a monopoly conglomerate, trading around the world, able to dictate its own future development, ignoring both competition and challengers. There were no rival "bubble" companies to compete with the vast monolithic edifice Law created. By contrast, the British were far more biased towards private enterprise and free trade.

From the start the two companies espoused very different aims. John Law recognised the limitations of a precious metal currency unaided by a paper money, for financing an expanding economy. His theoretical concept of national wealth creation, as we saw, encompassed the whole economy, backed by the authority of the State. He aimed to stimulate the lethargic real French economy by the expansion of paper money backed by the value of the nation's real assets – initially using the land itself, rather than by gold and silver held in vaults. When Law obtained the trade monopoly for the vast New World region of the Louisiana Territory, the erroneous view that it contained gold and silver mines was falsely assumed to provide further asset-backing for the paper note issues.

Ironically, both schemes depended for success on holding up the level of their shares. Law hoped, by holding the share price high, to keep interest rates low in France, while the fraudulent South Sea directors needed a high share price to repay the bribes they had made to get their scheme onto the Statute book, to create a "fund of credit" for their own future use and to increase profits for the Company.

Relying on his view of the strong linkage between money and the real economy, Law saw no difficulty in welding and interlinking his new paper issuing banking system with the commercial activities of the Mississippi Company. To demonitise the bi-metallic coinage, he used the newly created bank notes to support the Mississippi share price. Murphy thinks that it was Law's decision to use the Banque Royale to support the price of Mississippi shares which caused Cantillon to lose confidence in the System in August 1719, about 14 months after the two economists first met.

In England the Bank of England remained outside the control of the South Sea Company, although there had originally been an unsuccessful plan for the latter to take over the Bank. Since the South Sea Company could not use newly issued bank notes to increase the price of its stock, it resorted instead to increasing the velocity of circulation of money. This it achieved by repeatedly lending money on highly advantageous terms to purchasers of its shares. However, through its own banker, the Sword Blade Bank, the directors were able to introduce extra credit into the circulating money supply, which greatly enhanced the inflationary nature of the stock market boom. This interesting difference reveals how exceptionally easy it is to introduce a financial pump during a stock market boom. In 1720, the pump was activated for the Mississippi Company by printing bank notes; for the South Sea Company, it was activated by extending credit on an ever enlarging basis.

The principal directors of the South Sea Company had a more limited goal than John Law, namely, their own financial enrichment. John Blunt, chief architect of the scheme to convert the national debt, did all he could to prevent the credit he created from escaping, into either rival bubbles or other genuine enterprises. Where Law inadvertently operated an open credit pump, spreading like a burgeoning chain reaction throughout the national economy, Blunt and other dishonest directors specifically intended to create a strictly closed circuit, purely to support the price of South Sea stock. Several ministers of the Crown unwittingly acquiesced in this. The Company's conversion plans involved injecting about £5 million of new money (10 times the injection of 1719), into an already booming economy – unlike the torpid French economy, overburdened by rigid financial inefficiencies and excessive state debt. In England, a simultaneous reduction in interest rates accompanied this large money injection, again through the machinations of the South Sea directors. This provided more liquidity than the economy could possibly absorb, in the short term, in genuine production.

Circulating paper bank notes were a key feature of Law's scheme. If the note issue is not strictly controlled, however, it acts as a source of credit, as the same note represents money to both parties; it is counted as delayed cash by the issuer and acts as immediate cash for the user. Unfortunately, both Law and the Regent falsely concluded, from the early success of Law's grand "System", that unregulated paper could entirely supersede a precious metal currency. This view was rapidly seen to be flawed. One commentator bitterly summed up the extent of Law's failure in these words: "This traffic in paper, which was indeed a snare and a chimera, has ruined the kingdom more than all the wars of Louis XIV."

Ironically, the greed and narrow-mindedness of the South Sea directors saved England from a rampant paper money inflation, although they created a credit inflation which led to a period of outlandish conspicuous consumption and massive property price rises around London. The extent of the disaster almost brought down the newly established Hanoverian accession of George I.

However, the steadily growing English device of parliamentary control acted as a safety valve that was non-existent in France. It enabled the Government to restore the fortunes of the most hard-pressed victims of the South Sea Bubble and punish the perpetrators. By contrast, France suffered severely from the failure of Law's experiment. The insolvency of public finances remained an acute issue throughout the century, due to an endless succession of hugely expensive wars. The deep-seated distrust of banks that Frenchmen naturally felt after their experiences with the Banque Royale made it impossible to properly formalise state borrowing in France throughout the eighteenth century. The Bank of France was not to be recreated until it was reborn as part of Napoleon's wide-ranging fiscal and administrative reforms, during the two years (1800–2) when he was First Consul of France.

CHAPTER SEVEN

MISSISSIPPI MADNESS

The rue de Quinquampoix, which is their Exchange Alley, is crowded from early in the morning to late at night with princes and princesses, dukes and peers and duchesses etc, in a word all that is great in France. They sell estates and pawn jewels to purchase Mississippi.

Mr Pyot, a clerk at the British Embassy in Paris, September 1719

In earlier chapters, various aspects of the Mississippi Bubble have been introduced; the war-induced national debt crisis as its primary direct cause, the background conditions, some of the anecdotal evidence for the madness of crowds, and ways in which the French share speculation resembled and differed from its English contemporary, the South Sea Bubble. This chapter covers the main events of the French bubble showing how they tie in with the eight phase crashes model and the extra features we identified in Chapter 1.

I believe it is too simplistic to dismiss the Scottish projector, John Law as a reckless adventurer. His financial manipulations certainly became rather complicated, so we must not get waylaid in the obscure details of his manoeuvres at the height of the speculative excesses. Our aim is simply to reveal how closely the Mississippi events tie in with the major features we might expect to occur in a pure financial chaos episode based on the chaos features introduced in Part I.

Law's Legacy

For posterity, John Law has a mixed reputation. The sum of his achievements is caustically captured in Viscount Erleigh's 1933 edition of *The South Sea Bubble*.

John Law of Lauriston invented gaming counters and modern banking, though time alone will show which is to be his more permanent memorial. Many volumes have been written extolling him as a genius, and as many more decrying him as a charlatan. The truth probably lies between the two extremes; starting as an adventurous financier and finishing as a financial adventurer, he was by nature something of a genius and by necessity something of a charlatan, but the undeniable fact remains that in the space of little more than four years he had risen from an exiled Scottish gambler to be Controller-General of Finance to the Regent of France.

At the height of his powers he was fêted and admired by the greatest notables in France. Lady Mary Wortley-Montague, a prodigious writer of the age, summed up his triumph in October 1718,

> I must say I saw nothing in France that delighted so much as to see an Englishman (or at least a Briton) absolute in Paris; I mean Mr Law, who treats with Dukes and Peers extremely de haut en bas and is treated by them with the utmost submission and respect.

Montgomery Hyde, in *John Law* (his biography of Law), suggests he had the mind of an inventor, being attracted to novelties. Law rejected criticisms that his views mainly opposed the established tradition. He disputed the idea that gold was the sole repository of wealth. Like many people fired by ambition, he knew exactly what he wanted to achieve and exploited every fortuitous chance to bring his schemes to fruition.

The Scheme is Launched

The ideas Law had published in his book, *Money and Trade Considered*, were set before the Scottish Parliament in summer 1705. Introducing them, Law noted,

> There need be no speeches to show how much a sufficient stock of money, or a good fund of public credit, which is the same thing (money being but the counter of commerce), would be serviceable to the people and trade of the Kingdom, or how it would tend to the honour and justice of the Queen [Anne] and Parliament to pay off and clear the debts of the Government so long and so justly due to the Army and Civil List.

His proposals contained all the seeds of his future commercial and banking ideas. He attributed Scotland's poverty to a lack of capital and sought to increase her financial resources by large issues of paper money based upon the credit of a bank. This banking link, he reasoned, would give the paper the value and efficiency of circulating coin.

The Scottish Parliament rejected his revolutionary monetary plans, so he toured Europe, trying to persuade various Kings and Emperors to adopt them. His efforts fell on deaf ears, until in May 1716, the French Regent, weighed down by the insoluble nature of the State's debts, allowed him to establish a private bank, the Banque Générale, in Paris. This "foot-in-the-door" opening was all Law needed to set him on his path to executing the most far-reaching dirigiste monetary policies of the age. His System developed by a process of rough improvisation, in response to unpredictable vagaries in the prevailing conditions. As the main events slowly progressed, there were four key stages although it is impossible to know if Law had a neatly phased introduction to his System in mind as his schemes took shape:

1. To establish a commercial bank which later became a pseudo-central bank. Its prime function was to issue bank notes to replace specie (metallic gold and silver) as the chief medium of exchange.
2. Involvement in national debt management operations, through the founding of the Company of the West (Compagnie d'Occidente).
3. A combination of monetary policy and debt management operations by progressively linking the activities of the bank and his commercial company. The two vehicles were eventually merged in December 1719.
4. The use of changes in the French exchange rate to induce holders of specie to substitute their metallic coinage for his bank notes.

At the outset, despite his theoretical leanings, Law may never have visualised what he would achieve in just four years. He did not have a free hand with his experiments because the Regent, his backer, was struggling with the Parlement to consolidate his own power base. Law began cautiously, keen to display the success of his approach and so gain the Regent's confidence. No doubt he hoped as the Regent won more victories over the opposing Court faction, Law would get permission to implement more of his plans. Faced with the Regent's political constraints, Law's schemes had to advance opportunistically.

Although he acted mainly by improvisation, it is clear that Law remained continually focused on his primary objective to increase employment prospects in the French economy through expansionary monetary policies. Initially, his impact on the economy was minimal. It was only when he entered stage two in the progression of his System, namely, the start of debt management operations, that his strategies began to change the underlying structure of the French financial system. The main stages in the development of his System are outlined in Table 4.

The First Step – Establishing Banque Générale

Originally, Law tried to persuade the Regent to set up a state bank, but while his patron was sympathetic, Parlement was hostile. His first

Table 4 The development of Law's System

Date	Bank	Company	Acquisition
May 1716	Banque Générale		
August 1717		Company of the West	
July 1718			Tobacco Farm Lease
December 1718	Banque Royale		Company of Senegal
May 1719			Company des Indes et de la Chine
July 1719		Company des Indes	
			Mint rights
December 1719	Merger of Banque Royale + Company des Indes		

Source: Murphy, A., (1988). Reproduced by permission of Oxford University Press

scheme therefore, had to be greatly modified. The plan to create a joint stock private bank was accepted, with Law subscribing the bulk of the capital from his own resources. (He used some of his huge gambling fortune won in the capitals of Europe, before his arrival in France.) He agreed to defray the initial overhead expenses and carefully regulate the note issues. He saw the resulting increase in the circulation of currency as having a beneficial effect on trade and re-establishing confidence by creating money of a fixed value. As most people in France had never seen or used a bank note, early scepticism was to be expected. Bank notes were then circulating in only five European states (Holland, Sweden, Genoa, Venice and Great Britain), but in every case paper notes were a corollary to the circulation of specie. In no country had a paper currency completely taken the place of metal coinage. This was the innovative monetary leap towards which all Law's efforts were now directed.

On setting up the bank, he had three key objectives: first, to restore commercial confidence; secondly, to provide a facility for nationals and foreigners alike to deposit funds with complete security; and thirdly, to arrive at a position where his notes would be circulating freely throughout France and abroad. At this point he was convinced they would act, in effect, like universal bills of exchange. By the end of 1717, Law had achieved these three goals. The bank could afford to pay its shareholders a half-yearly 7 per cent dividend; it had been able to reduce its commercial discount rate from 6 per cent to 4 per cent as money became more plentiful. By exercising scrupulous management, both the bank's and the nation's fortunes were beginning to prosper. Law's reputation for prudent financial control rested on an astute policy. The bank issued notes that were repayable on sight, with silver coin at the value of the notes at the time they were issued. This brilliant strategy sent his notes to an immediate premium over the State's precious metal coins which were repeatedly being debased by the hard-pressed Government, forever short of cash. Moreover, this confidence-building master-stroke by Law ensured that although the bank had a capital of only six million livres, he was able to issue 50 or 60 million with equanimity.

Many critics contend that Law's efforts would have been resoundingly successful if he had avoided the trap of entering the debt management arena. However, according to Murphy, there were two reasons why setting up the Banque Générale on its own did not give him a broad enough base on which to build the next phase of his scheme. First, the bank was grossly undercapitalised and secondly, there was a massive overhang of government debt in the bond market. The initial capital of the bank was to be 6 million livres (£383,000 sterling) subscribed in four instalments of 1,200 shares of 5,000 each. The effective capital base was only around 3.3 million livres however, because three-quarters of it had been subscribed not in specie, but in the new government debt instrument, the state notes, billets d'états. In the market, these were so discredited, they stood at a discount of around 60 per cent. As only the first instalment was actually paid up, the bank began its life with only 825,000 livres (£52,000 sterling).

Expanding the money supply from such a slender base would have been impossible, due to the vast amount of state debt in circulation. The capital base of his bank represented no more than 1.125 million l.t. (livres tournois, the French unit of account) in nominal terms; there was approximately 250 million l.t. of billets d'états, plus perhaps 215 million l.t. of other "papiers royaux" representing other forms of government debt in existence, plus some substantial long-term debts in the form of annuities.

Stage Two – Founding the Commercial Empire

Law needed a second vehicle to give him a greater base from which to expand the money supply and lower interest rates. The opportunity to create his commercial Company of the West arose from the efforts of the wealthy financier Crozat to surrender his lease over Mississippi trade in 1717 to meet his enormous tax bill. By this time, his concession had grown to extend 3,000 miles upstream and to include all the territory lying between the Alleghenies on the east and the Rocky Mountains on the west. It extended from the Gulf of Mexico to the French possessions in Canada. Law's stature had risen in tandem with the reputation of his bank. In April 1717, his standing rose further when his notes were decreed acceptable for paying taxes.

In August 1717, Law founded the Company of the West (Compagnie d'Occident). It was granted the trade monopoly over the vast Mississippi region, erroneously thought to be rich in gold and silver mines. The initial capital of the Company was set at 100 million livres, with an issue of 200,000 shares at 500 livres per share to be subscribed in state bonds (that is, the deeply discounted billets d'états). Although the nominal market capitalisation of the company was 100 million l.t. the shares could only be bought with discounted billets d'états, so its effective market capitalisation was far smaller (in the region of 30 million l.t. (£1.5 million sterling)). This put the market cost at between 140 and 160 l.t, as the discount varied between 68 and 72 per cent of the billets d'états. Even so, the average share price of 150 livres is minuscule compared to the huge rise in the market valuation of the shares by 1720 as we saw in Chapter 2 in the tale of the poor widow, Madame Chaumont.

Law's principal aim with the issue of this first tranche of shares in the Company of the West was to convert the floating short-term government debt, held in the form of discounted billets d'états, into longer-term debt. On being paid up, the billets d'états were to be converted into perpetual annuities carrying interest at 4 per cent, while the original bonds were to be burned. This arrangement had advantages for both shareholders and the Government. The shareholders would receive the same rate of interest as they had on their bonds, while looking forward to profits as the development of the Louisiana colony progressed. The Government gained relief of one-half of the floating debt and Law, for his part, hoped that by showing how part of the debt problem could be alleviated by this type of conversion, he was preparing the ground for later phases of his hugely ambitious System; these it turned out, were not to be introduced until 1719. Although Law was supremely confident on the outcome of his plans, the Company of the West was not initially popular with the public. In fact, for almost two years its shares were quoted below par, at prices below 500 livres per share.

At this stage of its development, the French System was copying the South Sea scheme, as the essential original feature of both was the granting of a trading privilege in exchange for the Company's conversion of government debt at a lower rate of interest. Even if Law was aware of the close way his Company was modelling the English South Sea Company, from this point forward, his scheme followed an independent course, and the South Sea Company then became an imitator of Law's unfolding schemes. The way in which the two schemes diverged illustrates the chaos notion of sensitive dependence upon initial conditions introduced in Chapter 3.

The Combination of Monetary Objectives and Debt Management

During 1718, Law started to take measures to foster his macro-economic designs. He achieved this in several stages but we do not know if he was following a definite plan. Probably, with his gambling flair, he was adept at quickly evaluating any openings that cropped up, and turning them to his advantage, because his end objectives were always to the fore. First, he entered into a series of acquisitions, to expand his commercial trading interests. Simultaneously, he was able to convert Bank Générale into the quasi-central bank, Banque Royale. Thirdly, he managed to acquire the rights to the Mint over a nine-year period, and finally, he instituted the massive fund raising measures to finance all his acquisitions, including the Mint. It was the link between the Banque Royale note issuing policy and Law's launch of a series of highly attractive rights issues to finance his acquisitions that created the huge boom in Mississippi shares. To see how this masterpiece of financial engineering produced the speculative mania we must briefly sketch in its broad outlines, although our primary interest is to flesh out the features which enabled the boom to acquire an internal momentum of its own, that is, to become chaotic.

In January 1718 the company purchased the tobacco monopoly to supply the lucrative, widely popular snuff trade. Law obtained the trading rights for all ships and merchandise of the Company of Senegal. In March all Law's trading companies were consolidated into one trading conglomerate, later called the Compagnie des Indes. This gave him total control of France's entire non-European trade. With his ships, he began to organise colonisation of the Louisiana Territory.

In the summer, by royal decree Law's bank was to be transformed into a state bank, Banque Royale, by absorbing all the assets of Banque Générale. In short, his bank was to be nationalised. The Government now became responsible for the bank's note issues in circulation, standing then at about 12 million livres. Prior to the substantial increase in the note issue now being planned, an edict came into force altering the convertibility of the notes. The practice Law had implemented which had made his notes "as good as gold" was to cease. Instead of the previous arrangement whereby notes had been payable in bank money "of the weight and standard of the day", in future the link with a fixed value of specie no longer held. At the same time, the first step was taken towards achieving an inconvertible paper currency. By royal edict all payments above 600 livres were to be made payable only in gold or notes, not silver. As there was very little gold in the country at this time, this amounted to an enforced circulation of the notes. In December, the bank finally became Banque Royale under Law's total control although he lost his right to issue notes. Now only the Regent could authorise the note issue. Law was totally in favour of these new measures as he was convinced paper had superior qualities over gold as currency. Confidence in the bank notes was now widespread and he foresaw future economic benefits by making use of the notes compulsory.

The Boom Takes Off

By May 1719, Law was seeking ways to generate some momentum in the share price of his Company of the West, which was still trading at a discount. He organised the merger of all his trading companies to form the Compagnie des Indes. This action required additional finance as some of his acquisitions had large debts. He also needed to raise money to re-equip existing ships and build a new fleet to exploit the colonial trading opportunities of his commercial enterprises. To raise the funds, Law proposed his second issue of shares in the Company of the West, issuing 50,000 shares at 500 livres per share with a 10 per cent premium of 50 livres payable immediately. The shares were to be paid for in 20 instalments of 5 per cent each. On depositing the premium of 50 livres, plus one monthly payment of 25 livres anyone could receive an allotment. In other words, for a down-payment of 75 livres the investor was allocated one share priced at 550 livres. On 10 June, Banque Royale issued 270.7 million livres in new bank notes. This may have helped the share price rise above its par value of 500 livres. When the Parlement refused to ratify Law's expansion funding plans, the Regent brought them into force by a decree of council on 17 June, by which date the price of Mississippi shares had reached 650 livres. In addition to the incentive from a visibly rising price, two other strong enticements drew investors into the market to buy shares. First, the new issue was to be paid for by easy part-payments, of 20 monthly instalments at 25 livres each. Secondly, Law maintained interest in the existing shares through the rights privilege; existing shareholders would receive rights in the new shares. That is, buyers needed to own four old shares in order to purchase one new one. Thus, to obtain 10 shares in the newly named Company des Indes, it was necessary to possess 40 in the Company of the West. The old shares were soon popularly called mères (mothers) and the new shares, filles (daughters). The series of share issues is outlined in Table 5. In modern terminology, Law had made a rights issue to the holders of Mississippi stock to subscribe more capital to the Company.

These rights could be sold on the open market once the first instalment (25 livres) plus the premium (50 livres) had been paid. A decree of 27 July suggests that one needed only to pay the 50 livres premium, the first instalment being delayed until 1 September. Law encouraged growing support for the shares by these enticements. He was maintaining interest in the mères, enabling his wealthy sponsors, the Regent and his entourage, to enjoy significant capital gains on their holdings: and he was offering a cheap route into the shares for newcomers, who could buy the filles by monthly instalments when existing holders of the mères came to realise some of their profits by selling their partly-paid filles. Issuing

Table 5 Share Issues (in Livres) by the Mississippi Company

Date	Share	No. issued	Cost	Nominal	Terms
June and Sept 1717	Mères	200,000	140-160	100 mill	Paid for in billets d'états
June 1719	Filles	50,000	550	25 mill	20 instalments 4 old for 1 new
July 1719	Petites filles	50,000	1,000	50 mill	20 instalments 4 mères + 1 filles for 1 new
26 Sept 1719	Cinq-	100,000	5,000	50 mill	10 instalments of 500
28 Sept 1719	cents	100,000	5,000	50 mill	As above but mainly for office holders
2 Oct 1719		100,000	5,000	50 mill	As above
4 Oct 1719		24,000			
Total		624,000		325 mill	

Source: Murphy, A., (1988). Reproduced by permission of Oxford University Press

partly-paid shares provided leverage for investors to make capital gains that were a multiple of their initial investment. For example, if the shares rose to 1,000 livres (which they did by mid-July 1719), the holder of a partly-paid fille who had only paid the 50 livres premium, could make a profit of 450 livres, i.e. 1,000 less 50 already paid and 500 due for the outstanding instalments. By selling his fille, he made a return of nine times his original outlay.

For a full cash down-payment of 550 livres, an investor received a 10 per cent bonus, and this attractive device added to the cash the Company derived from the initial monthly payments. The effect of the new decree, converting the Company of the West into the Company des Indes, with all these attendant attractive marketing devices, was precisely as Law had anticipated. In an excited rush to become eligible for the rights, there was an immediate run on the old shares, sending their market value rapidly higher. The issue of the filles was soon over-subscribed, while the mères continued to change hands at ever rising prices. More than 25 million in specie was soon deposited at the disposal of the Company.

Shortly after, Law prepared to issue the third tranche of Company shares. A Royal decree of 20 July awarded the profits of the Mint for a nine-year term to the Company of the West for which it was to pay 50 million livres over a 15-month period commencing in October. On 25 July, Banque Royale's note issuing powers were increased by 240 million livres. The next day, at a general meeting of the Company, Law raised the dividend on the shares in 1720 to 12 per cent (that is, 60 livres per share of 500 livres), payable in two half-yearly payments. On 27 July, the second rights issue was launched, to raise 50 million livres to pay for the Mint transaction.

Within a few days, Law had accomplished a great deal: he had increased the money supply with the new note issues; he had promised a high dividend to raise enthusiasm for the shares, which was reinforced by floating more shares onto the market on terms which encouraged investors to make use of the additional availability of credit he had arranged. At this point, Richard Cantillon began to doubt the long-term prospects for Law's System. He recognised that the massive new bank note issues would generate an unstable situation by ushering in a rampant currency inflation. He sold out of his entire Mississippi holdings in August 1719 and then left France for Italy. For this timely act, he was later hailed as one of the most prescient analysts of Law's System.

The terms of the second rights issue in July 1719, were as attractively set as those of the first, issued in June. Another 50,000 shares were issued at a price of 1,000 livres per share, with a premium of 500 livres on the nominal price of 500 livres. To be eligible to subscribe for the new issue a purchaser had to possess 4 mères and one fille. The new shares were immediately dubbed petites filles (grand-daughters). Once again, more leverage was applied to the escalating share mountain, as the new rights were to be paid for in 20 monthly instalments of 50 livres. To encourage holders to take up their "rights" the share register was to be left open for 20 days but this concession was completely superfluous. By 29 July, the shares had risen to 1,500 livres and the urge to acquire them was intensifying by the day. A frenzy of speculation now took hold, as investors scrambled to gain access to all three forms of share; mères, filles and petites filles. During the summer of 1719, consequent on restructuring his commercial empire, the price of all Mississippi stock rose with a bewildering rapidity. Shares which had been quoted at 1,000 in July, had bounded ahead to stand at five times that value by September. Unfortunately, there is no formal index for the share prices at this stage, and before August 1719 quotations are difficult to find, but Murphy draws on several sources detailed below to indicate the extent of the surge:

17 June	650	(McFarland Davis)
25 July	1,300	(Piossens)
29 July	1,500	(Piossens)
1 August	2,250	(Dutot)
9 August	2,330	(Giraudeau)
14 August	2,940	(Giraudeau)

Source: Murphy, A., (1988). Reproduced by permission of Oxford University Press

The issue of new bank notes by Bank Royale during 1719 was closely linked to the new share issues. Dutot's statistics indicate how the note issue was expanded:

1719	Note issue in livres
5 January	18,000,000
11 February	20,000,000
1 April	20,940,000
22 April	51,000,000
10 June	50,000,000
25 July	220.660,000

Source: Murphy, A., (1988). Reproduced by permission of Oxford University Press

Dutot calculated that the market value of 624,000 Mississippi shares on 29 November 1719 was 4,781,750,000 livres tournois (the average price per share was 7,663 l.t.). The speculative fervour was nowhere near its peak at this stage, however. The final market value by May 1720 would reach an astonishing 6.24 billion livres.

By autumn 1719, the climate looked serenely right for the next stage of Law's ambitious scheme. He offered to lend the King 1.2 billion livres at an interest rate of 3 per cent to take over the State's long-term debts. These were held in the form of rentes (government bonds) and the remaining billets d'états. Law proposed that this loan-cum-conversion scheme would utilise the services of the Mississippi Company. The new shares were issued during the autumn of 1719, in three tranches, totalling 300,000 shares at 5,000 each, amounting to 1.5 billion livres. In fact, an additional 24,000 shares were issued, making a total of 324,000 shares in all. They were to be paid for in 10 monthly instalments of 500 livres, and quickly acquired the nick-name of the cinq-cents. The three preceding share issues had yielded a nominal total of 107.5 million livres in money and billets d'états. If the cinq-cents had been fully paid up, the company would have received an additional 1.5 billion livres (£58 million sterling) although in practice, this amount was never fully raised.

Techniques to Encourage the Boom

Law used the successful marketing techniques he had employed with such stupendous success for his earlier share issues. There was the lure of small part-payments coupled with the long drawn-out period of several monthly instalments extending for almost a year. This created hugely geared capital gains in the rising market. When the monthly payment dates began to cause problems for investors, they were further relaxed to make instalments payable on a quarterly basis. Law now introduced the concept of bearer securities to provide anonymity of ownership, a useful way of avoiding any future onerous tax demands. At a later date he also provided low interest rate loans by Banque Royale, an additional facility of easy credit which assisted the leverage. Added to all this great incentive to buy, the twice-yearly dividend was an attractive inducement for investors to recycle cash funds into the Company by reinvesting in the new share issues as they came onto the market. Then there was the introduction of primes, a type of option that operated briefly early in 1720.

Although options transactions were known to London investors, Law was the first person to introduce them in France. He himself had used an option in the spring of 1719 as a means of advertising his schemes to the general public. At a time when the shares were standing at a discount of 50 per cent, Law purchased the right to "call" for 200 shares of the Company at par (500 livres) in six months' time. By this contract he had agreed to pay the holders of Mississippi shares 100,000 livres, the par value of their shares, after a period of six months, although the shares were then worth only 50,000 livres. As an act of goodwill, he deposited 40,000 livres immediately, which he would forfeit if he failed to take up the shares at the agreed future date. This 40,000 acted as his premium for the options. His intention with this action was to attract speculative dealings in the shares to bring them favourably to the public attention, but with his fertile gambling instinct, he was also able to make a hefty profit. The shares gradually rose, returned to their par value and beyond, so that before all his contracts had matured they were worth 10 times their par value.

In October 1719, the Company announced its capital funding was complete. No further issues would be made. The total issue of shares now stood at 624,000, with a nominal value of 325 millions. However, as all the shares had been sold at a premium, except those in the original flotation of the Company of the West, the actual value was nearly six times that amount, approaching 1,800 millions. With receipts estimated at 82 million livres per year, the Company was in a position to pay a handsome 16 per cent dividend, of 130 livres per 500-livre share. This would have sufficed in normal circumstances, but circumstances were now anything but normal. The majority of new investors had paid almost 5,000 livres for their holdings, offering only a minuscule dividend of 1.5 per cent.

Of even greater significance, the huge growth in both the share and bank note issues had produced the situation which Law was so conscientiously working towards. Namely, that holders of all other forms of wealth in French society, including the old forms of government debts and gold and silver coinage, were remorselessly being subjected to a loss of alternative outlets for circulating currency. In effect, as his commercial empire reached its maximum size, all investors found themselves deprived of practically every outlet for investment except those that led up to Law's System.

The Burgeoning Money Supply

By the late autumn of 1719, Law's impact on the creaking French economy seemed like a fairy-tale transformation. The corrupt, haphazard fiscal system, permanently short of money and dogged by monstrous debts had been replaced by a wide range of imaginative changes. Banque Royale had issued one billion livres in bank notes, making money far more widely available. The bulk of the national debt had been taken over by the Company and the interest payments on it reduced, first to 3 per cent and then 2 per cent. The trading companies had been successfully reorganised into one efficient conglomerate and given fresh injections of capital to make them financially sound. Finally, the Louisiana venture, holding out the potential for amazing profits, was gathering a larger following of interested supporters.

In acknowledgement of his achievements, Law was made Controller-General of Finance in January 1720, marking the peak of his successes. In a country as conservative and reactionary as France, it was unprecedented for any foreigner to achieve this status. Even though Law had now become naturalised in the land of his adoption, no foreigner had ever been appointed to such a high and powerful office. He was, in effect, Prime Minister, second only in power and importance to the monarch. He had secured a prominent position in banking and commerce, as well as at court. He was, briefly, the most famous, highly esteemed and sought-after person in the realm, coincidentally as the share price peaked at 10,010 on 8 January 1720.

The driving impetus for buying Mississippi shares arose from Banque Royale's continuous increase of newly created bank notes. It was no mere coincidence that the bank expanded its note issue by 50 million livres on 10 June, a few days before the issue of 50,000 filles at 550 livres per share in the Company's first rights. Later, the note issue was again expanded by 221 million livres on July 25, just two days before the second rights issue of 50,000 petites filles shares at 1,000 livres per share was made.

The link between the issue of new shares and bank notes during 1719 shows how Law hoped to meet his two key objectives. First, to lower interest rates to boost economic activity; and secondly, to replace

France's entire gold and silver currency with a paper currency system. Because he was set on driving down the interest rate, he had to abandon control over the money supply. By pushing up the price of Mississippi shares (which reduced their yield), Law hoped to reduce the cost of converting the State's debts into Company shares as the rate of interest was forced down. At a price of 5,000 livres the expected yield on the Company's shares was 4 per cent, but as the price rose higher, so this yield declined. To obtain an interest rate of 2 per cent, Law was committed to supporting the high price of Mississippi shares at the same time as providing liquidity to the stock market through the expansion of the note issue. Bank notes in issue rose dramatically early in 1720, as the great final conversion tranche of Mississippi shares went into circulation. By May 1720 notes in issue had reached 2.1 billion livres.

The exact quantity of specie circulating in France early in 1720 is not known. An order at the end of February declared that "of the specie coined in the Mint there must be above 1.2 billion in specie in the Kingdom". By May 1720, Law had increased the money supply by 175 per cent. However, the boom in the shares of the Mississippi Company had served to monetise them, since they were an additional source of paper "money" circulating in the economy. The total value of the shares now stood at around 5.4 to 6 billion livres.

The Company had set up its own office for share transactions, ostensibly to prevent innocent investors being duped by "sharks" exploiting them in the notorious rue Quincampoix, where the shares changed hands rapidly between the throngs of jobbers and investors continuously clustering there as this street housed many important bankers. However, the deeper purpose of the official bureau was to provide state support for the share price to prevent it falling below a certain minimum floor price. By making the shares highly attractive through this policy of artificially holding up the share price, Law had greatly expanded the liquidity of the economy and in the process had in effect, monetised Mississippi shares. As everyone clamoured to possess the shares they began to acquire the characteristics of circulating money. In his desire to implement his policies, Law employed a series of opaque manoeuvres and market manipulations that unleashed a stock-jobbing fever of unprecedented proportions. Like a contagion of madness, it raised the temperature of the French investing community to a dizzy but unsustainable crescendo of impossible expectations.

The System at its Peak

As the System swung into top gear, the whole economy began to loosen up. After centuries of indolence, it was operating on a "high". With the huge expansion of bank notes, money was plentiful. Speculators with foresight to realise the good times would soon end, began cashing in their holdings to buy more tangible assets. Some cautious investors, servants and others of lowly means, whom we met in Chapter 2, were delighted to turn their inflated paper assets into something more substantial.

Others, including Lady Mary Herbert and her faction, fared less well. They suffered the mortifying experience of watching their paper fortunes rising, only to see them evaporate entirely away in less than one year. Foreigners who did sell out would have transferred their gains abroad, but most of the money stayed in France, where it fuelled a rampant boom in land and property prices, jewels, clothes, furniture, horses, carriages and works of art. Employment prospects rose encouragingly, to serve the growing demands for luxury life-styles and expensive commodities sought by the newly enriched. Far-sighted holders of bank notes began to exchange this paper for specie coinage. The Prince de Conti, in an effort to discredit Law, ostentatiously sent three wagons of notes to Banque Royale to transport away his gold after the exchange. Rumours on this and similar scare stories increased during the spring of 1720, planting the first real seeds of doubt on the viability of the System.

The Rush Towards Collapse

Although it is clear Law's System was advancing at a breakneck speed which virtually guaranteed its imminent demise, at the time each step in its development appeared to follow a natural progression, to the evident delight of Law himself. In a letter to the *Mercure de France* in February 1720, he recognised the simplifying unity of his schemes, when he wrote, "One sees here a sequence of ideas which develop one from the other and which, more and more, make one aware of the principle on which they are based." His remarks are reminiscent of Churchill's "one darn thing" quote, with the added irony that Law's confidence was certainly misplaced, and "one darn thing," was sadly much nearer to the spirit of the soon to unfold disaster. Although this outcome was almost deterministic, due to the speed with which his schemes had been implemented, there is no doubt from the evidence that his prime preoccupation was the well-intended aim of correcting the problem of widespread under-utilisation of resources in France by reforming its sluggish monetary system.

By mid-1719, Law had succeeded in attracting widespread interest in his schemes, but from his actions we can see his thinking throughout was still dominated by his theoretical concepts. The collapse, when it came, was triggered by a rapid series of decrees issued between February and March of 1720. Taken together, some of them had contradictory goals.

They were intended to continue his programme of financial reform, but in the event, they proved so destabilising that they tipped the whole expansion process into reverse. It underwent a dramatic collapse that was as abrupt in origin as the previous rise had been.

When the ill-fated decrees were issued in bewilderingly quick succession, public confidence in the System slumped in tandem with the price of Mississippi shares. A mad scramble ensued to convert paper money and shares into coinage and thousands of investors were ruined. Law was peremptorily dismissed from office and ignominiously forced to flee from France. None of his later actions or correspondence points to any evil intent. On his escape, with just 2,000 louis, he left all his liquid assets in France, disdaining to take anything of major value with him.

His spring decrees have been popularly judged as crisis measures, revealing a fatal indecisiveness on Law's part in his vacillating responses to the first creeping doubts now emerging about his System. Critics claim he introduced these edicts to prevent the whole house of cards from collapsing. As the rout set in during spring 1720, even contemporary sources, in the broadsheet press and in satirical prints, lampooned Law as a maverick alchemist, trying to foist essentially flawed and unworkable reforms upon the already tottering French economy. Murphy, however, thinks the decrees dovetailed into Law's grand reforming strategy to demonetise specie in the French economy and keep interest rates low. On any rational appraisal, and knowing that Law's theoretical idealism was centred on financial innovation to stimulate the real economy, it is hardly credible that he set out purely to create an unsustainable mania in Mississippi shares. His character and aims appear to support Murphy's view.

The Objectives of Law's System

If his actions were ill-judged, Law's key objectives remained consistent. However, to accomplish his twin goals he needed to both maintain public enthusiasm for Mississippi shares, in order to keep the interest rate low (a high price for the shares was accompanied by a lower dividend yield); and to encourage people of wealth to prefer bank notes to specie.

To reduce interest rates he had to support the Mississippi share price at a high value, so the yield on them would fall. This yield represented the rate of interest at which investors could convert their holdings of public sector debt into Company shares. However, this policy was bound to run into trouble if more investors wanted to sell than to buy shares. That situation would make it impossible for Law to maintain a low interest rate, unless he artificially supported the high price of Mississippi shares.

On his second problem, to demonetise specie as a circulating medium of exchange, previous disappointments made his task far more difficult. There was a long history of monetary manipulations by the French State which had fostered a widely-held distrust of circulating coinage. As the authorities were forever grappling with excessive levels of debt, one expedient to which they frequently resorted was to tamper with the values of the coinage, invariably to the detriment of public holders of those coins. Worries about recurrent revaluations (augmentations of the metallic coinage) was a constant brake on trading activity, as merchants could be ruined by a sudden detrimental change in the value of the currency. For a state servicing a large public debt, an augmentation was a quick route to debt-reduction as less specie was required to repay outstanding loans. In hindsight, the débâcle of the Mississippi collapse was a formative experience for French investors. It etched itself deeply into the public consciousness, so that they have subsequently held more of their wealth as gold than investors in other industrial nations.

Gold and silver metal coins formed the bi-metallic circulating media of exchange, as the louis d'or and the silver ecu, while the unit of account was the livre tournois (l.t.). This unit of account was an abstract device in the monetary system used to obviate the need for quoting the prices of goods in terms of both metals. A similar system operated in England; the pound sterling served as the unit of account although no such coin existed in the 1720s. The nearest coin was the golden guinea, worth 21 shillings (one pound and one shilling). An imaginary unit of account had a real impact on monetary affairs in a highly indebted country like France because both contracts of employment (for setting wages) and repayments of debt (for all manner of loans) were expressed in livres tournois. Arbitrary changes in its value relative to the bi-metallic media of exchange were frequent and invariably detrimental to citizens, while helping the State to balance its accounts. Law used the process of re-peated diminutions (devaluing specie relative to the money of account) not as a fiscal measure, but to advance his long-term goal of demonetis-ing specie while maintaining a low interest rate policy.

To achieve his twin aims together, Law had to hold a precarious balance between three different monetary variables, controlling them by turn. The three variables were the rate of growth of the money supply (through the quantity of circulating bank notes), the interest rate (through control of the Company's share price) and the exchange rate (the value of the French currency versus foreign currencies for de-monitising specie). Alternating control between these three central criteria generated immense contradictions in his policies and drastically destroyed confidence in his two circulating paper instruments, the shares and bank notes. In spring 1720, Law issued three conflicting decrees on 22 February, 5 March and 11 March. As the contradictory nature of these issued edicts dawned on anxious investors, the System spun into a horrendous free-fall.

The Beginning of the End

The Government's undertaking to buy any shares on offer at 9,000 livres was keeping the printing presses working non-stop. The economy was flooded with bank notes, generating a rampant inflation. A period of retrenchment was clearly desirable. At a meeting of Mississippi Company shareholders on 22 February, Banque Royale was merged with the Company, and the young King (Louis XV) sold his holdings of Company shares at 9,000 livres a share, the official support price for shares. However, the final measure of 22 February seemed an implicit acknowledgement by Law that his monetary policy was out of control. For the meeting decided to abolish the Company's office for the purchase and sale of shares (le bureau d'achat et de vente). The office had been extensively used to support the Company's share price by purchasing shares at 9,000 livres each. This support operation involved printing a huge quantity of bank notes. By closing the office Law was signalling an end to this support. He also announced that no new issues of bank notes would be made without approval by the Council in a general meeting of the Company.

Anticipating that this decree would precipitate a move out of shares, Law took two extra measures. On 25 February, hoping to stop people converting their share sales proceeds into specie, he announced an augmentation of specie, raising the gold coin (louis d'or) from 25 to 30 livres with other coins. This action was meant to warn holders of specie of an imminent diminution, whereby specie would be worth less in terms of the money of account. On 27 February, the signal that holders would have losses if they did not move out of specie and into paper notes was reinforced when Law proclaimed a prohibition, limiting the holding of specie to only 500 livres per person. By this decree the bank's inspectors could search private homes and confiscate gold or silver coins found there. Heavy fines were to be imposed on hoarders of specie. As a method of inspiring confidence in paper money, this measure was predictably counter-productive. It provoked a caustic remark from Lord Stair, the British ambassador in Paris, "there can be no doubt as to Law's catholicism, since he established the Inquisition, after already having proved transubstantiation by changing money to paper".

These decrees were designed to lock wealth holders into a choice of either bank notes or Mississippi shares. Specie was now scarce, and circulating bank notes had almost universally replaced it throughout France. Moreover, shares in the Mississippi Company were virtually the only form of quasi-government debt available to investors. They had formerly held a range of public sector paper but these had all been channelled into Mississippi paper through Law's acquisition policy for the Company des Indes. However, the swift decline in the share price in response to his 22 February edict brought howls of outraged protests from all sections of society, from princes to petite bourgeoisie now suffering losses on the market.

The Collapse of Law's System

Law's measures of 22 February, designed to halt the artificial share price support operation and arrest the over-expansion of the money supply, simply opened the flood-gates to torrents of protests. The effect on the Company's share price was dramatic. Mississippi stock lost 26 per cent of its value in one week, falling every day from 9,545 livres on 22 February to 7,825 on 29 February. The impassioned uproar against Law's decisions threatened to undermine the Regent's government. Saint Simon's observation captured the ugly public mood, "There was a most violent disturbance. Every rich man thought himself irrevocably ruined, either immediately or in the not too distant future; every poor man saw himself beggared."

By 5 March, with public clamour against the 22 February edict unabated, Law reversed the hated decree by stipulating that the Company's office for buying and selling shares would be reopened under the new name of bureau de conversions. Shares would again be purchased at a guaranteed price of 9,000 livres each. At this level the rate of interest had fallen to a little over 2 per cent consistent with his twin goals. In guaranteeing the share price at 9,000 livres in notes, he was forced to abandon money supply control. Access to metallic coinage was severely limited, suggesting the bank note monetisation was almost complete. If so, Law probably judged that the money supply problem was obsolete.

If this were his assessment, he was rapidly to be disabused of it after the ill-fated 5 March decree was made. A wild stampede to sell shares occurred when the office for conversions reopened. Confidence in them had taken a hard jolt by the rapid volte face. The selling onslaught signalled the public view that the shares were overpriced at 9,000 livres each. In printing further tranches of bank notes to satisfy the growing demand to sell shares, the uninhibited inflation was ratcheted upwards by yet another turn. Prices of all commodities, but especially food and other basic essentials, soared to fantastic heights. During the next two months 1,500 million livres bank notes went into circulation to pay for returned shares. Total notes in issue by the late spring reached a nominal value of 3 billion livres.

Inconsistent Edicts

The 5 March edict also prohibited all further dealings in options or primes, to check speculation. On 22 March, Law arranged to close the notorious rue Quincampoix. During 1719, while he was eager to stimulate enthusiasm for Mississippi shares, feverish activity there had been to his advantage. Banque Générale had been installed at number 65 in 1719. Now, however, with the share price falling, the rue Quincampoix was a natural breeding ground for hysterical rumours of every sort. Once the infamous street was closed for all share transactions, it was easier to extend the prohibition within a few days to all other districts in Paris. By these measures the era of unbridled speculation was over, but sadly, the final reckoning still lay ahead.

A final decree of 5 March was an announcement of a further augmentation of the currency from 36 to 48 livres for one louis d'or. It implied a new series of diminutions of specie against bank notes, this time with the primary motive of total demonetisation of specie. With specie no longer acting as a medium of exchange, people would be locked into the choice of either bank notes or shares. On 11 March, the decree to formalise this was made. There would be a swift demonetisation of gold by 1 May, and a phased diminution of silver in monthly instalments from 80 livres a marc to 30 livres a marc by December. This meant that from 1 May until December, the French economy would operate solely on a paper money supply, modestly augmented by silver coinage. By this edict, France became the first country in the civilised world where a man could not repay a debt or conduct any normal transaction with gold or silver coin.

Law's final demonetisation proposals had implications for foreign exchange transactions which were important for foreign investors in Mississippi shares. It implied a progressive revaluation of the French livre, denominated in bank notes, against foreign currencies denominated in specie. For example, it was predicted that the exchange rate for the silver ecu would rise from 13 pence to 50 pence sterling by the end of December. Simply stated, investors always gain in foreign exchange transactions if they move out of their own currency into one that is about to strengthen against it. However, Richard Cantillon, the banker, realised that certain conditions had to be met for this prediction to hold. First, the bank notes must maintain their value, and secondly, the devaluation of the silver coinage, promised under the 11 March decree would have to be carried out unfailingly every month. Cantillon was doubtful if these two conditions could be met and so was not convinced the French currency would appreciate in value.

The inconsistencies of Law's monetary policies now stood exposed. On 22 February, he promised not to expand the money supply to maintain confidence in the bank notes, now acting as a national paper currency. Yet only 15 days later, he promised to control the interest rate, offering to repurchase Mississippi shares at 9,000 livres in an attempt to boost confidence in the shares. By this about turn, however, he implicitly admitted the money supply could not be restricted as the 22 February edict had promised. Moreover, on 11 March, his pledge to raise the exchange rate of the French paper currency stood in contradiction to the need to continue over-expanding the money supply while holding the interest rate steady. An over-expansion of the money supply in an open economy usually causes a balance of payments deficit, which causes a decline in the exchange rate. That is, increasing the money supply leads to a fall in the exchange rate, not a rise, as Law was anticipating. Although Cantillon never referred to Law's System in his economic writings, it is clear that he recognised the intellectual arguments that were involved. Cantillon realised it would be impossible to keep the interest rate low by expanding the money supply while at the same time intending to revalue bank notes relative to specie.

Most French investors, however, were apparently impressed by Law's ability to maintain the speculative bubble. Between 7 and 30 March, a total of 45 million livres of specie were converted into bank notes at Banque Royale in Paris, while another 50 million livres were converted into bank notes in the provinces between 1 March and 13 April. Within six weeks, Law's measures had succeeded in converting one-twelfth of the estimated specie money supply into bank notes. On the surface, then, it seemed that gold specie was indeed being demonetised, bank notes were growing in popularity, and the French exchange rate was confidently expected to rise, as Law had decreed. However, the statistics show that Law's policy of prohibiting the holding and use of large sums of specie was only partially successful. By May 1720, the public held 2.1 billion livres in bank notes while Banque Royale held or was about to print another 600 million livres, but the bank held only 21 million livres in silver, 28 million in gold and 240 million in commercial bills. Despite massive open market support operations to guarantee the price of shares at 9,000 while stipulating the phased diminution of specie by another massive increase in the paper money supply, Banque Royale had virtually no specie reserves.

This was the tangible evidence that Law's ideal of a financial system based exclusively on a paper circulating currency was not yet wholly acceptable in France. Of course, the entire project had taken on the aspects of a financial whirlwind, and it is perfectly possible that a much slower pace of change would have ultimately brought a successful outcome. Indeed, events during the nineteenth century confirm this, since the paper currency that Law foresaw as an ideal circulating medium is now a routine pecuniary fact of life throughout the world.

Faced with the partial failure of his experiment, Law must have realised the measures he had introduced in March were basically flawed. The plan to phase in diminutions of silver to make paper money acceptable while building up the reserves of Banque Royale was on the point of collapse. To avoid this, Law introduced his corrective measures in May.

He was now grappling desperately to keep his system afloat. Resorting to a confidence-holding device that central bankers in years to come would repeatedly employ, Law chose a holiday to announce bad news. During Whitsuntide, on 21 May, a decree was published stipulating a phased reduction of shares and bank notes over the period from May to 1 December. The dates and reductions are shown in Table 6.

The phased diminution of the silver marc, decreed in March, had intended a reduction from 80 livres to 30 livres by December 1720. Now, on 21 May, shares and bank notes were also to be reduced with an immediate reduction of 11 per cent followed by 50 per cent for the bank notes and 44 per cent for the shares. Clearly, the March decrees had been over-ambitious and the May decree was intended to allow for a mixture of notes, shares and specie to circulate in the economy.

The Knock-out Blow

The infamous 21 May edict produced a monumental public outcry. It spelt the death knell for the "System". People finally confronted the unpalatable prospect that paper shares and notes in their pockets would be worth no more than about half their current value within six months.

Table 6 Reductions in shares and bank notes under 21 May decree

Dates	Shares	Bank notes	Reductions in silver March 11 decree
Prior to decree	9,000	10,000...100	80
21 May	8,000	8,000... 80	65 (May 1)
1 July	7,500	7,500... 75	55
1 August	7,000	7,000... 70	50
1 September	6,500	6,500... 65	45
1 October	6,000	6,000... 60	40
1 November	5,500	5,500... 55	35
1 December	5,000	5,000... 50	30

Source: Murphy, A., (1988). Reproduced by permission of Oxford University Press

It was beyond normal comprehension to accept that one's worth would not be cut in half as a result of this decree. And although it was a mere tinkering with figures, so that **within France** the purchasing power of 50 livres in December would be roughly equivalent to 100 livres in May, the psychological impact was devastating.

With a stunning naïvety, Law tried to explain this truism to the shaken populace, by insisting that no one would be harmed by the May decree. As the reduction in shares was only four-ninths, it was less than the bank note reduction (50 per cent) and specie (66 per cent). However, the fall in value was real enough in certain respects, for example, for the French when travelling abroad. Moreover, for some investors, wealth had indeed been cut in half, since bargains struck during the inflation would now have to be paid for with the devalued currency. Lord Stair, reporting back to London on the reception of this financial bomb-shell, declared Paris was like a town taken by storm. He estimated the loss to British subjects alone at £3 million.

Living in a state run as a totally authoritarian regime, where the ruler's power is unlimited, Law had been deceived into believing that his monetary reforms could be imposed as a matter of course. What he had failed to grasp is the fragility of public trust which can sometimes reach snapping point. Widespread trust was the real cement holding his shaky enterprise together. By suddenly undermining public confidence in the values of shares and paper bank notes, Law's corrective measures had precisely the opposite effect to what he had intended. Far from stabilising the System, his decree finally capsized the whole rickety structure. It marked the decisive turning point, the onset of total collapse.

Confidence did not suffer an instant decline, only ebbing slowly away, as the fall in the Mississippi share price reveals in Table 7. From June to November the monthly highs for the shares indicate a gradual descent. The June high of 6,300 fell to a July high of 5,403, then to 4,724 by August, 4,167 by October and 3,967 for November. In this respect, the slide in the value of Mississippi shares differed from the collapse in the South Sea shares which, after the peak, suffered an immediate and precipitous plunge. The reason was the acute prevailing shortage of specie in France. Investors were unavoidably locked into holding a choice of either bank notes or shares and the values of each tended to fluctuate as investors oscillated between dwindling confidence in the one as opposed to the other.

The Reconstruction Begins

With a meteoric speed, euphoria turned to revulsion against Law and his schemes. The edicts could not be enforced due to a spirited public

Table 7 Mississippi Company's share price

Date	Month high	Month low
June 1720	6,350	4,517
July	5,403	4,450
August	4,724	4,367
September	5,133	4,167
October	5,167	3,200
November	3,967	3,300

Source: Murphy, A., (1988). Reproduced by permission of Oxford University Press

protest. The Parlement refused to register the edict and after a few ago-nising days, it was revoked. Hastily, on 27 May, the Regent withdrew the previous decree of 21 May; two days later, he demoted Law from the office of Controller-General of Finance. The prohibitions on holding gold and silver were revoked and an augmentation of the bi-metallic specie was announced, to counter the former diminutions. As a crisis measure, the bank ceased to make payments in specie. In modern terminology, the bank went off the gold standard.

The excessive creation of liquidity had a more marked effect on the French exchange rate. It dropped from 20 pence sterling in mid-May to 6 pence by September and was unquoted for the last three months of the year. The greatest crisis for the collapse in the price of Mississippi shares is shown when they are expressed in sterling. In French livres, the shares fell from 10,010 livres in January 1720, to below 4,000 by November. However, the sterling price of Mississippi shares fell from over 300 in January 1720 to under 50 in September. Within a few months of his System reaching its zenith, virtually nothing remained of Law's astonishing brain-child except the legacy of a severe inflation-induced depression.

Mississippi Chaos

From start to finish the entire Mississippi saga can be illustrated by chaos as described in Part I, and viewed in terms of the eight-phase model of crashes outlined in Chapter 1. This eight-phase model can be clearly identified, although, in practice, some of the phases get packed together as events often unfold with a bewildering rapidity. This is what we might expect, for the model is a simplified version of reality, designed to help us unravel the complexities of real situations. In the real world, events may get jumbled, as they go tumbling along at a hectic, unstoppa-ble pace. The model depicts the developing tragedy of a sluggish, dor-mant system that has been jolted into life to become completely destabilised. Hence, it moves remorselessly through the eight stages, descending into chaos as events unfold. We shall therefore now review the Mississippi Bubble using chaos concepts and marking out the eight stages of the crash model as they emerged.

Before the Bubble

By 1717, the first phase of the Regent's sweeping financial reforms had produced a deeply entrenched economic paralysis. So draconian were his reforming measures, he had rendered the French economy almost moribund. Trade and industry were severely curtailed and the lack of a circulating currency in which the public could trust was an impediment to business activity. The State was almost bankrupt and confidence, along with the whole rickety economic superstructure, was acutely depressed. In chaos terms, this describes a complex damped system that is collapsing in upon itself under the pressures of a dominant negative feedback. Each contributing element reduces activity, adding another spiral to the negative feedback loop operating within it, thereby weakening it slowly towards a state of total inertia.

Phase One – The Trigger: Law Intervenes

This dampening is a gradual self-feeding process. It can only be arrested by introducing a positive feedback loop, powerful enough to neutralise the potent negative impacts. Law's intervention was the trigger in the ensuing bubble drama. His actions initiated the train of aggressive events that led to the climax of the crash. To fulfil his primary objectives, he was anxious to re-energise the torpid economy. Using the chaos mechanisms that underpin real activities, he could only achieve this by overwhelming the prevalent powerful negative feedback that held the economy in its ever-tightening grip. To break this negative spiral, he had to generate more activity within the sluggish economy.

Phase Two – Easy Credit Fuels the Boom

Law's first objective was to open a bank, boost confidence in it, and make his bank notes widely accepted for general trade and business. He saw rising confidence as a positive antidote to the negative torpor afflicting the economy. By June 1719, with evidence mounting daily that phenomenal returns could be made with virtually no effort, interest in the Company's shares suddenly began to escalate. This enabled the uptrend of the rising share price to swiftly become established. We can therefore identify early June 1719 as the moment when Law himself deliberately changed the nature of his evolving System. In the space of just a few months, it went from a relatively calm, stable state, attracting only moderate interest, to a frenetic, rampantly unstable state with mass public participation.

By his actions in bringing to market a sequence of attractively packaged rights issues in quick succession, with a series of very small down-payments and many follow-on instalments, he not only maintained the interest, he initiated a mounting hysteria to possess the shares at any price. To be eligible for the new issues, purchasers had to own some of the old, thus enhancing the hectic demand for both old and new shares. In double-quick time, the drama moved on through phase three of the crashes model, with inflationary share price rises, to phase four, pure speculation.

Positive Feedback and the Share Price Uptrend

As the intensity for owning the shares gathered greater momentum by the day, the positive feedback loop swung into overdrive. In an uptrend, the main response of a rising share price is a further rise, while sellers hold back, hoping to sell later at even higher prices. When everyone is a buyer and sellers hold back, a stock shortage develops, adding yet an-other turn to the spiralling positive feedback loop. The buying frenzy appears to be self-feeding, but this is simply reflecting the reality of the intense positive feedback mechanism now working its way feverishly around the system. Law exploited the speculative mania he had un-leashed with his sequence of rights issues, confident that demand would far outstrip supply, so essential if he were to keep the uptrend intact. The succession of new share issues, each linked to a large issue of new bank notes to facilitate the take-up of new shares, set in motion a potent chain reaction of a rising share price to accompany each flotation in turn.

So enthusiastically were these issues received that within a matter of about five months, by November 1719, the market value of the Company exceeded 4.75 billion livres. And whereas shares were changing hands for around 650 livres each on 17 June, by late November each share had reached a value 10 times that sum, fluctuating between 5,800 and 7,400 livres, depending on availability.

The Financial Pump

While it was necessary for Law to arouse a great interest in the invest-ing public to buy his shares, this stupendous spurt within a matter of five months could not have occurred if people had no cash with which to buy more shares. Providing cash was possible only because Law had access to a bank printing press. Through his direct link with Banque Royale, he could introduce into his expanding System the dynamism of a fully operational chaotic pump. By repeatedly feeding additional bank notes into circulation, he established an open financial pump that spread with explosive speed through the entire French economy. The massive note issue, coupled with the outpouring of new share issues swiftly produced a gigantic driven system, surging furiously towards its precarious climax, and the price of Mississippi shares spiralled completely out of control. As in all true chaos situations, the equilibrium of sellers matching buyers had been irreparably disturbed by the abrupt emergence of a financial pump; its action is shown in Figure 21.

The direct link of excess credit stoking a boom and bust in financial assets is the second stage of the eight-stage model. It marks the second phase in the evolving substructure on the route to chaos and is followed in short order by a dramatic inflationary rise in the price of consumer goods and financial assets. This is stage three of the typical crash model. Both the excess credit and its rapid impact on the price of financial assets are essentially chaos features of the expanding boom. They constitute the

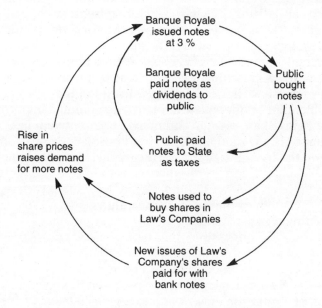

Figure 21 The financial pump of the Mississippi Bubble

financial pump and the positive feedback loop of rising prices. Indeed together this element of excess credit (the pump) and its resulting inflationary impact (the positive feedback loop) are integral aspects of the classic formula for the repetition of crashes over 300 years of industrial financial history.

Law's Financial Pump

Preparing the ground in the run-up to the share issues, Law arranged for the Banque Royale to put 180 million livres of bank notes into circulation between January and July 1719. Each share issue was accompanied by an issue of new bank notes, further fuelling the pump. When the final huge issue of 324,000 shares was launched in November 1719, another deluge of notes was discharged into circulation. Law's decision to support the share price on a plateau of around 9,000 livres during January to March 1720, seriously distorted the market and the note issue had to be increased yet again to absorb all the selling and keep the share price stable and high. By May 1720, a glut of 2.1 billion livres was circulating.

Once a financial pump is set in motion, the boom/bust cycle becomes predictable because the emergent structure is intensely unstable. It cannot support itself in this volatile state. The timing and details in each example will vary, due to the chaos feature of "sensitive dependence on initial conditions". On the detailed sequences, they will be intrinsically unpredictable, but the determinism of the long-run behaviour of such events is evident from the historical record.

The trick is to recognise the chaos elements that have been introduced to enable the pump to drive the system up to its inevitable peak and crash. The operation of the financial pump flips rational investors into a manic state through a phase transition event. Excessively irrational behaviour follows the creation of the financial pump because people begin to succumb to the lure of easy credit and exaggerated expectations.

Phase Three – Inflation in Assets

In France during the Mississippi speculation, asset prices, especially in stocks, bonds and property, rose astonishingly, and prices rapidly lost contact with fair values. There were manic scenes with crowds of people frantic to buy shares. Ostentatious consumption and a burgeoning growth in debt to buy financial assets were visible signs of the rising instability as we observed in Chapters 1 and 2.

Phase Four – Overtrading and Nonlinear Speculative Gains

This marked the onset of stage four in the crashes model, with over-trading and the emergence of pure speculation with increased borrowing to participate. Early in 1719, Law had introduced the idea of options to stimulate interest in Mississippi shares by entering into a large call option contract. His derivative instrument relied on the chaos non-linearity effect of a small outlay producing a large result. The gearing gives the investor credit as the outlays are small in relation to the possible returns. With a true gambler's instinct, Law's spring 1719 options on the shares were worth more than 10 times their par value of 500 livres (in excess of 5,000 livres) when they matured in September 1719, as the share price moved into a strong uptrend. His options illustrate the non-linear gearing effect on the plus side.

Speculation and the Lure of Huge Gains

The sorry tale of Lady Mary Herbert's insatiable urge to speculate illustrates the reverse result; magnified losses from a relatively modest outlay. In January 1720, she entered into a contract to convert 70 old Mississippi shares, each valued at around 9,250 livres, (worth 647,000 livres) into 600 call options or primes, valued at 1,050 each (worth 630,000 livres). This contract gave her access to a greatly expanded quantity of new shares. The nonlinearity and gearing could now operate either in a positive (producing a gain) or in a negative (losing) direction. If the market had risen further, the shares may have reached 12,000 livres. At this level, the 70 original shares would have been worth 840,000 livres, but the primes would probably have risen livre for livre with the rise in the underlying shares, taking them up to a value of 3,800 livres ([12,000 − 9,250 = 2,750] + 1,050). Her 600 primes would then have been worth 2.28 million livres. Unfortunately, her speculation began at the January peak; the market was set on a steady descent and her losses were greatly magnified.

The actual state of her affairs was complicated by the sheer extent of her dealing, most of it on borrowed money secured as loans. Murphy tabulates a prodigious total of her accumulated debts (on loans and losses) at £172,385 by mid-1720. However, to show the implications of her options deal, we know that by June, the shares were worth roughly one half of their January total. At June's highest price of 6,350, although her 70 old shares were still worth 350,000 livres, the primes value would have probably shrunk by more than half, to less than 500 livres each, assuming she had been able to cancel out her bargain. At 500 livres each prime, her investment of 600 primes would then be worth only 300,000 livres, but it would have been worth much less, if the primes fell below 500 livres.

Prospects for substantial nonlinear gains also featured strongly in the persuasive marketing ploys Law used in June 1719, to successfully float his new share issues. The small initial down-payment and the lengthy instalment plans for purchasing the shares were providing a form of credit for both small and wealthy investors alike. This credit would not have been available if all the shares had to be fully paid for at the outset. But, due to its geared effect, the easy purchase terms gave early investors the opportunity to lay out just a modest sum, which quickly resulted in spectacular returns. As we saw, the purchaser of a partly paid fille bought early in June 1719 on the initial downpayment of a mere 50 livres premium, could make a profit of 450 livres by mid-July, a gain of nine times his modest outlay within about one month.

The Phase Transition for Investors

Phases four and five, with speculation rampant, mark the **onset of a phase transition in the behaviour of the majority of Mississippi investors; it denotes the point at which, collectively, they changed from a rational to an irrational state**. Their outward behaviour in the frantic buying of shares and audacious displays of newly acquired wealth was the manifestation of this phase transition event. They were physically the same people but they exhibited entirely different characteristics to their previous conduct before the financial pump energised their greed motives. The daily spiral in the price of Mississippi shares rendered them number-drunk, making it impossible to maintain a rational concept of what represented "fair value" in the shares. Not everyone would succumb to this mania, nor would they all respond exactly in unison, but for the majority, the greatest urge now was to speculate immediately – to buy at any price – on the optimistic assumption that shares could quickly be sold on for a magnificent instant gain. The period when most investors were at the greatest risk of succumbing to a phase transition response would have been from mid-1719 to 22 February 1720, with the share price sprinting ever upwards, as the System slid remorselessly towards an unstable climax.

Phase Five – Crowds Pile In: The Market at the Peak

Early in 1720, the buying frenzy escalated even further, carrying the share price up briefly above 10,000 livres. In the run-up to this summit event when boom turns to bust, the level of mass participation increased. Law's fame spread quickly and fantastic tales of incredible fortunes being made on a daily basis drew people into Paris, as if it were a magnet. Thousands flocked in from the provinces and from abroad to join Parisians in their clamour to buy shares.

Chain Reactions for the Mississippi Company Affairs

The chain reaction effect was noticed by Law himself, when he observed in the *Mercure de France* in February 1720 how each step in the development of his grand design seemed to follow in a sequence of progressions. This unity in his planning obviously appealed to his mathematical leanings, but it is squarely based on the chaos effect of a chain reaction in the unfolding sequence of events.

Determinism

As the share speculation reached the peak, massive runaway positive feedback loops destabilised the market, sending prices to unsustainable heights and the collapse became inevitable. The chart for the soaring Mississippi share price (see Figure 22) shows the bubble-like nature of the rapid rise and swift decline, but it is distorted by the relatively long period between March and May 1720, when the price was officially supported at 9,000 livres. This chart pattern is not a convincing depiction of a strange attractor for this bubble event. However, it does endorse the consistent graphic appearance of the boom/bust scenario. There is invariably a rapidly rising trend, on high volume of participation, to reach a peak. This produces a characteristic pattern, in this case taking the form of a modified head and shoulders. This graphic format has a distinct, recognisable chart appearance, a strange attractor, no less, for the Mississippi Bubble. It depicts the long-run behaviour of the whole event. Points that do not lie on the strange attractor will be drawn towards it, so that, over time, the full pattern should emerge unless some unpredicted element intrudes, when the pattern will fail.

Order Descending into Chaos

For the Mississippi crisis, as the speculative mania took hold, the mix of initial order in the damped, depressed economy gave way to scenes implying the onset of a rapid descent into chaos as the financial pump

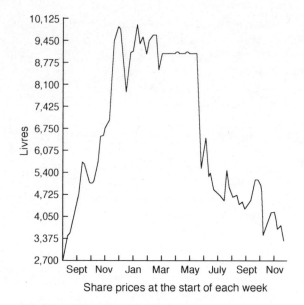

Figure 22 Mississippi Company's share prices (August 1719 to November 1720) showing the distortion to the price action by holding the price steady at 9,000 livres from March to May 1720.

Source: Murphy, A., (1988). Reproduced by permission of Oxford University Press

wrought its damage. Thousands crowded into the small city of Paris at the height of the boom. Frenetic activity occurred in the cramped over-crowded rue Quincampoix where shares were traded. The exploits of numerous speculators suggest mass hysteria was gripping the investing community.

As the climactic peak arrived, the chaos of the ensuing collapse took hold, although there was a brief interlude before the massive selling crescendo got underway. This was the sixth stage of the model, when the first doubts began to surface. We shall examine the history of the spiralling decline that replaced the boom in Chapter 9, but first we will look at how the English bubble unfolded.

CHAPTER EIGHT

THE SOUTH SEA FIASCO

The demon stock jobbing is the genius of this place. This fills all hearts, tongues, and thoughts, and nothing is so like bedlam as the present humour which has seized all parties... No one is satisfied with even exorbitant gains, but every one thirsts for more, and all this is founded upon a machine of paper credit supported only by imagination. . . .

Letter from Edward Harley to his brother, Robert Harley
24 June 1720 (1 day after South Sea shares peaked)

It seems incredible that two unprecedented financial bubbles occurred simultaneously in 1720, but the two financial manias that swept through France and England had essentially the same root cause: the high costs of the War of the Spanish Succession. Both bubbles are uniquely interesting in themselves and in their comparative histories, which illustrate the chaos concept of sensitive dependence on initial conditions. From the same peace, both attempted to solve the debt problem, and each solution was similar yet different in many ways, but both episodes reveal the key features and onset of chaos as discussed in general in Part I and in the last chapter on the Mississippi Bubble. Here, we shall follow the chequered tale of the South Sea saga, beginning with its incorporation in 1711.

Founding the New Company

In England, raising long- and short-term credit to finance William III's extravagant wars had grossly increased speculation. The credit arrangements were arbitrary, primitive and disorganised. Apart from its prime purpose of raising money to continue the wars, the Bank of England was founded to reorganise the ramshackle state credit and ease the problems of transferring money to the armies in Europe to provision them in these never-ending wars. By offering to raise and supply money to the King to consolidate future credit facilities, the Bank's directors, part of the powerful Whig faction which was also the party in office at the time, had become an important political force. In 1711, these political considerations prompted Robert Harley, soon to be Earl of Oxford, to found the Tory-based South Sea Company, as a counterbalance to the Whig-oriented Bank.

Initially, there was no dishonest intent in the founding of the Company; it was yet another attempt to alleviate the growing national burden of prosecuting the continental wars. In keeping with its grandiose trading aspirations the Company acquired a coat of arms and South Sea House, its splendidly imposing headquarters office. This spacious building was situated in the City, at the corner of Threadneedle Street and Bishopsgate. In its founding Charter, the Company agreed to take over £9.5 million of the national debt in return for a monopoly of trade to South America and the islands of the Pacific, territories thought to possess unlimited riches. Prospects were greatly enhanced in 1713, when, under the celebrated Assiento Treaty, it acquired from Spain the monopoly of importing Negro slaves into Spanish America, a move thought to greatly enhance future prospects. However, the Spanish soon violated the treaty, its benefits never materialised, and the Company did virtually no trading. Its impressive prospects met a sceptical public reception as the shares, with a par value of £100, stood at a discount at £77.5 shortly after the Charter was granted.

The Conversion Scheme is Hatched

In 1718 the recently crowned Hanoverian King George I became the Company's new Governor, adding his royal prestige. For the first few years, opportunities for trade were constrained by the lack of a formal peace treaty with Spain. Meanwhile, the fortunes of the rival Bank of England were rising strongly. By 1717 it had gained a significant role in the national credit system, as its founders had intended. They were now contemplating expansion, along the lines newly introduced by John Law in France. By 1719 John Blunt, one of the Directors, saw expansion possibilities for the South Sea Company, with opportunities for monetary gains by adopting measures similar to those underway in France. He realised schemes for conversion of the national debt would increase the fortunes of both the Company and its Directors. News of massive price rises for Mississippi shares spurred his efforts. The meteoric rise in Mississippi stock was an endorsement for Law's policies. The obvious improvement in France's fiscal position, together with evidence of a newly risen inflationary prosperity, helped to encourage public enthusiasm for the Directors' plans, which were launched in January 1720.

The initial plan was to convert the entire national debt, of £51.5 million, into Company shares to abolish the entire debt over a 25-year period. This ambitious scheme was soon scaled back as it involved the virtual take-over of both the Bank of England and the East India Company, whose combined holdings of government debt amounted to £6.6 millions. Pressure groups in both influential institutions were sufficiently powerful to block this result. The fortuitous failure of the South Sea Company to take over the Bank of England prevented the English Company from following the disastrous course taken by the Mississippi Company with an excessive expansion of the money supply as its chosen route for supporting the share price.

The Benefits from Conversion for the Government

As with the French scheme, the South Sea Company's proposal to take over the national debt promised benefits for both sides. The advantages for the Government were considerable. The state of its existing liabilities was appalling, comprising a rag-bag assortment of irredeemable and redeemable securities with varying rates of interest, together with debt held by the Bank of England (£3.4 million) and the East India Company (£3.2 million). Thirty-one million pounds of government debt was in private hands. It consisted of £16.5 million as redeemable securities and £15 million as irredeemables. The latter included both short- and long-term annuities, with the Government committed to pay a specified amount of interest annually for a set number of years. The high interest payments on these annuities were an expensive burden on the Exchequer. An interest rate of 9 per cent was paid on the short annuities, due to expire in 1742, while the long annuities, paying 7 per cent, would expire between 1792–1807. They were termed irredeemables as they could not be repurchased or converted into redeemable debt without the express authority of the holders. This restriction explains the importance the Directors attached to efforts for persuading a majority of private annuitants to convert their holdings into South Sea stock.

The South Sea plan would help the Government by consolidating all the securities at a lower rate of interest. The State would owe the South Sea Company a debt equivalent to the converted stock, but it would be uniform, redeemable at the Government's option, and have a lower rate of interest. Initially, the Company offered to convert all the debt, including that held by the Bank of England and the East India Company, into a stock on which the Government would pay 5 per cent interest until 1727 and 4 per cent thereafter. There was to be an immediate lump-sum payment of £3 million for the right to convert the debt. This proposal offered yearly savings to the Exchequer of £542,000 in reduced interest payments. John Aislabie, Chancellor of the Exchequer, strongly supported the scheme. He planned a sinking fund for the £542,000, to wipe out the debt within 25 years.

The Benefits from Conversion for the South Sea Company

To achieve short-term relief on government interest payments plus the long-term prospect of eliminating the entire national debt seems like financial alchemy, with substantial potential benefits to both parties. Yet once the mechanisms underpinning the conversion scheme are understood, it becomes lucidly clear why the fraudulent Directors went to such extreme lengths to support the price of South Sea shares.

The nominal capital of the Company would increase by the amount of the debt exchanged. However, there was no stipulation in the agreement on the **price** at which the Government stock should be rated for the purpose of that exchange. For example, if £100 of South Sea stock was exchanged for £100 of government stock, the capital of the company grew by £100. With the stock at £200, the Company could convert the entire £32 million of government stock by issuing just £16 million of its shares. At a price of £200 the Company could issue another 16 million new shares, raising £32 million of capital for its own purposes. Any price above £100, therefore, offered it the potential for a "fund of credit", through the gap that emerged between the actual issued and the potentially issuable capital of the Company.

The size of this potential "fund of credit" that might be raised for its own account, depended upon two factors: first, the total amount of Government debt converted into South Sea shares; and secondly, the price at which government debt was converted into the shares. The new "fund of credit" would be greatest for the largest amount of government debt converted at prices above £100. Although potentially £32 million could be achieved, if all the privately held government debt was exchanged for South Sea shares, it was clear that through general inertia alone, many private holders would need strong inducements to agree to convert their holdings.

The nominal price of South Sea stock was £100. If all the outstanding debt was exchanged for South Sea shares at £100, the Company would have no fund of credit and both the Company and its shareholders would have made losses on the conversion scheme. The Company loss would be considerable, since it had promised to pay the Government £3 million to take over the debt. The shareholders would also suffer a loss, by accepting a lower rate of interest than that which was paid on their annuities prior to conversion. At a conversion price of say, £200, the equations looked completely different. The issuable capital of the Company would increase by £16 million, and, assuming all this was sold at £200 per share, the Company would secure a fund of credit worth £32 million to use for its own investment purposes. At a conversion price of £300, the potential fund would be £64 million, and so forth, as the stock rose to £400, £500, or even higher. The miracle of exponential compound gains looks as tantalising today as it certainly seemed to the avaricious Directors in 1720.

Two major points of the Government's agreement with the Company, as incorporated in the Act, virtually ensured the directors would pursue a fraudulent course. First, the Act failed to place any statutory limit on the height to which the share price was allowed to rise, and it made no provision for sharing any excess profit above a set level between the Company and the Government. The second omission was even more serious; for the Act wholly failed to define the precise terms to be offered to annuitants for conversion of their holdings into South Sea stock. In the noisy clamour to reform the nation's ramshackle public finances, scant attention was paid by Members of Parliament in debate to the niceties of the scheme. The Directors went to great lengths to gain MPs' support, with bribery through spicy share allocations, which may explain these oversights.

The money raised by issuing new shares was not profits *per se*. It was extra capital the Company could use to buy new assets on which to make more profits. During 1720, as it swung into action, the Company issued £10 million of stock in money subscriptions at issue prices of £300, £400 and £1,000. The cash it would receive if all the calls had been met was £75 million, a vast investment fund, virtually a monopoly of new funds for investment purposes coming onto the market. It is doubtful if such a massive fund could have been invested in profitable ventures. Indeed, investment in its designated trading area, the South Seas, would take several years to produce results, but these inconveniences were not the dominant concerns of potential South Sea investors as the Company "hype" swung into action.

The Scheme Takes Off

Early in 1720, the scheme ran into fierce opposition from the Whig-backed Bank of England. They made a £5 million counter-bid and agreed on a quicker reduction to a 4 per cent interest rate. By a crude Dutch auction of competing offers, the South Sea Company finally out-bid the Bank. It would pay £7.75 million for the right to take over the national debt. This was the public cost of securing Parliamentary approval, but behind the scenes outrageous bribes to the influential, including members of the cabinet, MPs, peers and court favourites, had added another £1.3 million in hidden costs. To cap the rival Bank of England bids, plus bribes to ensure the Bill reached the Statute books had hugely increased the Company's initial liabilities. Such immense indebtedness explains the pressure the Directors were under, inducing them to resort to reckless methods for maintaining the share price.

The Need for Cash

An Act of Parliament was necessary to endorse the successful scheme, and it duly passed through the House of Commons on 2 April with a majority of 172 to 55, with consent from the House of Lords on 7 April, by a majority of 82 to 17. The Bill received the Royal Assent that day.

Prolific letters and documentation available from the period allow us to catch an intimate glimpse of just how simple it was for even the most level-headed bystanders to become sucked up in the whirlwind of speculative mayhem that now ensued. As we saw in Chapter 2, no less a rational person than the brilliant scientist, Sir Isaac Newton and the great Robert Walpole were both tempted to re-enter the market at the peak. And Parliamentary involvement was extremely high. To ensure the scheme became law, the clique of fraudulent directors granted potential supporters fictitious holdings of stock at highly favourable prices prior to the South Sea legislation being passed. The share price had risen sharply, anticipating a successful passage through Parliament. Once the Act received the Royal Assent, the Company credited the holders of the imaginary shares with sales at the higher market prices so their "profits" could be paid out without any purchase money changing hands. Beneficiaries of this substantial bribe included John Aislabie (the Chancellor of the Exchequer), Charles Stanhope, John Craggs, the Earl of Sunderland, and other prominent politicians. A "slush fund" of ready cash was needed now, to pay out these bribes, and this was secured by inviting subscriptions for shares in cash, within a week of obtaining the Royal Assent. Any efforts directed at converting the national debt took second place to the immediate need of raising enough money to reward these influential supporters. Robert Knight, the Company's cashier, kept a special book, "the green book", for allocating stock without payments to the King, the Prince of Wales and some ministers of the Crown, to enable them to take "profits" later, although evidence suggests the King paid for all his shares in full. Many entries in the books were entirely fictitious, but most of the advantages from the Government had been purchased by the Directors with gifts and money inducements to serving ministers of the day. John Aislabie, the Chancellor of the Exchequer, in charge of the Bill on its passage into law through the House of Commons, acquired £70,000 of stock through this fictitious device.

The Money Subscriptions Begin

The price of South Sea stock was 130 in the first week of January 1720 and 180 by the start of March. The country was bracing itself for the coming boom as wild rumours spread from London to the provinces. "South Sea is all the talk and fashion," Mrs Windham wrote to her relatives in Norfolk, "The ladies sell their jewels to bye, and hapy are they to be in. . . . But first the dealers are the greatest gainers. . . . Never was such a time to get money as now." As the boom raced on, the rising share price reflected the growing delirium. When the Government chose the Company's conversion scheme rather than that proposed by the Bank of England, the shares began to leap ahead. In early April, during the Bill's passage through both Houses, the share price fluctuated between 250 and 380 but soon shot up to 400 when the Bill was passed before profit-taking pulled it back below 300. On 7 April, with the Royal Assent, the stock stood at 335. The price was soon roaring up again when the Company announced its First Money Subscription, swiftly followed by the first loan offer. On 14 April, two million of South Sea stock at £300 a share were offered, hoping to raise £6 million. This was the first of three immensely successful money subscriptions the Company made in quick succession within the brief space of 10 weeks. A further two money subscriptions, one in August and one in September were desperate measures by the cash-strapped Directors to keep the Company afloat.

As with the Mississippi scheme, to ensure success for the Directors' prime objective, namely, raising public interest in the shares, all the share issues were attractively marketed to entice the public to buy. In this first subscription, only a cash down-payment of 20 per cent was required, (just £60). Alternatively, bonds of the East India or Sword Blade Companies could be offered. The remaining £240 was to be met by eight calls of 10 per cent at two-monthly intervals (£30 per call). These easy, irresistible terms meant a small down-payment of only £60 immediately secured rights to a South Sea share with a market price at the time of well above £300 and rising daily.

On 20 April the Company announced the terms of its first loan. It agreed to lend a total of £500,000 to existing shareholders at the rate of

£250 each for each £100 stock (then worth £330 per share). A maximum borrowing limit of £5,000 per person was set. To illustrate the attraction of this loan, consider the position of a favoured investor who could immediately borrow the maximum £5,000. He acquired rights to 125 shares when the Second Money Subscription for shares was announced soon after, on 29 April. This highly geared position promised large capital gains as the share price headed rapidly above £400 in response to the surfeit of tempting offers.

Two weeks after the First Money Subscription, on 30 April, annuity holders were invited to subscribe, by registering their securities for transfer into South Sea stock, although no terms for this transfer were announced. Indeed, these terms, so crucial for investors planning to exchange their government debt for shares, were only published on 19 May. The Second Money Subscription was announced on 29 April, just nine days after the first loan had given investors ample ready cash. The formal issue was for £1 million of South Sea stock at £400 per share, although actually a total of £1.5 million was issued. Again the terms for this offer were delightfully easy, to encourage widespread public participation. The down-payment was 10 per cent (£40) with the balance payable at three- to four-monthly intervals. South Sea stock was now rising meteorically as these money-spinning offers, appearing in rapid succession, whipped up a euphoric bull market.

The Company hoped to raise £10 million through the first two money subscriptions, but as there had been an over-issue of stock on both occasions, the total issued amounted to £12.5 million. Very little of this money was forthcoming immediately, however, as the easy payments meant the cash would trickle into the company over several months. The over-issue of shares was officially attributed to a communications failure between the issuing clerks registering subscription receipts. In reality, it allowed Company insiders to realise substantial profits through retrospective share issues to themselves and their supporters.

Deliberate Methods to Fuel the Boom

From the outset, the Directors faced the need to maintain the South Sea share price, to achieve the largest possible "fund of credit" on the conversion of government debt. This meant fuelling the stock market boom with continuous injections of liquidity into the market. Without sufficient credit, the buying surge would fizzle out, a situation they were keen to prevent at any cost. The Directors had no direct link to the Bank of England, which was hostile to their whole operation, so they could not resort to the relatively easy process of printing bank notes to support the share price, as Law had done in France. The techniques they devised involved increasing the **demand** for additional buying by whetting investors appetites while deliberately restricting the **supply** of available shares.

Recycling the Funds

To encourage buying the Directors adopted attractive marketing ploys, imitating many of the Mississippi Company's successful tactics. They maintained buying interest to sustain the price momentum with small initial down-payments coupled with lengthy payment periods for the money subscriptions, to motivate small investors, while offering tempting loans to entice richer investors to take up highly geared positions in the stock. Their underlying share support strategy relied on the circulation of money in the economy. The more money in circulation, the faster prices of everything else will rise. An increase in money acts like adding water to wine. The more water you add, the more wine there will be, but as it will be far weaker than it was at the outset, you will need far greater amounts of the diluted wine to make you drunk. Similarly, increasing the amount of money in circulation which cannot be utilised in genuine new production, simply forces up the price of all commodities, creating an inflationary boom. There are several ways to support the boom. Printing more notes is only the most blatant direct route to increase money in circulation, as the total number of available notes rises. This produces the old cliché, "too much money chasing too few goods". Lowering the interest rate has a similar effect. Cheaper credit releases into the economy some of the money that would have been used for debt repayments. This money can be saved or spent. Cheaper credit adds to the amount of freely circulating money, as it encourages more borrowing. The money can be double-counted. When lent, it is a spendable loan to the borrower while remaining on the lender's books as a debt that will eventually be repaid. So this same cash is a store of "money" to both parties. Magically, it now belongs to two different owners and so has a magnified effect on the cash in circulation.

A third technique to support an inflationary boom stems from any means of increasing the rate at which notes circulate in the economy. As money passes more rapidly from one owner to another, it produces exactly the same result as an over-expansion of the money supply. The quicker money circulates, the greater the number of "hands" through which it passes, allowing a far greater number of completed transactions. It gives the same result as if there were actually more notes around, simply because of the extra speed with which it changes hands. While merely an illusion, this effect increases spending and trade.

The broad strategy the directors adopted to restrict supply while increasing demand centred on an increase in the velocity of circulating money. This was achieved by raising funds through three highly successful Money Subscriptions (a further two in August and September were mainly attempts to shore up the failing enterprise). They then rechannelled this same money back to shareholders in three loan offers, enabling them to re-use the same money to buy more shares. The Directors had access to almost unlimited credit from their bankers, the infamous Sword Blade Company, and approximately £5 million was pumped into the market as credit, to lubricate the wheels of this money-go-round dynamo. Raising money with this technique and keeping it within the narrow Company orbit, the directors increased the circulating velocity of money. Although there was bound to be some seepage, they had, in effect created a closed recycling money loop, shown in Figure 23.

The loans served an added purpose since **they greatly restricted the supply of shares on the market**. Borrowers had to lodge their existing holdings of stock with the Company as collateral for the loans, thus withdrawing large numbers of shares from the available supply. Three loans were made on 20 April, 20 May and 1 June. The close link between the loans and new subscription offers ensured the borrowed funds were

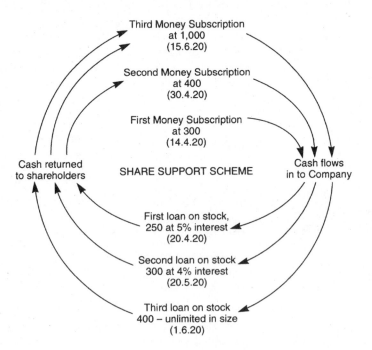

Figure 23 The closed money circuit for South Sea Company shares

recycled directly back into shares, around the narrow loop, with minimum leakage. This is clearly seen from the dates for the first three
money subscriptions on 14 April and 30 and 18 June.

Another ploy the Directors used to limit the supply of stock while
interest was maintained at fever pitch, was to **delay until December** the
issue of South Sea shares to annuitants and holders of redeemable stock
who had registered their securities for **exchange in April or early May**.
This delay kept a large block of newly issued South Sea shares off the
market and prevented the annuitants selling out early. While the directors master-minded the delicate balance of reduced supply and rising
demand, lavishly wild rumours on improved trading prospects for the
Company circulated in the market, together with stories on increases in
the dividend, and expectations of further increases. The South Sea Bubble was swiftly moving into top gear.

Rising Expectations

The 19 May announcement of terms for the conversion of annuities had
been eagerly awaited. It was pivotal to the Directors' plans. Annuitants'
stock was not to be converted at par; instead the Company would convert
the government debt at a price of £375, creating the possibility of future
large share issues for its own account. The scheme was made attractive to
annuitants by offering them 32 years purchase for long-term and 17 years
for short-term stock. These were generous terms relative to the original
prices annuitants had paid for their stock. With South Sea stock now
moving above 400 in the scramble to buy, the incentives to convert looked
overwhelming. So enthusiastically was the news received, within six days
of the announcement a quarter of annuitants had accepted the terms and
lodged their government holdings at South Sea House.

The good news for the Directors, at a price of £400, meant double the
quantity of stock could be converted than at £200. Each conversion of
stock at a higher price increased the potential size of the fund of credit as
more government stock would be converted in exchange for smaller
amounts of Company stock. To meet the flood of paperwork, 70 clerks
and 28 additional staff were assigned to handle the rush. In a letter to
Earl Stanhope, Secretary Craggs described the seething pandemonium
surrounding South Sea House.

> It is impossible to tell you what a rage prevails here for South Sea Subscriptions
> at any price. The crowd of those who possess the redeemable annuities is so
> great that the Bank, who are obliged to take them in, has been forced to set
> tables with clerks in the street.

The Bubble Companies Explosion

Mouth-watering prospects for instant gains aroused a frenzy of stock-jobbing activity in Exchange Alley during the summer of 1720. Unlike the French situation, where Law's acquisition policy had virtually scooped up all the opposition trading companies into the orbit of his monopolistic Mississippi Company, free enterprise thrived in London. Venture capitalists had been flourishing for years and were a growing force. Between September 1719 and September 1720, public subscriptions for about 190 bubble companies had been opened. Of these, only two, Chetwynd's and Onslow's insurances achieved charter status on 4 May, but this was granted only after they had jointly contributed £600,000 towards extinguishing the arrears on the King's Civil List. Both these insurance companies survive to this day as the London and the Royal Exchange Assurances respectively.

As excitement mounted, interest in stocks became international, from Dublin to Hamburg. South Sea prices were quoted in local broadsheets, like the *Plymouth Weekly Journal*. To take advantage of this heightened interest, there was a dramatic mushrooming in the numbers of copy-cat companies, most of which were not officially incorporated and many indeed were outright swindles. Rapidly dubbed "bubble companies", they advertised themselves in the daily broadsheets now circulating freely in London. During May and the first fortnight of June, over 100 were advertised, despite the Bill then passing through the House of Commons to suppress them. Newspapers doubled in size to carry all the notices. On 7 June, there were 23, by 9 June, 24 and another 15 on 10 June. Many made weird, impossible claims for wealth creation and were patently fraudulent or simply hoaxes. Yet as the South Sea share price shot ever upwards so did shares of these aspiring upstart imitators. Their extraordinary claims reveal the span of the collective mania now spiralling out of control. There were companies to supply Deal with fresh water, for the planting of mulberry trees and the breeding of silkworms in Chelsea Park, for trading in human hair, for insuring of horses, for draining bogs in Ireland, for making oil from sunflower seeds and for a wheel of perpetual motion.

The Bubble Hysteria

As we saw with the ferment exploding in the rue Quincampoix as Mississippi shares daily scaled new heights, so now the environs of Exchange Alley were crammed with a seething pack of jobbers, yelling, scurrying and gesticulating as they darted to and fro between the many coffee shops where trade was briskly transacted. Aristocrats and courtiers, both men and women, readily identified by their richly elaborate costumes of silks and velvets, ribbons and lace, with swords and voluminous wigs, jostled among the less well-accoutred mobs and the lower classes, all clamouring to buy.

One oddity was the ease with which married women participated in the speculation, through the quaint omission of any law to restrain them. This oversight sheds an amusing light on how rapidly the contagion of popular share ownership was spreading. The abruptness with which public involvement in capitalist enterprises exploded onto the scene is nowhere so visibly apparent than in this legal anomaly. Among many who availed themselves of this fleeting opportunity were ladies of the Prince of Wales's Court, the Duchess of Rutland, the Countess of Gainsborough and the formidable Sarah, Duchess of Marlborough. There was even a bubble company exclusively for the patronage of women which exorted the fashion-conscious to buy only British-made goods, in an effort to relieve distress in the woollen and cotton industries.

Ostentation Booms

The ostentation of sudden affluence was blatantly flaunted everywhere. One journalist noted,

> since the hurly-burly of stockjobbing, there has appeared in London 200 new Coaches & Chariots, besides as many more now on the Stocks in the Coachmakers' yards; about 4,000 embroider'd coats; about 3,000 gold watches at the sides of whores and wives; and some few private acts of charity.

As the London season reached its climax, lavish jewellery displays and other conspicuous trappings of instant wealth abounded. At a celebration to mark the King's birthday, the portly Duchess of Kendal wore a dress covered in gems worth £5,000, while a feast to commemorate his elevation as a Knight of the Garter cost the Earl of Sunderland £2,000.

One ominous sign of the spiralling credit inflation was the rise in land prices. Around London, land fetched nearly 45 times the annual rent. So close was the correspondence of property prices with the South Sea share price, it was noted in auction rooms to encourage bidders. Loss of advertising revenues in the broadsheets after the Bubble Companies Act was passed, prohibiting their promotion to the public, was soon compensated for by a stream of notices of estates for sale. At least one bubble promoter is known to have become an instant estate agent to handle rising demand. And foremost among those rushing to own landed estates were officers and directors of the South Sea Company, who had made fortunes in the run-up to securing the Royal Assent back in April. Between June and September, Gibbon and Chaplin spent £20,000, and Houlditch nearly double that. Deputy Cashier Surman made purchases of land worth almost £180,000 in the summer and autumn. Not all his contracts were completed, but they related to 27 properties in nine counties. Sir John Blunt, chief projector to the South Sea conversion scheme was busy buying land in June and in August he arranged to buy even more.

The Mania Spreads and Foreigners Join In

The delirium spread from London to the provinces, where men mortgaged their estates to purchase shares. From as far afield as Ireland, Lady Molesworth wrote, "I believe most of our money is gone over to the South Sea stock, for I never saw it so hard to get in my life." The cynical comments of Edward Harley, writing on 21 April to his brother Robert Harley, Earl of Oxford, illustrate London's mood. "The great doses of opium that are swallowed by the stock-jobbers have intoxicated the whole town, so that what becomes of the peace or trade is very little regarded." Normal business was virtually grounded. "There are few in London," wrote Edward Harley, "that mind anything but the rising and falling of stocks." As the Directors' bloated propaganda machine swung into over-drive, the English boom radiated out further, spreading beyond the provinces across the Channel, attracting continental speculators. Nobility who, a few months earlier, had crammed the rue Quincampoix, now flocked to London to participate. French notables to arrive included the Abbot of St Agnes, the three sons of the Governor of the Austrian Netherlands and Counts Bareta and Constansana. The ubiquitous Cantillon came, eager to add a second, South Sea fortune to his substantial Mississippi gains, and promptly achieved that goal.

To participate in the lucrative money subscriptions, Sir Theodore Janssen had a long list of subscribers from Geneva, Paris, Amsterdam and the Hague, while the list of Lambert, the MP, had many French names. The banker Martin who subscribed £500 in the absurdly generous June Third Money Subscription made this acerbic comment: "Though I believe if you had been in town you would scarce have had the courage to have ventured, but when the rest of the world are mad we must imitate them in some measure." The Canton of Berne had placed £200,000 of public funds in the Company at an early date, and now sold out for a handsome profit of £2 million. The infamous Beau Joseph Gage who gained and lost a huge fortune in Mississippi stocks, had arrived, to try his luck with South Sea shares, as did members of the Scottish Whig nobility. They, a few months earlier, had been among Law's greatest supporters. Several appeared in Knight's notorious green book, where favoured notables received fictitious purchases; among them was the Earl of Rothes, appointed as Lord High Commissioner to the Church of Scotland on 16 April, a few days before he cleared a profit of £18,500 from a fictitious holding allocated to him in March. Other Scottish nobles quickly on the scene were the Earl of Haddington, the Duke of Montrose, and the Lords Dunmore and Hyndford. Dunmore, Hyndford and Rothes were among those who borrowed huge sums from the Company's loan facilities and promptly reinvested them.

Another prominent group to appear were army officers, ever ready for a gamble and perennially short of money. Among their number were the two Campbell brothers, John and Peter, relations of the Duke of Argyll. Thirteen large advances to colonels and brigadiers were made in the first loan, with many more entered in later loans. During July, their immediate command to return to barracks was a contributory cause of the drying up in the buying demand for the shares when the peak had passed. Cantillon was highly sceptical of the long-term prospects for South Sea stock. He had instructions to sell some put options for Lady Mary Herbert. He wrote to her on 29 April, the day before the Second Money Subscription of £1.5 million South Sea stock was issued at £400, explaining that the grossly speculative mood made it hard for him to sell them.

> People are madder than ever to run into the (South Sea) stock and don't so much as pretend to go in to remain in the stock but sell out again to profit. . . . I see nor hear no encouragement to concern your Ladyship in anything on this side where there appears but a melancholy prospect for those who shall stay in the last.

On 19 May, the day of the announcement of the new conversion of annuities, Cantillon purchased £2,500 capital South Sea at 372 for Lady Mary, although, as he told her, he deemed the prices of all stock to be "extravagantly high". The annuities conversion announcement drew a rapturous reception, producing a manic boom in shares quoted in Exchange Alley. They leapt from 400 on 21 May to 890 by 2 June, as the market was once again flush with cash from the third loan offered on sensationally easy terms. As the share price careered along its giddy path to a 24 June peak of 1,050, the rise was patently financial magic to Lady Mary Herbert. She had watched the price of her shares gallop up from 372 to 1,050 in just 34 days, despite the pessimistic cautions expressed by Cantillon. Repeatedly, his actions reveal him as an ultra-cautious investor. By always taking his profits too soon, he missed out on the most meteoric rises of both the Mississippi and South Sea Bubbles. His theoretical grasp of the economic flaws of both schemes convinced him they could not survive long-term, and calling the peak was presumably as difficult in 1720 as it has always been.

Exuberance Peaks

Sarah, Duchess of Marlborough, was convinced, "that this project must burst in a little while and fall to nothing." She sold out early in June, creaming off £100,000 in profits and refused to be persuaded to reinvest in the further money subscriptions. Instead, she now invested in bank and insurance shares. Alexander Pope, yet another cynical observer of the rising speculation crescendo, wrote:

> At length corruption, like a general flood
> Did deluge all, and avarice creeping on
> Spread like a low-born mist and hid the sun.
> Statesmen and patriots plied alike the stocks,
> Peeress and butler share alike the box,
> And judges jobbed and bishops hit the town,
> And mighty Dukes packed cards for half-a-crown
> Britain was sunk in lucre's sordid charms.

Jonathan Swift penned a satirical poem, drawing attention to the scale of South Sea madness sweeping Europe:

> Ye wise Philosophers! Explain,
> What Magick makes our Money rise,
> When dropt into the southern Main;
> Or do these Jugglers cheat our Eyes?

And he predicted:

> The Nation then too late will find,
> Computing all their Cost and Trouble,
> Directors Promises but Wind,
> South-Sea at best a mighty bubble.

With speculative ferment swirling around South Sea stock at fever pitch, about 117 bubble companies were launched between April and May. Huge premiums were possible as small down-payments and exaggerated claims in the hastily printed prospectuses combined with market mania to make every launch a raving success. In this hot-house atmosphere of raw greed, many bubble companies emerged from a vision of future material progress, but this was far ahead of the technological capacity then available to achieve it. The upstart bubble companies threatened the South Sea directors' plans, by diverting cash from their share support operation. Even the prices of its two great rivals were rising in tandem, adding to their concerns; Bank of England shares rose from 150 in January to 260 in June, while East India stock reached 440 from 200. The biggest price surge was in insurance stock. Walpole and Secretary Craggs had been buying them in February when Chetwynd's insurance was only 4; from 20 early in May it hit 50 by the month-end, in which time Onslow's had also more than doubled.

The South Sea Bubble at the Peak

In response to the second loan offer, cash poured out of Knight's office and the share price soared. By the end of May, more than half of the annuities had been lodged with the Company in exchange for the promise of about £3.25 million in stock. The Company's paper profit was £20 million. The share price reached 495, soaring to 610 on the yet more favourable third loan terms. This loan came right after the second, breaking the sequence of each money subscription followed by a loan, as it was issued ahead of the Third Money Subscription. By introducing even more liquidity to the market, this final loan greatly added to the freely available speculative money. It produced the most massive stimulus of any action so far and sent the share price rocketing up to 870 within a matter of days. Table 8 shows the 1720 sequence of all five money subscriptions and three loan offers.

Accolades For Fraudsters

As January 1720 saw the pinnacle for Law's Mississippi Company, so June 1720 was a high point, a fleeting moment to savour in many respects, for the South Sea Company and its miscreant Directors. With uncanny repetition, the train of propitious events sounds so familiar, it is almost as if there was a rerun of the same French script, now in English: "the sorry saga of two Johns". Blunt's crowning triumph came on 11 June; as prime projector for the conversion process, he was created a baronet. Momentarily emulating the illustrious Law at his hour of glory, Blunt stood at his summit of success. However, while Law savoured the ephemeral success of his "System", Blunt saw riches beyond his wildest imaginings with gains made on his share issues early in the scheme's

Table 8 Money subscriptions and company loans-on-stock

1720	Event	Details
14.4	First Money Subscription:	£2 million new South Sea stock at 300 20% payable on application. Balance payable over eight two-monthly instalments. Partly paid stock went to a premium.
21.4	First loan-on-stock:	£0.5 million lent at 5%. An advance of £250 was made for every £100 stock placed with the Company as security.
30.4	Second Money Subscription:	£1 million new South Sea stock at 400, payable in instalments.
20.5	Second loan-on-stock:	4% interest instead of 5%. An advance for £300 for each £100 stock deposited as security.
1.6	Third loan-on-stock:	Unlimited in size and advanced £400 for each £100 deposited as security.
15.6	Third Money Subscription:	Set at 1000, 1/10th now and the next instalment not due for over one year.
27.8	Fourth Money Subscription:	20% on application, balance over two years
12.9	Fifth Money Subscription:	went to an instant discount.

evolution. Again, as with the collapsing French drama, the apotheosis for Blunt marked a transient distinction; on 11 June, Parliament, having finally sanctioned legislation on the motley swarm of rival bubbles, issued a proclamation warning that severe punishments awaited stock-jobbers or projectors who actively continued to promote bubble companies after the end of June. This was to have dire repercussions for the success of Blunt's scheming endeavours.

However, for one brief moment of elation, with the share price at its zenith by 24 June, the entire Board of Directors were fêted by politicians, ministers, nobles and ladies for the valuable patronage they could bestow; for it was they who decided the allocations on each new money subscription, fertile with the allure of boundless gain. They chose who should participate and who was to be excluded. "We have made them Kings," wrote Brodrick, the MP, to the Irish Lord Chancellor Middleton, "and they deal with everybody as such."

Cash Problems for the South Sea Directors

Amid these accolades, however, a more immediate concern faced the Company Directors early in June; they needed to have £5 million in cash as available funds to re-lend to shareholders for the third loan offer, announced on 1 June, directly after the second loan offer had been made, with no new money subscription in between. This anomaly was swiftly rectified when the Third Money Subscription was launched on 15 June, soaking up the recycled funds from willing stock holders who had received £400 for every £100 of stock they had lodged with the Company on 1 June. Early in June the Company announced that the transfer books would be closed for at least a month at midsummer to allow the stock bonus to be worked out. This temporarily depressed the share price as it imposed a firm settlement date on current deals. This brief drop created the left-hand shoulder on the head and shoulders pattern for the chart. (see Figures 16 and 24 on pages 139 and 230).

The unprecedented scale of the Third Money Subscription of 15 June marked the apogee for South Sea finance. The subscription was for £5 million South Sea stock set at 1,000. The terms were so absurdly generous that even rational investors, including the King himself, Robert Walpole and Sir Isaac Newton, were inveigled back to reinvest large amounts of their previous gains in this most tempting of all the money subscriptions issued. The extent of the inducements is gauged from the remarkable fact that the current share quotation in Exchange Alley was around 750. Yet subscribers were willing to pay 33 per cent more than the current price of the original stock. The lure of the exceptionally easy payment terms had worked its magic. As the euphoria reached boiling pitch, the prevailing view was that the shares could move even higher, so subscribers would sell out at a profit before they need find the cash payments to meet further calls. The subscription lists read like a Who's Who directory of the English élite. This was the moment when King George I insisted on reinvesting his earlier South Sea gains, but he was in good company, since the subscription lists contained over half the members of the House of Commons and the Lords.

The irresistible inducements that made this blatant disregard for "fair value" possible were the extremely favourable mix of a small down-payment coupled with exceptionally easy-staged instalments spread over a lengthy period. A modest down-payment of £100 was coupled with the rest in half-yearly instalments starting on 2 July, 1721. The gearing gave newcomers a chance to buy South Sea stock for just £100. Despite a 6-year payment period, the goal to raise £50 million was inordinately ambitious, yet the whole offer was allocated within the day as the share price stormed up to its peak a week later. Despite the high price at which it was pitched it was a resounding success, making an instant premium of 60 per cent and the share price reached 780 in Exchange Alley. This issue marked the zenith for South Sea Company financing. The peak, with quotations around £1,000, was reached in mid-June in response to this spectacular offer, reinforced by the closing of the Company's transfer books, which allowed a startling rebound in the price to occur. With the books closed, there was no constraint on speculators to comply with their bargains, and they went absolutely berserk. Market quotations rocketed to 1,000 with stock changing hands at different prices at opposite ends of Garraway's coffee house. This event created the "head" on the charts. This phase lasted only a few days, but a flood of speculative credit kept the price above 900 for several weeks.

Remaining holders of the national debt were invited to register their titles with the Company ready for conversion. Over £14 million of redeemable debt was deposited with the company. By 24 June the Company was grossly overvalued, but any fear of collapse was skilfully warded off as the Directors used their well-tested expedient of recycling funds to the market over the following five weeks. In July 1720, as shares in the French Mississippi Company went into acute decline, the shares in South Sea and the fleet of English bubble companies hit new peaks each week. In mid-July, the highest ever price offered for South Sea stock, 1,100, found no buyers. By the end of July, the original stock was 930 but the Third Subscription had reached 1,330. And other major companies whose shares were freely traded including the rival Bank of England and East India stock, were also joining in the boom.

Over to Amsterdam

In this hot-house setting of compounding capital gains, the speculative lunacy now leapt across the Channel to Holland. Amsterdam, with its excellent banking and financial facilities offered investors a range of securities in Dutch, English and French stocks and options. It was a sophisticated cosmopolitan financial centre where traders of several nationalities worked side by side in the narrow, winding Kalverstraat, dealing in shares of the Mississippi, South Sea, East India and West India Companies and Bank of England stock. By July, a 12-hourly relay of messengers ran routinely between Helvoetsluys and Harwich, reporting market news. Aristocrats descended *en masse*, upon the cramped Kalverstraat. Nobles decked out in their finery, or their appointed agents, thronged amid the crush of dealers, jobbers and brokers; the Princess Dowager Duchess of Orange Nassau, Prince George of Hesse-Cassel; the Tsar's envoys, Princes Kourakine and Dolgoroucki; the agents of the Queen Mother of Spain, and, of course, the redoubtable Cantillon, eager to scoop a third great fortune into his mounting pile. Despite discouragement from the authorities in some towns, the contagion of new issues proved irresistible. A crop of native promotions of mainly financial companies, emerged in June and July; many were for insurance and some of them survive today. The raw excitement spilled over into Hamburg, where the Exchange was crowded at all hours of the day and another crop of new issues appeared, mainly in insurance, with prices shooting ever upwards.

The Beginning of the End

On 4 August, with the South Sea share price hovering between 870 and 900, the second offer for conversion of the remaining annuities plus an offer for redeemable securities was made, but by 24 August, despite all the money so far raised, yet another money subscription was deemed necessary to buy stock on the Company's account to maintain the share price which was again sinking as a result of the Directors own secret selling. Another 1.25 million stock, issued at a price of 1,000, brought the total to four extant money subscriptions on which periodic calls for payment were being made. In tandem, however, the public was also making similar payments to the plethora of small bubble companies that had rushed to the market to exploit the manic interest in new issues. The over-all market valuations of shares, roughly estimated at a prodigious £500 million in total, was now completely out of balance with the actual amount of capital being supplied.

In August, when the Company announced the final conversion terms, they were based on a stock value of £800 instead of £375. This was agonisingly disappointing for new conversion applicants; it meant they would receive less stock and a smaller hedge against collapse. The share price underwent a sudden ominous dip on the news. This coincided with a massive demand for credit for calls on the whole constellation of new bubble issues flooding the market. The South Sea Company found itself competing directly with these little upstart companies for the limited quantities of funds available for investment on the market. This dip coincided with the second or right-hand, shoulder on the head and shoulders pattern of the chart.

The Collapse Begins

On 18 August, the first proceedings against four bubble companies began. Blunt, acting for the South Sea directors, issued writs against the York Building, the Royal Lustring and the English and Welsh Copper Companies. The writs demanded they close down in default of proving their activities were in strict conformity with the charters under which they were purported to trade. They were accused of misusing or changing the status of their original charters, an accusation that was quite brazen, since the South Sea Company itself was just as guilty of this charge. And what was one to make of the status of the South Sea Company's bank, the curiously named Sword Blade Company? Originally set up with a charter to manufacture hollow sword blades, but finding the market for these somewhat thin, it had turned itself into a bank. Ironically, none of the four Companies targeted for legal action by the South Sea directors was a true bubble company, since they all had charters. The accusing Directors claimed the companies were not acting in accordance with their original charters, while totally disregarding the fact that both the South Sea and Sword Blade Companies were similarly in breach of their original charters and so, equally at fault. By initiating legal action, the Directors' hoped to stop cash leaking from their closed circuit for supporting South Sea shares, as investors sought out profitable positions in other companies. And, unfortunately, even though the Lords Justices granted the order, another difficulty swiftly arose, since three of the four companies immediately ceased to trade. Abruptly, their shares became worthless, wiping several million pounds off the paper wealth of those unlucky investors left holding them at this moment of demise.

The Trigger for Collapse

Lamentably, the merest prospect of legal action planted an anxious confusion in investors' minds, suddenly unsure which companies were bubbles, to be avoided, and which were not. If companies with charters could face legal action, how much more damaging would be the actions against companies without charters? Investor bewilderment coincided with the first serious doubts as to the long-term success potential of the South Sea Company. The writs prompted an immediate collapse in share prices, not just of the affected companies three of which were now worthless, but also of other companies without official charters. Many investors held a wide portfolio in several small bubble shares plus their South Sea stock, mainly bought on credit. Facing steeply falling prices, they could not ride out the drop and were left heavily indebted to their bankers, with inadequate security for their loans. This was particularly true for the three companies now pronounced insolvent as a result of enforcing the writs. Many investors were therefore driven to sell some or all of their South Sea holdings to cover losses on these worthless shares and repay bankers' loans. Enforced sales caused a precipitous drop in South Sea stock. Within a week of issuing the writs, South Sea had fallen to 810; 12 days later, on 30 August, it was 755.

To arrest this alarming decline the Company set a 30 per cent dividend for 1720 which briefly checked the downward slide, but an additional 50 per cent guaranteed dividend for the next 10 years drew attention to the poor yield at current prices. To pay this dividend the Company would have to make a profit of around £15 million per year, yet it had not even begun trading in the South Sea area. In effect, as was now becoming clearer, the South Sea Company was little more than a vehicle for financial manipulation. News on the dividend allowed the price to recover to 815 on 31 August and 780 ex the dividend (that is 830), on 1 September. By late August, the Directors again faced a cash crisis and issued the Fourth Money Subscription on stiffer terms than the previous issues. Twenty per cent was due on application in what was, effectively, a rights issue, available only to existing stock holders. Reflecting the gathering storm, the premium never rose above 20 per cent. This poorly supported issue raised just £250,000 in cash.

The Stampede Out of South Sea Shares

The late August rally only lasted two days and then the price plunged towards 750. By 6 September the stock had fallen 50 points, but went on falling. Soon, Fourth Money Subscription bargains were trading on a 20 per cent discount, the share price slithered to 575 and confidence was rapidly evaporating. Most shareholders were now losing money. George I had reinvested £66,000 in South Sea stock in the rapturously acclaimed Third Money Subscription of mid-June. The value of his investment had shrunk to less than £10,000 by November.

During September, the flood of investors deserting the stock became a stampede. On 9 September the share price crashed through the 600 level, marking an important psychological threshold. This 600 support level was of crucial significance as many banks during the summer bull run had lent funds to investors on collateral of South Sea stock valued at 600 or above. As the price moved below 600, many banks called in their loans. More investors became forced sellers of stock, magnifying the spiral of downward pressure on the falling share price. Between 15 and 19 September, these sales accelerated the decline, and the share price plunged to 380. The fall was further magnified by the South Sea directors' illegal practice of selling stock deposited with them as security for loans, hoping to buy it back more cheaply as the price sank lower. European support was rapidly withdrawn. The collapse of Law's system had re-imposed orthodox banking in France but the lack of gold was extremely pressing. During September, the London representatives of French bankers sold large amounts of South Sea stock to repatriate bullion to France. Dutch bankers anxiously advised their London agents to sell out. By late September, when an emergency Bank of England rescue package was organised, the shares were down to 370.

To add to the gathering gloom, during September, the Company's banker, the Sword Blade Bank was forced to close its doors. As in many such banking crises, a swift knock-on effect from the Sword Blade Bank collapse hit confidence and the Bank of England faced a severe run on its funds. By only the narrowest margin did the Bank itself avoid a threat of closure. The demise of the Sword Blade Bank terminated the South Sea Company rescue plan in mid-November. The Bank of England had only reluctantly agreed to this rescue and soon took advantage of the Sword Blade collapse to withdraw its support. By now the South Sea share price had sunk back to 135; the price it had been in February 1720, before the Bill was passed. In true bubble fashion, the share price had risen and collapsed again within a brief eight months.

Demands for an inquiry could not be silenced. By December, the House of Commons was insisting on a Company investigation. In January 1721 its Directors were called before the House to answer questions on its affairs and the cashier, Robert Knight, fled to the continent. Within months of the mid-June 1720 peak, the share price had slumped back to its 1719 level. Almost nothing remained of this dazzling adventure, except the tortured legacy of the 1721 Parliamentary Inquiry, an acute recession, an impoverished army of disgruntled investors thirsting for revenge and Thomas Guy's new hospital in the City of London. Plus, of course, all the books written to record the fraudulent escapade.

South Sea Chaos

From the outset, the brief South Sea drama is so packed with evidence for chaos in action, it can be completely described by the language of chaos, as was the French bubble. Again, the eight stages of the typical crash model are visible in the unfolding sequence of events. We shall therefore review the history of the South Sea Bubble to expose its chaos foundations.

For years after its 1711 foundation, the Company was virtually inert. The predicted lucrative trading opportunities with its South American trading area did not materialise when the Spaniards reneged on the treaty. For years nothing untoward occurred. The Company was passively dormant; in chaos terms, it was a complex damped system subdued into a static lethargy by the prevalent negative feedback.

Phase One – John Blunt Intervenes

To acquire his dishonest fortune, the projector, John Blunt treated the slumbering Company as modern ambitious entrepreneurs would treat a shell situation, although modern directors are severely restricted by Parliamentary legislation to prevent them acting fraudulently. To re-activate a quiescent shell, money, new management and a new direction for the reconstructed enterprise must all be injected. The corrupt South Sea directors achieved all these three goals. First, they obtained an Act of Parliament to authorise a new direction, namely, to take over the national debt. Secondly, they raised money from the issue of several highly successful money subscriptions. And thirdly, they allocated the day-to-day running of the Company's affairs to a small coterie of "insiders" committed to their fraudulent aims. The scheme hatched by the Directors amounted to the introduction of a positive feedback loop into the dormant company. Their plan constituted, in effect, the first stage of the crashes model discussed in Chapter 1. It was the first, triggering shock event which launched the Bubble on its route towards extreme instability. As we saw with Law's scheme, the monumental speed with which the Directors re-activated the Company generated a breakneck boom, flipping the system abruptly from damped to driven using the device of a financial pump. And in the process, they grossly destabilised it and took it to the edge of chaos.

Nonlinearity at Work

Opportunities for substantial nonlinear gains, where the modest input is not directly proportional to the greatly enlarged gains, featured prominently in the appealing marketing methods used by the Directors in April, May and June, to entice the public to subscribe for shares in the newly revived Company. The helpful facilities of very small initial down-payments and lengthy instalment periods, allowed a small outlay to rapidly result in enormous gains for investors who bought early into the scheme, because of the strong gearing effects of the payments arrangements. For a small down-payment of £60 an investor in the First Money Subscription of 14 April, secured the rights to a South Sea share currently worth over £300. By holding it until 2 June, that is, before the next instalment of £30 was due on 14 June, this share could be sold for £360. If the full £300 had been due to be paid on 14 April, the gain would have been 20 per cent. As only £60 pounds was paid, the gain within six weeks was £300 pounds, five times the initial outlay.

The nonlinear gains attraction also operated for the three hugely successful loans-on-stock issues made consecutively in the months of April, May and June. They operated marvellously to the advantage of a wealthy speculator whose credit-worthiness, or links to the small clique of insiders, allowed him to borrow the maximum £5,000 on 20 April. This lucrative facility offered the immediate right to acquire 125 shares on easy payment terms, in the Second Money Subscription announced nine days later, on 29 April. If the loan were repaid by the sale of the 125 shares early in June, before the next instalment of £40 per share fell due, the return would have been a staggering £25,000 after allowing a deduction of £45,000 for the nine unpaid future instalments. A further deduction of about £5,030 was necessary, to repay the loan plus the interest due over about six weeks. The outright gain, which had incurred absolutely no capital outlay by the investor since he was using borrowed funds, amounted to the princely sum of £19,997, a great fortune in 1720 terms. The trading antics of Edmund Waller reveal that this example is not a vague theoretical case. He brought virtually no money to the market, relying instead on the credit he was able to raise from his position as son-in-law to the Chancellor of the Exchequer. Through the entire boom, his drawings on the Sword Blade Company were over £750,000 and surviving accounts show his turnover with six stock-brokers reached £300,000. Almost all his trading was on credit. He has the doubtful distinction of offering South Sea at the peak price of 1,100 on 10 July, but found no buyers.

Nonlinearity worked its marvellous magic for enthusiastic South Sea investors throughout the heady summer of 1720. The introduction of two loan issues consecutively, on 20 May and 1 June, without an intervening money subscription to soak up the flood of available cash pouring into the market, meant that the loan issue of 1 June, which was unlimited in size, produced an enormous nonlinear effect on the rising share price. It shot up from 600 on 2 June to 870 within a matter of days. This splendid nonlinear trick was repeated on 15 June, when the mouth-watering Third Money Subscription was announced. It received a rapturous reception. Investors went absolutely wild in their agitation to subscribe, sending the price of the existing shares from 750 to the peak of 1,050 within a week.

Positive Feedback in the Share Price Uptrend

Naturally, as evidence mounted daily that phenomenal, virtually in-stantaneous gains were achievable in South Sea shares, interest in them soared. With the uptrend of the rising share price well established, the added incentives of a sequence of further share issues punctuated by loan issues, sent it to stratospheric heights in no time at all. As the hysteria to gain possession of the shares gathered greater momentum, the positive feedback loop swung into overdrive. During the uptrend, a rising share price fuels more rises; sellers hold back, waiting to sell at even higher prices. If the majority are buyers and sellers are in the minority, a stock shortage emerges, adding yet another twist to the accelerating feedback loop. As we saw, creating a stock shortage was one of the key devices used by the directors to maintain buying momentum in the shares.

Phase Two – Easy Credit and the South Sea Financial Pump

The self-feeding buying mania is a chain reaction. It reflects an intense positive feedback loop in action. The Directors exploited it by inundating the receptive market with three money subscriptions and three loans on stock within three months, from 14 April to 15 June. With the string of new issues establishing a rising trend, the price rose swiftly, from around 380 on 14 April, to 1,050 by 24 June. This frenetic buying was engineered by the rapid sequence of share and loan issues made by the South Sea directors.

With access to unlimited credit facilities from the Sword Blade Company, the Directors introduced into the market the potent dynamism of a fully operational chaotic pump. However, it differed from the pump Law unleashed in France, as his direct link to the Bank Royale enabled him to feed repeated new bank note issues into circulation, perfectly timed to support his attractively marketed rights issues. The South Sea directors had no direct access to a bank which would issue millions of new notes. Instead, they harnessed the three loans-on-stock issues to three new share issues to produce a massive credit-creating boom. In total, a credit injection of £5 million flooded the economy. Their financial pump relied on this abrupt input of cheap, abundant credit, supplied via the Sword Blade Bank connection. The Directors deliberately intended to recycle funds from the Company to investors via shares and so back into the Company in a tightly controlled loop. The action of the pump, clearly evident in the ensuing speculation, is shown on Figure 23 on page 210.

This strictly closed circuit recycled money round a narrow loop of new loans to pay for new shares, and was intensely energetic in action. So swiftly did it emerge, the boom was soon careering helter-skelter towards a climax, as the price of the shares roared up erratically to the June peak. As with Law's boom, and all chaos driven situations, within a few months, the financial pump had suddenly turned a becalmed damped system into a turbulent driven system. The equilibrium of sellers and buyers throughout the Company's early years, was unceremoniously swept away by the abrupt emergence of this financial pump.

Phase Three – Inflation and the South Sea Chain Reactions

In the stock market the euphoria gripping South Sea shares spread in a contagious chain reaction in many directions. First, it created a mushrooming bevy of imitator bubble companies, clamouring for the attention of gullible speculators. Secondly, it drew large numbers of eager investors to London from the provinces and continental Europe. All the shares of other companies traded in London rose in tandem, and the chain reaction of the boom spread to Amsterdam and Hamburg, fuelling further rises in all the London quoted companies readily traded there. These ripples stemmed from the growing credit boom and the self-feeding influence of the boom.

In the economy, the chain reaction effect was equally impressive. The furore over share prospects fuelled newspaper sales carrying increasing numbers of advertisements for new company issues. This and associated growth in spending levels was beneficial for trade. Demand for consumer goods and property rose. Conspicuous consumption was soon evident in sales of luxuries. The credit-induced inflation exploded into life around London and the home counties. In terms of chaos mechanisms, this inflationary boom is squarely based on the chaos effect of a chain reaction, where huge profits on rising financial assets created an artificial wealth effect. It provided incentives and ready cash to radiate extra spending out on other goods. This marked stage three of the typical crashes model, where the large credit input results in a strong inflationary surge. There was an accompanying mushrooming growth in speculation and in debt to purchase shares, in the scramble to become wealthy enough to own all the other enjoyable material luxuries whose prices were now booming, marking stage four of the crashes model.

The Phase Transition for South Sea Investors

The emergent structure of the boom is essentially unstable; indeed, it becomes chaotic because the activity never settles down. It undergoes continuous unpredictable change from one second to the next. I believe it is the introduction of a vigorous financial pump which abruptly plunges investors from a rational into an irrational mental state. During phase four, with speculation rampant, many underwent a phase transition event which tipped them abruptly from rational to irrational behaviour. As they arrived in strength in Change Alley, their conduct revealed this phase transition event. Outwardly, they were the same people but their behaviour showed a profound shift. They exhibited entirely different characteristics to their previous conduct before the financial pump energised their delirious urge to become instantly rich. This phase transition occurs during the period of overtrading, pure speculation and the growth of borrowing to buy shares (phase four of the crashes model) and on into phase five when the uninitiated public join in. It depicts the unfolding period when the majority of rational investors become irrational as they get swept up into the manic intensity of a stock market phase transition and the market becomes chaotic.

Once a financial pump is set in motion, the boom/bust cycle becomes predictable. On reaching this volatile state, it is poised at the edge of chaos. It is now almost impossible for the system to regain stability through a measured return to normality. Moreover, once it is totally unstable, any sudden unexpected shock may rapidly tip the system into chaos. However, in each case, the timing and specific details will vary, due to the chaos feature of sensitive dependence on initial conditions, as these will be unique for every example studied. On the detailed sequences, they will therefore be essentially unpredictable, but the determinism of the long-run behaviour of such events is evident from the historical record. The extreme instability presages a dramatic collapse. The share price is moving remorselessly along the path of its long-run trajectory, which is the chaos strange attractor for its unfolding behaviour.

Phase Five – The Bubble at the Peak

During these intoxicating summer months, as the surging share price rocketed towards its fleeting summit phase five of the crashes model emerged, with mass participation of the gullible public plunging in. With speculative excesses increasing, the trail of order descending into chaos is equally clear. Thousands of people from London, the Provinces and Europe, jostled in a tiny sector of the City around Change Alley, intent on making quick fortunes. Dozens of competing bubble companies, launched in May and June, exploited the intense interest. Activity in Change Alley reached frenetic proportions.

The subscription lists embraced the very cream of British and European society, and thus, we surely cannot assume these irrational souls were all foolhardy inveterate gamblers by nature. In their normal pursuits as leading figures of the age, they were immeasurably rational. What emerges from the evidence of the lists is that the temptation to be sucked up into this hysterical mania was, for the majority, absolutely irresistible. Yet there must be a deeper explanation of why so many sane people were suddenly driven to an avaricious insanity. In the colourful language of deterministic chaos, all those who were now caught up in the infectious delirium of the moment underwent the curious switch of a phase transition. They were provoked by the outrageous inducements to subscribe. And so appealing was the speculative prospect of instant gain they became number-drunk. They were quite incapable of assessing "fair

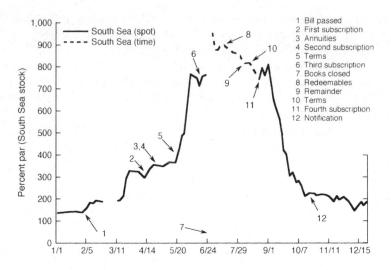

Figure 24 South Sea Company share prices to show how they were affected by the main events for the Company during 1720

Source: How the South Sea Bubble was blown up and burst, L. D. Neal, in *Crashes and Panics: The Lessons from History,* edited by E. N. White

value" for the shares on offer. Indeed, **with the subscription price around £300 more than the current price of the stock,** they were relying on a continuing upward share price to allow the small down-payment and lengthy instalment scheme to produce their handsome nonlinear gains. From the depth and breadth of participation, it is clear the urge to subscribe resoundingly overwhelmed any caution about the risk of loss. With this orgy of interest spanning a wide spectrum of the credulous public, phase five of the crash model had most definitely arrived.

Determinism

As the share speculation reached its climax, massive runaway positive feedback loops destabilised the market. Prices hit unsustainable heights and a dramatic collapse became inevitable. The chart evidence for the South Sea Bubble, together with other examples of crashes from this century, reveals the consistent appearance of the boom/bust scenario seen in terms of the rising/falling share price. There is invariably a rapidly rising trend, on high volume of participation, to the peak. This acquires the characteristics of a head and shoulders, or a double or triple top formation. This graphic format suggests there is a distinct and recognisable chart appearance, a chaos strange attractor, for the speculative hysteria of the South Sea Bubble. The chart pattern for the South Sea Company share price is a typical head and shoulders formation.

The head and shoulders chart pattern depicts the long-run behaviour of the system and is a powerful influence; points not lying within its orbit will be drawn towards it by the momentum of events. The South Sea Bubble is so well documented and of such a short duration that it neatly encapsulates a small discreet episode with an identifiable beginning and a definable end. It is therefore possible to note the events that affected the share price and produced the familiar head and shoulders chart shape. This sequence has been added to the annotated chart in Figure 24.

As the slumping fortunes of South Sea stock continued, order was falteringly re-imposed by a hesitant and gradual self-reorganisation on the part of the authorities. This was possible because, unlike the out-moded French arrangements, the British Parliamentary system was linked to a constitutional monarchy. Parliament became the self-organising focus, imposing a reasonably just reconstruction. The dramatic collapse can also be expressed in the rich language of chaos, as we shall see in the following chapter, when we discuss the detailed events of the crash and the aftermath for both 1720 bubbles.

CHAPTER NINE

THE AFTERMATH

> I have often wished that these bank notes were consigned to hell fire. They are much more of a worry than a help to my son, and it is impossible to describe all the evil that has resulted from them. . . . I should like to see Law go to the Devil with his System and I wish he had never set foot in France.
>
> The Dowager Duchess of Orléans

The collapse of 1720 has been described as the first international economic crisis because speculation during 1718–20 spread so widely. It affected financial centres in France, England, Holland, northern Italy and Germany. The distress caused by the bubbles was deep and widespread. How it rippled through the two economies of France and Britain is the main topic of this chapter. With the two projects running virtually in tandem, it was obvious that the author of the Mississippi scheme came to be associated in the public mind with the fraudulent South Sea directors, but it is patently clear that Law was not a swindler, whereas a small coterie of directors of the South Sea Company clearly were. Because of the close proximity in the dates of the two bubbles, Law has come down to posterity tarred by the same fraudulent reputation as the promoters of the South Sea scheme. There are, however, several important differences between these two historical scenarios.

The Louisiana enterprise was founded on a project of true substance enjoying a trading monopoly over the entire French overseas Empire. Efforts to build a colony in Louisiana, while slow to make progress, did ultimately succeed. The fledgeling town of New Orleans owed its origin to the establishment of the colony, and today, its ultimate importance cannot be doubted, but from the outset in 1711, the South Sea venture had no promising commercial prospects. The outbreak of war with Spain in 1718 put a premature end to the trade potentials with Spanish America. From its formation, with no useful trading purpose, the Company was heavily over-capitalised at £10 million. The excessive size of its capital base left it vulnerable to fraudulent practices if its management were so persuaded. By their actions, the South Sea directors' dishonesty caused incalculable harm to the Tory party, whose leaders backed the enterprise. The popular link of Law to this English corruption harmed his reputation for posterity, but he himself summed up the truth in a single statement when he said, "The South Sea directors have worked **against** England; I have worked **for** France.'

Dog Days for the Bubble Companies

Bubble events inevitably live up to their name. The end, whenever it finally comes, is usually dramatic, unexpectedly abrupt and totally unforeseen by the trusting, ever hopeful majority. Towards the peak, smart investors sell out to greedy newcomers, but, if the majority thought a crash was due, more people would be early sellers and it might be averted. If there were more sellers willing to forego future expected gains and less holders harbouring outrageous hopes, fewer investors would be left in a collapsing market, caught totally unprepared. We can recognise this helpful early warning period, after the huge run-up in prices, when the panic is, literally, on hold as it were, in both the Mississippi and the South Sea Bubbles.

Phase Six – Early Nagging Doubts

Law's System peaked in January 1720, but the serious collapse did not begin until May, in response to the infamous 21 May edict. The South Sea Company downfall set in slowly around the end of June 1720, but the first ugly drop in the share price occurred in August, when investors took fright over ambiguity in the infamous Bubble Act legislation; the final collapse developed in September. This pause of a few months between the moment of greatest confidence and the onset of its abrupt evaporation is evident in both examples. It depicts the arrival of phase six in the typical crashes model, when early nagging doubts appear. Now, although the majority are firm holders, enough disbelievers emerge as sellers to prevent the share price from soaring away to even more ridiculous heights.

Mississippi Winners and Losers

The imposition of Law's grandiose System in such a short time frame was bound to throw up a motley group of winners and losers. When formulating his ideas, Law realised it would create beneficiaries as well as losers. Among the groups to face severe hardship were the outright speculators, many of whom were financially ruined. Others to suffer included the enormous army of inefficient tax-gatherers, the rentiers owning government stock and the labouring classes. Even the band of the notoriously successful investors were affected, when the Regent imposed severe plans to tax the new Mississippi millionaires.

The economic historian Earl J. Hamilton compiled a commodity price index to assess economic hardship created by Law's System. Using a 1716–17 base for his index on foods, raw materials, staple household goods and building materials at wholesale prices, his analysis sheds light on those most at risk from imposing a paper currency regime. For example, between May 1716, when Law's Bank Générale was set up, and November 1718, prices rose by only 8.7 per cent. By September 1718, Hamilton's index was 100.6, but had risen to 116.1 by July 1719. In September 1720, it had soared to 203.7, suggesting prices almost doubled in two years. Yet, in the two-month period of December 1719 to January 1720 prices rose 34.8 points, or 25.5 per cent.

Hamilton also complied indices of money and real wages for Parisian labourers over this same period. Money wages stood at 107.2 in September 1718; by July 1719 they had risen to 125.8 and they too reached their peak in September 1720 at 161.9. Therefore, while prices were in the process of doubling, wages only rose some 50 per cent, indicating the severe hardship suffered by this group of workers during the monetary inflation. Once again, however, the greatest disparity emerged in the short period of December 1719 to January 1720, when money wages actually remained unchanged while prices romped ahead. Judged in terms of real wages, that is, after adjusting for the inflation, the deterioration in the labourer's position is starkly clear, even allowing for seasonal variations for reduced wages and higher living costs during winter. From 107.7 in September 1718 and 113.7 in July 1719, the figure slumped to 84.8 in September 1720 and was only 68.0 by the start of 1721. The crucial December 1719 to January 1720 period showed a drop of 17 points, from 91.4 to 74.4.

Hamilton's findings across the country, in Toulouse, Bordeaux and Marseilles reflected similar results to the situation prevailing in Paris, but the index rise was most alarming in Marseilles, exacerbated by the outbreak of the bubonic plague. The French labouring classes, therefore, certainly suffered under Law's System, but the intensity of their hardships were short-lived. In Paris, by July 1721 commodity prices stood at 124.9, money wages at 124.7 and real wages, adjusted for inflation were at 115.1. Moreover, although hard to quantify, the boom accompanying the paper currency experiment may have provided greater employment opportunities than usual, which might have countered some of the fall in the values of real wages.

For the winners, the ports of Lorient and Nantes undoubtedly enjoyed a booming prosperity, with 2,000 vessels registered at Nantes in 1721, compared with fewer than 1,350 in 1703. The build-up of the French Royal Navy began in 1719 with an order for the construction of five ships at Brest, plus orders at Rochefort, Le Havre and Toulon. A slimmed-down version of this programme survived after the System collapsed. By December 1719 the Compagnie des Indes had over 30 ships (excluding frigates and brigantines), more ships than the British East India Company owned. Colonising efforts in the Mississippi region survived the crash, although, clearly, a very long time scale was involved in properly exploiting the commercial advantages there. Law obviously failed to appreciate the huge time-lag between founding a colony from scratch and obtaining the financial benefits that would flow from its successful establishment.

On the domestic front, the boom produced some notable improvements. There was a renewed emphasis on the cultivation of wheat and a consequent reduction in the threat of famine. More land was cleared and rural building projects were begun. Large-scale construction plans for roads, the Provence canal and the canal joining the rivers Loire and Seine were started. Paris gained from the building expansion coupled to Law's System. Many elegant houses in the place Vendôme, the place des Victoires and the Palais Bourbon owed their origins to it. In 1720 Law himself bought land in the prestigious place Vendôme in seven lots. He built houses here, most of which he sold on straight away, but one block comprising four houses he retained. Ironically, in 1723 two of these properties were purchased by Abraham Peyrenc de Maras who had made 60 million livres in the bubble.

The Mississippi Downfall

Law's ill-fated 21 May edict met an outbreak of raw panic. He failed to carry the people with him in his crude efforts at internal devaluation. Confidence was shattered by the plan to cut the value of all the shares and notes in circulation. The run on Banque Royale that followed was so immense it was forced to close its doors for 10 days. Payments resumed on 1 June, but only notes of less than 100 livres denomination were honoured. Within days, a restriction to ease the suffering of the poor was introduced, and one 10-livres note per person, could be exchanged for specie. The working class, with notes of the lowest denomination, had difficulty in exchanging them for even basic necessities. Fear of hunger kept crowds of desperate people thronging the streets around the bank's imposing premises, where previously crowds of eager speculators had congregated daily, in a state of high expectation. Orders reinstating the holding of gold were issued on 1 June, with the share price at 5,000. Twenty five million new notes of 10 livres each backed by revenues of Paris were issued. As a confidence-raising gesture, the old notes were publicly burned. By 10 June, the bank reopened for the exchange of notes for coin, mostly in copper as gold was still in acutely short supply.

Tempers and impatience rose with the summer heat. On 9 July, mobs outside the bank flung stones at the soldiers. Similar disturbances continued for days. Among the jostling crowds, many people were injured and some trampled to death. In the early hours of 17 July, troops guarding the Palais Mazarin (now the Bibliotheque Nationale), where the bank was situated, charged the crowds with fixed bayonets. With 15,000 frantic people packed in the rue Vivienne, leading to the bank, 16 were suffocated, crushed to death trying to enter the building to exchange notes for coins. An enraged mob, discovering the corpses at dawn, rushed to the Palais Royal, to vent their anger on the Regent while others surrounded Law's house, screaming abuse and hurling stones at his windows.

To escape the fury of vengeful mobs, Law, greatly shaken by the rank hostility openly expressed against him, took shelter in the Regent's Palace. Here, for months he was protected by a detachment of Swiss Guards, virtually under house arrest for his own safety. His fears of crowd reprisals were well founded when news came that a coach had been smashed to pieces on the merest suspicion that it might belong to him. Meanwhile outraged members of the Parlement became an ugly lynch mob, intent on hanging Law, as soon as he could be found.

Law and his family faced the fury and frustration of the crowds throughout this long ordeal. The Regent's mother wrote, "Law is like a dead man and his face is as white as a sheet. I expect there are times when he wishes he himself were on the Mississippi or in Louisiana." Ribald verse and numerous lampoons proliferated, satirizing Law and his System. One jest produced an apposite synopsis of the System:

> My shares which on Monday I bought
> Were worth millions on Tuesday, I thought.
> So on Wednesday I chose my abode;
> In my carriage on Thursday I rode;
> To the ball-room on Friday I went;
> To the workhouse next day I was sent.

From midsummer, there was desolation in Paris. To add to the gathering sense of dread, on 31 July at Marseilles, two dockers unloading wool from a ship from Sidon in the Lebanon, were discovered to have contracted bubonic plague. Within days the town was ringed with a cordon to contain the epidemic. All over Europe, quarantine regulations featured in daily newspapers, alongside the latest financial reports. Compounding the misery, the plague epidemic spread northwards through France. As the months passed, with the paper currency rapidly losing its value, Law, once the most celebrated man in France, became universally the most detested. A new finance minister was appointed to reinstate orthodox finance for the public accounts and re-establish public confidence in money.

To improve the currency situation, notes valued at 700 million livres were withdrawn, exchanged for municipal bonds and other forms of security held by the bank. Yet despite his earnest efforts to save the System, with the loyal support of the Regent and others who had made fortunes from it, Law's struggle to sustain it soon failed. The notes steadily lost favour as the Mississippi share price fell, and by the end of summer they were at an 80 per cent discount.

Finally, admitting defeat, the former monetary system was imposed by an edict on 10 October, the day Banque Royale closed its doors permanently and the paper currency was publicly burned. Gold and silver would be in use again from 1 November for all commercial transactions, and bank notes could not be used in any sort of financial transaction: the young Voltaire sarcastically observed that paper money was being reduced to its intrinsic value. This final edict brought Law's experiment to an abrupt end less than four years from its beginning. Relief was palpable for both Regent and Parlement, when Law finally fled France in December 1720 with all his grandiose schemes overthrown.

By 1 January 1721, the national debt was still a colossal 3.1 billion livres (£224 million) with annual interest at 3.2 million livres. France would take more than a generation to recover from the effects of this traumatic adversity. Although Law was widely condemned by contemporaries as a greedy adventurer exploiting the embedded weaknesses of the French economy on the death of Louis XIV to line his own pockets with a fortune, his subsequent actions in leaving all his assets behind in France on his escape, belie this harsh judgement.

Errors in Law's System

The collapse of the Mississippi Company and closure of Banque Royale guaranteed Law a poor press for prosperity, but there were some long-term benefits which counter the dogmatic "catastrophe" verdict of his System. France experienced a real element of economic revival. Some of the slack in the labour market was taken up, more land was cultivated and capital invested in major construction projects. Law was certainly a visionary in his belief in the use of paper credit to serve as the life-blood of industry, trade and commerce. Modern reliance on paper currencies has completely vindicated his views.

His greatest error was to push through his programme of reform at such breakneck speed, it was impossible for either the economy or the populace to adjust quickly enough to all his measures to avoid a catastrophic collapse. He paid scant regard to the role that increased savings might have played in stabilising the situation he created with the massive injection of paper money. He also ignored the basic human instinct to set aside resources to cope with future needs. He failed to appreciate the considerably long introductory period his System would require to allow positive signs of wealth creation to emerge. These would include a growing population, higher manufacturing productivity and more employment opportunities. The gradual industrialisation of Britain over many decades in the nineteenth century, in tandem with the widening use of paper bank notes and credit, indicate the necessary time scale required. Even there, it was not a serene procession, for it was accompanied by many setbacks and intermittent banking crises. A streak of impatience in Law's nature left him exposed to the great temptation to rush the pace of reforms faster than the fragile economy could possibly handle.

Kindleberger suggests Law's operations were a mistake based on two profound fallacies: first, his notion that stocks and bonds are actually money, and secondly, his view that issuing more paper money as demand increases is not inflationary. He confused the increasing demand for paper money with an increase in real wealth. This stemmed from his belief that money is a means of exchange rather than a measure of value, when in effect, paper money performs both of these functions, not either one or the other. His main difficulty was to regulate the speed of the inevitable inflationary boom and correlate it with his overall economic strategy. His commitment to low interest rates fuelled the boom, especially through his misguided efforts to "peg" the price of shares at 9,000 livres in the early months of 1720, instead of allowing them to find their own level. The frequent adjustments to the value of the coinage – 26 alterations in 1720 alone – and his instant volte-face over the 21 May edict, were almost guaranteed to annihilate public confidence.

According to Murphy's analysis, Law's economic policy rested on an irreconcilable inconsistency, which Cantillon had shrewdly recognised, as we saw in Chapter 7. Law's objective of keeping interest rates low by expanding the money supply could not be reconciled with his aim of raising the exchange rate of the French currency. An over-expansion of the money supply in an open economy would cause a balance of payments deficit and a consequent deterioration in the exchange rate. Most crucially, however, Law failed to acknowledge the need for people to slowly build up confidence in the novelty of his bank notes and the shares. Indeed, he thought it was possible to compel people against their will to maintain their faith in these, the two main instruments of his schemes. He genuinely believed that panic selling of the Mississippi securities on the stock exchange could be checked by legislation. He placed too much faith in the arbitrary power of despotic authority and far too little on the influence of public opinion on monetary matters, relying too much on the rigid in-built attitudes that dominated life in France. Ironically, he anticipated the French dirigism of state management by a few generations. This misconception is amply testified by his own words. As he himself observed, "It is a fortunate country where action can be considered, decided upon and carried out within twenty-four hours instead of twenty-four years like England."

Listing all these elementary failures in his System and its implementation, it was therefore probably inevitable that the reforms he introduced, especially in the field of taxation, should have been unceremoniously swept away in the ensuing débâcle, and should have found almost no faithful advocates after his exile from France. Yet Law was unshaken in confidence for the long-term viability of his reform measures. In his last letter to the Regent while he was still in France, he wrote, "For the rest, time will show that I have been a good Frenchman. The institutions that I have founded are under attack, but they will survive, and posterity will do me justice."

Debt Deflation – The Mississippi Fall-out

The Mississippi mania brought many evils in its wake. Prices rose phenomenally, with a massive increase in gambling and a general loosening of morals. An edict prohibited public gambling, under heavy penalties, but it remained popular especially in the so-called market of St Germain near the Latin quarter on the left bank of the Seine. Here gambling establishments of all kinds flourished unashamedly. According to the writer, Buvat, 60,000 livres were commonly staked on a single throw of the dice or turn of a card, with the players contemptuously sporting fist-fulls of notes. A few unlucky speculators committed suicide when the French bubble finally burst, but the majority turned to crime or gambling to recoup their losses. There was an alarming increase in lawlessness, robberies and crimes of violence. Eleven people were killed or robbed in Paris within the space of a few days. Dismembered parts of corpses were regularly dragged from the Seine, after people had been murdered for their money, hacked to pieces and then dumped into the river. The ferocious crime wave rapidly spread to the provinces. Masked highwaymen infested the roads and robbed travellers of their valuables.

As part of the mopping up process to restore the State's finances after Law's System had collapsed, the authorities resorted to a similar much-hated Visa measure to the one they had imposed in 1716, shortly after the death of Louis XIV. The despised Paris brothers who had organised the 1716 Visa to improve the Government's financial position were again put in charge of the 1721 Visa. After their inquisitorial investigations, a similar, but even harsher, reduction in security values was implemented. On 15 September 1722 a wealth tax was introduced on the property of the largest Mississippians termed, "les hommes nouveaux". Four classes of "actionnaires, millionaires et autres Mississippiens" were identified. Within the top group of 46 leading Mississippi millionaires, Cantillon was listed as number 21. His gain was calculated to have been about 20 million livres. At the September 1722 exchange rate this was of the order of £630,000. The tax to be levied against his estimated gains was 2.4 million livres. He stayed out of France during this period, to avoid paying this tax, but the authorities put out an order in January 1723, to proceed with the sale of his French property, to cover his tax liability to the State. He did not return to France again until September 1728. This 1723 order may have applied to Law's properties also, allowing Abraham Peyrenc de Maras to buy up two of his place Vendôme houses.

Dog Days for the South Sea Company

The sad ruination of the South Sea Company after the July peak tells a similar tale of hardships and general despair. The major difference with the Mississippi demise was the appalling speed of collapse for South Sea shares, from August to October, in a headlong rout. The main reason was the sweeping impact of the lack of alternatives in France which virtually locked the public into a choice between shares and bank notes, falsely supporting their value. As South Sea share price slumped in a precipitous downward spiral, reliance on credit was nakedly exposed. With the fall, more collateral was wiped out, forcing more creditors to sell stock onto a falling market. This added further selling pressure to the accelerating trend. Losses were piling up on both the shares and on contractual obligations that many investors faced for further instalments on partly-paid South Sea and bubble company holdings. In the ensuing panic, share prices plunged in even the most soundly-based companies. Thousands of small investors had been attracted into South Sea stock by the small initial down-payment, together with easy follow-on instalments for further payments. The ever rising share price had lulled them into the false assumption that they would sell their shares into the rising market before having to find more payments. During September the falling share price was accentuated by underhand tactics of the corrupt South Sea directors, who sold the stock short. They dumped shares deposited with them as security for the loans onto the market, hoping to buy them back again more cheaply as the price sank.

Outraged investors facing new repayment calls, together with those who bought stock in August at the highly inflated figure of 800, began demanding changes in the terms of their obligations, to adjust for mounting losses. A riotous shareholders' meeting on 20 September failed to resolve this dispute. The rights of late-comers were vigorously opposed by those who had been in the stock since early spring and wanted no dilution of the terms. The Bank of England, whose business had suffered severely with the meteoric rise of the South Sea Company, was called in to arrange a rescue operation. Reluctantly, an agreement was thrashed out, and news of this rescue plan steadied the share price at between 350 to 400.

Unfortunately, on 22 September, an ominous development occurred, with the closure of the Sword Blade Company. Stopping of payments by the Company's banker was a heavy blow, sending the shares smartly down to 300. The Bank of England hastily revised its decision to assist the stricken Company. Having agreed to take South Sea stock at 400 in payment of £3,775,025-17s-10d of redeemable debt held by the Bank, the drop in the share price in response to the frightening news on the bank closure meant the Bank of England immediately would lose over £2 million by honouring its rescue plans. On 28 September, when news that the Bank would not honour its word reached Exchange Alley, South Sea stock fell to 200. At South Sea House, in the summer of 1720, the monumental efforts by clerks to cope with the issue and transfer of stock was ultimately defeated with the collapse. Confusion about ownership added to the slump. Bargains went unrecorded, creditors and debtors were ambiguous, repudiations were as common as defaults.

The Credit Implosion

During the autumn, a huge proportion, easily 66 per cent, of the credit-generating system that had grown up alongside the expanding economy, suddenly disappeared, creating a severe depression. Many aristocrats and influential people faced ruin. Some banks and stock brokers failed, shares in other companies and property slumped, land prices fell drastically, unemployment rose and firms were foreclosed. The depression reached Holland where bankers suffered from exposure to collapse in both Mississippi and South Sea shares. Meanwhile, conditions in France were shocking. Commerce ran at a trickle and the distribution of food and other essentials faltered. By the autumn of 1720, much of northern

Europe was gripped in the misery of a monstrously widespread and debilitating depression – a debt deflation. In England, millions of pounds of outstanding Sword Blade bank notes were almost worthless, but the paper currency element of the economy had mushroomed considerably to include an assortment of other paper; shares, bonds, notes, bills and receipts. They had all been subjected to an uncontrolled expansion during the boom. In both bubbles, expansion of credit and the rise of speculation in land and shares had advanced in tandem. The voluminous growth of notes in issue in France and the repeated offer of new loans advanced on ludicrously easy terms in England, supported by Sword Blade bank notes, generated a financial pump coupled to new share issues that swiftly drove asset prices to extreme heights and equally swiftly plunged them back to their pre-boom values as confidence suddenly evaporated. The explosive excesses and subsequent disorganisation of credit made both collapses virtually inevitable.

However, the predominant cause of the boom and subsequent bust was the facility with which too much credit without any asset-backing and minimal productive outlets, had been initially created and quickly destroyed. The hapless Europeans of 1720 were neither the first, nor surely will they be the last, to confuse credit with wealth for if a boom/bust cycle is to be avoided, credit must always rest firmly on a wealth-producing asset. However, once swept up into the mêlée of a credit boom, when people finally rediscover this timeless reality for themselves, they feel instantly impoverished and their experiences enter the public memory, often for generations into the future.

Desperate Measures To Survive

The collapse of the South Sea Company and the Sword Blade Company almost brought down the Bank of England. As the rush for cash reached fever pitch in September, the Bank faced a damaging run on its reserves when it reneged on its promise to buy South Sea shares at £400. Mcleod's *Theory and Practice of Banking* describes the crude defensive measures taken to avert outright failure. The Directors set their friends at the head of the cash queues, paying out at a snail's pace in sixpenny coins. The cash was instantly taken in via another, secret, door, to be re-deposited and again paid out by the same glacial counting procedure. In this way, the story relates, the run was held off until the Festival of Michaelmas (29 September). After the holiday, the run was over and the Bank survived. A similar story recounts the fading fortunes of the doomed Sword Blade Company. For a while it resisted repeated attempts to redeem its paper in silver. When the run began on 19 September, the bank ostentatiously brought up wagonloads of silver to inspire confidence and proceeded to pay it out at a slow-motion pace, in small change. One fortunate note-holder reportedly obtained £8,000 in shillings and sixpences before the bank finally closed its doors on Saturday, 24 September.

The Extent of the Involvement

The widespread scale of the disaster that now faced the English popu-lation can be gauged from the extent to which they had been drawn into the speculative contagion. It subsequently emerged that no fewer than 462 members of the House of Commons had been holders of South Sea stock at some stage during the year. Moreover, 138 of these had actually borrowed money from the Company in order to purchase further shares which they could not finance from their own resources. Of the 200 mem-bers of the House of Lords, no fewer than 122 had been investors. It was thought that of all the ministers and noble personages of the day, only the Dukes of Argyle and Roxburge and the Earl of Stanhope had stayed aloof from the rising mayhem. Despite his known belligerent objections, even Robert Walpole purchased South Sea shares. Many of these not-ables were first sucked into the scheme with the issue of the notoriously generous Third Money Subscription at the height of the mania. This issue was the high point for South Sea finances. Its terms were so out-standingly benevolent that it attracted enormous interest and support.

The subscription lists for the Third Money Subscription indicate the extent of the speculative epidemic sweeping England by mid-June. The Directors were each allocated a section of the subscription, amounting in total to four-fifths of the whole. This was to be apportioned according to the personal nominations of the individual directors. Among the il-lustrious subscribers was the King, disguised with the name of Aislabie's brother-in-law, Vernon. A great number of Courtiers were included plus famous names from the world of art and letters, in addition to half the members of the House of Lords and over half of the Commons. As only one-fifth of the issue was assigned for the general public, which was allocated in a single day, it had a certain rarity value, which helped it rise to a 60 per cent premium on the Alley when the books were closed.

The Debt Deflation – Depression Follows the Boom

The self-feeding process of a spiralling decline swung into effect during September as several banks failed, or were about to collapse, as many debtors could not raise cash to meet commitments on loans made to speculate on the rising market. As share prices fell, broking firms failed, bank failures spread, as did the numbers of personal and commercial bankruptcies. Many aristocrats were ruined and the sudden collapse in share prices led to massive shortages in circulating cash. Robert Walpole skilfully extricated himself from the débâcle, by leaving London before the panic ensued. Many others were seriously affected, staying in to the last. From his correspondence with his friend, Cantillon, we know the Duke of Chandos experienced a embarrassing cash shortage following the South Sea Company collapse. Cassandra, his Duchess, alarmed by the Duke's substantial losses, wrote to friends asking for loans ranging from £5,000 to £10,000, to tide him over the crisis. She herself had invested £11,000 in South Sea stock as part of her dowry on her marriage to the Duke in 1713. Her mother had an even greater stake. Cassandra writes of the desperation many must have experienced, in a letter to the Duchess of Grafton: "I can assure you that of the late general misfortune, I have had my share, since of the £20,000 which my mother subscribed for herself and friends, there has been only £2,000 allowed."

William Brydges, the Duke's cousin, in London during November 1720, wrote of a widespread prevailing distress.

> This town is in a very shattered condition, eleven out of the twelve judges are dipped in South Sea: Bishops, Deans and Doctors, in short everybody that had money. Some of the quality are quite broke. Coaches and equipages are laying down every day and 'tis expected that the Christmas Holydays will be very melancholy.

Victims faced the disaster in a variety of ways; as in France, there was a spate of suicides, including a wealthy merchant from the City, a notable stock-jobber and Charles Blunt, cousin to Sir John. The sudden death of Lady Margaret Creighton was seen as the result of grief at the loss of her fortune in South Sea stock. The Duke of Chandos reputedly lost £700,000; he tried to raise loans from Cantillon, as a short-term measure to stay solvent. The Duke of Pentland was so reduced financially he gratefully accepted the office of Captain-General of Jamaica. The famous portrait painter, Sir Godfrey Kneller, lost most of the fortune he had made from painting the fashionable elites of the age. Several goldsmiths and brokers, unable to meet their obligations, closed their shops, absconded and fled abroad.

The South Sea Fall-out

Adversity was equally widespread among tradesmen and the building industry, for huge stocks of luxury goods were now unsaleable and many expensive building projects, commissioned when prosperity seemed assured, were suddenly mothballed. Workshops were filled with partly executed orders for which there was now no hope of payment and prospects looked exceedingly grim. The depth of the depression can be judged from a letter by Edward Harley, Jnr to Abigail Harley on 20 April 1721:

> Nothing arises or increases here but uneasiness, discontent, and clamour which reigns in every part of the city. The Exchange is the least frequented place of any of it. Jonathan's and Garraway's empty, and no creatures but passengers to be seen in the Alley, nor any trade stirring but what belongs to common necessaries.

A rolling deflation took hold, as paper assets became worthless and fortunes evaporated overnight. Some indication of the extent of the Sword Blade support can be gauged from records of its transactions for the Company. The Directors tapped into a vast credit reservoir from their banker, to lubricate the staccato process of repeated subscriptions and money loans launched in quick succession. The Cashier, Robert Knight, had access to a seemingly over-flowing current account with the bank, operated in the name of Surman. From January to March, the bank provided credit of at least £100,000 a month; the Company used it for share price support during February and March, while the South Sea legislation was passing through Parliament. Between mid-April and mid-May, turnover was in excess of £1 million, and nearly £4 million in the following four weeks in this account as the bank made advances to the Company on the strength of subscription receipts. This prodigious credit, plus the Company's spare cash, was required as injections into the market when each of the three loan offers on existing stock were announced.

Chaos in the Collapse

The sequence of the collapse covers phases six – eight in the typical crashes model. In both the Mississippi and the South Sea Bubbles, we can identify the particular events which triggered phase six, the initial doubts phase. In the Mississippi saga it began with the share price peak in early January 1720, but phase seven, the selling flood, rapidly set in as Law issued a series of contradictory edicts, during February 1720, seriously undermining confidence in the System. In the South Sea story, the flood of bubble companies coming to market gave investors more choice. Having more competition, funds leaked to upstart companies, with falling support for South Sea shares. This created the first appearance of a set-back as phase six. In both bubbles, the onset of phase seven coincided with the rapid chain reaction of anxious selling, ushering in a widespread distress among investors. This began with contradictory edicts in February/March in France and the issuing of writs against four other companies on 18 August in England, Finally, in both examples, there is phase eight, the huge distress of the panic sell-off. This occurred during investor mob reactions in July in Paris, and early in September in London, when the fall of the price below 600 triggered massive selling by banks holding shares as collateral linked specifically to that price.

As we saw with the upthrust of the boom in both the Mississippi and South Sea Companies, the classic features of the collapse can all be described in terms of chaos. It played a dominant role because chaos is, I believe, the driving force for the market's behaviour, in both directions. As with the boom, so with the collapse, and chaos is again the over-riding factor. In each case we can identify a specific trigger which sent the share price spinning downwards. As noted, the Mississippi Bubble peaked in January 1720, but the panic collapse was delayed until May. Similarly, the South Sea Company fortunes peaked in June, but the collapse was delayed until August. The two triggers, which we will now examine, were both examples of the chaos phenomenon, popularly called the Butterfly Effect. Here, a small initial event ripples through the system, setting off a chain reaction of events that escalate in intensity and distribution as they proceed but the range and extent of the reaction are unpredictable.

Mississippi Butterflies

The notorious 22 February decree issued by Law had an unpredictable result. It set in motion a powerful chain reaction that rapidly culminated in the abrupt and totally unexpected demise of his entire project. Although the edict was intended merely to arrest the share support programme, to allow shares to find their own level in the market, the implication so alarmed investors, it had an instant disastrous effect on Mississippi share prices; they plunged 26 per cent in a week. The outcry of rage that greeted this decree forced Law into a complete volte-face, a total reversal of his policy. Yet, despite announcing a series of conflicting edicts confidence in his system remained unwavering. His reputation was so assured, investors could not contemplate his failure. As late as March and April, most Mississippi investors, including the ever-optimistic Lady Herbert, Joseph Gage and their friends, retained their faith in prospects for impressive gains from their holdings, completely oblivious to the imminent arrival of a shocking reversal to their paper fortunes.

The contradictory edicts Law announced on the 5 and 11 March, were finally capped by the offensive 21 May edict. It resulted in another chaos Butterfly Effect, this time inflicting the totally unexpected fatal blow. Due to the unrelenting storm of protest and vilification of Law that accompanied this decree, it could not be enforced. It unleashed an extreme, ongoing crisis. The ill-fated decree was hastily withdrawn within a week, Law lost his office and his exceptional status, and Bank Royale went off the gold standard; it ceased to make payments in specie. With this acute crisis of confidence went the downward sliding share price; it had lost around 65 per cent of its January value by November when it stood at around 3,500 livres per share. At this date, Law's System was in tatters and the old monetary order was limpingly being reinstated.

South Sea Butterflies

A similar fate befell the South Sea Company, again through the sudden emergence of a Butterfly Effect. The trigger here was the first proceedings against four companies accused of misusing their charters. This unfortunate miscalculation was made by John Blunt, when he issued writs on 18 August. The wording of the infamous Bubble Act was vague, leaving the way open for challenges, even for companies that did have charters in addition to those that did not and were now illegal. The Directors must have been overjoyed when the writs succeeded; three of the four accused companies were actually forced to close. Their pleasure, however, was tantalisingly brief. Rather than clearing away the confusion posed by the upstart bubble imitators, the dramatic result of Blunt's ill-considered act was to trigger a major slump right across the London stock market. It undermined confidence in all the shares trading in London, not just in unauthorised bubble companies and swiftly brought about the demise of the South Sea Company, the very company the Directors were intending by their action to protect. This ongoing chain reaction effect continued to ripple along through the aftermath of the Bubble. The horrific shock of the collapse ushered in a vociferous clamour for retribution by setting up a formal Parliamentary inquiry. Ultimately, the most fraudulent directors were seriously penalised, and their ill-gotten gains had to be repaid, while Robert Knight, the company's cashier fled abroad. The chain reaction of the gathering crisis involved the closure of the Sword Blade Company and almost forced the Bank of England to close its doors. The widespread London stock market collapse ushered in a severe economic depression in England and across northern Europe.

Furthermore, this chain reaction event, once set in motion by the onset of the triggering Butterfly Effect, produced the rapid and steep decline in the share price that marked it out as a bubble. Within a week, the price of South Sea shares had fallen from over 900 to 810, and by 30 August was down to 755. The stampede out of shares went into overdrive during September, in spite of desperate efforts by the Directors to save the Company. The extent of the Butterfly Effect is recorded in the dramatic collapse of the share price. From 880 on 18 August, the date the writs were issued, it had plunged to 150 by 25 September. Here again, this powerful chain reaction, which applies to both Mississippi and South Sea shares, can be described by the classic features of chaos.

The Positive Feedback Loop of the Crash

When panic reaches a crescendo, money can become almost unavailable. For overstretched investors, bankruptcy looms with a sickening immediacy; tenuous links between asset prices, solvency, liquidity and the search for cash stand starkly revealed. The process whereby a crash or a panic takes hold results from positive feedback. A fall in the asset price reduces the value of collateral. This induces the banks to either call in existing loans or refuse new ones. To square their positions and repay their debts, commercial houses, dealers or traders sell commodities; private individuals sell securities; industry postpones further borrowing, and asset prices fall still further. The selling pulls down share prices, resulting in a further decline in the value of collateral, which leads to more liquidation, and the process repeats itself again around the positive feedback loop. Firms fail, so bank loans become irrecoverable and banks fail. As banks fail, depositors, stricken with sudden fear for the welfare of their savings, withdraw their cash; this link was more crucial before deposit insurance was introduced. For the banks, deposit withdrawals mean further loans must be called in and more securities will have to be sold.

Suddenly, the demand for cash takes precedence over all other considerations. The urge to sell becomes obsessive, at any price. With the need for cash paramount, everyone urgently wants liquid resources – trading companies, firms, banks, brokers and investors. The worst performing assets are sold off first, but soon, even profitable securities have to be sold in the rush for cash. The icy shock of the crash is harshly exposed by the abrupt way in which the "paper" wealth vested in assets with ever rising prices dramatically evaporates, virtually without trace. This sudden "wipe out" is the stark financial image captured by the term "bubble". Ruination becomes a sudden fact of life for thousands of disillusioned losers.

Self-Organisation for the Reconstruction

In England, the Parliamentary system was coupled to a constitutional monarchy. In chaos terms, it acted as the self-organising focus, to counter the disorder of the precipitous collapse. The objective was to impose a roughly just reconstruction and the unexpected hero who emerged to master-mind this result was Robert Walpole. He was to become one of Britain's greatest statesmen and politicians, although his early career gave little hint as to his ultimately huge future success and importance. He was to hold office as the King's first minister for a longer period than anyone who followed him, occupying the position of chief minister for George I and George II during the 1720s and 1730s.

His opposition to the misconceived terms of the conversion scheme at the outset in February was later matched by a brilliant stroke of timing. He left London to return to his Norfolk family home at Houghton, just as the South Sea story was unravelling, in autumn 1720. His absence from the centre stage during the dramatic demise of the corrupt Company endowed him with a prescience for predicting imminent disaster and left him as one of the few notable politicians untainted by the scandal. Uplifted by his apparent sagacity, his reputation for foresight, wisdom and incorruptibility soared. There was an immediate demand to place him in charge of the forthcoming Parliamentary investigation into the entire fiasco.

Walpole faced a tricky balancing act when he came to clear up the mess left by the collapse of the South Sea Bubble. It was important not to destroy the Whig administration for fear of allowing the Tories to gain power. His first duty was to stabilise the situation and restore public confidence in the Government's ability to rebuild the economy. Although the banks themselves finally worked out a satisfactory resolution to the impasse, Walpole, with his sure grasp of the financial essentials, was able to impose a minimum stability within which the banks could tackle the underlying problems.

After the lengthy Parliamentary inquiry, both Parliament and the public were persuaded to accept a scheme of reconstruction. It summarily, and by a process of rough justice, put people back to their pre-boom situation. There were several large gainers and many equally large losers, especially among the directors. Robert Knight, the Company cashier, was banned from England for over 20 years. He was party to the names of all the notables who had deceitfully participated for their own gain. He was clearly an awkward embarrassment to guilty people in high places, since he knew all the details of their implication in bribes to launch the Company on its conversion career. Most remarkably of all, thousands of private bargains were statutorily cancelled or adjusted, to eliminate much of the imaginary wealth. This sensible act alone demonstrated the reality of the exercise of parliamentary sovereignty in England. Moreover, the fragile Hanoverian monarchy, so recently established after the death of Queen Anne in 1714, although closely implicated in the governance of the Company, escaped the ignominy of being overthrown by the gathering crisis.

The two 1720 bubbles are reasonably well-contained episodes, now confined to the annuls of history, so it would be reasonable to suppose that modern economies are more sophisticated and would not fall into the trap of over-expanding credit to create an inflationary binge. Yet when we turn to twentieth-century crashes, in Part III we soon discover that the themes we have examined in the Mississippi and South Sea Bubbles repeat themselves with an astonishing consistency. The same eight-staged phases of the typical crashes model are evident. And recognisable chaos, as we shall see, is again the dominant force driving these events to their inevitable sorry conclusion.

I think this consistency is important. When we read about the antics of 1720 irrational investors, we should not feel smug or self-righteous. Indeed, we should not think of 1720 bubbles as quaint historical anecdotes holding no relevance for us today. It should be an exceedingly useful exercise to examine them in detail for they hold up a mirror before us, showing a painful but sadly accurate reflection of ourselves, if only we care to look. And this is precisely what we shall now do, as we turn to explore some of the principal crashes and bubbles of the twentieth century.

PART III

Modern Bubbles
and Crashes

CHAPTER TEN

1929 AND ALL THAT

> Your truly conservative banker cannot be stampeded into unwary speculations by the hysteria of a boom. He sits tight through 1926, 1927 and 1928. Unfortunately, he begins to come into the market in 1929. . . .
>
> Fred Schwed, *Where Are The Customers' Yachts?*

By September 1929, the history of Wall Street was already peppered with several previous crashes, many of a serious nature, but the Great Crash in October rapidly entered the legends of folklore by breaking all existing records. It was manifestly the most extreme incident of its kind to that date. It retained this morbid reputation for pre-eminence until it was overtaken in ferocity and magnitude by the October 1987 crash. And even as late as 1979, when Galbraith wrote the fiftieth anniversary edition of his seminal account of the 1929 Wall Street crash, the suggestion that another such awesome event, but now on a truly global scale, lay only eight years into the future, would have seemed to most commentators outrageously unlikely.

The immensity of the 1929 crash quickly gained recognition as a milestone event, because the depression into which it imperceptibly merged, had a catastrophic effect on the lives of millions of people, not only in America, but throughout the industrial world. It was the most formidable depression the world had yet seen. During the early 1930s capitalism itself was under increasing attack and verging indeed on extinction, since it was so manifestly seen to be failing in its formative heartland, America. Wide-scale suffering and privation almost led to open revolution. And the spectre of starvation was faced with fearsome dread by some of capitalism's most ardent advocates, the "huddled masses" – refugees who had fled Europe in their millions for the unbridled opportunities America was known to offer.

The slow build-up to the crash was merely one stage in a progression – a lengthy chain reaction of events. The ending of the First World War in

1918 was a seminal moment. Despite the horrific carnage of the war, industrial nations desperately wanted a quick return to the pre-war easy-going normality. Eagerness to eliminate harsh war-time deprivations spawned an unsustainable boom. It rapidly lost momentum, leading to a sharp and painful slump that hit America between 1920 and 1922 from which a creeping recovery slowly began; but even by 1922 America's mood had lightened. Many thought their compelling capitalist dream would swiftly materialise; as the mounting feel-good factor flourished, with rising output and economic growth, so did personal wealth. It was a time of mounting optimism and self-assurance.

The long boom and lengthy demise on Wall Street during the 1920s and early 1930s mark the incident out as a crash, rather than a bubble. Yet the eight-staged phases of the typical bubble drama are all evident, as are the dominant chaos features we identified in the 1720s examples. With the experiences of Mississippi and South Sea fresh in our minds, as self-contained case histories, we shall discuss the entire 1920s saga in terms of the underlying driving forces of chaos and the eight phases that expose the deeper structure of these historic events.

The Optimistic Mood of 1922

As heinous memories of the First World War slowly receded, a wondrous sense of optimism swept across the industrial world in the 1920s. The sense of light-heartedness was captured by the evocative phrase, the "Roaring Twenties"; it sparked the most extravagantly speculative boom ever known. Nowhere was this rising optimism more apparent than in America, where a growing conviction took root that this time a permanent prosperity was assured. People seriously began to think good times would continue uninterruptedly on an ever upwards trend. This pronounced period of prosperity came to be known as "the new economic era".

Although wages did not rise greatly, prices held steady and the num-bers of affluent people were increasing. Production and employment rose strongly in a vigorous surge. The explosive growth underpinning the euphoria was reflected in the key figures for national activity given in Galbraith's account. The number of manufacturing firms rose from 183,900 in 1925 to 206,700 by 1929. The value of their output increased from $60.8 billions to $68 billions. The Federal Reserve Index for indus-trial production had only averaged 67 in 1921, but it hit 110 by July 1928 and 126 in June 1929. Between 1921 and 1929, national income grew from $64,000 to $87,800 million. Gross National Product (GNP) topped $100 billion in 1929 for the first time and unemployment fell from 11.9 per cent in 1921 to 3.2 per cent by 1929.

Ordinary American families began enjoying a higher living standard. They were better fed, better dressed, had more leisure opportunities and travelled widely. They began to buy their own homes, as easy credit facilitated purchases through mortgages. Mass production factory techniques blossomed, through the pioneering skills of Henry Ford and F. W. Taylor. Family cars became an affordable luxury, as did a host of other delectable consumer goods and household gadgets. So confident were Americans in the mid-1920s that two in every three households installed electricity and then rushed out to buy a clutter of swanky electrical appliances. Lamps, refrigerators, washing machines and toasters sold in millions. Americans developed a passion for antiques, like oak furniture and *objets d'art*. Rising pay packets made even these luxuries affordable. Cautious middle-class people abandoned their long-held fear of debt and began to acquire models of amazing new inventions now flooding onto the market. Their love for the radio as a source of home entertainment was one exciting passion to emerge. In November 1920 there was only one radio station; by 1923 more than 500 broadcasting stations were operating. Radio shares in the late 1920s enjoyed one of the greatest surges, even in a market where everything was rising phenomenally.

At first, there were few outward signs of economic strain, but some discouraging trends were emerging. Net farm incomes declined during the period; although average earnings for industrial workers rose by 30 per cent, in 1929 they were still less than the annual $1,800 estimated as the minimum wage to maintain a family at a decent living standard. Again, over 60 per cent of all personal savings were made by a small proportion of families with incomes in excess of $10,000 a year. The Republican administration did not attempt to effect fairer income distributions. And while industrial production was rising, the hardship experienced by the poorest groups largely passed unnoticed. Despite the boom, many within an increasingly affluent society did not share the rising prosperity.

Two groups in particular did not enjoy a rising income: the farmers, facing over-production, high costs and restricted export markets; and industrial workers, whose wages rose at a slower rate than corporate profits and dividends. The international financial situation was also unbalanced. During the First World War, America became a creditor nation; its gold reserves rose from 25 per cent of the world's supply in 1913, to almost 40 per cent by 1921. Weakness in the system was exacerbated in 1925, when Britain returned to the gold standard at a rate which overvalued the pound. In 1925, the Federal Reserve Board lowered interest rates in an attempt to check the inflow of gold from Europe, and stimulate investment prospects within America.

Phase One – The Trigger of the Florida Land Bubble

America was indisputably a land of golden opportunities. Many Americans harboured a secret 'get-rich-quick' ideal. During the 1920s this potent urge went into overdrive, fuelled by the Florida land bubble which exploded into life in 1925. This boom was fomented by the arrival of many practised speculators. Yet despite their sophistication, the extraordinary efforts of Charles Ponzi, the infamous Bostonian financier were outstanding. His plan was to develop a suburb west of Jacksonville by subdividing building lots and selling off **the right to buy** for a 10 per cent down-payment. The boom centred not on the land itself but on "binders" or the right to buy it at a stated price. This right to buy was effectively a derivative instrument. It derived its value from the underlying land in Florida, but it operated primarily as an option. It could be traded on its own account, without any need to actually buy or sell the piece of related real estate. Derivative instruments, as the 1720s examples revealed, were custom-built for wild speculation. And so it was in 1925 for clients of Charles Ponzi.

The great novelty of Ponzi's "right to buy" scheme was that it allowed plots of land to change hands almost as fast as company shares can be traded on a stock exchange. This so facilitated the buying and selling of land plots, it enabled the speculation to increase at a phenomenal rate. Unfortunately, by autumn 1926, the buying fervour was running out of potential new recruits, when two severe hurricanes in the region dealt confidence a hard knock and the mania fizzled out. In essence, the Florida land boom signalled the prevailing American mood for risky financial adventures, in the same way that the widespread attractions of gambling provided a congenial backdrop to allow a build-up in speculative momentum during the 1720 bubbles.

Galbraith's data from his book *The Great Crash* show share prices were still at modest levels in the early 1920s. With the prospect of rising company earnings, however, there seemed every reason for them to rise. A gentle uptrend in prices began to establish itself in the second half of 1924. *The New York Times* industrial average for the prices of 25 leading shares stood at 106 at the end of May 1924; it had risen to 134 by the year-end. On 31 December 1925, it hit 181. There were several set-backs during 1926, and the year ended at 176, but optimism and share prices were both rising again by early 1927. The demise of the Florida land bubble, plus a drop in interest rates in 1925, may have been a trigger (phase one in the eight-staged crashes model), to set Wall Street on its crash-prone course. Opportunities for speculation blossomed with the Florida boom and this mood may have transferred to New York stocks after the demise of the Florida hype, just as French and Dutch speculators flocked to

England to participate in the booming stock market there when the Mississippi decline began during May and June of 1720.

Phase Two – The Lure of Easy Credit

When Britain returned to the gold standard at the overvalued rate of $4.86 in 1925, its trade situation was adversely affected. Gold was seeping out of Britain and Europe, to America. To arrest this, a deputation of European politicians, lead by Montagu Norman, Governor of the Bank of England, travelled to America in the spring of 1927, to urge America's central bankers to adopt an easy money policy. The Federal Reserve Board obligingly cut the rediscount rate from four to 3.5 per cent. The Federal Reserve, which misguidedly maintained a ruinous policy of easy money for far too long during the speculative phase of the boom, bought up government securities in huge amounts from banks and private investors, already awash with plenty of cash. The glut of surplus funds soon found its way to Wall Street, first in a modest flow, and ultimately in a deluging torrent.

There was an almost eerie repeat of this magnanimity by the world's biggest creditor nation, exactly 61 years later. Only the cast of characters is different, but since they appear to be reading from an identical script, it comes as a shock to realise that the 1988 actors may not have read the 1927 script. In both cases, the world's current biggest creditor country, America in 1927, Japan in 1988, tried to help out a reserve currency nation in severe trouble; British sterling in 1927, US dollars in 1988. In both cases, the end result was a mighty boom, followed by a calamitous crash.

In his account of the crash, Galbraith is scathing in his criticism of commentators who blamed the subsequent speculation squarely upon the blunder of an easy money policy. However, history and chaos theory are not on his side of the argument, although I believe **a cluster of factors must be operating in conjunction before a true bubble event emerges.** Yet from the evidence it is patently clear that a large injection of credit at appetisingly cheap rates can soon become a drug of addiction to wealth-hungry investors. In terms of the typical eight-staged crashes model, it introduces stage two, when ready access to easy credit energises a financial pump and fuels phase three of the model, the inflationary rise in consumer goods, property and financial assets. The positive feedback loop of many buyers, flush with cash, chasing a limited quantity of consumer and luxury goods, land or financial assets is the chaos mechanism that drives prices quickly up to unrealistic heights.

When conditions are right, cheap credit acts as a chaos financial pump, forcing prices around the positive feedback loop in ever faster spirals, so that the cost of financial assets and consumer products reaches excessive and unstable levels. In double-quick time, this pump stimulates imaginative new financial innovations, new companies and mass participation by the uninformed public. Galbraith claims that cheap money is not the main culprit for a speculative mania, since there have been numerous occasions when the existence of plentiful cheap money did not lead on to such a damaging outcome. From our discussions about chaos driving markets to excess, it should now be clear that his objections revolve around two key chaos features.

First, there is the problem of the sensitive dependence upon initial conditions, the famous Butterfly Effect. And secondly, of course, leading on from this chaos-induced chain reaction of small changes spiralling their way through the entire system, is the plain unpredictability factor inherent in such events.

History shows that during a deep depression, as in the 1930s, low rates of interest on their own, will rarely be a snare to entice people back into a buying binge on borrowed funds, since memories of the acute pain and distress this caused will still be only too fresh and levels of indebtedness far too high. A more recent example is the futile efforts of a weak Japanese government to reactivate a moribund domestic economy, five years after the bubble burst in Japan in January 1990. This inertia persisted despite numerous attempts to kick-start the economy with reflationary packages and interest rates falling to a miserly 0.5 per cent. Effectively, the huge elimination of wealth following on from both the Japanese 1980s bubble and the 1929 crash left fewer people with free cash to indulge in speculation, regardless of interest rate levels. In both instances, the economy was mired in a savage debt deflation from which it can only recover very gradually. People are holding greatly devalued assets bought at far higher prices during the preceding boom. And at such times most investors are suffering from debt-aversion. While reducing their debt exposure nothing can induce them to increase it until the ghastly memories of their over-borrowing escapades have faded completely away. The 1930s depression wiped out vast amounts of money, mainly through bank closures. Millions faced starvation or lived precariously on the bread-line. Thousands of company directors, bank officials and professional fund managers suffered serious monetary losses in the aftermath of the crash. In such circumstances, a speculative hysteria will be totally abhorrent. Cheap money on its own can never completely set the scene. What is needed is a chain reaction of events which together conspire to swing the entire episode convincingly up into a boom/bust mode. In short, the chaos-inducing features only come into force when all the first few stages of the typical crashes model emerge, one after another; then chaos can swing into action under the growing impetus of its own momentum.

Financial Innovations – 1920s Style

The structure of US industry and business underwent a profound transformation during the 1920s. First, a shift in the financing demands of
corporations forced commercial bankers to seek out new areas of revenue. And secondly, the growing investment trust sector brought thousands of new, generally inexperienced investors into the market. As
large, new capital-intensive firms emerged, they sought to raise funds for
expansion from retained earnings and by issuing new shares, a feature
commonly seen in boom/crash scenarios. Accordingly, commercial
loans as a percentage of total earnings assets of national banks declined
from 58 per cent in 1920 to 37 per cent by 1929. Facing this lost loan
business, the banks sought new areas of fee income. Regulations barred
them from investing directly in industry and they could not trade openly
in equities. As their traditional role as intermediaries shrank, they compensated by focusing on assisting the share-buying public. To do this
they set up wholly owned security affiliates, which could enter freely
into all aspects of investment banking and brokerage. The number of
such affiliates grew rapidly. In 1922 only 10 national banks had security
affiliates. This had risen to 114 by 1931. They could trawl their huge pool
of depositors, searching for potential clients.

For small investors without enough capital to buy a diversified portfolio, the investment trust sector growth met their needs. Prior to 1921,
there were only 40 investment trusts. Over the next eight years, their
number swelled by another 730. By 1927 another 140 had emerged, in
1928, 186 and in 1929, another 265. From 1921–4 new trusts attracted
about $75 million, but the total jumped to $1 billion between 1925–8 and
another $2.1 billion entered the market in 1929 alone. By this time, total
assets under management were $4.5 billion. The new trusts were often
closely interlinked with the parent firm's operations, acting together in
the purchase, distribution and underwriting of issues. This close association and the enormous leverage and pyramiding that occurred in the late
1920s led to some serious abuses and excessive volatility.

However, the investment trusts did serve a useful role, by acting as
conduits for savings to industry. They also allowed thousands of small
investors to become asset-owning capitalists, acquiring a well-diversified
portfolio of stocks. In the capital markets, the amounts of new issues of
stocks increased, while issues of bonds and foreign security declined.
This is a feature of all bull markets. Rising share prices encourage new
companies to come to the market and existing companies to tap it for
funds to support expansion plans through new share issues. Figures
reveal a massive growth in new domestic US stock issues. From $1,474
million in 1927 to $5,914 million in 1929.

Phases Three and Four – The Boom Accelerates

In January 1928, the industrial index stood at 245, the same level at which it briefly stabilised in November 1929, after hitting a peak on 3 September of 452. Early in 1928, however, as the huge credit explosion got underway, it was clear the nature of the boomlet had changed. Instead of a genteel gain in prices, punctuated by modest profit-taking pauses, the index rose, and sometimes fell, in startling, volatile leaps. In chaos terms, the steady-state of a gently rising market had been replaced by the early signs of rampant instability.

The loss of balance is an early warning sign that the market was bordering on the edge of chaos. From 1928, the movements of the index reveal this growing instability. In March alone, the industrial average rose almost 25 points. Frederick Lewis Allen, in his seminal account of the 1920s, *Only Yesterday*, dates the start of the boom to precisely 5 March. On this day, General Motors' stock began its steep ascent, as did RCA (Radio Corporation of America). These shares were favoured by some of the big speculators, including W. C. Durrant, Arthur Cutten and John H. Rascob. General Motors' prospects were especially good as Ford, still a private company, had closed down in 1927 to retool the Model A.

Interestingly, the surge in prices was most marked in a few favoured sectors, notably the electric utility industry, the movies and radio. Movie and radio shares were the high tech sectors for the 1920s. From a few dollars, RCA soared to over $400 a share. Yet it had no earnings and paid no dividends. When the market finally crashed in October 1929, these highly favoured stocks, especially General Motors and RCA, felt the full force of the collapse. The share price of RCA took almost 30 years to recover to its 1929 high. As we have noted, companies in the early stages of development, with start-up losses and no profits, are the most difficult investments to value. They frequently move to very high valuations on the strength of a promising story alone.

Back in the spring of 1928, however, gyrating share prices suddenly became hot news, featuring daily in front page headlines. Phase three, the inflationary surge in stock and commodity prices, was emerging. Expert traders began to make considered pronouncements about the future prospects for the thriving economy, observed by Professor Dice, who was pleasantly impressed by their "vision for the future and boundless hope and optimism".

With increasing euphoria, a trail of milestone "all-time highs" along the route swept the boom rapidly towards phase four, overtrading accompanied by massive borrowing in order to speculate. The level of participation illustrates one such progression of rising "all-time highs". On 12 March 1928, the volume of shares traded reached a high of

3,875,910, but this was easily superseded by 27 March, when the total reached 4,790,270 shares. The magic 5 million figure was comfortably exceeded on 12 June, when 5,052,790 shares changed hands. Tied to the primitive technology of the age the ticker, recording every trade, fell nearly two hours behind the market. To compare this milestone event with volumes on Wall Street in the 1990s, the daily total of shares traded has grown almost 100 fold, to around 350 to 450 million per day.

Another all-time high was sparked by the landslide election of Herbert Hoover as Republican President in November 1928. The ecstatic market promptly celebrated with a "victory boom". On 16 November a huge buying surge hit Wall Street, with 6,641,250 shares traded. This ebullient endorsement of the new President was almost repeated on 20 November, when trading reached 6,503,230 shares. However, if investors had known of Hoover's acute antipathy to trading, their response may not have been so exuberant. In his memoirs, he condemns speculation in the most vitriolic terms. "There are crimes far worse than murder for which men should be reviled and punished."

Although enthusiasm waned slightly during December, the industrial average still posted an annual gain of 86 points, up from 245 to 331 by year-end for yet another historical record. The magnificent total of shares traded on the New York Stock Exchange for 1928 hit a staggering 920,550,032, as against 576,990,875 for 1927. New records were being set as 1929 began. Early in January alone, on five separate days, the number of shares changing hands exceeded the big round number of five million, but evidence for repeated new records on the trading front pales into insignificance beside the figures for a phenomenal growth in margin trading, now gripping the investing community. This was another expression of phase four in the crashes model, with rampant borrowing specifically to purchase shares.

Nonlinearity – The Gearing Route to Super-profits

The chaos-basis of nonlinear gains and losses was explained in Chapter 3, and examples of it in operation were seen for both 1720 bubbles. Nonlinearity operated as a powerful force for outright speculation on Wall Street predominantly through two important routes: margin trading and the explosion of new investment trusts. In chaos terms, the substantial gearing element inherent in these two financial devices creates the extremes of instability which ultimately shoot the system up to an untenable peak. At first, nonlinearity fuels the boom upthrust, as people see paper profits rising exponentially. Euphoria feeds upon itself with a rising enthusiasm. A prosperous glow radiates out like ripples in a pond; wherever there is a share to buy, there is someone ready to buy it. Investors become number-drunk, and no longer able or even willing, to calculate "fair-value".

Traders, investors and speculators may all experience a phase transition event – tipping them from a rational to an irrational investment state of mind. The determinism of the crash emerges, although the timing of events is still extremely difficult to judge. With the onset of the panic, the entire gearing effect operates powerfully in reverse. Both borrowers and lenders now face the prospect of total liquidation, often at a frightening speed. When everyone is a seller, at any price, the collapse becomes almost instantaneous. This is why the panic is so horrendous. The system has become chaotic. It cannot settle down at all until the selling avalanche has subsided and a new stability can slowly begin to develop.

The Margin Trading Bonanza

For 1929 lenders, loans for margin trading appeared to offer a virtually risk-free return, with the shares themselves as collateral, and the call margin for extra protection. If the price fell, more margin had to be put up by the speculator until he was wiped out, but as the money was repayable on demand, the lender felt confident he could recover all his or her capital even when shares had to be liquidated to repay the loans. As speculative excesses roared on, US corporations, individuals and foreigners were drawn towards this treasure trove of easy money, not to invest, but to lend to the margin traders. By early 1929 loans from all these other sources equalled loans from the banks, but during the year, non-bank loans grew much faster. This indirect contribution to soaring Wall Street prices reflects the mounting role that outsiders, including foreigners played in fuelling the boom. With the advent of twentieth-century methods for transferring money between nations, it was no longer necessary for foreigners to flock to New York to participate in the boom, as their 1720 counterparts flocked to Paris, London or Amsterdam. Nor were they confined to simply buying shares or derivatives, for now they could act as lenders to the margin traders, in the mistaken belief that their actions were risk-free. Since much of this loan money evaporated into space during the week of the October crash, these interest-hungry lenders were indulging in rampant speculation without so much as purchasing even one share, secure in their false hopes this money out on loan was "safe".

As many thousands were lured into joining the margin trading gravy-train, either as lenders or borrowers, we will briefly look at how it worked in practice. The buyer on margin uses his newly acquired shares as collateral for the loan he had arranged to pay for them. The buyer enjoys all the benefits of full ownership to his stocks, including their earnings, for the prospect of securing a capital gain. Interest due on his loan is the only charge to consider, always assuming of course, that the market continues to rise. This, as we saw in the 1720 bubbles, is the magic of nonlinear gains. In 1720, issuing loans-on-stock, for the specific purpose of allowing further investment in shares, was much favoured by the South Sea directors. Their procedure operated in almost precisely the same way on Wall Street, two centuries later. To illustrate the huge potential from a reasonable outlay that was achievable on Wall Street, Galbraith suggests a speculator who paid an average of 10 per cent to carry his holdings of RCA through 1928 would have seen a gain of 500 per cent on the value of his investment. This is the golden nonlinearity scenario, but it can rapidly turn to ashes if the market encounters a serious set-back. Now the steep nonlinearity of losses prevails and the multiplier gearing works in reverse. In the panic, shares are dumped at any price and both lenders and borrowers can swiftly face ruin.

A Deluge of Loans

Although margin trading as a form of rampant speculation had excited the Directors of the South Sea Bubble with their tempting three loans-on-stock offers, it reached an altogether vaster scale during the boom of 1928–9. It became one of the most potent fuels stoking the self-sustaining price rises and, in the process, more "all-time high" records were hit with monotonous regularity. In an effort to dampen the hysterical enthusiasm, the rediscount rate at the New York Federal Reserve Bank was raised to 5 per cent in January 1929, but the momentum of the boom needs a far more decisive action to bring it to a halt. And brokers' loans to support margin traders charged any rate of interest from 5 per cent to a level of 10 or even 12 per cent. While on 26 March 1929, the rate on call money reached its peak at 20 per cent, indicating that high levels of interest charged would not alone reduce the margin mania.

From Galbraith's account, the growth in brokers' loans tells the story. Early in the 1920s the volume of loans ranged between $1 and $1.5 billion. By early 1926, it reached $2.5 billion, remaining at that figure for most of the year. During 1927, another increase of about $1 billion occurred, and by year-end, the loans totalled $3.4 billion. Although this was an astonishingly huge amount, the real expansion was just about to begin. This should not surprise us because, as we saw, the boom really took hold during 1928, and as new records were repeatedly set for volumes of shares traded, so the growth of new loans mushroomed to exorbitant levels. Loans reached $4 billion by 1 June, $5 billion by 1 November, with a year-end total of $5.7 billion. During January 1929, brokers loans rose by a vast $260 million. In the summer, brokers' loans were increasing at the rate of $400 million a month, and by the end of summer, the total exceeded $7 billion of which more than half came from corporations and individuals, both at home and abroad. On 3 September, when the market peaked, call money was 9 per cent and new loans amounted to $137 million in one week. During September, although the end was imminent, brokers' loans increased by almost $670 million, by far the largest increase of any month to date.

This astonishing escalation in margin trading reflects the move to phase five in the crashes model, as mass participation by the credulous public took hold. Yet one of the most surprising facts about this episode of collective US madness was the relatively small core of active speculators in the market. In a 2 March 1996 article, Robert Sobel in the *Weekend Money FT*, suggests figures for 1920s share ownership are unreliable. The Treasury estimated that 4–7 million people owned shares by 1929, but active investors held many issues, so the statistics are not clear-cut. J. K. Galbraith considers that only 1.5 million people in a population of about 120 million had any active association with the stock exchange. By October, the number of committed speculators was probably below a million, while numbers of margin trading accounts were around 600,000 and the value of shares listed on the New York Stock Exchange was $90 billion. (In the mid-1990s with the population at around 250 million, Americans collectively owned $5,000 billion in stocks, bonds and mutual funds.)

What emerges, surprisingly, from Galbraith's detailed analysis is the lack of a broad participation in the mass hysteria as the market drew ever closer to its inevitable top. Public interest was excited by a speculative mania as an acclaimed reality in the life of American culture and the rise on rise of Wall Street perfectly captured the nation's optimistic mood. Constantly rising share prices epitomised the spirit of the age.

Although Galbraith's analysis suggests the peak emerged without mass participation, the public mass involvement was actually there, but one step removed, as it were. With front-page headlines in the daily press, drawing attention to the soaring price of stocks, everyone, investor or by-stander alike, enjoyed the warmth of steadily rising prosperity, almost by implication. And then, behind the small army of active speculators, stood a massive supporting group, the lenders of loans, who, in their thousands, and from banks all over Europe, were also participating indirectly, by advancing loans to support share buying on the ever upwardly rising market.

The Investment Trusts Explosion

The phenomenal growth of investment trusts is the other prime example of the nonlinearity route to geared returns in the 1929 boom. It was a huge compounding engine for generating monetary excesses. Compound interest must surely be the eighth wonder of the world. The ultimate irony of both its rise and demise sprang from the fact that people buying into investment trust stocks were effectively investing in companies collecting funds to finance their own speculation. The similarity to the marketing ruses of John Law and the South Sea directors is no accident. For the circularity of investors chasing new issues which inspired yet more new issues was the self-same money-making loop that Law and Blunt exploited 200 years earlier, producing, sadly, almost identical results, but Wall Street's investment trust mania enhanced the action of a far more powerful financial pump than even they had been capable of creating. As with the mushrooming of bubble companies in England around 1720, so on Wall Street in the booming 1920s, there was a similar mushrooming in numbers of new investment trusts floated onto the New York Stock Exchange to exploit profitable opportunities thrown up by the continuing boom.

Investment trusts can borrow to buy more shares and, in a rising market, the fixed interest on their loans provided the gearing whereby the owners of the trust's equity, after paying the fixed interest on the loans, got all the benefits of the rising share price. During 1928 and 1929, US investors embraced these imaginative financial instruments with mounting enthusiasm. They watched in stunned delight as the magic of leverage sent investment trust stock prices surging ever higher. Over 40 years prior to the 1920s, investment trusts proved themselves to be highly successful collective funds for small British investors, but this innovative investment approach had only recently reached America. Now, as the boom intensified, the trusts slowly acquired a more prominent profile in New York. These trusts invest in other quoted companies on the exchange. As their shares are freely traded on the stock market, prices are usually determined by supply and demand, but they typically reflect a discount to total assets. On liquidation, the value of all the ordinary shares in the trust's portfolio will amount to more than the total capitalisation of the trust itself. The difference is the discount. However, if demand is really strong the trust's shares can sell at a premium.

In 1928 and 1929, US investors who rushed to buy investment trust shares, saw the miracle of nonlinearity at work on the prices of their holdings. In 1929 the Exchange required a trust to notify the market only once a year of the names and values of its underlying stocks, reminiscent of the 1720 English bubble company promotion of "an undertaking of great advantage, but nobody to know what it is". The refusal to disclose its holdings was considered a sensible precaution to avoid fuelling a roaring boom in securities bought by the trusts. The ruling may have backfired, as lack of information probably added to the buying frenzy. In the early months of 1929 an amazing statistic was added to this unfolding story; approximately one new trust appeared on each business day. In total, 265 new trusts joined the market that year. The enormous flood of purchasing power accompanying the explosion of new trusts is revealed by the figures. In 1927 the trusts sold $400 million worth of securities. By 1929 they had marketed an estimated $3 billion, representing at least one-third of all new capital issued that year. By autumn 1929, as the market neared its peak, the total assets of all the trusts exceeded $8 billion. They had increased approximately eleven-fold since 1927.

Nonlinearity with Investment Trusts

For small investors, collective trusts have the advantage of allowing a modest investment to be widely spread over perhaps 100 or more shares, thereby reducing risk. The other great benefit is leverage, which introduces the chaos nonlinearity effect of a small outlay producing the potential for huge gains – or losses. Galbraith illustrates the miracle of gearing with a trust established in early 1929. Say it raised capital of $150 million, through one-third common stock, one-third from the sale of bonds (paying a fixed interest) and one-third from preferred stock (where holders get preferential treatment on dividend payouts if the trust cannot afford to pay a dividend to all shareholders). After investing its initial capital of $150 million, a booming market might increase its assets within a year by 50 per cent. The portfolio assets would then have a value of $225 million. As the bonds and preferred stock together would still only be worth $100 million, the $50 million of common stock would have grown to $125 million, a gain of 150 per cent although the total assets of the entire trust had only risen by 50 per cent.

The Leveraged Pyramid

The sudden explosion in numbers of new trusts coming to the market during 1928–9 was primarily due to this compounding growth effect of leverage. If the common stock of a trust could appreciate by 150 per cent in a relatively short period, this could be greatly enhanced if this same stock were held by another trust employing similar leverage. The increase then could be in the region of between 700 and 800 per cent from the initial 50 per cent asset increase. Usually, a new investment trust was sponsored by another company. Lucrative profits came from sponsor-ship, included management fees for the trust, commissions for trading its securities and useful premiums on the purchase price at launch. As prices rose on Wall Street, the public craving for new issues ensured a steady launch of investment trusts found an enthusiastic reception. So strong was this demand, almost all new trusts sold at a premium to the issue price, to the profitable advantage of the sponsoring company. By 1929, many different types of corporation had discovered the non-linearity route to bountiful profits offered by investment trusts. They blossomed by the sponsoring efforts of investment banking houses, com-mercial banks, brokerage firms, securities dealers, and pre-eminently other investment trusts.

The geometric progression of gains that could accrue from investment trusts holding shares in other trusts resulted in a rush to sponsor new trusts which would then sponsor other new trusts, and so on around another lucrative loop. Having launched one trust and retained a share of its common stock, the capital gains achieved through leverage made it a relatively easy exercise to launch a second, much larger trust, which further enhanced the gains, and so on around another whirl, with yet a third, even larger trust launch. Although to the cynical outside observer, it looks as suspect as it patently was, when the fervour of a raging bull market provides the backdrop, the process assumes the appearance of a one-way ticket to financial success. Even the sober-suited professionals in the City – any city – rapidly become mesmerised by the attractions of monopoly-like gains.

Almost exactly 60 years later, the suave Japanese financial community walked this very same route of incestuous investment trust pyramid-building with virtually identical strides. Unfortunately, both the 1920s American and 1980s Japanese speculators in investment trusts ignored, or were blithely unaware of, the implications of where their path to certain riches would lead.

Succumbing to the Phase Transition Event

How is it possible for astute bankers, financial experts and celebrated leaders to get sucked into this money morass? I believe it is explained by their quixotic transformation into irrational investors. And on Wall Street in 1929, irrational investors were everywhere. They were not simply doormen, porters or shoe-shine boys, clambering onto the money-making roundabout at the peak, as the legend of the Great Crash would have us believe. The records are unequivocal. Directors of the banks, insurance companies and investment trusts were prominent professionals with good reputations for reliable money management. Nor were they resident only in America; bankers all over the industrialised world sent money flooding into America on behalf of their clients, to fuel the margin trading glut. Their behaviour in the boom is only explicable in the terms of chaos concepts. What we observe as phases four and five of the crash profile emerge, is the metamorphosis of perfectly sane professionals. A phase transition pitches them headlong into an absurdly irrational state. They become number-drunk speculators, with a blazing desire for instant wealth-creation.

In Goldman, Sachs and Company We Trust

The case of Goldman, Sachs and Company describes this lunacy, hooked on leverage that thrived under the investment trust banner in 1928. In its endeavours to tap the public's fervent desire for new issues it trod the well-worn path the two Johns, Blunt and Law, had travelled over 200 years before. The similarities are astounding, so faithful is the repetition. In December 1928, the company issued 1 million shares in a new Trading Corporation at $100 a share, all originally bought by Goldman, Sachs before 90 per cent of them were sold on to the public at $104. There was no leverage at this stage, as neither bonds nor preferred stock were involved; merely a modest, but healthy premium to the issuing company of $4 per share. By 4 February, the stock was selling for $136.50 and on 7 February, it reached $222.50. At this figure, its value was approximately twice the current worth of all the securities, assets and cash it owned. And this astonishing rise in its value was mainly due to the fact that the Trading Corporation was buying its own securities in large quantities.

Two months after it first floated the original 1 million shares, more stock was sold and following a merger, the assets of the enlarged Company amounted to $235 million, for a gain of over 100 per cent in two months. By 14 March, the Trading Corporation had bought 560,724 of its own shares for an outlay of $57.02 million. A fierce positive feedback loop was now operating. By buying its own shares, the Trading Corporation forced up the price of those shares, making its total assets more valuable, which allowed it to buy more stock. This tightly closed loop helped the share price to rise miraculously.

On 26 July 1929, the Trading Corporation launched the Shenandoah Corporation with an issue of $102.5 million which was reportedly oversubscribed seven times. This new issue included leverage with the sale of some preferred stock. The initial issue price was $17.50, but it opened at $30, reaching a high of $36, to stand $18.50 above its issue price. (By

December, when leverage was working in reverse, the price was just above $8.) In August, the second leveraged investment trust from the Goldman, Sachs and Company stable was launched. This was Blue Ridge with a capital of $142 million, sponsored by its stable mate, Shenandoah. Of its 7.25 million shares, plus a hefty issue of preferred, Shenandoah subscribed a total of 6.25 million. Two days later, with the acquisition of a West Coast investment trust, and another mammoth issue of $71.4 million of stock, Goldman, Sachs had issued more than $250 million of securities in under one month. This gargantuan effort stood at the pinnacle of the new era finance. It is reminiscent of the formidable growth in new issues promoted by the two 1720s "Johns". Both Law and Blunt launched massive new issues into a tide of rising market delirium, to tap the mounting craze to participate in the effortless marvels of huge nonlinear returns.

Phase Five – Wall Street at the Peak

The need to keep in touch with events on the Street had never seemed greater than during the summer of 1929, so reminiscent of events in 1720 in the rue Quincampoix and Exchange Alley. As Alexander D. Noyes noted in *The Market Place,*

> Brokers' offices were crowded from 10 am to 3 pm with seated or standing customers who, instead of attending to their own business, were watching the blackboard. In some "customers" rooms it was difficult to get access to a spot from which the posted quotations could be seen; no one could get a chance to inspect the tape.

Being out of touch with the market was a tiresome inconvenience. Fortunately, the ticker service now operated right across the nation while a local telephone call could be made from almost anywhere for an up-to-date quotation. By August 1929, even the problem of staying informed while crossing the Atlantic to Europe had been solved. Some efficient brokerage houses installed branches on the big transatlantic ocean liners for the benefit of their travelling investor clients. The famous beautician, founder of a cosmetic empire, Madame Helena Rubenstein, reputedly lost over $1 million dollars when she sold a massive holding of Westinghouse shares on a transatlantic crossing during the week of the crash.

An anonymous poet on the editorial staff of the *Spokesman-Review* in Spokane penned a ditty to commemorate the novel ocean-going broker facilities, as quoted in Galbraith's account of the crash.

We were crowded in the cabin
Watching figures on the Board;
It was midnight on the ocean
And a tempest loudly roared.

. . . .

"We are lost!" the Captain shouted,
As he staggered down the stairs.

"I've got a tip," he faltered,
"Straight by wireless from the aunt
Of a fellow who's related
To a cousin of Durant."

At these awful words we shuddered,
And the stoutest bull grew sick
While the brokers cried, "More margin!"
And the ticker ceased to tick.

But the captain's little daughter
Said, "I do not understand –
Isn't Morgan on the ocean
Just the same as on the land?"

Yet during the summer of 1929, before the peak came lurching into view, those who expressed alarm or concern at the rate the debts were mounting were dismissed as pessimists or plainly unpatriotic for inferring the price of stocks was too high. There was no cause to worry over the rising tide of debt. In this day-dreaming world of money-go-round, defending the level of loans consisted primarily of defending the level of prices in the market. It prompted a series of wholehearted endorsements for ever rising prices from streams of worthy public figures. The silly quotes season had arrived.

Phase Six – Early Nagging Doubts

With the boom in full swing, most of the ominous signs lurking in the background were completely ignored. A year earlier it had become evident that the commodity price level had begun to fall, that productive capacity was not being fully utilised, and that construction had declined. Market prices had begun to drop in Europe, even as the American boom went surging on. As in the 1720s, when the first creeping doubts arrived they heralded phase six of the crashes model. In 1929 it emerged with a hideous flourish. From nowhere, a chaos Butterfly Effect appeared, ushering in a fierce chain reaction that radiated widely out from one low-key event.

On 7 February, the Federal Reserve Board issued a sombre warning to the public on the danger of speculative credit. Almost instantaneously came news that the Bank of England was raising the bank rate from 4.5 to 5.5 per cent in an attempt to reduce the flood of money pouring into America to provide loans at 12 per cent for Americans who wanted to hold common stocks on margin. *The Times* index dropped 11 points on the day, to record another 5 million shares traded session, and suffered a further plunge the following day. Investor nervousness reached a crescendo when the Federal Reserve began holding daily meetings but refused to issue any statements to the press. An unprecedented Saturday morning meeting on 23 March unleashed a torrent of selling. *The Times* industrial average dropped 9.5 points, and banks began curtailing their loans in the call market. This action sent the rate on brokers' loans to 14 per cent.

The situation worsened on 26 March, and a wave of fear swept through the market, with the Federal Reserve Board maintaining a demoralising silence. The records for shares changing hands in one day crashed, along with the prices of shares. As 8,246,740 shares were traded, prices reached a 20–30 point low on many shares, the industrial index lost 15 points at one stage, and throughout the trauma of the sell-off, the antiquated ticker machines lagged way behind the active market. Due to the unprecedented volume, speculators and investors alike were operating in total ignorance, because prices were certain to be lower than those showing on the ticker. As trading ended for the day, thousands of terse telegrams were winging their way from nervous brokers to anxious investors, ominously marking a new stage in the boom. Contrary to all the previous communications brimming with optimistic phrases, these telegrams were demanding more margin. On 26 March, yet another record was notched up. The rate on call money reached its all-time high for the 1929 boom at 20 per cent.

This exceptional set-back for the market should have presaged the full collapse. It stands almost on a par with the early February edicts issued by Law to stem the mounting monetary inflation in France, but, in true chaos fashion, on Wall Street, the imminent panic was averted, almost single-handedly, by Charles E. Mitchell, the Chairman of the Board of the National City Bank. In an interesting angle that links him to the South Sea Company directors, Mitchell, one of the most influential bankers of the day, was speculating on a massive scale for his own account. Clearly, he had a vested interest in maintaining the boom. He announced to the press that the National City Bank would loan money as necessary to prevent a dangerous crisis in the money market. His words brought instant comfort and the market rallied strongly in a huge nonlinear leap.

On the following day the National City Bank put $25 million into the call market, $5 million when the rate was 16 per cent and an additional

$5 million for each percentage point above that. A few days later, in its monthly letter, it clarified its action, by recognising the dangers of over-speculation, but wishing to avoid a general collapse in the securities market that would have a disastrous effect on business. This uncomfortable dilemma, the central predicament facing the Federal Reserve authorities, was the reason for their deafening silence during this time. With frantic overtrading on Wall Street, they had to decide whether to support the raging boom or terminate it and face the possibility of a crushing collapse.

From our discussion on the 1720s bubbles, we can see that the Board had allowed the speculation to run for far too long. Exorbitant levels of margin trading plus the grotesque excesses of hundreds of newly issued investment trusts bent on pyramid-building had generated the all-too-familiar financial pump. Undoubtedly, the mania was already irreversible. The typical chaos scenario was dominant, irrational investors were overwhelmingly in the ascendant and the chaos was deterministic; the inevitable ending had become predictable. It was foreshadowed by the sheer scale and strength of the boom that had been building. Faced with the action of the National City Bank, the Federal Reserve withdrew to the sidelines, awaiting the final collapse, but the speculators had regained their collective nerve, and the boom roared on. From 1 June there was no turning back.

Swindles and Fraudsters

We have already mentioned the collapse of Clarence Hatry's financial empire in September 1929. This London-based fraud involved forged certificates when Hatry tried to raise funds to finance a large steel conglomerate he planned to float on the stock market. During the summer, while trying to raise the £4 million he needed, Hatry illegally used some of his cash to support the value of his company's shares in the declining market, as the South Sea directors had done 200 years before. Desperate to raise the balance of cash he needed, when share prices were falling, Hatry resorted to a criminal offence; he raised loans from banks on the security of shares that had never been sold. By 19 September, the value of his shares having plummeted, he had debts of £19 million on assets of just £4 million. On 16 December, Hatry and his associates were committed to trial at the Old Bailey, where he was sentenced to 10 years imprisonment.

About this time, on the other side of the Atlantic, another fraud was being hatched by some of the officials and staff of the Union Industrial Bank in Flint, Michigan. This involved a gigantic swindle, using depositors' cash to speculate on the New York Stock Exchange. All the members of this scam had different reasons for wanting cash; one had a sick wife, another had heavy gambling debts. Over a period, more than $2 million was stolen to play the market. By May 1929, the strength of the market had enabled the embezzlers to repay half of the stolen $2.5 million with well-placed investments in RCA and in a food stock. Other investments went so well that the total sum outstanding had shrunk to $62,000 by August. Unfortunately, luck and set-backs in the market now turned against them. A series of losses, plus the adverse market reaction to the failure of the Hatry empire, brought their total losses to $1.5 million by the month-end. By 24 October, the embezzlers were down a hefty $2 million, which swelled to a horrifying $3.6 million in the débâcle of 29 October. The bottom had fallen out of the market and there was no way the money could be repaid. The main stock holder and Chairman of the bank, Charles Mott, who was a senior officer of General Motors, was an honourable man. Instead of declaring the bank insolvent, he travelled to Detroit and drew out $3,592,000 from his private account to replace the deficit. The embezzlers received custodial sentences ranging from six months to 10 years in the Michigan State Prison.

Phase Seven – The Downturn Arrives

The mini-crash on 24 October represented the onset of the selling flood. It was the signal for the loans pyramid to disintegrate. The wave of selling sent prices spiralling down. A record of nearly 13 million shares changed hands. To check the decline, bankers and politicians stepped in amid high publicity to steady prices. One alarming aspect of the plunge in prices was that the ticker was hours behind the action. It was after 7 o'clock that night that the ticker finally finished recording the day's misfortunes. The lights blazed in Wall Streets' offices as clerks battled to record the day's business.

Churchill's Ring-side Seat

On the night of the crash, Bernard Baruch, the famous Wall Street investor, was entertaining Winston Churchill, then on a lecturing tour of Canada and North America with his son, Randolf. Baruch introduced Churchill to some 40 leading American bankers and financiers. Next day, Churchill visited the New York Stock Exchange to witness the unfolding catastrophe. From the apartment block where he was staying he later recalled that under his own window, "a gentleman cast himself down fifteen storeys and was dashed to pieces, causing a wild commotion and the arrival of the fire brigade."

Phase Eight – The Great Collapse

The end, when it came, was horrendously alarming in both the scale and magnitude of its impact. During the week of the crash, 23–30 October, values fell, margin accounts were liquidated and the volume of brokers' loans fell by more than $1 billion. Corporations and out-of-town banks called home over $2 billion. The days of investing in the risk-free call market were definitely over. Although there was a temporary lull on Wall Street, after the shock of the 24 October sell-off, on 29 October the selling pressure returned with a frightening gusto. On this day, known to posterity as "Black Thursday" more than 16 million shares were sold and prices plummeted. Great blocks of shares came onto the market, offered for whatever they would fetch. In the first half hour, sales were at the rate of 33 million a day. In many issues, there were enormous sell orders and absolutely no buyers. Again, the ticker lagged the market; at the close it was two and a half hours behind.

The day of 29 October was etched in the memory of many who experienced it. Huge blocks of stock, 25,000, 50,000, 100,000 shares, were dumped on the market for whatever price would be offered. As there was hardly any buying support, no matter how far some stocks had fallen, floor brokers found their pockets bulging with unexecuted orders still to sell at the close of trading. Some financial specialists, like John V. Bouvier III, who were supposed to provide buying support when none was forthcoming, faced the spectre of ruin if they complied strictly with this function. Accordingly, when the closing gong sounded, their wastepaper baskets were also stuffed with unexecuted sell orders. Analysts calculated if all orders received that day had been executed, there would have been a 20 million share liquidation, which would have driven prices to even lower levels than were actually reached. Massive drops in prices across the board marked the extent of the calamity investors now faced. General Electric had fallen 28 points on the day, Auburn Motors sank another 60 points, Allied Chemicals lost 35 and Electric Auto Life plunged 45 points. Across the length and breadth of the nation, millionaires and aspiring millionaires were in shock, their dreams shattered by the savagery of losses set on that awful day.

In the febrile climate of summer 1929, the investment trusts had invested heavily in each other. When the crash came, their true incestuous nature stood revealed. The leverage went into steep reverse and the stabilising effects of their huge cash reserves proved hopelessly inadequate to stave off disaster. Nonlinearity in reverse proved a harrowing trial for bankers, company directors, investors and speculators alike, since everyone had been simply projecting additional gains well into the future. Look, for example, at the chain reaction catastrophe that overtook the Goldman, Sachs and Company investment trust empire. The fall in the price of Blue Ridge had a knock-on effect on Shenandoah. The collapse in the share price of Shenandoah decimated the share price of Goldman, Sachs Trading Corporation. As share prices fell so did the value of the investment trusts' portfolio of stocks. If half the shares were preferred, when the asset values fell by half, the common stock value was completely wiped out. Mr Sachs, giving evidence before a Hearing in 1932 on Stock Exchange Practices, cited the current price of Goldman, Sachs and Company's Trading Corporation shares (initially launched at $104 on 4 December 1928), as approximately $1.75. During the last week of October, investors rapidly learned the sickening reality that the law of geometric progression works just as effectively in a negative as in a positive direction.

However, even this sobering discovery was not the starkest lesson that the 1929 crash taught. In earlier crashes, there had been a sudden and abrupt beginning, with an equally clear-cut finale. As Galbraith points out, the tragedy of 1929 was that there had been a slow and gradual build-up in momentum to the peak, taking years. After the October crash, however, the worst continued to worsen in such a mischievous way that scarcely any escaped unscathed from the great débâcle. Many were rapidly wiped out. Those with larger funds paid the calls in the expectation that the bottom had been reached, and ultimately, because it hadn't, they too often faced ruin. Finally, those wily investors who had withdrawn before the first crash struck, entered the market to pick up bargains. In another murderous decline, bargain hunters saw values drop to a third or a quarter of their purchase price.

From its August 1929 high of 449, The New York Times Industrial Averages fell to 224 by 13 November and hit 58 at the ultimate low in July 1932, which proved to be a floor. The Dow Jones Industrial Average (DJIA), monitoring 30 major stocks traded on the New York Stock Exchange, went into freefall, plunging by 79 per cent as the country suffered through the tormenting traumas of its deepest ever recession. As investors continued to believe the upturn must surely now be in sight, no one could ever guess that the bottom would not finally arrive until July 1932, a period of nearly three years of remorseless falls since the October 1929 débâcle.

The glacially slow origins and extensive aftermath explain why this Wall Street débâcle was never termed a bubble, but the great reliance on margin trading and support for new investment trusts issues were the two principal innovative devices that allowed the onset of chaos to occur. The rickety structure powered to an extreme peak, which was swiftly overwhelmed by the crash. The pyramiding of the investment trusts aggravated the instability. They relied for stability on the prosperity of the parent company; any weakness there would be reflected in the financial structures superimposed above it and could, as was soon seen, result in a complete collapse. We know this to be the onset of massive fluctuations that ensues when the critical point at the edge of chaos is reached. It is a classic illustration, analogous with the pile of sand grains example discussed in Chapter 5.

Debt Deflation – The Wall Street Fall-out

In the melancholy reckoning that followed, the banks realised that many of the loans they had so willingly provided would never be repaid. Consumers realised they were hugely over-borrowed. A swingeing debt deflation took hold. This is a credit vortex; the underlying value of an asset, such as a house, land or a financial security, has fallen faster than the value of the associated loan. Once a debt deflation sets in, it is incredibly hard to dislodge. There is little that governments can do to reinstate the vanished wealth, except to support the most essential parts of the economy while the inching process of recovery unfolds. In a severe debt deflation, sales of goods and services fall away, there are serious shortages of cash and profit margins are squeezed across the range for manufacturers and businesses. Credit is based on trust; if trust evaporates, it can only be regained by a grindingly slow process of gentle renegotiation. Meanwhile credit becomes almost unobtainable, although interest rates may be at abysmally low levels. In the 1930s rates were 2 per cent in Britain and 0.5 per cent in America, but borrowers remained most reluctant to take on loans, even at these levels and bankers were equally reluctant to accept new loan business. It is no accident that the word "depression" is used both by economists and psychologists. For the depression of the 1930s generated a profound apathy in its victims as the economy became increasingly more paralysed. A 1994 UK television series on the Great Depression showed amazing film footage of the period, with scenes of hungry citizens driven almost to rioting point, as conditions continued to deteriorate and the authorities seemed hopelessly inadequate in their muted response.

The financial system cracked under the strain. Companies cut back in an attempt to survive, demand fell, unemployment rose and degrees of genuine poverty and hardship reached unprecedented levels in Europe and America. The democratic Western world was gripped by a vicious debt deflation which produced unprecedented levels of suffering. Over 1,300 banks closed their doors in America in 1930 and another 3,700 in the next two years. Every economic indicator reflected the collapse. The manufacturing production index fell 28 points between 1929 and 1932, GNP in 1929 dollars fell from a peak of $104,400 to $74,000 million in 1933, automobile factory sales fell from 4.5 million in 1929 to 1.1 million in 1932.

By 1932 9 million people had lost their life savings. Unemployment, less than 1 million at the height of the boom, rose to over 13 million, a shocking 24.9 per cent of the labour force by 1933. People were undernourished, or near to starvation. The birth rate dropped dramatically, from 18.4 per 1000 population in 1920 to 2.7 per 1000 by the early 1930s, the lowest level in American history. The spreading misery was calamitous. Squalid shanty towns, dubbed Hoovervilles, of cardboard and rubble rose on the outskirts of most cities; breadlines often stretched round entire city blocks in queues for relief at charity stations; scavengers sifted through the rubbish in city dumps searching for edible scraps.

The Wall Street crash sent ripple effects throughout the free world. The scale of the wipe-out was a blow to international confidence on a magnitude which completely dwarfed the damaging effects of the 1720 bubbles. The early euphoria in America of "vision and boundless hope and optimism" lay dashed, especially so as it slowly dawned that the crash had heralded the onset of a mega-economic slump. Whether the two events were a cause-and-effect progression is not relevant, since the reality of the depression following hard on the heels of the crash ensured the morbid reputation for the latter and the accolade of "Great" for both events. The collapse in US share prices had drastic repercussions on confidence and world trade, with confidence shattered and trust evaporated on a world-wide scale.

Business activity declined in those European economies which had been heavily dependent on US loans and credits. These economies were only just reviving from the ravages of the First World War. The contraction in trade was a severe blow to their continuing recovery. Primary products and commodities fell in price. This had a serious knock-on effect as producers of these raw materials in the developing world now had less incoming revenues with which to purchase key manufactured goods from the industrialised world. Investment and trade dwindled alarmingly. As all the developing, the European and US economies contracted, the first major consequence was a rapid rise in world-wide unemployment. In May 1931, a Viennese Bank, Credit Anstalt, failed, sparking a crisis of confidence in Germany and a run on the central German bank, the Reichsbank. This sent ripples of a banking collapse through Europe, to Britain and ultimately on to America.

The Slow Reconstruction Begins

With around 12 to 13 million people out of work, America was desperate for a new beginning. This now arrived under the imaginative steward-ship of the Democrat, Franklin Delano Roosevelt. Elected as President in 1932, on the promise of full employment in peace time, he ushered in the era of faltering reconstruction and the New Deal. Under his leadership, America embarked upon a series of major public works projects and job-creation schemes. His guarantee of full employment took years to de-liver, and 10 million were still without work in 1938. The rise of Hitler and America's rearmament programme to assist Britain in the fight against Hitler, finally solved the 1930s unemployment dilemma, but Roosevelt's role in restoring the American economy to health cannot be understated.

In the month prior to his inauguration, banks were failing in droves, and gold and currency was being withdrawn from circulation at the alarming rate of $15 million per day. The Government had already lent $850 million to the banks and now began lending to the railways. On 4 March 1933, the day of his inauguration, Roosevelt made his ringing address to inspire the nation, "We have nothing to fear but fear itself". On his inauguration day, without any legal authority, he closed every bank in the country. Circulating money ground to a shuddering halt and his rule as a benevolent dictator had begun.

When he came to the centre stage, America's crisis of self-confidence was in extremis. In terms of chaos, the entire system was mired in a stultifying paralysis. His role was to reawaken democracy and recreate an entrepreneurial economy out of these unpromising ruins. Ironically, his method of re-imposing order on this debilitated structure was to ask and be given emergency powers by Congress, and to rule for the next two years as a benign autocrat, attempting to rebuild the nation through his National Recovery Administration.

It Couldn't Happen Again

During the long upswing years following the Second World War, when Western Europe was rebuilding itself and global economies grew hand-somely, the thought that another such international crisis could occur was so remote as to be literally unthinkable. Yet, this strange cycle of a six-year boom followed by a mega crash, was not to be a unique 1930s incident. There are differences between the crashes of 1929 and 1987, of course, but there are many similarities as well. We have already noted that the behaviour of stock prices during the two periods was extremely close, even to the length and extent of the rises which were almost identical.

Other similarities arose from the major changes in the structure of industry and widespread financial innovation affecting both boom periods. These similarities are quite striking, at least, they would be seen as such, if we did not know that both crashes were chaos-induced phenomena and therefore, once the chaos mechanism was in place, they followed a predictable path. How this strange recurrence worked itself out in 1987 is the topic we shall now explore.

CHAPTER ELEVEN

1987 – THE GLOBAL CRASH

October. This is one of the peculiarly dangerous months to speculate in stocks. The others are July, January, September, April, November, May, March, June, December, August and February.

Mark Twain

Very few investors, brokers or politicians seriously thought the enormity of the October 1929 crash could ever be repeated. Yet we seem to be condemned to repeat similar mistakes at long-term intervals. Major misjudgements appear to skip a generation. Because they haunt the memories of the children, they can only return in strength to mock the efforts of the grand-children. Peter Lynch, the fabled manager of the mighty Fidelity Magellan Mutual Fund recounts in *One Up On Wall Street*, his first-hand experience of the mood of Americans caught up in the Great Depression during their most impressionable years.

> Most of my relatives distrusted the stock market, and with great reason. My mother was the youngest of seven children, which meant that my aunts and uncles were old enough to have reached adulthood during the Great Depression and to have had firsthand knowledge of the Crash of '29. Nobody was recommending stocks around our household.

Marty Zweig, another renowned 1980s fund manager, who runs a multi-billion dollar group of mutual funds, grew up in the 1940s and felt close enough to the Great Depression for it to have made a lasting impression on him. He recalls dinner conversations often returned to its harrowing themes, observing, "that dreadful period and its great bear markets are always on my mind whenever I deal with stocks."

The market has only a limited long-term memory, and history book lessons are not as searing and unforgettable as bitter first-hand experiences. The surprise is to discover how long the echoes of these memories persist. Lynch points out that distrust of stocks was the prevailing American attitude throughout the 1950s and 1960s. During this period, however, the stock market tripled and then doubled again, as the global post-war recovery got into its stride.

Yet, even if the circumstances differ in the detail, people's behaviour is uncannily constant. The irrational investor is a true survivor, emerging unscathed to revisit every panic or crash.

Although we have shown it is the onset of chaos in the market that drives gullible investors into a deranged mentality, when we examine the recent history of the October 1987 crash it is still hard not to be amazed by the uncanny resemblance it bears to the Wall Street crash that preceded it, by almost 58 years to the day. One statistic, out of many, illustrates this repetitive theme: both crashes were preceded by a substantial price rise in the nine months to September; 31 per cent in 1929 and 32 per cent in 1987.

If progress is measured in size, then 1987 was certainly a far more impressive event, for although it began on Wall Street, it sent colossal shock waves reverberating around the 24 hour trading clock, as noted in Chapter 1. It was a panic of global proportions.

Today, cynics are quick to accuse the presiding authorities of failing to learn from history. Yet, to be fair, although they made a major contribution to the build-up to the 1987 crash, when faced with the awesome reality of it's presence, the main Governments of the industrial nations took instant steps to arrest the haemorrhage of fear. By a speedy response and united effort to restore confidence through reduced interest rates, they signalled to the financial markets that this time around, they would take all necessary avoiding actions to forestall a repetition of the ghastly depression years of the 1930s.

Accordingly, during 1988, the stock markets of the major industrial nations gradually recovered their nerve, and climbed steadily to new highs during the 1990s. That is, except for Japan. The sorry tale of Japan's continuing bear market is covered in Chapter 12 but its roots lie firmly buried in the history and aftermath of the 1987 crash, because, in true chaos fashion, one thing leads on to another, . . . and so it goes.

Background to the Crash

As with the Wall Street crash of 1929, the background to, and onset of the boom in 1986, the rapid move to the peak and the crash itself, can all be explained in chaos terms. As the detailed story is reviewed, therefore, we shall note these chaos features as they occur. This account of events surrounding the crash of 1987 draws heavily on Brian Reading's book *Japan, The Coming Collapse*. The general conditions in the run-up years before the 1987 crash show strong similarities to the 1920s situation. Just as the slow-burn recovery of the 1920s emerged from the erratic trading environment thrown up by a short, sharp but unsustainable post-First World War boom, swiftly followed by a two-year slump, so the build-up to the 1987 crash had an equally long and chequered history. Moreover, both boom periods saw substantial financial innovation for industry and commerce.

Recession Precedes the Boom

In the early 1980s the economies of both the developed and developing nations were severely hampered by the second large oil price rise to occur in six years. In a modern industrial state, rising oil prices rapidly translate into increasing levels of inflation. The added costs for heating, lighting and fuel permeate through every sector of the economy: in agriculture, with swift increases to food prices; in manufacturing, in the costs of dozens of products that are derived from petroleum; in industry, where petroleum products make up the raw materials for all manner of industrial output; and in the household, where domestic budgets are increasingly strained by additional expenditure on every household activity and cost.

The dramatic impact of rising oil prices cannot be underestimated as a source of increasing inflation for modern manufacturing nations. The ensuing recession was a harsh epilogue to the turbulent, inflation-ridden 1970s, when governments espoused expansive state intervention, deficit financing and were committed to full employment. They constructed enlarging welfare systems to support the weakest members of society, while borrowing heavily to honour their promises on benefits and hand-outs. This reckless mood – borrow now, pay later – was untenable for dealing with massive dislocation costs, such as the two oil price rises of 1973 and 1978.

The deep recession of 1979–81 became a sluggish economic backdrop that preceded the onset of chaos. Once appropriate triggering devices were in place, chaos could emerge from this lethargic recessionary state of underactivity. In percentage terms, however, the second oil price rise was less severe than the first. Between 1972 and 1974 prices quintupled, but from 1978 to 1980 they little more than doubled. But since the 1978 starting level was much higher, in absolute terms, the effect on import prices was almost as bad, especially in Japan which was totally dependent on imported oil.

The Japanese Export Miracle

The adverse effects on the Japanese economy are of particular importance to the way events developed because decades of remorseless growth by Japan's export manufacturers fuelled an angry backlash from America. Unfortunately, the adjustments the Americans demanded ultimately destabilised the entire global economy. Japan had been remarkably successful in coping with the first oil price rise. The higher oil costs were mainly absorbed by lower profits and reduced real wages between 1972 and 1974 as manufacturers chose maintenance of global market share as their top priority. Although their readjustment efforts were incredibly successful, Japanese inflation soared, ultimately peaking at 25 per cent.

The Japanese were even more adept at coping with the second oil price rise of 1978. For two years, inflation was restrained by a stringent monetary policy, staying below 10 per cent. The yen exchange rate recovered after only a brief fall. As with the previous oil price rise, the costs of higher oil prices were absorbed in lower wages and profits, thus preventing an inflationary surge. Once again, Japan's substantial presence in export markets was upheld by this policy, with her exports more competitive than those of other oil importers, where monetary discipline in response to higher oil prices was far more lax. So harsh was the necessary adjustment to the rise in oil prices that even under this tight regime, a worsening in the terms of trade still forced the Japanese current account balance into the red. Yet in volume terms, the trade balance showed a strong improvement. Activity did not collapse; growth merely slowed. Unlike most of her industrial competitors, Japan avoided the slide into a serious recession.

Changing Monetary Moods

Brian Reading points out that the climate of the early 1980s was coloured by a sober realism, a "financial correctness". The Keynesian ideas of the 1960s and 1970s had produced extravagant government borrowing and debasement of the currency through persistent and rising inflation. Some countries managed to avoid the worst excesses of over-borrowing and inflation, most notably Japan and West Germany (before the 1989 East/West Unification). However, the far-reaching broad effects were similar in all the industrial countries, but they were much worse in the English-speaking nations of America, Britain, Australia and New Zealand. Early in the 1980s, in response to the two oil-induced shocks, this Keynesian approach became untenable. The mood of governments changed, especially in America, with the election of Ronald Reagan as Republican President, and in Britain, where Margaret Thatcher became Tory Prime Minister in 1979. They wholeheartedly rejected the Keynesian method of deficit-financing and an increasing government involvement in the running of the State which they thought was stifling the incentives of a free enterprise society. They now declared that this former approach was an unworkable solution to the problems of late twentieth-century democracies. Out went the inflationary psychology of living beyond one's means. The new creed was to be monetarism, with strong currencies and a balanced budget.

Unfortunately, in both America and Britain, the 1980s demands for balanced budgets and less government spending and borrowing were never fully practised. Public rhetoric about strong government finances and reduced state interference in the economy proved merely a cosmetic front. While extolling the virtues of sound money, the Republican Reagan and Tory Thatcher governments both embarked on a period of unprecedented monetary reform. Through programmes of financial liberalisation and deregulation, introduced during the early 1980s, governments in America, Britain and then, belatedly in Japan rapidly lost control of the crucial monetary levers.

Cheap credit coupled with their loosened grip on money, led to a massive speculative surge in financial and property assets primarily in the Anglo-Saxon economies of America, Britain, Canada and Australia, and latterly in Japan. A period of phenomenal financial instability ensued world-wide. In the second half of the 1980s, the yen soared in value, while the dollar collapsed. In 1987, with quixotic abruptness, investors suddenly recognised the gross overvaluation of assets. Stock and bond markets crashed. Only Japan, urged on by truculent US politicians, failed to heed the messages of the crash. During 1988, Tokyo became enmeshed in a manic speculation which created the conditions for the subsequent Tokyo stock market bubble.

Phase One – The Trigger for the Long 1980s Boom

One of the greatest bull markets of the century exploded into life in August 1982. In that month, Mexico halted its massive interest payments due to the world's major banks on huge debts piled up in cheap dollars that had suddenly become completely exorbitant to service, now the dollar was booming. The Mexican debt crisis followed hard on the heels of a small but pivotal banking crisis. In July, the Federal Insurance Corporation closed down Penn Square Bank in Oklahoma and seized its assets, sending shock waves reverberating around the tightly-knit banking world.

Paul Volker, then Chairman of the Federal Reserve Board, had been implementing a stringent three-year regime of ultra-high interest rates to squeeze inflation out of the US economy. Now he faced a desperate crisis. He foresaw an impending global catastrophe could be unleashed if other newly industrialising nations followed Mexico's example. Many Latin American countries were in the same dilemma, with all their vast dollar-denominated debts having been arranged during the late 1970s, when the dollar exchange rate was incredibly low. The combination of Volker's drive to restore the domestic American economy to financial health, and Reagan's rhetoric on sound money and deregulation to limber up the over-burdened entrepreneurial heartland of US capitalism, had sent the dollar soaring, making these formerly cheap Latin American internationally raised loans hugely expensive to service. As interest payments became increasingly onerous, levels of developing country indebtedness escalated greatly.

In February 1982, Freddie Laker's internationally trading airline company, Laker, went into liquidation, as his expansion plans using borrowed cheap dollars ran into these same high-dollar interest repayment buffers. A back of the envelope calculation estimated that $500 billion dollars had been lent by banking syndicates to the newly industrialising nations, recycling the billions of petro-dollars flooding into the coffers of the newly enriched OPEC oil nations, after the huge oil price rises of 1973 and 1978. The bank syndicates had made the ludicrous, but false, assumption that sovereign state borrowers never go bankrupt, and thought their lending was "safe". Unfortunately, all the various syndicates were using the same international banking groups, including Citi-Corp, one of America's greatest banks, Chase Manhattan, and British banks, like Barclays and National Westminster. With such enormous cross-linking between members in different syndicates, no one now knew what the total exposure amounted to. An international debt default chain reaction looked possible.

A changed attitude to tight monetary policy was Volker's answer to prevent the Mexican debt crisis snowballing out of control. If Mexico decided to default on its debts, most of which were held by major banks of the international community, other debt-ridden nations in Latin America, Asia and the communist bloc would surely follow. This nightmare scenario threatened the solvency of the whole banking system, with the spectre of a world depression similar to the early 1930s, when the Federal Reserve tightened money supply precisely when it should have eased it.

By early 1982, Volker was considering a relaxation of his tight money policy. He had hinted, at the end of February at official intervention to halt the dollar's extraordinary rise which was causing a massive dislocation in the currency markets. The dollar's seemingly unstoppable rise simultaneously saw the DJIA index break into new high ground, at 1,299. His indications that there would be a more flexible approach to money supply was a trigger event of 1982 that ushered in the start of the world-wide equity boom. The knock-on effect of his decision to reverse his deflationary stance was a bout of euphoria on the global stock and bond markets. The DJIA index soared from a summer low of 770 to hit 1000 in early October when Volker suspended the money supply target he had been monitoring. This move publicly heralded his abandonment of the three-year experiment to target money supply. The markets went wild with excitement and the great 1980s bull market was truly underway.

Phase Two – Easy Credit with American Liberalisation

One of the greatest underlying changes during the early 1980s that had a profound destabilising impact on the boom was the decision in the two main Anglo-Saxon economies of America and Britain to introduce sweeping measures for financial deregulation and liberalisation. By the mid-1980s, Japan's superior trading performance raised the spectre of a trade war, but President Reagan's revolutionary fiscal policies (which cover the Government's budget measures of spending and taxing programmes) obligingly saved Japan from this threat. He had been elected on a promise to install dynamic supply-side policies to solve America's sluggish growth problems. This experiment was designed to remove government's oppressively heavy hand from America's wealth-producing manufacturing sectors while at the same time reducing the huge nation-wide dependence which had slowly built up on government welfare spending. In theory, this approach made excellent sense; in practice, efforts to reduce the state hand-out side of the budgetary equation quickly ran into irreducible problems with well-informed middle-class vested-interest lobbies.

To free up the economy, Reagan planned big personal tax cuts to improve work incentives, to be matched by deep cuts in public spending, for a neutral end result. Taxes can be cut at a stroke, to wide acclaim, but cuts to government spending run into the buffers of sophisticated pressure groups, hooked on huge government support programmes like healthcare, pensions, unemployment and sickness benefits. Failure to reduce government spending produced a lop-sided outcome. Lower taxes were welcomed but high government spending went rolling along at previous levels, buttressed now by huge rises in defence spending, to restore US morale after the traumatic set-backs suffered under President Carter's stewardship.

The sums never balanced, creating a major distorting impact on the US economy, but the administration was committed to its lax (low tax) fiscal policy. The Federal Reserve countered this by adopting a tight monetary policy (raising interest rates to ensure there was no credit surge as consumers spent their large tax rebates). The years of the early 1980s were beset by exchange and financial market turbulence. Volker, the Federal Reserve's powerful Chairman, pursued a policy of tighter monetary control, to eliminate the inflation mentality that had dogged growth prospects during the late 1970s.

Reagan's supply-side reforms lowered the after-tax cost of borrowing, increasing the demand for credit. To limit money supply growth and combat inflation, Volker raised US interest rates. The combination of easy tax policy and tight money attracted an inflow of foreign capital to take advantage of high interest payable on US government stocks, collectively known as Treasuries.

Prosperity Flows where the Money Goes

Substantial flows of volatile money came from Japan when exchange controls ended in 1980. Between the third quarter of 1980 and the first quarter peak of 1985, the dollar rose by an average of 60 per cent against other currencies, although it only rose 20 per cent against the yen. The effects of this currency shift were dramatic. US manufacturers were priced out of world markets, and foreign imports flooded in. Between 1981 and 1985, the US current account went from a $7 billion surplus, or 0.2 per cent of GNP, to a deficit of $122 billion, (3 per cent of GNP). Expecting great improvements from the supply-side programme, economic growth had been optimistically forecast at 5 per cent a year. Domestic demand did rise by a little under 4 per cent, but due to the deteriorating trade balance, GNP growth fell short of the forecast 3 per cent.

The Overvalued Dollar

One-quarter of extra spending by Americans between 1981 and 1985 went on additional imports. The overvalued dollar shrank US exports, neutralising the cut in the after-tax cost of company borrowing which had been expected to create incentives for greater work effort. The manufacturing sector was severely disadvantaged; investment in new plant and machinery fell, but the service sector was largely unaffected by foreign competition. The strong dollar encouraged a boom in office building, shopping malls, hotels and leisure complexes. The deteriorating US payments balance occurred as the economy was recover-ing from the 1980–2 recession, so entrepreneurs were actively looking for profitable ventures. They ploughed considerable capital into these domestic situations where growth prospects looked extremely appealing.

Phase Three – The Inflationary Surge in Asset Prices

The US stock market anticipated the imminent peak in the dollar. It began a powerful resumption of the bull market in the second week of January 1985. Perhaps it may have belatedly begun to celebrate two discount rate reductions made by the Federal Reserve Board on 21 November and 21 December 1984. During 1986, the Board implemented another four cuts in the discount rate over a period of six months. As the cost of borrowing fell, the levels of debt in the economy began to rise remorselessly, while government bonds and equities enjoyed a substantial rally. The bull market had swung into a higher gear.

The changing fortunes of the dollar/yen relationship were another cause for celebration by the global financial markets. During the summer and autumn of 1985, the dollar moved gently down from its Y260 March peak. In September the G5 (group of five major industrial nations) agreed at the Plaza Hotel in New York to co-operate in a "managed and orderly depreciation of the dollar". This signalled a united policy to push the dollar lower to allow the huge US economy to act as the locomotive for reviving world economic growth.

In Britain, the pound's plunge in 1984 towards $1 had undermined the government's anti-inflation policy. The retail prices index rose to 7 per cent, twice its 1983 level. This was a *de facto* reflation, carrying all the disadvantages of higher prices with no benefits to unemployment and high public spending levels. However, growth was well established, interest rates were slowly falling and there were record retail sales, in spite of mounting levels of consumer debt. By the end of November, with the oil price falling, optimism rose in the markets, along with the prices of stocks. The new FT-SE 100 index swept through 1,400 and the DJIA crossed 1,400 for the first time ever; it ended 1985 at 1,546.7, for a rise of 27.5 per cent.

Markets continued strong into 1986, with two mega-bids in London, one for Distillers (the drinks company) and the other for Imperial Group (the tobacco giant); each changed hands for around £2.5 billion. The surge continued into February, even though the oil price had dropped below $10 dollars which might have been expected to prompt another British interest rate rise, but gilt-edged yields fell below 10 per cent, suggesting lower, not higher interest rates. The Dow breached 1,700 on the last day of February. The Federal Reserve lowered the discount rate to 7 per cent in early March. In Britain the March budget provided yet another market boost. The basic tax rate dropped by 1 penny to 29p and the target rate of 25p was reaffirmed, promising further tax rebates to come. With thresholds and allowances also raised the budget gave a £1 billion boost to consumers, where it was likely to be spent on extra consumption. The M3 target for money growth was raised to a range of 11–15 per cent. With the introduction of Personal Equity Plans (PEPS) and a drop in interest rates to 11.5 per cent The *Financial Times* pronounced this "a budget for equities". Within days, the markets had taken the message on board. The FT 30 index rose above 1,400, the Government securities index was above 90 and the Dow Jones crossed 1,800.

Low Oil Prices Fuel the Boom

The oil price fell below $10, a level not seen since 1974. (Energy prices fell as an oil glut increased with the recession.) The fall threatened problems in the US banking system, with huge loans committed to the energy industry. In Britain, oil revenues were forecast at less than £3 billion in 1986–7 compared with £11.5 billion in 1985–6. In April, with money supply running at 20 per cent, UK base rates were cut to 11 per cent, explicitly signalling that the authorities had abandoned monetary targeting. This was confirmed in May; with the rate of money growth rising yet more sharply, this did not prevent interest rates from falling to 10 per cent. Nigel Lawson, Chancellor of the Exchequer, was driving a financial pump. The election timetable became a weightier issue for economic policy. Unemployment was static, despite a Retail Prices Index of a modest 2.8 per cent, but falling manufacturing output and continuing recession implied falling oil prices were not stimulating economies as fast as politicians wanted.

Ignoring the Warning Signs

To promote re-election prospects, politicians faced the dilemma of combining low inflation with rising employment. According to the Butler-Miller Paradox (so named after the two economists who had detected it) people are prepared to hold more money when inflation is falling as it represents a better store of value. This means a larger money supply will be needed to finance activity. However, the store of liquidity built up as inflation falls may not be held over the long term, and as it is spent it adds to the excess liquidity already being pumped into the system. This hampers efforts to reduce the inflation that follows excessive rises in liquidity.

The warning signs were clearly spelt out at the time, but a raging boom is a chaos-induced event. It develops its own internal momentum, feeding off itself with enormously powerful positive feedback loops that drive it to ever greater instability extremes. Investors by mid-1986, were not perturbed by worries about excess liquidity in the monetary system. The wonderful new world of low inflation, low interest rates and cheap oil was the financial alchemy of the day. It promised a cornucopia of economic growth. This alone justified the ever higher prices that people were willing to pay for shares, and encouraged an accompanying property boom.

The Trump of Trumps

There were numerous contenders for the title of Property King during the mid-1980s, but one man, almost single-handedly, illustrated the explosive growth in US domestic building projects resulting from the over-valued dollar. Donald Trump's mercuric rise to celebrity-status became the stuff of legends. His glamorous, luxury life-style reflected his mushrooming wealth, to billionaire proportions, on the back of a flood of property deals. He had a master's touch for property development, buying or building skyscrapers, hotels (including New York's most famous – the Plaza), and casinos, mainly in Atlantic City. His towering ego matched the scale of his building efforts. Virtually everything he owned was Trump something – Trump Tower, Trump Castle, Trump Plaza, Trump Airlines. When he sponsored a cycle race, it was Tour de Trump. His extravagant life-style and intriguing marital affairs became objects of notoriety as press-worthy as his building and buying extravaganzas.

In the "capitalist-as-hero decade" of the 1980s, he was seen as Midas reincarnate. Everything he bought turned miraculously to gold, until, like the legend of Midas, the story turned sour. The book he co-wrote, *Trump: The Art of the Deal*, triumphantly explained how deal-making should be done. The 1987 crash came just too late to be included in it, but he managed, like Houdini, a brilliant escape, exiting the market a few days before the crash. Sadly, his property empire suffered in the 1989–91 recession, when all the debt-laden property empires were exposed to the twin squeeze of falling revenues and rising interest payments.

Property Bubbles

However, America was not the only democracy smitten by a property bubble. In Japan, a similar story for the late 1980s made home ownership exorbitantly expensive and in Britain, the housing market had, for years, been distorted by tax concessions. In the late 1980s, with the Lawson pump at full throttle this distortion acquired a savage new momentum. Figures given by Roger Bootle in *The Death of Inflation* flesh out the detail. In 1986 when general inflation in Britain dipped temporarily to 2.4 per cent, house prices were rising by 16 per cent nationally and 24 per cent around London. Between 1970 and 1992 house prices rose 13 times in Britain and six times in America and Japan due to inflation; real house prices rose by an average of 2.5 per cent a year in Britain and Japan. But from 1985 to 1990 real house prices in Britain rose by over 9 per cent.

Britain's property price spiral created a horrific bubble within a decade, with devastating consequences for millions of disadvantaged home owners. And in true bubble fashion, a new word entered the financial lexicon; negative equity. This shock-horror condition arises when a house is worth less than the price initially paid for it and the associated debt becomes greater than the diminished value of the property. To a property-owning democracy nourished in the reassuring bosom of an all-embracing welfare state and a post-war housing boom which ensured property was a one-way bet to massive financial gains, this dramatic turnaround was a bitterly cruel experience. Encouraged by a lax government attitude to home ownership, the number of people in private rented accommodation fell from 20 per cent of households in 1970 to about 8 per cent by 1991. Between 1980 and 1992, the number of mortgaged properties rose by over 50 per cent; from 6.2 million in 1980, to 9.8 million by mid-1992. This total represents 50 per cent of all households. Between 1980 and 1990, house prices more than doubled. In 1983, the Halifax Building Society estimated the average house cost £30,898. By July 1989, at the peak of the bubble, it cost £70,588. In 1993 negative equity peaked at a total of £10.8 billion. By mid-1995, building societies were repossessing houses at a rate of 1,000 per month and 1.5 million people were suffering from a negative equity, perhaps as much as or in excess of £5,000 per home. As in every case, the negative overhang is a strong dampener on market activity.

Inflationary Excesses and the Louvre Accord

Throughout 1986 and into 1987 the dollar continued to fall. The American administration decided to resolve the trade war impasse with Japan by practising benign neglect of the currency. Instead of intervening as it fell, they simply watched passively, hoping, no doubt a lower level for the dollar would help to correct the burgeoning US twin deficits; on the trading account and the Government's own budgetary account. The 1985–6 collapse in oil prices encouraged their stand, as they thought that would check potential rises in domestic inflation. The slide was disconcerting; no bottom could be seen to the abyss into which the currency was falling. Japan was not alone in fearing that the dollar's fall would greatly overshoot. Meeting in the Louvre in Paris in February 1987, finance ministers of the G5 decided the time had come to prop up US currency. They declared that the dollar has already fallen "within ranges broadly consistent with underlying economic fundamentals".

For depreciation to eliminate America's growing external payments deficit, it was necessary to release resources at home by reducing domestic demand. The Americans needed to save more and spend less. The administration totally failed to bring about this vital switch from spending to saving. Congress took very limited action to bring the budget deficit under control. Trade volumes on exports had improved, but only modestly; and not sufficiently to offset America's deteriorating terms of trade caused by the dollar's fall. Import prices rose faster than import volume declined, so that the import bill simply grew larger. The US current account deficit consequently widened even further; to $145 bn in 1986 and $162 bn in 1987.

Foreign private investors were reluctant to lend to America to plug this payments gap. They demanded the bribe of higher US interest rates to encourage them to invest. This would be a reassurance that the G5, by their concerted actions, could halt the dollar's fall. The Federal Reserve Board, however, decided interest rate policy on purely domestic grounds, with no intention of raising rates to satisfy the demands of foreign governments. It chose to ignore the external pressures being applied. When private investors boycotted the dollar, believing it was still overvalued, central bankers set out to prove them wrong. They intervened on a massive scale to support the dollar; from February to October 1987 they bought 100 billion dollars on the world's foreign exchange markets, spending equivalent billions of their own yen, D-marks, francs and pounds. By this action, therefore, the US twin deficits were largely financed by Japanese, German, French and British government borrowing.

Phase Four – The Boom Accelerates into Mania: The Edge of Chaos

Government borrowing provides the reserve base on which bankers are able to expand credit. Official intervention to support the dollar in 1987 substantially increased money supply growth in Europe and Japan. It allowed America to continue neglecting problems, rather than correcting them. Had the dollar's fall continued, America would have been forced either to raise interest rates to protect the dollar, or tackle the huge twin deficits sooner to correct the on-going devaluation. The consequences of international intervention were thus disastrous. Stock market shares, bonds and property prices had been rising since the early 1980's encouraged by the new mood of monetary stringency that they thought the US and UK governments were pursuing. Now, however, in tandem with the cheap dollar and cheap oil, these enormous monetary excesses in 1987 set in motion by the international bankers, fuelled a horrendous speculation.

The Financial Pump

Having seen, in earlier chapters, the striking examples of the 1720 bubbles and Wall Street in the mid-1920s exposed to the ruinous effects of a potent chaos-induced financial pump, it is easier to recognise the awesome monetary blunder the international banking authorities had embarked upon. By injecting the equivalent of $100 billion into the global economy at a time when supply-side policies of deregulation and liberalisation were already putting surplus cash into consumer's open pockets, they set the world's financial markets on an inevitable course. They accelerated an existing pump, already operating from the combination of cheap oil and the cheap dollar. This intervention marked the onset of the slide into chaos, with all the deterministic outcomes we know will follow.

Rampant Speculation Mania

Shares on international stock markets and global property prices responded energetically to the monetary excesses of 1987, fuelling speculation that was financed by a monumental build-up of debt at all levels, from which some areas of the industrialised world were still suffering even in the mid-1990s. Stock markets boomed. Property prices soared. Antiques, collectables and fine art fetched breath-taking prices at auction. Ordinary shares rose to spectacular heights and a new word entered the financial dictionary – junk bonds – paying punishingly high rates of interest. Markets soared as the junk-bond-induced frenzy sent corporate take-over activity to a fevered pitch. Between December 1986 and August 1987, share prices on Wall Street climbed 43 per cent, to a peak not seen again until early 1991. London's market surged in tandem, with the FT-SE 100 index rising 45.5 per cent, while Tokyo climbed 42 per cent through to October. The economies of Europe, Scandinavia, the Asian tiger emerging economies, Australia, Canada and New Zealand all joined in. Inflation generally began to accelerate, spurred by a rebound in world oil prices from their 1986 lows.

Imaginative New Trading Ideas

True to the bubble-building pattern, a clutch of new buzz-words emerged. Three key innovations stamped their imprint on the "greed is good" 1980s credo; leveraged buy-outs (LBOs), junk bonds and portfolio insurance through program trading. These were relatively simple concepts, masquerading as state of the art financial engineering. The lure of program trading and portfolio insurance rested on the widespread use of computers to monitor asset prices. The central rationale was to impose discipline and eliminate emotion from trading by feeding automatic buy and sell prices into the computer. Such a system works well in theory, but proved horrendously destabilising when everyone pushed the sell button simultaneously on 19 October.

The beauty of both the leveraged buy-out and the junk bond strategy was squarely based on the exceptionally lucrative geared advantages of nonlinear returns. These operate with a wondrous predictability, due to the fundamental chaos-basis of financial markets. And, with an equally predetermined regularity, they can clock up massive losses with the same facility as the gains emerge, whenever the underlying conditions reverse. Accordingly, when the 1989 recession set in, with rising interest rates and falling revenues, the ugly side of the nonlinear relationship suddenly sprang into focus. The geared balance sheets of the highly leveraged buy-out companies plus thousands of companies, stuffed to capacity with junk bonds and other imaginative borrowing instruments, were incredibly over-stretched. Many collapsed under the sheer excess of debt. Others struggled to survive, trapped by onerous terms of massive refinancing deals which had become acutely necessary.

In the true chaos tradition of an unfolding chain reaction, the long, drawn-out struggle for survival was one of the key elements that destabilised the global banking system in the late 1980s, and led to the build-up of the international bond market bubble of 1993, covered in Chapter 13.

In investment philosophy, the age-old saying "The bigger the rewards, the greater the risk", should never be ignored. Throughout the last four centuries, time and again, once a miracle of new financial creativity has rocketed to centre stage, its risk–reward ratios are irrevocably changed. No matter how inspiring the potentials for gain appeared at the outset, in responding to the dynamo of the gathering herd instinct, the rules of the game undergo a subtle shift. In the euphoria of the moment, this will escape the attention of all but the most alert participants. Early comers enjoy the spectacular benefits to be gained by this novelty, but later arrivals are virtually condemned to suffer. And the impossible lure of the financial pump can turn the most moderate and cautious investor into a sizzling speculator, an uninhibited gambler. In this respect, sober-suited bankers in 1985 were kindred spirits to those in 1928 – sometimes even the names were unchanged.

The Leveraged Bug

The name most synonymous with LBOs was Henry Kravis, a legend on Wall Street. By the mid-1980s, his company Kohlberg Kravis, founded in 1976, controlled more than two dozen companies acquired on borrowed money. In principle, the leverage buy-out strategy was remarkably straight-forward. A small group of senior executives, working with a Wall Street partner, such as Kohlberg Kravis, proposed to buy out its company from the public shareholders on borrowed money. Together, the Wall Street experts and company's management bought the company by raising money from banks and from the public sale of securities. As the craze grew, this was primarily through junk bond issuance. The debt was to be repaid from cash flow arising from normal company activity, or by selling off unimportant parts of the business, cutting it back drastically to its profitable core functions.

Enthusiasts argued that leveraged buy-outs unlocked company value that was unrecognised on the financial markets. Steep debt schedules ensured the company grew leaner and fitter across all its operations. Leveraged buy-outs were a superb money-maker: the calculations were stunningly simple; they could be done on a table napkin, over a dinner to discuss the project. A purchase price of say, $90 per share was the starting point. Then an estimate of the company's cash flow over the next five years was assessed and compared with the debt necessary to buy the company. To make the figures balance, various peripheral parts of the business could be sold off.

And then, on the other side of the napkin, of course, you could list the benefits, primarily in fees. For the Wall Street partner, there were fees from selling bonds to finance the deal, up-front fees, for advising and money-lending, plus a "success fee", when the deal was completed. This could amount to between $100–200 million in total. In addition, there were fees for the divestiture programme – splitting off unwanted businesses and selling them on to meet the debt repayments. And then there would be follow-up fees. For years to come fees would result from refinancing the deal, fees for continuing advice offered and fees for simply keeping the show on the road.

And to add gilt to the gingerbread, there was the phenomenal prospect for both parties to the buy-out, of wonderful returns from their new investments. As the newly empowered shareholders of a LBO company, there was no limit to the amount of capital gains that would accrue from buy-out adventures. Seen in this light, when the sums were so delectable, it is not surprising that leveraged buy-outs were immensely popular and soon became very hot news on Wall Street. Among the greatest advocates of LBOs, the feeling was strong that everyone stood to gain, reminiscent of Will Payne's remarks in January 1929: "a gambler wins only because someone else loses, but with investment, all gain." The 1985 version of this utopian philosophy, the argument went like this: the undervaluation of the stock would be solved. The current shareholders would get a handsome pay-out. The Wall Street partner gained the kudos of another successful deal and the incumbent management would become rich beyond their wildest imaginings through the miracle of gearing.

Critics of the procedure claimed it was stealing the company from its true owners. They fretted over the monstrous corporate debt mountain created when the company was taken into private hands. Could this arrangement produce better returns from companies that were considered by their buy-out supporters as undervalued? Inevitably, the interest payments were so astronomical, expenses had to be cut to the bone. Many departments, such as research and development and new project planning, tended to be axed to repay the debts. It may have been purely a pyrrhic victory, but the slide into the 1989 recession gave the last laugh on leveraged buy-outs to the doubters.

Junk is Junk

Junk bond mania went hand in hand with the advance of the leveraged buy-out fashion and the unbridled growth of financial skulduggery, mainly on Wall Street, but also in London. The undisputed emperor of the junk bond market was Michael Milken. In a lightning rise to fame, vaguely reminiscent of the Scotsman, John Law, Milken almost single-handedly took this idea from the drawing board into the board-rooms of thousands of medium-sized American companies, creating in a matter of months an entirely new multi-million dollar securities market in the process. By the early 1980s, it had grown from almost nothing to $200 billion, with Milken's firm, Drexel Burnham Lambert alone funding a record number of take-overs, through mammoth junk bond issuance.

Milken's astute idea was based on a study of the past records of distressed bonds. These traded for much less than their face value because the issuing company had encountered difficulties. Such second-hand bonds offered great investment opportunities, as the hugely discounted price gave buyers a much higher yield than they would get from more secure investments. The extra reward compensated buyers for any risk that the issuing company might default on its obligations. Milken's analysis of past records convinced him that the chances of default were, in many cases, lower than was suggested by the level of return; they had been over-discounted for the risk. He jokingly called these devalued instruments, "junk" bonds, a joke which he later came to regret. He considered them great investments because the potential rewards outweighed the risks.

This creative alchemy launched an enormously important second-hand market for high-yielding bonds. They were issued by second-rank companies who could not raise funds by using top Wall Street firms as they did not have blue-chip creditworthiness. In the liberated environment of Reagan's supply-side experiments, the atmosphere was exactly right for thrusting entrepreneurial companies of modest size to make ambitious projects and expansion plans. The Reagan incentives stimulated an urgent need for capital among medium- to smaller-sized businesses, whose credit rating was not high enough to allow them to raise funds through normal Wall Street financing channels.

Milken's great breakthrough was his claim that the risk–reward profile on the high-yielding bonds had been incorrectly evaluated. His analysis suggested that the higher return paid on the bonds more than offset the risk of default from these less than blue chip companies. In this assessment he was to be proved hopelessly misguided in the short term by the turn of events, but the mood of the times was in his favour and the craze for junk bonds was swept along by a mounting tide of euphoria. By filling this evident niche in the capital markets, many of Drexel's clients, who were modest fringe financiers at the start of the decade, became multi-millionaires when they used junk bonds to launch highly leveraged take-overs during the mid-1980s.

As the new market expanded in the mid-1980s, Milken himself became the most powerful financier of the age. His decisions could mean the difference between instant wealth and overnight ruin for businesspeople locked in delicate corporate take-over battles. At the peak, his personal fortune was in excess of $1.1 billion, earned in salary and bonuses between 1983 and 1987, plus trading and investment profits. When at the pinnacle of his powers, his command over the market was awesome. No other junk bond dealer could compete with his ability to place, almost overnight, a billion-dollar issue by an acquirer, often only one tenth the size of his target. While he was active, Drexel dominated the junk bond market, controlling around 70 per cent of it. Milken's role, like a modern-day John Law, loosened up the corporate scene through creative financial engineering, wielding an awesome power in the process.

By mid-1996 Richard Lapper in the *Financial Times* of 26 August reported a revival in junk bond appeal. A total of $59.4 billion of bonds were issued in 1993, but by August 1996 $42 billion had been issued for the year to date suggesting the 1993 total would be exceeded by the year end.

Mega-deal Mania

In the mid-1980s, Drexel backed T. Boone Pickens, the Texas oil magnate, in his attack on Gulf Oil, to force a merge with Chevron. Pickens lost the deal, but the $400 million he made in the attempt was a handsome monetary compensation. In April 1985, Nelson Peltz and his partner Peter May, backed only by a controlling interest in a minute company called Triangle Industries, used a pile of Drexel junk bonds to buy National Can, a major American industrial corporation. With an initial equity of $100 million in the Triangle company, a staggering $565 million of debt was created to clinch the deal. Triangle's 1984 revenues were only $291 million, compared to National Can's $1.9 billion. Following this deal, Peltz and May controlled an empire with revenues of $4 billion.

During 1985, the deals flooded in, one following another in breath-taking audacity. In August 1985, Ronald Perelman bought cosmetic giant, Revlon, for $900 million and in December Carl Icahn bought the airline TWA for $1.2 billion, with $660 million in junk financing from Drexel. With this avalanche of intoxicating deals behind it, Drexel catapulted itself from obscurity to become, by 1986, the richest firm on Wall Street with after-tax profits of $545 million. Facing such unprecedented competition, some of the most discreet Wall Street houses shed their conservative image to keep abreast of this upstart interloper in their midst. Firms like Morgan Stanley, and none other than Goldman, Sachs and Company, began to finance big deals with their own money. They initiated "bridge financing" at great risks to themselves to secure a share in the lucrative business now almost monopolised by Drexel.

By this time, the new face of Wall Street, inspired by imitation, wore the ugly mask of avarice, flaunted by Drexel. Connie Bruck, author of *The Predators' Ball*, which charts the rise of Drexel, describes in the language of a typical phase transition, the fate that now befell some of the most conservative corporate chieftains and the staid and stolid investment banking community. Dark-suited bankers who for years, had carefully nurtured trusting relationships with blue chip clients turned into "prowling egos, hungry for the next deal", with ever increasing dollars attached.

At Drexel's 1986 Predators' Ball, with his star high in the ascendant, Milken boasted to his audience that their combined net worth probably exceeded $3 trillion – a figure approaching the GNP of the United States at the time. His salary alone for 1987 would be an incredible $550 million, more than the GNP of some developing nations. Milken spelled out his assessment of the impact his astounding idea had wrought on American finance when he told his group, "Capital is no longer scarce. The scarce resource today is management, knowledge, vision, dealing with change."

Scandals Aplenty

The link between Drexel and the arbitrageur, Ivan Boesky, only came to light when Boesky was tried and sent to prison in 1988 for three years, after pleading guilty to a charge of conspiring to make false statements to the Securities and Exchange Commission. He also paid $100 million in civil penalties to settle insider-trading charges. He had been an active participant in a series of large UK bids in 1986. After weeks of rumours, a British Department of Trade and Industry investigation in December was ordered into the Guinness take-over of Distillers. This was closely followed by the revelation that Guinness had "invested" $100 million in Boesky's arbitrage pool of funds. It was Boesky's agreement to co-operate with the authorities on a wide-ranging investigation into criminal activities on Wall Street that exposed unsavoury aspects of Milken's deal-making. Recriminations and investigations rumbled on for the next three years.

Drexel's critics claimed junk bonds were creating "a casino society", transforming corporate America with high-risk debt to finance rickety mega-deals. They saw the vindication of their complaints later in the decade, when a growing number of debt-laden companies collapsed and the junk bond market slid into disrepute, along with the reputations and fortunes of Drexel and its master-trader, Michael Milken. By 1990 the boom had soured. Milken was indicted on 98 charges ranging from fraud, to market manipulation and insider dealing. And his firm, Drexel having pleaded guilty to six felonies and paid $650 million in fines, filed for bankruptcy. It defaulted on loans of $100 million and had to stop making markets in 220 stocks and liquidate its positions.

Many of Milken's most enthusiastic clients, disparagingly termed sycophants by the critics, were Savings and Loans executives, the US equivalent of British Building Societies. During the mania, they bought millions of junk bonds and were unceremoniously destroyed by their own investment folly as their companies collapsed in tandem with the junk bond market in the early 1990s. Their reckless investment in ultimately worthless junk bonds contributed to the monumental Savings and Loans financial crisis for which the American tax-payer will foot a bill perhaps in excess of $900 billion over the next 30 years.

Computers Take Control

Several significant reforms had been put in place after the October 1929 crash, trying to ensure there would never be a repeat. Deposit insurance was introduced to allay the fears of bank depositors, disclosure rules for new issues were tightened up, the Securities Exchange Commission was set up (chaired by Joseph P. Kennedy in a poacher/turned gamekeeper role), and a Banking Act in 1935 gave the Federal Reserve extra powers. Yet this battery of defence mechanisms failed to prevent the repeat, because, when overtaken by a driving financial pump, different innovative exploits were invented and played a pivotal part during 1987. Two such culprits, widely blamed for triggering the crash in the impassioned debates that following it, were the new techniques of programmed trading. These included portfolio insurance and market index arbitrage.

Active traders were increasingly resorting to computerised strategies to decide their buy decisions, after a market rise (i.e., once a trend was firmly established). Conversely, these strategies automatically trigger a sell decision after a market decline (i.e., signalling when the trend was broken). Traders relying on computerised signals might experience a heightened sense of security. Unreliable emotions have been superseded by a sophisticated computer discipline. They might be willing to over-trade, confident the automatic sell signals would release them systematically from the market before a serious decline began. This poses an added danger for traders using portfolio insurance that they will accept greater risk than is prudent, because of their genuine faith in the programmed trading concept. By October 1987, the capital involved in programmed trading had reached the enormous sum of $60–80 billion, which could have set off a chain reaction of selling, once the market declines took hold.

The other fashionable block trading idea that came to prominence was index arbitrage, based on index futures. This area of activity had grown fantastically during the mid-1980s, after index futures were introduced in 1982 and index options in 1983. Traders took advantage of the simplicity of handling one mega-contract, which represented a huge block of stocks in the group of companies listed in that index. A willingness to enter into these large trades had become more attractive in America by reductions in the costs of trading after the 1 May 1975 switch from fixed to negotiated commissions. By 1986 the annual share trading volume on the New York Stock Exchange had grown seven-fold since 1975. Of this total, block trades represented 50 per cent of traded shares, about three times greater than their share in 1975. This massive increase in reliance on rapid large block trading was bound to make an impact in unsettled markets, since it was a destabilising force in its own right. When everyone planned to sell, an unprecedented order imbalance in several large stocks would result, which would contribute to the sense of alarm and add fuel to the avalanche of selling in a self-perpetuating loop.

America's Economy at the Peak

Reagan's supply-side liberalisation programme, dubbed "Reaganomics" achieved some substantial gains; the recovery begun in 1983 continued through his second term in office, and into the Bush administration of 1988–92. The rate of inflation fell from an average of 12.5 per cent in 1980 to 4.4 per cent by 1988. Unemployment fell from 7.1 per cent to 5.5 per cent, and an astonishing 18 million new jobs were created. The prime interest rate fell from 15 per cent to around 9.3 per cent. The reduction in tax rates was equally impressive. When Reagan entered office in January 1981, marginal tax rates (the rate at which the last dollar of income is taxed) had been 70 per cent. This was cut by more than half, to 33 per cent at the end of his second term.

There was a price to pay for this superb prosperity, however. Private national wealth rose by only 8 per cent in the six years after the recession. This compared unfavourably with the 31 per cent growth in wealth – almost four times as great – that occurred between 1975 and 1980, a period scathingly termed inflation-prone and unproductive by Reagan. Then the flaws and failings must be added to the reckoning.

The national debt had ballooned alarmingly, almost tripling to $2,684.4 billion and the trade deficit more than quintrupled in size, to $137.3 billion. These swollen twin deficits were partly the result of the huge tax cuts and military build-up, without the compensating welfare programme reductions, but they were compounded by the relentless rise of the dollar as American manufactured goods became uncompetitive on world markets. During Reagan's second term, America became a debtor nation for the first time since 1914. The administration was now a hostage to the fickle investment inclinations of foreigners. They were financing the trade deficits with loans and purchases of US stocks, bonds, land, factories, buildings, companies and property. Moreover, the monopoly-sized amounts of dollars in these twin deficits ensured that America rapidly earned its place as the greatest ever debtor nation on earth. The lasting legacy of these debts is still unclear.

Phase Five – The Pinnacle in Sight

Reagan's policies reflected his personal priorities, which were shared intuitively by mainstream populations throughout the industrial world. Ironically, this view may have promoted the ever rising euphoria for permanent prosperity in the run-up to the October crash. Reagan saw economic recovery based on lower tax rates in America as a spur to similar moves in other industrial nations. He wanted to expose the economic bankruptcy of the command economies of the communist world. He was right on both points. For him, capitalism is a cornucopia of material bounty forever overflowing. He played a key role in promoting the growing prosperity of the West, in stark contrast to the abject failure of the Soviet experiment. However, he left the bill to finance this largesse to future generations, although it is still possible, as he hoped, that America might grow its way out of indebtedness.

The World Economy at the Peak

In Britain, Chancellor Lawson's 1986 autumn statement announced public spending increases of £10 billion over the next two years, with privatisation asset sales of £5 billion a year, for the next three years. The Public Sector Borrowing Requirement (PSBR) at £7 billion for 1986–7 would be unchanged, implying he might spark a pre-election mini-boom. The low PSBR was largely illusory; it arose from the Government's privatisation policy with continuous asset sales filling the public purse. Public spending had risen steadily over seven years; it was higher now as a percentage of Gross Domestic Product than in 1978–9, in the last year of the Labour Government. Pronouncements on "sound money" merely paid lip service to low inflation; the reality was the same old mischief as before.

Cynics said the Chancellor had abandoned monetary and fiscal restraints and was ready to accept devaluation to encourage a consumer spending boom, so the Tories would be re-elected. Against a background of financial scandals, for insider dealing involving Morgan Grenfell and Guiness, the Christmas rally appeared on cue, taking the FT-SE 100 up to

1,679, for a gain of 23.5 per cent for the year, while the Dow recorded a gain of 22.5 per cent, closing at 1,896.

Reagan expressed an unquenchable faith in America in one of his famed off-the-cuff sayings. "Someone once said that the difference between an American and any other kind of person is that an American lives in anticipation of the future because he knows it will be a great place." This saying astutely sums up the mood of gathering optimism pervading the global financial markets at the start of 1987.

By February, investors everywhere were unsuspectingly being sucked into the vertiginous slipstream of the intense financial pump the international authorities had unleashed. Hopes were high for persuading the key surplus countries of West Germany and Japan to stimulate their economies sufficiently to make a decisive dent in their huge trade imbalance with America. Markets were happily taking a great deal on trust, surging to new highs by the end of January. The DJIA burst through 2,000, for the first time; Japan's Nikkei Dow went through 20,000 and the London FT-SE 100 had broken above 1,800.

A Sceptical Reception for Doubters

For every commentator making cautionary noises, there were several eager to justify ever higher prices. The problem of high-growth rates in average earnings were rationalised on the grounds that they were merited by improvements in productivity and overtime working in key industries. Levels of output were thought to be understated, as they gave too much weight to declining industries, like ship-building and steel, with insufficient weight to high-growth sectors, like media, pharmaceuticals, consumer goods producers, retailers and electronics.

Worries over the value of the dollar re-surfaced, as it renewed its decline. This might force the Federal Reserve to impose a further squeeze, thereby snuffing out the delicate young recovery. The optimists, all committed bulls awaiting the next great upwards leap in the markets they were now confidently expecting, quickly explained away this risk by pointing out that it was the duty of West Germany and Japan to take on the role of "locomotor" for the world economy, by adopting additional stimulatory measures.

London Joins In

The boom in London, still the world's third-largest financial centre after New York and Tokyo, had begun to accelerate during 1985. A record

£6 billion was raised, up 72 per cent on 1984, with new issues including the niche fashion house, Laura Ashley. The price earnings ratio at the offer price of 135p, was a heady 23, but this did not deter hopeful investors. Queues of more than 100 yards long formed on the day the prospectus was issued, and the offer was 40 times over-subscribed. On the first day of trading, the shares touched 200p and closed with a premium of 59p.

The Privatisation Bonanza

Excitement in London was fomented by the Tory Government's privatisation agenda and the new issues band-wagon. Both went rolling along, gathering momentum, right through 1986 and into 1987. New investors were drawn into the stock market by an imaginative television advertising campaign, blatantly drumming up support for privatisation issues. The stock market began to be viewed as an unbeatable money-making machine. Even the scandals had a positive influence; they added spice and drama, risk and mystery to the exotic investment process.

Long queues formed outside the issuing houses, waiting for the all-important prospectus documents, so the proper investment decisions could be made. Multiple applications became an essential ritual for thousands, especially for the Government's offerings of public sector companies now being sold into the private sector on highly attractive part-payment arrangements. An application invariably produced an instant profit, handsomely geared, because it was solely linked to the small initial down-payment. The novice army of first-time small investors naturally viewed the Government's privatisation policy as a one-way bet, orchestrated by the Tories to fulfil their election pledge to turn Britain into a share-owning democracy. Doesn't it all sound ridiculously familiar?

By early March, markets were surging strongly to new heights. The FT-SE 100 crossed 2,000 for the first time, anticipating a "give-away" budget to soften up consumers ahead of the expected general election which the Tories were hot favourites to win, for a historic third term. Right on cue, budget "give-aways" included another 2p off income tax, dropping the basic rate to 27p, while allowances and thresholds rose. The Chancellor was widely praised for using half his buoyant revenues to reduce borrowing and half to cut tax rates. The PSBR for 1987–8 was only a modest $4 billion. Economic forecasts were rosy, expecting 3.5 per cent growth in the non-oil economy and inflation down at 4.5 per cent by year-end. Growth in M0 (bank deposits with the Bank of England and coin in circulation) was to be targeted at a range of 2–6 per cent, and the current account deficit was thought unlikely to exceed an acceptable £2.5 billion. Within a week of the budget, base rates fell to 10 per cent. A passing anxiety was the rapid growth in consumer spending and private credit, but it could readily be rationalised by the thought that, unlike corporate and government borrowing, consumer borrowing is eventually repaid.

Interest rates had fallen to 9 per cent with two further reductions by early May. Sock Shop, a niche retailer, was floated on the UK stock market at 125p and was over-subscribed 53 times, opening at more than double the issue price. Tie Rack, another niche retailer, did even better; it attracted subscriptions of over £1 billion for the 12.5 million shares on offer. Rolls-Royce, the Government privatisation of the month, was hugely over-subscribed, opening at 147p on the partly-paid shares, against an offer price of 85p. Moving against the trend, and with a masterly sense of timing, Preston Rabl, a co-founder of WPP, the advertising group, placed his 5.6 per cent stake with institutions in May, while in July, Saatchi and Saatchi, the two brothers running the other major UK advertising company did the same.

The Conservatives achieved their third consecutive general election win in early June, and the stock market was ecstatic. It celebrated the victory with a one-day rise of 40.2 points on the FT-SE 100 to a record 2,289.5, while the DJIA advanced in sympathy to 2,377.7. At this level the yield on equities was about 3 per cent, one-third of that obtainable on long-term government stocks, and this, in itself was yet another record. Money supply growth of M3, now a discredited government indicator, was running at well over 20 per cent a year, oil prices were firming, commodity prices had stopped falling and earnings growth was edging up above 8 per cent. Consumer spending hit record levels and house prices were roaring ahead, along with prices of other real assets. Amid the burgeoning euphoria, warning signs were evident, but few took any notice or avoiding action.

The Japanese market tumbled 10 per cent between June and July, but its rapid recovery to yet another new high was viewed as a confidence vote in world share prices, since prices in Tokyo were the most expensive of all the major markets. The indices peaked in London on July 16, with the FT 30 at 1,926.2 and the FT-SE 100 at 2,443.4. The DJIA also hit a peak that day at 2,496.97, but it continued rising to its top at 2,722.42, reached on 25 August. Conditions in London had deteriorated sooner, on the shocking news of a dramatic rise in the trade deficit to £1.16 billion, with a steep rise in imports. The yield ratio now stood at 3.3, higher than the peak in 1972. A huge and growing settlement backlog built-up, aggravated by small investors vigorously trading in penny shares with a monumental appetite for rights issues. Remember the tables set up outside South Sea House in 1720 to cope with the share transfer backlog during the infamous South Sea Bubble?

A Rush of Rights Issues

Cautionary signs of investor fatigue were now visible to those with eyes to spot them, as a glut of rights issues hit the London market. These rights issues were primarily to fund a string of mega-deals where companies with highly-rated share prices could afford to pay extravagant sums to take over other companies without having to borrow. The rosy gloss applied to every offer enabled the purchasing company to use its shares instead of cash in the take-over mania now afoot. The stream of rights to fund acquisitions became a flood emerging with greater audacity than the prodigal Law had achieved in Paris in 1720. The London 1987 version amounted to around £3 billion – £837 million for Blue Arrow, £177 million for WPP, £700 million for Midland Bank and £500 million for BAA. The first of these to be announced, by Blue Arrow, the employment agency company, in the first week of August, was the biggest ever rights issue launched on the London market. The take-over of Manpower, America's largest recruitment agency, meant raising £837 million. *The Financial Times* described the take-over plan as one of "stunning audacity", since Blue Arrow had only joined the junior UK market, the Unlisted Securities Market, three years before, at a capitalisation of £3 million and still only had net assets of £21 million. *The Financial Times* warned that the excess liquidity in the system which made such deals possible carried the dangers of increased leverage, making any set-back highly risky. Wasn't this exactly what Richard Cantillon had tried to explain to Lady Mary Herbert way back in 1720? But, as ever, when investors have been driven crazy by exposure to a ferocious financial pump, warnings fell on deaf ears.

The clouds were certainly gathering when WPP announced its £177 million rights issue (to help finance a bid for J. Walter Thompson) had only been 35 per cent taken up. A surprise rise in interest rates of 1 per cent two days later, in response to "domestic monetary conditions" sent the FT-SE 100 back to 2,261.5 on the day, and the underwriters were clearly panicking over how much stock on this gigantic flood of rights issues they would be left holding.

London rallied again in September, although the next set of horrendous trade figures for both Britain and America were another ominous sign, but the torrent of rights issues continued unabated into October. There was a £777 million bid by the banking group, TSB for the Hill Samuel Fund Management business, plus AB Food's £767 million offer for S & W Beresford, a £2 billion break-up bid by Benlox for Storehouse and, perhaps the most brazen bid to emerge, the Saatchi & Saatchi abortive effort to take over the massive Midland Bank. The atmosphere had become frenetic by October, with many investors wary of selling on a rising price in case something special was about to happen, and fearful of selling on a falling price in case they missed the surge in the share price that automatically followed a bid.

Silly Season Quotes

By the time the DJIA hit the August peak, the only debate on Wall Street was how soon it would reach 3,000. One leading financial magazine wrote an article with the immensely optimistic title, "Dow 3000: not if, but when". With the use of that brilliant but infuriatingly frustrating yardstick, hindsight, we can now supply the timespan for this prescient prediction; 3,000 on the DJIA, not imminently in the autumn of 1987, as was fondly hoped, but in the autumn of 1991, fully four years later, and with the heart-stopping crash intervening. In the closing days of 1991, the US market leapt for joy when the Federal Reserve unexpectedly dropped the discount rate by a full point, to 3.5 per cent. This action was seen by the world financial community as a signal that a recovery in the US economy from the 1991 recession would kick-start the rest of the world. This was the start of the great global bond market bubble discussed in Chapter 13.

Back in the super-charged bull market atmosphere of mid-1987, the optimists were competing among themselves for the distinction of becoming the most accurate, and hence influential, guru in town, by producing a market projection which would be closest to the actual outcome, in due course. The DJIA at 3,500 was seen as a foregone conclusion, but 4,000 seemed perfectly possible, since prices in New York and London looked so much cheaper than the absolutely outlandish quotations on the Japanese Tokyo market.

Other newspaper headlines that suggested the silly season was at hand included such gems as, "Selling panic makes stocks 'dirt cheap'", "Companies find good deals in own stocks", "Slide reminiscent of years ago, but analysts unruffled this time", "Buyers are back", and "Investment clubs seize buying opportunity".

Phase Six − Early Nagging Doubts

All manner of explanations were suddenly on offer, once the gigantic melt-down of the crash finally materialised late in October. As we know, there was an initial trigger for the onset of the boom, way back in 1982, when the Mexican debt crisis threatened to sabotage the entire international banking system. Again, the trigger for the onset of chaos was provided early in 1987, as a direct consequence of central bank intervention in the markets to support the dollar. By September 1987, there was a gradual withdrawal of funds from America by Japanese investors, to finance their applications for shares in the second tranche of the NTT privatisation offer. As noted in Chapter 2, Japanese investors' anxieties and actions undoubtedly weakened confidence in the market, so it became vulnerable to any sudden unacceptable shocks.

The Japanese Impact

When we discussed the irrational investor in Chapter 2, we noted that although the Japanese investors did not cause the October crash, they played a significant role in the build-up to the drama. Japan's key role as events unfolded demonstrates the interdependency which ties the world's main capital markets together. Japanese actions during the autumn of 1987 in their attitudes to the NTT second issue were almost a re-run of the South Sea boom. Institutional and private investors obviously expected to make additional gains from NTT holdings. Like bemused South Sea investors calculating future gains from applying for the enticingly lavish Third Money Subscription in June 1720, Japanese investors reasoned that the share price was bound to rise, as the Government was committed to successful privatisations.

By April 1987, the first tranche of NTT shares were trading at Y3.2m each, a profit of 160 per cent in two months for investors who had obtained shares at the launch. Only favoured stock broker clients would have gained this profitable advantage, however. At Y3.2m per share and the P/E above 300, the total capitalisation of NTT was $340 bn.

Japanese Butterflies

The second NTT tranche was due for sale on 9 November at a price of Y2.55m per share ($18,000). The total cash to finance the entire tranche amounted to Y5.7 trn, or ($35 bn). This would cover almost the whole cost of the planned July fiscal package. In the autumn, Japanese investors who were holding US bonds decided to repatriate funds by selling these bonds. Nicholas Brady, Chairman of the New York investment bankers, Dillon, Reed & Co at the time, thought the immediate trigger for the October crash was the vast numbers of Japanese investors who sold US government bonds, thereby destabilising the relationship between the bond and equity markets. Other factors – the twin deficits and the missile attack incident in the Persian gulf – were, he estimated, just minor incidentals.

The concerted sales by Japanese investors of vast amounts of US government bonds drove the yield on a 30-year Treasury bond up though 10 per cent. This had a knock-on effect on the yield gap prompting action by US investors who little realised that the major reason for plunging share values resulted from the proposed November sale of NTT shares in Japan, about 6,700 miles away. It caused huge capital flows across the world's financial markets. Nor would this effect have been possible earlier in the decade, before the Japanese liberalised their financial system. It may have been one mighty big butterfly, but it is an example of the chaos Butterfly Effect, none the less.

Phase Seven – The Selling Flood

When a stock market is nearing a big reversal, it is operating in a far-from-equilibrium state. When the turn finally comes, the majority of people are fully invested and thinking the wrong way. This link of extreme instability at the edge of chaos and the wrong consensus view rapidly tip the system into an acute chaotic response. And this duly arrived during the second week in October to produce phase seven of the crashes model with a succession of stock market falls.

Phase Eight – A Global Chain Reaction Panic

There had been many warning signs earlier, with the summer market peaks, but most investors, so typical of those enthralled by ever rising prices, had disregarded any warning indicators. Now the signals could no longer be ignored, but most investors were patently bemused by the course events were taking. Although there were several days of heavy selling, marking phase seven of the model, the real selling deluge, which marked the onset of phase eight, did not occur until a few days later. On 19 October 1987 the bubble burst. As Wall Street crashed by 22.6 per cent stock markets around the world plunged in its wake. Tokyo fell 15 per cent on the next day. The crescendo panic of selling in phase 8 of the 19 October crash was a classic chaos event – a chain reaction, powered by a very vigorous positive feedback loop. Even today, people remember that sequence of crash events as a "domino effect", or by the more visual image of a "Mexican wave". Both pictures conjure up the idea of markets crashing around the globe in step with the 24 hour trading clock. As the markets opened in each new time zone, so the crash went reverberating on, over that catastrophic Monday and Tuesday. Eloquent phrases are attractive in presenting these moving events. However, I think in the time-honoured tradition of Shakespeare's quotation, "A rose by any other name would smell as sweet", it surely must now be time to use more scientific terminology. If we consistently use chaos terms to describe these key financial dramas, we will begin to recognise how widely they apply. And knowledge is the first weapon in our defence against unwittingly recreating these unstable market conditions where chaos can unfold.

Japan Builds a Bubble

The Americans and Europeans quickly realised no recession would follow the October crash, and early in 1988 they tightened monetary policy by raising interest rates. Nigel Lawson, however, delivered £6.6 billion of tax cuts in 1988. Japan's current account was still rising, pressure for trade retaliation was intensifying and the US presidential election was due in November. The Americans persuaded the Japanese to maintain a lax monetary policy. Interest rates in Japan stayed at a record post-war low until May 1989. In 1988 as the US economy slowed, Japan's economy flourished. Domestic demand rose by an average 6 per cent from 1987 to 1990, but 5 per cent of that was purely asset price inflation. The Japanese were embarking upon the oldest game in the capitalist repertoire, they were cultivating their own unique version of a financial bubble following in the footsteps of generations who had gone before. How they modified the plot to suit their special temperament is the topic for Chapter 12.

CHAPTER TWELVE

JAPANESE BUBBLES

How can a share with a price-earnings ratio of 40 be called cheap? Ah, but this
is Japan, the brokers say. Japan is different – everybody knows that.
Bethan Hutton, *Weekend Money FT*, 12–13 August 1995

One of the most astonishing rags to riches stories of the second half of the
twentieth century is surely the emergence of Japan as the fifth richest
country in the world by 1995. Exactly 50 years earlier, in August 1945, the
Second World War came to a shuddering end after two Japanese cities
had been utterly demolished. Hundreds of thousands perished or sustained mutilating burns, amid heaps of smouldering rubble with the
dropping of two atomic bombs. Japan lay in ruins, humbled by defeat.

Rising From the Ashes

The Japanese surrender was a turning point of enormous significance in
the history of the world, but, equally as a vital watershed for Japan, it is
an appropriate starting point for our look at the Japanese financial bubble which burst in December 1989. The remarkable post-war history of
Japan perfectly illustrates the powerful chaos concept of order recreating
itself out of a state of utter disarray and confusion. The new Japan was
able to develop characteristics that helped it to achieve an economic
miracle and attain the role of the world's major creditor nation by the
1990s.

Japan's defeat involved the first invasion and occupation in the entire
history of this fiercely proud people. They were taught to regard their
land as sacred, so the effect of defeat was doubly traumatic. Nevertheless, the new Japan rose vigorously from the ashes of despair. The shock
of abject defeat offered some advantages, which the Japanese swiftly

recognised and equally quickly exploited. The bombing devastation allowed her to rebuild the entire national infrastructure almost from scratch. The opportunity to create a modern industrial nation state was eagerly grasped; this became a propitious moment to catch up with the West. In 1945, Japan was not truly classed as a developed country; it had not undergone an industrial revolution to match the powerful spurt of industrial development that had occurred in nineteenth-century Britain, America and Western Europe.

With the chance to make a totally clean start, as it were, this was the perfect time to craft a new state. Modern manufacturing plants and offices rose from the oceans of rubble, but the transformation went deeper, even than that. This was an auspicious moment to restructure the entire society, by introducing a sweep of modernising approaches. They included more democracy on several fronts; for the general populace, for the democratic organisation of government departments and policies, and for abolishing the rigid old "caste" system. Merit would matter more than accident of birth. Under this Westernised regime everyone stood a fairer chance of self-improvement. Greater emphasis was placed on better training and education. The results of this quiet revolution have been astonishing. When Japanese people are asked to say to which sector of society they think they belong, about 90 per cent consider themselves to be "middle class".

Economic growth was encouraged by a combination of government and private enterprise initiatives. American assistance, again both from government and private sources, proved to be equally decisive. Japanese banks made commercial loans easy to obtain and the Government offered tax incentives and high depreciation allowances. We can flesh out Japan's remarkable resurgence in the modern world with some comparative figures for growth once the initial difficulties of adapting to her defeat had been overcome. From 1950–65, overall economic growth averaged 10 per cent annually in Japan, against 6.1 per cent for West Germany, 5.3 per cent for France, 2.4 per cent for England, and 2.3 per cent for the United States. Japan's Gross National Product (GNP) rose from $1.3 billion in 1946 to $15.1 billion by 1951 and swept on to more than triple ($51.9 bn) in 1962. By 1968, it had shot up to a staggering $167 billion.

The phenomenal success that has followed from Japan's modernisation owes a great deal to the dogged Japanese character. They are a proud, hard-working people, who value their elders, place considerable emphasis on family ties and loyalty, and view authority and tradition with high esteem. This rosy picture has recently become more blurred, as Japan has struggled to come to terms with the astounding success of its post-war development. After 1945, the Japanese began concentrating their main energies on building up their domestic industries in preference to encouraging inward investment from abroad. Although, during the early phases of their regeneration, they were exemplary copy-cats, improving on the design and marketability of similar products produced abroad, as their economic miracle progressed, the Japanese became adept at developing their own new products and making highly profitable innovations, especially in the lucrative area of consumer products. These range from motor cycles, automobiles, radios and televisions, to the vast spectrum of electronically controlled consumer goods: hi-fis, videos, CD-players and camcorders.

Again, the statistics tell the story of Japan's unfolding domestic affluence. Average wage earners have seen a vast improvement in their real incomes. Taking 100 as an index for the year 1934, they had lost almost half of their income by 1946 (51.9). It took them another eight years, to return to their 1934 income levels (99.5), but by 1962 their earning power had more than doubled (215.2).

Development has been extremely rapid, but also somewhat patchy. The great emphasis on manufacturing was a brilliant master-stroke. The ruling authorities speedily recognised that the industrial base of a modern nation is the power house for wealth creation. It is doubtful if they had read that Britain was the "workshop of the world" during the great nineteenth-century economic miracle of Britain's glory empire days, since very few government officials would have read European history in any detail. Nevertheless, a Japanese version of Britain's former economic success was, in essence, what they achieved. Competition between the various manufacturers was strenuously encouraged, and this further enhanced progress in these vital export-leading industries. Although in the early days the main impetus was simply to provide consumer products for the domestic market, the superiority of the products, coupled with the cheap yen, launched Japan on its export-generating economic miracle – one of the most impressive growth stories of the twentieth century.

However, less attention was paid to the service side of the economy. Even today, distribution and retailing in the economy are fragmented and relatively inefficient. Living costs are astronomically high, compared to the West, partly because domestic retailing is poorly organised. And, as the 1995 Kobe earthquake tragically revealed, the infrastructure modernisation did not extend to the mainly residential areas of the towns and cities, where most people still live in minute, poorly constructed wooden houses in ramshackle streets.

The country is seriously overcrowded, with 123 million inhabitants living on a string of islands where a population of half that number would be a reasonable density. A quarter of the population lives in

Tokyo. Travel in Tokyo is a continuous nightmare. Roads into and out of the city are so incredibly choked with traffic, even short journeys can take hours through constant jams. There are no off-peak trains because every one is filled to bulging point with commuters day or night, but they are clean, unspoiled by graffiti, safe, reliable and punctual almost to the second. Airline seats have to be booked months in advance because Tokyo's Narita airport has not expanded to keep pace with Japan's ballooning growth. The layout of residential areas is completely unstructured, turning the centre of every city into an anonymous maze, as unfamiliar to natives, including taxi-drivers, as to foreign visitors. The houses have paper-thin walls, and are astonishingly cramped, generally no bigger in overall size than the average living room in a Western home.

The Japanese are masters of making the best of these trying conditions. Although there is a shortage of land, a lack of natural resources and living costs which leave Westerners breathless, they seem quite unruffled by such irritations. The economic miracle has brought unimagined wealth to many Japanese. A couple in Tokyo can pop out for an evening meal and easily spend £500 on an ordinary dinner. Houses in standard Tokyo suburbs cost around £500,000, while a minuscule apartment in a drab part of town costs around £250,000.

America certainly played a role in helping Japan to recover after the war by offering export incentives and ensuring the forcible devaluation of the currency. In 1950 the yen's value was fixed at Y360 to the dollar (chosen to denote the 360 degrees of the circle – the image of Japan as the land of the rising sun). This equated to Y1,010 to the pound. A weak currency is a boon for a major exporting nation, such as Japan was now to become. This tremendous advantage worked in its favour for almost two decades, laying the foundations for Japan's economic success.

Since 1973, when restrictions were lifted, the yen has strengthened greatly, albeit with wild fluctuations as the exchange rate has see-sawed violently throughout this period. By March 1996, the dollar bought only around Y105 rather than Y360. Some argue that the dollar has begun a fall marking its terminal decline, similar to that of the UK pound sterling during the first half of the twentieth century. If so, then the yen could possibly strengthen even further.

The Bubble in Outline

We have covered some of the preliminary stages to the onset of the bubble in earlier chapters. In summary, we might say that for Japan, the entire 1980s boom, with all its global ramifications, evolved from its tremendous post-war successes; it became the long-term build-up to

Japan's flirtation with the chaos of a massive bubble in financial assets. After the débâcle of the October 1987 crash, the principal trigger event for destabilising the Japanese financial markets was the insistence of the American authorities that Japan should maintain a low interest rate policy to reduce its massive trade surplus.

By agreeing to this benevolent act Japan surely could not have known what an incredible *déjà vu* situation it was creating. Its main aim was to improve the tense diplomatic relations with America, its most influential ally, thrown up by decades of astonishing export success. However, Japan was now repeating, and tragically, with the same dire consequences, the accommodation agreement reached between Europe and America in 1927. At this time, American exports were dominating the global market place. European governments used similar special pleading to persuade America to lower interest rates, to help their post-First World War recovery. Hindsight is a cruel companion. It throws up explanations years after they can be fruitfully acted upon.

During the late 1980s, threatened with trade warfare, Japan tackled the symptoms of its structural trade surplus with the palliative of cyclical reflation. As its budget deficit was still worryingly large, the burden of reflation was thrown upon an easy money policy. By the late 1980's the economy was awash with credit, cheaper and more plentiful than ever before. This produced the "bubble" economy, with a monumental inflation in all manner of financial assets. It finally burst in January 1990, amid a striking procession of scandals.

Phase One – Build-up to the Boom

The 1980s were bedevilled by exceptional bouts of currency exchange rates and financial market turbulence. In particular, America and Japan, the two largest economies, were caught up in a trial of strength over the extent of Japan's excessive trade surplus, most of which was accumulating through imports to swell America's burgeoning trade deficit. The two trade scenarios, America's deficit and Japan's surplus, became complementary parts of a whole, with the dollar and yen currencies engaged in a perennial yo-yo, swinging erratically from over- to undervaluation by turns. History indicates that recently, falls in the yen have all been accompanied by the Japanese money supply rising faster than its US counterpart.

Although this unsettling situation has continued into the 1990s, a point we will return to in Chapter 13, its impact on events during the late 1980s had a profound influence on the build-up to the Japanese bubble. As one example, the rapid rise in the yen was the parallel of dollar weakness that began in March 1985.

Like the opposing sides in two tug-of-war teams, both parties were impatient to secure the best conditions for their trade and economic growth prospects. A declining currency helps manufacturing profits for exporters in two ways. First, foreign profits, translated at a lower exchange rate, mean higher profits when expressed in the domestic currency. Secondly, a weak currency increases the competitiveness of exports and reduces the attraction of imports. While this is a longer-term benefit, it can have a substantial effect. This weak currency environment was the background that enabled Japanese manufacturers of motor cycles and cars, radios and televisions to demolish the global competition during the 1970s and create the bedrock of Japan's amazing post-war growth. Conversely, the strong rise of the yen since 1990 has encouraged an astonishing renaissance in America's trade performance, while the dollar has been weakening greatly against both the yen and the German Deutschmark.

The Rising Yen

The broad moves of the yen–dollar relationship give an indication of the problems currency volatility created. The yen hit a low of Y260 to the US dollar in February 1985. It climbed rapidly to Y160 two years later and then rose gently to a peak of Y120 by the end of 1987. The soaring yen threatened to price Japanese exports out of world markets. By 1986 the domestic economy was facing a grim recession. Naturally, the rise in the yen after March 1985 produced howls of anguish from Japanese industrialists and exporters. As the mirror-image effect, in 1986 the US current account deficit, in volume terms, stopped rising and began to decline. The stimulus which rising exports had given to the Japanese economy was withdrawn. Making profits from manufacturing suddenly became frustratingly difficult. Growth came to an abrupt halt and fear of recession spread nationally. Industrial production fell and real GNP growth slowed to 2 per cent. Industry's profits shrank and investment projects were slashed. The Government responded with additional *ad hoc* fiscal packages, but each year's budget remained severely tough, so that these seemingly reflationary interim measures were, in reality, simply reducing the absolute degree of fiscal deflation to which the economy was being subjected. The Japanese government's fiscal stance was essentially neutral. The main burden of reflation, therefore, to limber up the sluggish economy, fell upon monetary expansion, primarily through holding interest rates low over this prolonged period of the dollar's decline.

The dollar's fall proceeded throughout 1986 and into 1987, with the American administration ignoring its continuous drop. However, years of persistent pressure by the Americans for Japan to improve the performance of its domestic economy now fell upon more receptive ears. As the dollar peaked and then collapsed, internal reforms by the reluctant Japanese seemed unavoidable. They embarked upon a similar, albeit, far less wide-ranging version of a supply-side experiment. Tax reforms were introduced in 1987 and slowly, greater financial deregulation followed. This involved the dismantling of inward and outward restrictions over international capital markets that were thought to have contributed to Japan's inherent unwillingness to import more manufactured goods from around the world.

Phase Two – The Japanese Financial Pump

Managing financial reforms is clearly a mine-field for government officials. In Britain, removal of exchange controls shortly after Margaret Thatcher came to power in 1979 sent sterling soaring, to the detriment of British exporters. Financial liberalisation had destabilising repercussions on both the US and UK economies in the early 1980s, as we saw in Chapter 11. Now equally disturbing effects were executed by the authorities upon the domestic Japanese scene, under the banner of financial reforms and deregulation.

Japanese interest rates were progressively reduced. The Bank of Japan's official discount rate, at 5 per cent in early 1986, was cut to a post-war low of 2.5 per cent by early 1987. It was thought that rising capital outflows would moderate the yen's fall, while lower interest rates would stimulate domestic demand. However, lower Japanese interest rates did not work as expected on the value of the yen. The gradual liberalisation with low interest rates and poor returns at home encouraged ever more Japanese capital to flow abroad. The yen therefore grew weaker and undervalued once more, making Japanese exports cheap, while the dollar was strengthened.

Net long-term capital outflows from Japan doubled in 1986 and remained high in 1987, putting downward pressure on the yen. These were offset by short-term capital inflows and banking transactions. Confidence in the dollar was so weak that Japanese institutional investors reviewed the exchange risk of holding more dollar assets. While continuing to buy dollar assets, they began borrowing dollars with which to buy them. If they used yen to buy dollar assets, they sold dollars forward to ensure they got back into yen safely even if the dollar fell further. A forward transaction is a contract to exchange, from 3–12 months or more later, a given sum in one currency for another, at an exchange rate fixed when the contract is originally set up.

The progress made towards financial deregulation using low interest rates unleashed the Japanese version of a financial pump. This marked the onset of the slide into chaos by its financial markets; it contributed substantially to the speculative crisis which overtook Japan in the late 1980s. As liberalisation and deregulation proceeded at a leisurely pace during the second half of the 1980's, the Ministry of Finance gradually lost control. Later, it was learned, the Government had earlier brought pressure to bear on the top banks, and they ceased to issue loans for real estate speculation. Government actions and inactions are explicable in the context of the macro-economic and political pressures it faced, but the lack of control over Japan's money supply contributed to a period of major financial instability both at home and abroad. World financial markets collapsed in the crash of October 1987, but the Japanese financial pump was still in operation. Tokyo now became the centre of a manic speculation.

However, during the stock market collapse of October 1987, on 20 October alone, Y5.74 trillion ($400 billion) in value was wiped out. The severity of the October 1987 crash sent shock waves through the markets and governments of the Western industrialised nations. Everyone greatly feared a repetition of the horrific 1930s depression. In unison, therefore, the Governments abandoned their attempts to reduce infla- tion, concerned only to prevent the global economy sliding rapidly into a spiral of recession. With markets plunging all around the world, they relaxed their efforts to restrain money supply growth.

Phase Three and Four – The Boom Accelerates

These morbid predictions quickly proved unfounded. Indeed, with the fall in interest rates, the slow-burn recovery from the 1980–2 recession received its second wind. Prior to this the upswing had been driven by falling savings and rising consumption. The recovery in investment had been feeble. The early 1980's recession had left an excess of idle plant and equip- ment in its wake. Unemployment remained high and labour was plentiful. Not until the fifth year of the recovery did capacity utilisation reach levels at which it was profitable to invest for expansion. Belatedly, investment boomed, sustaining and reinforcing the upswing just when forecasters ex- pected it would end. Japan's GNP rose 6 per cent; Britain and America notched up 4.5 per cent; the laggards, like Germany and France each man- aged 4 per cent. It was the second fastest growth-year of the 1980s.

The Americans and Europeans began to tighten monetary policy again, raising interest rates early in 1988. Japan was the prime exception. Its current account had climbed to $87 billion in 1987. Pressure for trade retaliation was intensifying. The American congress with the Presiden- tial election due in November was turning more belligerent. Worsening trade friction between the two economic powers persuaded the Japanese to maintain a cheap and easy monetary policy a year longer than in other countries.

The Bank of Japan did not raise its official discount rate from its record post-war low of 2.5 per cent until May 1989. The results for growth and the balance of payments were highly pleasing. While the American economy slowed down, the Japanese economy carried on booming. America's real GNP growth dropped to 2.5 per cent in 1989 and below 1 per cent in 1990. Japan's growth accelerated from 4.9 per cent to 5.4 per cent. Of even greater significance, the Japanese current account surplus shrank to $36 billion in 1990, a mere 1 per cent of GNP, while the American deficit fell to $90 billion.

Phase Five – Mass Participation at the Peak

In the short-term the boom appeared to have solved some major Japanese problems. Savings fell, investment rose, output rose rapidly, and the payments surplus shrank. Japan was happy to be back on the fast-growth track. A transformation between 1987 and 1990 saw it move from being the world's slow-coach to the locomotion economy. Domestic demand rose 6 per cent on average over those three years, but only 1 per cent of this spilt over into higher imports which would help other countries to expand. Unfortunately, the other 5 per cent rise in output was not soundly based. It was caused by asset price inflation.

Share prices on the Tokyo stock market rose by 120 per cent in the two years following the October 1987 crash. The Nikkei index climbed from its post-crash low of 17,387 to a peak of 38,915 at the end of December 1989. The rise in property prices was almost as steep. Residential and commercial property values doubled between 1986 and 1989. Rising share and property prices made the one-third of Japanese citizens who owned everything effortlessly wealthier. The two-thirds who owned very little saw no point in saving money from their incomes. They could never afford to buy their own homes. Japanese consumers *en masse* went on a stupendous spending spree.

Personal savings declined notably as personal wealth rose. Household net savings dropped from 16.1 per cent of disposable income in 1986 to 13.8 per cent in 1990. Companies began to spend indiscriminately. Total investment rose by nearly 40 per cent in real terms between 1987 and 1990. The share of total investment in GNP increased from 31 per cent to 37 per cent. The share of plant and machinery investment rose from 18 per cent to 23 per cent. One bizarre expression of inflationary assets was the explosion of interest and prices among art connoisseurs. Buying top

European art suddenly fell into the price range of a surprising number of wealthy Japanese. During the boom years of the late 1980s four out of every 10 top quality paintings sold at the world's major auction houses winged their way to Japan. In 1990, at the peak of the buying craze, and before the Japanese recession really took hold, Japan imported Western art worth $3.4 billion. In one week alone, in 1990, one company boss, not a notable art collector, paid over $160 million for a portrait by Van Gogh and Renoir's *Au Moulin de la Galette*.

Capital spending by companies increased sharply as borrowing money involved virtually no cost. Diverted from their core manufacturing efforts, companies began making huge profits on stock market and land speculation. Investment projects were decided on the strength of their desirability without a thought on how they were to be financed. Money was simply no constraint. Initially, spending on investment was a damage limitation exercise. The strong yen made it imperative for Japanese manufacturers to move up market. They needed to develop and sell products that were technologically so advanced that they would still be saleable, almost regardless of their high price.

However, as the boom gathered momentum, labour grew more scarce. Cheap capital was used to replace it. Finally, one-quarter of all new capital spending was an alternative to higher wages. The productivity of capital fell as new facilities for workers were built – swimming pools, fleets of new cars, sports arenas. Remember Donald Trump on his building extravaganzas of the mid-1980s? Japan's investment boom added to capacity which, if not used to supply the home market, would certainly be switched to increasing exports again.

Japanese Tax Distortions

In *Japan: The Coming Collapse*, Brian Reading describes how the lack of an effective capital gains tax in Japan has encouraged people to seek capital growth rather than securing reliable income returns from their investments. Dividend payments in Japan are onerously taxed so companies continue ploughing back earnings into their business, in the search for ever higher capital growth. The result is a gross distortion in the fundamental statistics for Japanese companies. Extraordinarily high P/E ratios and minute dividend payments to investors mean Japanese companies do not easily conform to the usual analysis carried out by Western investors.

Japanese companies customarily pay out less than 25–30 per cent of their annual earnings as dividends, compared with up to 80 per cent for some American and British companies. For the individual investor, the temptation is simply to spend the tiny dividend, but retain shares which show good capital gains. The taxation discrepancy between the treatment of capital gains and dividends encouraged the boom. The expectation of continuing price rises was part of the taxation distortion produced by minimal dividend payouts. It coloured people's attitudes towards their investments. Having grown accustomed to constantly rising prices, the momentum for further rises was part of the self-sustaining mood in the market. Years of strong economic performance had programmed people to expect continuing and even greater tax-free returns. After the bubble burst, this ingrained attitude towards capital gains among Japanese investors began operating in reverse. It therefore produced the effect of extending the decline, as the poor yield on investments prolonged the disinclination to re-enter a market where investors saw scant possibility of further capital gains.

Imaginative New Financial Instruments

As the bubble emerged, the Japanese penchant as brilliant copyists swiftly surfaced. Familiarity with European history may have been minimal, but with the financial pump unleashed, Japanese-style innovations emerged at speed imitating, as we saw in Chapter 1 the "new" investment instruments of earlier booms. And, as the record shows, the Japanese trod a well-worn path that millions of irrational investors have trodden before them.

Converted to Convertibles

Like earlier innovative Dutch financiers, Japanese executives invented new financial instruments to take advantage of their rising share prices. The enthusiasm with which these novelties were employed reveals the mass participation at the peak. As the Japanese themselves increasingly entered the booming market, so also did investors world-wide, through the medium of collective funds, unit and investment trusts in Britain, and mutual funds in America.

One of the most imaginative new devices was the issue of convertible bonds. Brian Reading relates how both company and investor benefit; the advantage to the company has the ability to borrow immediately by issuing a bond with a life of four to five years: the bond buyer had the option, when the bond was repaid, of using the proceeds to buy the company's shares at a price that was set when the bond was initially issued. Warrant bonds, a variation on this theme, had conversion rights in the form of a warrant which was detachable from the bond at launch and could be sold separately. Depending on the terms of the issue, the right to purchase the company's shares could be exercised on a specified date or at any time within a given period. The purchase price was often as low as 5 per cent over the price of the company's shares a day or two after the warrant was issued. The investor hoped to make a great profit by exercising his rights, if the stock market rose. Locked into a mind-set that expected gains to continue well into the future, he was therefore willing to receive a nominal interest on the bonds during their lifetime, in anticipation of a huge gain on conversion.

The company received cheap cash now, foregoing the opportunity to possibly acquire cheaper funds later on. When the conversion rights were exercised, the company obtained funds to repay the bonds. This clever scheme was based on nonlinear gearing effects. The company hoped to gain from cheap loans; investors bought warrants, fondly expecting ever rising asset prices and fat returns. In the bull market, self-feeding optimism anticipates this happy ending. A market fall is the only glitch likely to ruin it. Then, the gearing works horrendously in reverse: the conversion rights will not be exercised; the company will be forced to borrow expensively to repay its cheap bond loans; and investors who were eagerly hoping to convert bonds profitably into shares will be major losers, with the convertible warrants worthless on expiry.

The issue of convertible and warrant bonds built up from a small start in the mid-1980's. From a level of $20–30 billion in 1986, companies raised $66 billion in 1987, $80 billion in 1988, and $126 billion in 1989. Interest on these bonds fell below 1 per cent by the late 1980's. Securities houses were major investors in warrant bonds, banks were not allowed to issue warrant bonds but they bought heavily into convertibles instead.

A Japanese Mississippi Bubble – Zaitech for Profits

Endaka was the Japanese term for a strong yen, as it doubled in value against the dollar between 1985 and 1988. The yen's strength ruined export prospects for Japan's entrepreneurs and encouraged government attempts to relieve the business downturn by making credit extremely cheap and plentiful. However, instead of borrowing the cheap funds to boost their capital spending, Japanese companies borrowed to speculate in the financial and property markets. The name given to their financial operations was "zaitech". It began modestly as a way of cutting costs when profits fell.

Zaitech operations turned out to be an amazing money-making machine that would have been easily recognised by 1720s and 1920s financiers. The more money companies borrowed to buy shares, the faster the stock market rose; the more the stock market rose, the larger were the zaitech profits that companies made; the larger these profits, the more their own share price rose. The market was pursuing one of its great illusions in the true bubble style we repeatedly saw operating in earlier examples. A pulsing financial pump was working flat out; rising share prices on the Tokyo stock market boosted company profits and earnings, while higher earnings then boosted share prices.

According to Brian Reading, in the year to March 1987, the top 10 industrial zaitech earners made pretax profits of $5.3 billion, with $3.4 billion solely from zaitech. The development of Tokkins was even more imaginative. With Tokkins, zaitech became an unerring money-go-round, in the traditional mode set by Law, nearly 270 years before.

Investment Trusts Japanese Style – The Tokkins

The rise in popularity of the "tokkins" shows how easily this lucrative idea could be espoused under the influence of an active financial pump. If company A holds shares in company B, these can be valued at cost, for tax purposes, only if company A does nothing with them. In Japanese tax laws, unrealised gains do not count as profits and are not taxed. If any new shares of company B are bought, however, all the old holding has to be revalued at the new price. This has the effect of increasing A's profits on which taxes will become payable. As Japanese companies often hold a wide range of each others' shares, this limits the extent to which they are willing to speculate on the stock market. The smart solution to this problem was to open tokkin funds held by trust banks. A company can put its own money into its own tokkin fund, to which no one else sub-scribes. If company A buys or sells company B shares through its own tokkin fund, there is no need for company A to revalue B's shares in its own portfolio. The tokkin pays it a dividend, earned from capital gains, on which A is taxed but it escapes taxation on unrealised gains on B's shares. These funds were immensely popular by the late 1980s. Ul-timately, the securities houses ran illegal tokkin funds, to by-pass the trust banks. The Ministry of Finance knew about these but took no ac-tion. The exact size of the illegal funds can never be fully known but it is thought they may eventually have grown to Y30–40 trillion by 1989.

Not the Best Policy

Another attractive device that mushroomed into prominence at the height of the boom was the "variable life insurance policy". Banks and

insurance companies launched these policies as a way to get around inti-
midating inheritance taxes and to maximise returns. Homeowners were
encouraged to mortgage their house to the lending institution to raise
money for a lump sum to buy the policy. Under the scheme, the policies
would cover inheritance taxes once the homeowner died. Policy-holders
were promised an annual yield of around 9 per cent on their investment,
about double the average for life policies in Japan. Unfortunately, the
returns were dependent on fund managers' investments in the stock
market. When this collapsed at the start of 1990, the risks were suddenly
exposed. Having borrowed to buy the policy, most of the 1.2 million
holders began to struggle to repay the loans, while the promised yield of
9 per cent remained just that – a promise that could not be fulfilled. As
late as 1996, disgruntled policy-holders were still attempting to persuade
the major banks and insurance companies to compensate them for their
losses or at the very least, renegotiate the terms of the loans which had
become an onerous burden to their holders, many of whom were
pensioners.

Foreign investors were also tempted to join the boom band-wagon
during the late 1980s, and the bubble-like performance of investment
fund manager's Invesco's Nippon Warrant Fund, reminds us of Lady
Mary Herbert's speculations in Mississippi options at the peak in 1720. In
similar leveraged fashion, the share price of Invesco's Nippon Warrant
Fund rocketed upwards from its launch in August 1986, for a 970 per
cent gain by the peak at December 1989. However, by March 1996, long-
term investors who did not bale out earlier had lost all their initial
capital, and were sitting on a real loss of 60 per cent.

The October 1987 crash should have come as a warning, but the cheap
money drug was intoxicating. With new financial instruments working
effortlessly to generate profits and massive concealed price manipulation, the Tokyo stock market carried on surging; it had climbed back
above its 1987 peak by March 1988. As it swung into top gear, the
monetary excesses grew to sensational proportions but Baburu, Japanese
for "bubble", only gripped the nation when the extent of frauds, corruption and malpractice surfaced with the stock market collapse.

Mass Participation as the Fraudsters Abound

The recent history of Japanese speculation is replete with scams and
scandals. What emerges from the evidence of the wide-ranging scandals
is the broad extent of public participation. The scandals were primarily
used to exploit devious company speculation to take advantage of
soaring share and property prices. So corruption, fraud and malpractices

of every kind ran rife among politicians, officials, brokers, businessmen and their employees. Anyone who could exploit loopholes in the system, legally or illegally now did so.

Sumitomo used Itoman in the late 1980s as a vehicle for property speculation. Forgery was behind some of the great art purchases, revealed when the art scam was uncovered. The massive Recruit bribery scandal broke in 1988, bringing down Noboru Takeshita's government in 1989. He alone collected Y151 million in donations and cheap shares. The Recruit Company, a real estate conglomerate, gave gifts of unlisted stock to a wide range of politicians, including Nakasone and Takeshita, among others, before the company went public. In the same way that fraudulent South Sea directors manipulated the market in 1720, after the public sale, the value of Recruit shares soared, and the favoured recipients were able to sell out, banking huge profits.

Kotana, a greenmail speculator, was arrested in 1990 for share rigging and blackmail. Frauds among several banks involved borrowing money against the collateral of forged securities. Foremost among these, at Fuji Bank, a leading Tokyo-based bank, fake certificates of deposit were used to raise Y700 billion (£3 bn) in illegal loans. In October 1991, Ryutaro Hashimoto, Japan's finance minister, resigned to acknowledge responsibility for the plethora of stock market and banking scandals, while the Diet, Japan's parliament, passed a package of stock market reforms to prevent such wrong-doings being repeated.

The bank frauds, although widespread, were different from the highly publicised securities industry scandal, where brokerages compensated favoured clients for their investment losses. Over 20 securities brokerage firms admitted to paying more than $1.5 billion in improper compensation to prominent customers for losses they had suffered. This magnanimity was purely to retain these special investors as clients. Their behaviour was at first held to be improper, not illegal, but Parliament prepared legislation to outlaw such underhand practices because public opinion was incensed by them.

When the Sagawa Kyubin affair was revealed, so many financial and political scandals had surfaced, new allegations were losing their capacity to surprise. Sagawa Kyubin's claim to fame was the sheer scale of wrong-doing. During 1992, alleged breach of trust offences involving Y528 billion (£2.2 bn) quite dwarfed the 1989 Recruit stocks-for-favours saga and the Lockheed bribery of the 1970s. The 70-year-old founder of the group, Kiyoshi Sagawa, built up his trucking company over decades. Despite entangled links between gangsters and politicians with Sagawa Kyubin, it was found to have supplied about Y80 billion in payments to over 100 politicians including many past Japanese ministers to help it negotiate through endless red tape delays.

Stories of deals between the company's second in command, Hiroyasu Watanabe and key political figures revealed the extent of corruption. Through dummy companies, Watanabe channelled Y528 billion in loans and loan guarantees out of the company for speculative property and stock investments. Another Y59 billion went to companies where he had a personal interest and another Y85.7 billion to companies linked to his assistant, Saotome. The recipients of this largesse could no longer repay their debts when the value of their assets plunged during the 1990 market collapse. Both Watanabe and Saotome resigned and were arrested. Sagawa was shocked by the extent of the financial malpractices. He feared many of the outstanding loans would never be repaid.

One unlikely anti-heroine of baburu was 61-year-old Ms Nui Onoue, a star turn in one of Japan's greatest ever single bank scandals. She was dubbed "a mystic Ivan Boesky" from her obscure habit of holding a weekly seance at her restaurant in Osaka's Minami entertainment district, to make contact with the spirits. At dawn, after listing the names of companies they revealed to her, she acted promptly, to invest in the "tips" they offered her. Is this the ultimate insider dealing? Reputable Japanese banks lent her hundreds of billions of yen, although her restaurant's annual turnover was just Y1 billion. Rising Japanese interest rates in May 1989, and the collapse of the stock market during 1990 brought to light 13 false certificates of deposit valued at Y342 billion (£1.5 bn) from Toyo Shinkin Bank, which she used as collateral for her loans.

Madness in Property Prices

Together with exploding rises in share values, an unbridled property speculation ensued as bizarre as the share price frenzy. Residential and commercial property values doubled between 1986 and 1989. Real house prices (after inflation) rose 12 per cent a year between 1985 and 1990. Rising share and property prices were a magnificent way to grow passively rich. A novel mortgage emerged, to cater for ever steeper price rises; like planting an avenue of oak trees, a 100-year mortgage enabled people to buy a property outright, for their descendants to own and enjoy, but mortgage repayments spanning three generations is not the only oddity in property values in Japan, where small landowners can be millionaires and many Tokyo families live in apartments the size of one large British lounge.

The absurd values placed on Japanese property can be judged from a few examples in Brian Reading's account, *Japan: The Coming Collapse*. The high-class Ginza shopping and night-club district is the most extreme case he quotes. In 1990, it reached Y50 million per square yard. To buy the area covered by a one dollar note placed on the ground in the Ginza, 10,000 more notes had to be placed on top of it. The price is astronomical because the opportunities to buy land in this area are as rare as snowstorms in the Sahara. The average price of a 70 sq m condominium in Tokyo reached Y70 million at the market's peak in 1990. Prices elsewhere in Japan are lower. For Osaka, they are about 80 per cent of Tokyo prices. At 1990 values, Japan was worth four times more than the whole of America, which is 25 times bigger. This means that at a Y130 = $1 exchange rate, Japanese property prices are 100 times US prices. And the land occupied by the Emperor's palace in Tokyo is worth more than the whole of California. Again, as with financial assets, land is not held for income, but for capital gains. Over 35 years, from 1955–90, residential land prices in the six largest Japanese cities rose 200 per cent. During that period, wages rose 21 per cent and consumer prices only 5 per cent. The Japanese soon realised that what you own, not what you earn, is the secret of wealth. Some astute Japanese owners became more rapidly rich in the late 1980s than at any time since the end of the Second World War.

Property fervour is neatly reflected in golf club membership prices, because golf is a popular Japanese leisure pursuit and members jointly own their golf courses. The Japanese are obsessive golfers. There are over 1,700 golf courses, more than 350 under construction and over 900 in various stages of planning applications. In 1988 the going rate for the most expensive club, Koganei, reached Y280m ($2 million). Between 1982 and 1985, the Nikkei index for the cost of club membership in the Kanto area doubled. Between 1985 and 1987 it trebled. The peak hit 948 (base = 100 in January 1982) in March 1990, after rising 50 per cent in eight months. The stock market collapse proper began in February 1990 with golf club membership prices falling two months later. By June 1991 the index was down 300 points, or one-third from the peak.

As part of the property mania, in 1989, Sony, the Japanese electronics giant, bought the Columbia film studios in Hollywood. This gave Japan its first foothold in foreign media, but it caught a raw nerve with Americans who saw it as a slow process of conceding its economic destiny to Japan. A year later Sony was followed by Matsushita, when it purchased MCA, owner of Universal Studios, for $6 billion. At the time, this was the largest single investment ever made in America by a Japanese firm. Between them, Sony and Matsushita now controlled a quarter of the entire American film business. Their motivation was strictly financial. Buying film studios was a natural next step for the world's leading electronics manufacturers. It was the quickest route to securing the enormous film libraries the movie studios own. These provide over 3,000 films which can be made into video tapes to sell along with the video cassette recorders the manufacturers produce.

The Japanese Jusen (Savings and Loan) Débâcle

Unbridled investment in property during a stock market bubble is a well-proven route to riches-then-rags, which is certainly not confined to twentieth-century financiers. As we saw, extensive property buying was high on the list of coveted assets for South Sea Company directors in 1720. In an almost mirror-image re-run, the parlous condition of Japan's housing loan companies, the jusen, came to light during 1995, to stand along-side the American Savings and Loans débâcle that is set to cost the American taxpayer so dearly over the next decade.

By early 1996, seven jusen were known to be almost bankrupt, over-whelmed by a mountain of non-performing loans acquired in reckless property-related lending during the bubble era. The Government's attempts to win Parliamentary approval for their rescue plan, to spend Y685 billion ($6.47bn) to bail out the country's failed jusen, provoked rare outbursts of public outrage. Opinion polls suggested up to 90 per cent of voters were hostile to the use of taxpayers' money to rescue what they regarded as incompetent and unscrupulous bankers.

The statistics for Nippon Housing Loan (NHL) under its long-standing president Mr Keiichiro Niwayama, illustrate the extent of the collapse. Three-quarters of its loan book was known to be bad. In four years, from 1991–5, it had lost the equivalent of more than eight times shareholders' equity. The share price had fallen from Y2,310 in 1990, to Y40 (37 US cents) by March 8 1996. Its liquidation was to be financed by the donation of public funds.

Reflecting on this spectacular annihilation, Mr Niwayama was disdainful of the part others had played in his company's downfall.

> Everyone is looking for someone to take responsibility for this crisis, but it is certainly not all our fault. The blame lies with the banks that created the companies and the government which created the financial conditions that led to our failure.

Reviewing the history of NHL in a leading article on the jusens on 19 March 1996, *The Financial Times* suggested that

> An examination of the history of Nippon Housing Loan reveals the extraordinary web of relationships between banks, bureaucrats, politicians and big business that brought about its failure. Culpability for the jusen collapse lies, in fact, with almost everyone involved in the functioning, supervision and management of the Japanese financial system.

As we have seen with the long catalogue of scandals, corruption, fraud and monetary excesses, Japan's financial system is truly holistic; the interconnectivity of all its constituent parties ensures that both the boom and the collapse will acquire a "global" dimension, because the ramifications from one element cascade through the whole system in a ripple-on effect, as we saw in Chapter 5 with the sand-piles example. As the Japanese bubble clearly demonstrates, when there is such a widespread holism in the system, both boom and bust will have enormous repercussions for the whole economy.

The Japanese Government had gradually come to realise a rescue plan was essential to restore confidence in the battered financial system. It enlisted support from US treasury secretary, Robert Rubin, to urge the Parliament to accept the scheme, to safeguard international financial stability. For better or worse, the extensive globalisation of the world's markets has now drawn everyone into the growing sand-pile. The holism has assumed a universal quality that could, under the right conditions, ripple through all the world's markets.

Phase Six – Early Nagging Doubts

A stock market collapse is always traumatic; it was doubly so for the Japanese who had put 50 years of unremitting effort into becoming economically successful. Finally, however, the bubble burst at the end of 1989. For the first two months confidence seeped steadily away, before prices began a more serious decline. The early slide in prices coincided with a drop in other key international markets, in America, Europe and the emerging areas of the world. This broad decline tended to mask the truth that the Japanese bubble had peaked.

Phase Seven – The Selling Flood

While all the markets responded adversely to Saddam Hussein's August invasion of Kuwait, the selling in Tokyo had become stronger and more determined as the year progressed. The Tokyo stock market ended 1990 with share prices 40 per cent lower. At the worst point during the year, on 1 October 1990, the Nikkei index was down to 20,221, at almost half its December 1989 peak. Property prices also fell, but more modestly. Even after interest rates began to rise in May 1989 and particularly through 1990 while the stock market plunged, the easy investment spending went on. Due to the lag in investors' perceptions, it took a long time before the message finally got through that money had become scarce and expensive. Investors suffered an information delay, so investment went on rising long after the conditions which supported it had changed. Domestic demand growth did not slow down significantly until 1991. When it did, the old problem of excess savings reappeared. The Japanese balance of payments surplus began to rise once more. Despite a Gulf War support payment of $9 billion, Japan's current account surplus rose to $73 billion in 1991, 2 per cent of GNP. By the end of the year it was running at an annual rate of $120 billion.

However, during 1991 the stock market slide continued remorselessly so that prices reached a six-year low of 14,309 in August 1992 on the eve of a government announcement of measures to reflate the economy. This produced an eight-day rebound of 25.6 per cent. Within two years a conspicuous collapse in share trading, ever soggier land and property prices, announcements of poor financial results by key companies, plus the never-ending tales of major business and political scandals had severely shaken national pride. Talk of a total collapse in the country's financial system was commonplace. The debt hangover was, and remains, astronomical. Wildly varying estimates for bad debt levels were common-place. The banking system was thought to be nursing so many suspect and doubtful debts that solvency for some was still questionable. From being the world's biggest stock market, Tokyo fell back again into second place, behind New York, exposing the fragility of the earlier rise; soaring Japanese land prices fed the share-buying boom which generated profits and collateral for greater land speculation, around the familiar loop. Money and oil were cheap, inflation was low and the economy boomed, until the entire scenario went into reverse.

The Horrors of a Major Debt Deflation

The Tokyo stock market never experienced a full-blooded crash because the presiding authorities were notoriously adept at manipulating the market by exerting pressure on banks or brokers, thereby muting the falling trend. However, while the free market collapse on Wall Street in 1929 took almost three years to create a base from which it could recover, the Tokyo market continued to suffer for well over five years, until mid-1995, as the Government wrestled with one of the most extreme cases of debt deflation that the post-war world has seen.

The Japanese bear market has proved to be a grim long haul. It is the worst economic downturn in more than 50 years. A series of well-intentioned reflationary packages were ineffective. As a result, a large discrepancy between the economic growth rates for Japan and the rest of the industrial world has widened considerably during the 1990s. From 1990–4 Japan grew by a mere 0.5 per cent annual average, while America was growing at around 3 per cent. During 1990 and 1991, extravagant consumer spending continued at its previous heady pace, while perceptions slowly caught up with reality. By 1992, the economy was clearly seen to be suffering a marked downturn. A Japanese survey reported a 65 per cent rise in business failures for 1991. Investments in land, property and stock from the boom years accounted for a huge proportion of company debt. By spring 1992, some of the most favoured stocks on the Tokyo Exchange failed to find buyers. Investors were suffering a severe bout of debt-aversion.

Signs of depression were everywhere. In December 1992, the largest hotel in downtown Los Angeles went into bankruptcy after the Mitsubishi Trading Company and an American partner defaulted on their $75 million mortgage. In the first half of 1993, Japanese banks in America saw their bad loans rise to 13 per cent of their debts, from 5 per cent in 1991. During 1993, Japan was experiencing the worst slump in the economy since the first few years following the end of the Second World War. Unemployment, almost unheard of during the growth decades, rose to a record level of 3.2 per cent by May 1995, with the traditional lifetime employment philosophy under serious threat. Levels of unemployment could rise even further. The all-pervasive sense of uncertainty among consumers meant demand in the economy stayed fragile and weak. Industrial production was depressed. No one can yet be sure if conditions will continue to deteriorate. The key feature of the on-going recession has been the remorseless fall in property prices as the bubble effect is slowly being unwound.

When foreigners bought shares on the Tokyo stock market, a rally prompted indebted institutional investors to sell shares into the rising market, to relieve their over-stretched balance sheets of capital losses on their share portfolios. Private investors, still nursing huge losses on their equity portfolios, also sold stock into the rising market, eager to get out as prices rose. The Japanese investor has become seriously risk-averse.

A massive deflationary cycle of declining demand for credit had been *in situ* over six years, from mid-1990 to 1996. Many asset values, in bonds, equities and property have been greatly diminished in the process. During this period, the Bank of Japan reduced interest rates almost to the vanishing point, in an attempt to revive the flagging economy. By 1995, interest rates were virtually at zero (0.5 per cent), yet memories of the financial suffering investors have recently endured suggest their spirits cannot be lifted by the enticement of ultra-cheap credit, unless they feel confident that the worst of the deflation is now over. By early 1996, investors still felt vulnerable to losses; the sense of fear that economic recovery would falter still appeared to outweigh prospects for enrichment from buying financial assets at current levels.

The ever present risk was that the positive feedback loop which underpins the downward deflationary spiral, might swing up into a higher gear. Even by late 1996 it could have rapidly accelerated if declining asset prices forced a greater retrenchment within the banking, household and corporate sectors, where almost everyone was still locked into many assets with falling values. Another twist around the downward spiral would trigger even more retrenchment, as the momentum of decline gathered pace each time around the loop.

Tentative Reconstruction Attempts

The Bank of Japan had been ineffectively trying to improve the economic environment for years, introducing reflationary packages at intervals. These have fallen considerably short of their goals to stimulate the sluggish economy back onto a more vigorous growth trend. In 1995, a run on Cosmos Shinyo Kumiai, the largest credit union in Tokyo, resulted in heavy property losses. This trigger event finally galvanised the authorities into action, fearing a chain reaction of bank failures if public confidence suffered too severe a knock. At the end of July 1995, public funds were employed to protect the depositors of Cosmos, to prevent a classic run on other banks developing.

By mid-1995, therefore, the Bank of Japan was acting with more determination to boost the supply of liquidity in the economy, primarily to haul the crippled banking sector off the looming shoals of insolvency. For by this time, the Finance Ministry had finally come to realise the scale of the banks' bad debts. In 1995, these were estimated to be in the order of Y50,000 billion (£355 bn). This huge amount, equivalent to a tenth of the whole economy, is the legacy of excessive lending during the bubble years. By spring 1996, it was clear that 17 of the country's 21 leading banks would end the year in loss. Between them they forecast Y3,300 billion ($33 bn) of losses after writing off Y7,000 billion of bad debts. By 1996, the banks had begun to account for their shaky balance sheet positions and many had provided for up to 75 per cent of their problem loans.

Back in mid-1995, the authorities began reassuring investors that none of the top 21 banks, nor those with national networks or international businesses, would be allowed to fail. These moves in effect presaged a more substantial role for the Government in the recapitalisation of the banking system, a role it had previously avoided. The hope was that this effort would give a boost to investors' shattered confidence. Other necessary measures were to include a programme to cut through business regulations that continue to stifle Japan's still traumatised entrepreneurs.

This was the dynamic approach successfully adopted by President Reagan and Mrs Thatcher to galvanise the American and British economies early in the 1980s, but it acquired a very bad reputation when it led to the boom/bust cycle of the mid-1980s. However, for a moribund economy, if it is introduced carefully, ever mindful of the excesses pitfall into which the economy can slide, it is still an excellent route for reactivating a dormant economy. The great mistake made by governments in the mid-1980s who imposed it on their societies was to allow the ensuing boom to get completely out of control.

The Japanese have repeatedly paid lip service to the need for deregulation. In 1996, the Economic Planning Agency published a document called "The Revival of a Dynamic Economy" which was unusually frank in recognising the required changes to end the recession. All attempts throughout the early 1990s were essentially confounded by the strength of the yen against all the major currencies, especially the dollar. As Japan's external balance evaporates, due to its hugely unfavourable terms of trade, the yen could collapse. This would rapidly achieve a resolution to Japan's entrenched economic woes, far more dramatically than could be achieved if the Bank of Japan just pursues its intervention in the currency markets, buying up dollars and selling yen. This policy produced minimal effects in the first few years of trying to escape from the clutches of the debt deflation plaguing the Japanese economy.

By midsummer 1995, the Bank of Japan finally admitted the enormity of the rebuilding task it faced; following the American example of the late 1980s, it became overtly expansionist in its monetary policies. Short-term interest rates fell to the minuscule rate of under 1 per cent and currency intervention was "unsterilised" (notes were printed to pay for the dollars) in a determined effort to expand the money supply. By early 1996 it was possible to detect that these concerted efforts would ultimately bring to an end the longest Japanese retrenchment and bear market since the 1960s. In February 1996, Japan's foreign exchange reserves rose by a record $17 billion, suggesting the Bank of Japan was a heavy seller of the Yen. Figures in March 1996 showed Japan's first current account deficit for five years, suggesting that the US–Japanese trade gap could continue to narrow. Economists at Goldman Sachs expected the Japanese current account surplus to fall to $54.9 billion in 1997, compared with $108.8 billion in 1995.

While pumping money into a closed domestic system may on its own restore a depressed economy to financial health, this cannot apply to Japan, which is part of the ever-more-closely integrated world economy. A prolonged period of holding Japanese interest rates at ultra-low levels tempted the American hedge funds to borrow vast amounts of very cheap yen. They converted yen into dollars to buy American Treasury bonds which offered a far higher yield than equivalent Japanese bonds. By late 1996, the unquantifiable effects of this massive new currency flow and bond-buying boom had not yet unfolded, but problems posed by inter-connectivity throughout the global economy suggested that the increased Bank of Japan liquidity could ignite other financial markets, thousands of miles away from Tokyo in as yet unimagined and dangerous chain reaction effects.

Even by spring 1996, evidence was already accumulating, in true chaos style, that the Bank of Japan's monumental efforts to restore the Japanese banking system to financial health were creating knock-on incipient problems elsewhere. Resorting once again to the financial pump by holding key Japanese interest rates at virtually zero, monetary excesses in other financial markets far from Japan, were almost by definition, bound to emerge.

As new bubbles surface, the endless saga goes rumbling on. Indeed, during the course of the early 1990s, bubbles of many hues were surfacing and subsiding in a constant stream. How this recent crop has fared is the topic to which we now turn.

CHAPTER THIRTEEN

BONDS, BEARS AND BUTTERFLIES

Investors are the big gamblers. They make a bet, stay with it, and if it goes wrong, they lose it all.

Jesse Livermore

In the contemporary financial scene, the interconnectivity of markets makes their inherent instability even more pronounced. As they lurch from one new bubble to the next, the magnitude of events and their dramatic consequences seem to be increasing both in size and scope. This may simply reflect our closeness to these happenings, but it may actually reflect the truly global nature of 24-hour trading. Actions in the Far East, in Europe or Latin America, can trigger serious reactions thousands of miles away, in America, South East Asia of Australia. So complicated is the global financial scene, no one can hope to understand how its various links intermesh together. This superficial ignorance introduces a hazardous dimension to all aspects of investing, even for small investors. There has never been a time when some knowledge of the underlying forces propelling these markets along has been more valuable.

The Devastation of the Bubble

Prosperity is more than just money in the bank; it is an attitude of mind, a psychological state of well-being. It acts as a natural antidote to depression. Bubbles and crashes destroy overnight the excesses of paper wealth that have given investors, savers and even borrowers a glowing sense of monetary well-being as the market climbs towards its ultimate top. The abrupt destruction of this wealth mirage is a demoralising experience. People suffer a period of intense financial shock, from which a faltering recovery can only gradually take hold. And so it was with the sudden collapse of the bond speculation that gripped the international investment community during 1993. Although the warning signs were clearly there for those who knew what to look for, it reached a short-term finale quite unexpectedly on 4 February 1994.

Although it is an example of a recent and topical global bubble, we shall look only very briefly at its main events, using a format similar to that adopted to explore each of the major bubbles and crashes covered in earlier chapters. We will not dwell too much on the detailed history, because the first and most important lesson that our time-travel forward from 1720 has taught us is one simple but crucially central idea. Events in a typical bubble/crash scenario are different yet unchangingly familiar. And this is our first marker for identifying future bubbles. When you begin to recognise the old familiar signals in the heroic stampede towards the peak, you now know you can confidently write the last pages of the script for yourself, even before they happen.

As the story unfolds it becomes astonishingly clear that despite the global nature of trading today on the financial markets, and the undoubted skills, knowledge and sophistication of the main participants, if you have followed the events of the earlier examples, the script will by now seem almost boringly repetitive. We will explore the background to the bond bubble, and the sequence of events that led up to its bursting, followed by the aftermath. As with all the twentieth-century examples we have examined, the chaos concepts will be introduced as they appear.

Build-up to the Bond Bubble

Unfortunately, governments in the major industrial nations had entered the 1989–91 recession with their finances severely over-stretched. The economic downturn aggravated their difficulties, because tax revenues were reduced and spending on social services, especially for growing numbers of unemployed, was involuntarily boosted. Facing this poor underlying financial situation, governments were forced to resort to a tremendous burst of bond issuance to cover rising deficits. In particular, the sound financial position of the former West Germany was suddenly undermined by unification with the much less developed communist East to form a united Germany for the first time since 1945.

Phase One – A Trigger Ignites the Boom

The initial trigger for the bond boom arose in 1989. It sprang from the Federal Reserve Board's anxieties over the health of the US banking system. This was afflicted by a surfeit of ill-judged lending, linked to the monetary excesses of the late 1980s, discussed in Chapter 11. In America during the exuberant 1980s, consumers, companies, local authorities and the central administration had collectively gone on a borrowing and spending spree which had left the nation seriously indebted to the banks and lenders of long-term housing mortgages, the Savings and Loans institutions (Savings and Loans are the US equivalent to Japanese jusens and UK building societies). The reckless lending practices of the S & Ls began before the Japanese jusen débâcle, but as we saw in Chapter 12, both followed a similar course and created similar dire results.

The most acute problem was posed by reckless attitudes to risk adopted by many Savings and Loans institutions. Countless S & L balance sheets were severely over-stretched. In a cavalier lending fiasco on a monumental scale, they had disregarded the first principles of cautionary banking; by advancing thousands of long-term, 20-year mortgages to the housing sector and borrowing to make these loans through short-term deposits, they created a crisis of confidence. In the early 1980s, they were paying depositors 15 per cent while borrowers were paying only 8 per cent, or less. The risks grew after the Government agreed in 1988 to Federal guarantees on S & L loans. This magnanimity backfired unpleasantly because, after 1988, many irresponsible Savings and Loans indulged in rampant speculation and management malpractice. Most had been prodigious buyers of junk bonds. The Reagan guarantee for all depositors removed the risk element from Savings and Loans calculations. Now several were technically insolvent. This scandal is the most expensive government-created calumny in history. By offering these hasty guarantees the Government has become America's largest private property owner.

Although this monetary impulsiveness mainly affected the Savings and Loans institutions, there were, additionally, deep-seated problems for the banking institutions themselves. Professor Tim Congdon succinctly summed up the seemingly perennial dilemma the banks face, in his February 1996 Bulletin, "The banking system seems to suffer from a peculiar incontinence. Whenever it has excessive capital, it expands lending until the need to write off the resulting bad loans eliminates the excess capital." Reckless lending policies by US banks in the late 1980s neatly illustrate his point. They were now gravely weakened by colossal levels of suspect debts. Appearing on bank balance sheets under the picturesque heading of "non-performing loans", most would probably never be repaid. In consequence, to restore the banking system to financial health, during the early 1990s, Alan Greenspan, Chairman of the Federal Reserve Board, operated a deliberate policy of low interest rates. From 1989 to 4 February 1994, America's main interest rates fell and then stayed low, to enable the banks to rebuild their fragile balance sheets.

Phase Two – Easy Credit and the Financial Pump

While it could never have been his intention, with hindsight we can see that Mr Greenspan created a massive financial pump by gradually reducing the key US discount rate over a five-year period to a 3 per cent low by late 1993. Everyone becomes a buyer in the hope of making quick gains and selling is delayed in the expectation that prices will rise even further. Reassured by the almost effortless accumulation of easy profits, the concept of "fair value" is heedlessly jettisoned. Conversion from caution to high risk-taking can affect the most cautious sophisticates and stolid professionals at the very moment when it lures in all the novices and outright speculators, just when the peak looms into view. The history of the 1993 global speculation unleashed by the Greenspan financial pump reveals this destructive process in action.

The official compliant attitude to low interest rates enabled the banks to borrow cheaply and invest the proceeds in higher yielding bonds. Through this policy, they were slowly able to accumulate large profits, thereby repairing their much debilitated balance sheets. Unfortunately, if interest rates are falling, even very slowly, over a considerable period of time, there comes a certain moment when serious-minded investors acting in tandem with more speculative types become duped by the lure of easy money and cheap credit; in thousands, they undergo a seemingly painless transformation, from a rational to an irrational investment stance, through the weird chaos mechanism of a phase transition. This effortless metamorphosis occurs indiscriminately; chaos is no respecter of persons, everyone can fall victim to its pernicious impact. The occurrence of a phase transition event marks the denouement in the operation of a financial pump, as the system flips frantically from damped to an unstable driven phase. On this occasion, the hands of America's central bankers were firmly on the throttle.

Profitable Proprietory Trading

The prolonged period of very low interest rates helped to pitch many professional bankers, brokers and fund managers into the realms of the "get-rich-instantly" brigade. New, previously underdeveloped trading techniques now became hot news – as the in-vogue trends of the day to be slavishly followed. Foremost, for the banks, perhaps, was "proprietary trading for their own account". This was a method of making profits in-house, without the bother of seeking out new loan customers, even though advancing loans is reputedly the banks' core business. It was the American version of "zaitech profits" beloved of Japanese businessmen in the late 1980s.

Innovative New Techniques

Other technical wizardry that shot to prominence at this time included some old ideas dressed up as new. Collectively they form the vast "derivatives financial markets". Briefly, they are forward contracts, covering foreign exchange dealings; futures contracts involving currencies, bonds or commodities; options contracts, as discussed in Chapter 3; and swops (or swaps) which are an ingenious method of raising loans in another country when no collateral is available. This latter market has grown so fantastically that by mid-1994 it was estimated to be over $10 trillion in value, nearly double the size of the entire US Gross National Product. However, in May 1996, *The Corporate Risk Management Handbook*, published in association with Price Waterhouse, the accountancy firm, calculated the notional principal of derivatives positions held by companies in the S&P 500 index amounted to $19,000 billion in 1994, of which 98 per cent was attributable to financial companies, such as banks.

Financial directors for huge multi-national corporations, for local authorities and financial institutions, especially the banks, became increasingly active in these new-fangled money-making instruments, until they belatedly discovered the serious downside risks to which they were exposed, or learned with horror that employing these financial instruments was outside the legal frameworks of their written constitutions or articles of incorporation. We need not dwell on the details of these imaginative creations. Suffice it to say, they fulfil one of the conditions we expect to emerge in tandem with the bubble mentality, namely a flood of weird and wonderful money-spinning methods that are quickly seen by active participants as modern advances outdating everything innovative that has gone before in the get-rich-quick arsenal.

The Hedge Funds Boom

The banks were not the only major players to discover the new-found strategy which Mr Greenspan's accommodating monetary policy was promoting; namely, borrowing cheaply and lending out the proceeds by buying higher-yielding government bonds. The enormously successful US "hedge" funds, which had come to prominence over the past two decades, were equally keen to exploit these profitable opportunities. If Mr Greenspan failed to recognise the chaos mechanism of the financial pump he had created, the key participants in the speculative bond bubble, the notorious US-based hedge fund managers, equally misread the underlying forces at work.

The original concept for hedge funds was to balance each position, by taking both a long (buying) and short (selling) position. Then as the trend in the particular asset or market they were following became clear, they would sell out of the losing position and buy more heavily into the winning position. Using this initial neutral strategy of covering both sides gave them their name; essentially, they were hedging their bets. It was a highly successful method of risk control. The hedge funds invest in a wide range of extremely liquid assets, including stocks, bonds, currencies and commodities. These funds have been a feature of US financial markets since the 1960s, but they rose to greater prominence over the past 10–15 years. Initially, they set up collective pools, offering to manage money taken onto their books in substantial amounts from exceedingly wealthy clients keen to find competent professional managers to produce ultra-high returns on their investments. To achieve this hedge fund managers often borrowed heavily (against the value of the fund's assets) to add a massive gearing boost to their trading positions. This is the chaos, nonlinear boost, which will greatly magnify the gains (and losses). The managers also use hedging techniques – primarily selling assets short – to enhance their returns. Several years of high profile and exceptionally successful speculative trading gave the hedge fund sector an immense notoriety. The publicity allowed them to build up funds of monumental sizes as new money from high-worth clients, usually with in excess of $1 million to invest, came pouring in to take advantage of their excellent management services.

Phase Three and Four – Asset Prices Rise as Speculation Grows

These funds, however, in their turn, also became unwitting victims of the Federal Reserve's financial pump. As they went through the phase transition experience, from rationally thought through techniques of investing to more risk-prone irrational speculating, the behaviour change increased the level of their trading aggression. They abandoned their original strategy with a hedging element to reduce risks. Now, when profitable opportunities appeared, they would take an immediate view on the future direction they predicted, and plunge into the financial asset they were targeting, to pin down rapid returns. The fabled George Soros, one of the most acclaimed hedge fund managers of the 1980s, coined an evocative description for this approach, "Going for the throat". This expression may derive from the hunting techniques of the big cats – lions, tigers and cheetahs. When hunting carnivores catch their prey, they grab it by the throat, aiming to sever the main arteries from the heart. By gripping the throat, and tenaciously holding on, the captured animal is soon killed.

Phase Five – Mass Participation and the Speculation Mania

As news spread in the press that bonds were surging, thousands of small investors clamoured aboard the soaring bond market money-go-round. In America, investors were dismayed by poor returns on their cash deposits as interest rates fell to their 1993 lows. They poured money into collective bond and equity mutual funds. Meanwhile, in Britain and Europe, interest rates also fell early in the 1990s, in response to the recession of 1989–91. This same switch of funds out of cash deposits and into bonds and equities therefore occurred in all the main European markets. The flood of European money was reinforced by vast amounts of American cash leaving America, as its citizens sought out profitable foreign investments to diversify their portfolios overseas. The global financial community was enjoying one of its great collective delights; it was chasing ever more exorbitant paper profits, thanks to the benevolence of the central banking fraternity.

The Bubble at the Peak

Predictably, rampant speculation drove asset prices around the world to fantastic levels. The yield on the benchmark 30-year US Treasury bond was driven down to 5.78 per cent in October 1993, its lowest level for a generation. As the yield moves in the opposite direction to the price of the bond, rising prices at the peak had produced magnificent capital gains. In the wake of soaring bond markets, stock markets roared ahead and another new craze for international investors shot to fame in the growing investment firmament. This was the emerging market story, where small under-resourced regions of the global village were slowly emerging into the golden dawn of a post-industrial new world. Areas like southern Europe, Latin America, parts of South East Asia, the fragmented post-communist world of Eastern Europe, and even China and

India, were suddenly seen as offering a counterbalance to investors anxious to diversify as a means of minimising risk. By spreading some of their assets into these less well-developed countries, so the argument ran, one could diversify the risk. If the major industrial markets hit a setback, the developing regions would remain unscathed, as their progress was thought to be out of step with and independent of the developed markets.

Evidence that the public had moved *en masse* into emerging markets, came from the latest American mutual fund figures. In January 1994 they showed net new sales of mutual funds (after deducting for their sales) reached $18 billion. Although this was the biggest monthly total, coinciding neatly with the looming peak at 4 February, the amounts of cash pouring in to the mutual funds coffers had been averaging between $8 billion and $12 billion every month for most of 1993.

If the general public was now participating in earnest, so indeed were the professionals. The amount of derivatives trading had grown monumentally and several US banks and institutions had exposures worth many times their underlying capital. In 1993, Bakers Trust had derivatives exposure worth $61.8 billion, roughly 13 times shareholders equity. A minute loss, tiny compared to the market, could potentially wipe out the bank. Other major US companies, including Chemical Bank, Citicorp, J. P. Morgan and Chase Manhattan all had derivative exposures 250 per cent in excess of their equity.

Phase Six – Early Nagging Doubts

Some canny investors were clearly already taking profits by late 1993, as the US bond market started to weaken from its October high, but the great investment wave went rolling on around the globe, sending stock markets in Europe, Asia, America and in the superbly fashionable emerging markets, up to vertiginous heights. However, warning signs of trouble were evident in other markets, for those alert enough to spot them.

In the early 1990s the mighty Olympia & York, the private investment company of the Canadian Reichmann family, began experiencing financial difficulties, primarily relating to its formidable plans to redevelop the London docklands region with the Canary Wharf project.

At its peak, Olympia & York had major international property interests plus a controlling stake in Abitibi-Price, the world's largest newsprint producer, and a huge holding in Gulf Canadian Resources, the oil and gas group. Yet, finally, in 1992, Canary Wharf went into administration, with debts of $15 billion, against a background of falling rents and property values. This financial disaster led swiftly to the break-up of the entire Olympia & York business empire.

There were several other straws in the "financial distress" wind at that time. The British and Commonwealth shipping and insurance giant, founded by the Cayzer family, ran into trouble when its acquisition for £417 million of the leasing company Atlantic Computer, was found to be worthless. By 1991, the entire group was in administration. Another to flounder in a blaze of mystery and hype was Robert Maxwell's publishing empire after his dramatic death by drowning. A similar fate of imminent failure appeared to loom for the heavily debt-laden publishing empire of Australian tycoon, Rupert Murdoch. It was feared his trading corporation could be on the point of collapse but through dogged determination and a long period of financial reconstruction, he managed to survive and prosper anew.

The Greenspan Butterfly Effect

On 4 February 1994, the music skidded to a nasty halt. When Alan Greenspan raised the key US discount rate by a miserly quarter per cent (0.25 per cent) the speculative bubble burst. Commentators thought his action was intended to send a genteel message to the markets that interest rates would need to rise slowly over the coming months. Instead, to add to his chaos financial pump, Mr Greenspan had now triggered yet another classic chaos phenomenon – the Butterfly Effect. Many months of severe disruption followed the seemingly innocuous initial rise in US interest rates because this modest act represented a major turning point in investors' perceptions of the future course of interest rates, for which they had been completely unprepared. One tiny interest rate rise in America gravely disturbed bond and equity markets world-wide over several months.

Phase Seven – The Selling Flood Begins

One minute interest rate change by the Federal Reserve produced a drastic rethink in sentiment across the world's financial markets because it signalled as clearly as any message could that America's lax attitude to monetary policy was over. With this innocuous message was also unleashed a selling stampede of astonishing size and rapidity, primarily for one simple reason. The initial rise in bond yields created an imminent crisis for the over-borrowed hedge funds. Rising yields, with their promise of fat interest payments, were currently of trivial interest to them;

they were not long-term holders of bonds. Their foremost objective was to make large, immediate capital gains from rising bond prices. Once they suspected the direction of future interest rates was up not down, the fund managers made a frantic dash to unscramble their heavily loan-related bond holdings.

Phase Eight – The Selling Stampede

We recognise this as the gearing element, working now in reverse, against the speculator. Born of long experience in their markets, hedge fund managers might quickly visualise the unfolding drama that confronted them. They knew the losses would start to rack up with frightening immediacy. They began unwinding their gigantic holdings, dumping bonds by the billion onto a reluctant market. Since their position in the market was so enormous, the change of direction in the bond market threatened to expose them to hugely damaging losses. As they rushed to reverse their long bond positions, they initiated a selling chain reaction as vigorous as the previous buying explosion had been. Large-scale selling triggered further selling in a mighty positive feedback loop as investors and speculators alike hastened to lock in their profits and buyers held back, waiting for prices to fall even lower.

Everyone holding bonds, including mutual fund managers, company finance directors, banks with proprietory trading departments, governments and local authorities plus the army of small investors were caught, unceremoniously, in the sudden slipstream of this selling avalanche. But if bond yields rise with a steep insistence, for whatever reason, the yield on highly priced equities stands nakedly exposed, by comparison, as totally unrealistic. This out of balance relationship had become the triggering event for the October 1987 crash. Similarly, in February 1994, the torrent of selling leapt across the asset markets, from the falling bonds, to engulf the excessively priced equity markets world-wide.

Whatever the background trigger event, the results are always the same. As the conflagration spreads, the top priority is to secure the profits or minimise the losses. Sadly, a leaden sense of inertia invariably descends upon the majority of investors and speculators exposed to a sudden switch in the direction of the markets. They are often caught completely unprepared for any fast-moving change, having made no contingency plans on how to cope with such an eventuality. Repeatedly, this ensures that the initial loss of potential profits swiftly becomes the onset of true losses, as prices plunge rapidly on the way down, falling below the original buying price for the assets on the way up. Now the selling avalanche increases, under the pressures of continuously sliding markets. The collapse of the bubble is a stark reality and everyone is facing unpalatable losses.

Some of the key derivatives players, who had wrongly expected interest rates to stay low, suffered sensational losses as the bond bubble unwound. In *Riding The Business Cycle*, William Houston lists 15 public and private institutions which together are known to have lost nearly $75 billion from derivatives trading in this period. They included Metallgesellschaft ($4 billion) and Kidder Peabody ($3 billion). Yet even these titanic losses had not brought the derivatives juggernaut to a halt. By the end of 1994, the total derivatives financial markets had reached the sum of around $50 trillion, double the entire annual output of the global economy. In addition, by March 1996 an estimated £1,230 billion was routinely changing hands every day in the foreign exchange markets. Moreover, in Britain a sudden rush of several building societies in 1995 to convert to banks was thought to be prompted by the high-profit opportunities that awaited them in derivatives, currency trading and interest rate swap activities. The Halifax, Woolwich, Alliance & Leicester and Northern Rock building societies were all hoping to copy Abbey National's success in building up "treasury operations" for proprietory trading. We can recognise this astounding expansion as evidence of the self-perpetuating growth to which complex, chaos-dominated systems are inevitably prone.

Unwinding the Bubble

The great puzzle that worried many financial analysts and commentators as the bond bubble collapsed, was why bond and equity markets almost everywhere, were anticipating future inflation rates in excess of 5 per cent when the dragon of inflation itself seemed by 1994 to have been holed up in its den, if not yet mortally slain. What these fundamentalists had ignored was that the several months of decline in the global bond and equity markets which followed the modest 4 February interest rate rise, was illustrating a well-established manifestation of chaos in financial markets – a damped, driven system. The ricochet effect from boom to bust is primarily a **technical condition in the market;** it will only finally abate when the entire system has somehow managed to restabilise itself.

The fundamental analysts had failed to understand that until the excesses of the financial pump boom had completely unwound, this technical condition would dominate all other aspects of trading behaviour. Until buyers and sellers were again roughly in balance, no fundamental assessments of the underlying situation would have any relevance. The concept of "fair value" is often a secondary factor when investors are struggling to preserve their capital during a financial collapse.

Both the enormous buying and selling episodes are examples of the driven side of a damped, driven system that continued to operate over several months, until the imbalance between buyers and sellers slowly returned to a more sustainable equilibrium. This finally restored the system to a short-term, relatively stable state and the concept of "fair value" could again become a relevant test of investment potential for investors and speculators alike. The international bond market gyrations may not be at an end, however. Over three years of great volatility (1993 to early 1996), the American long Treasury yields have been on a hectic switch-back. In 1993 they fell from 7.5 to below 6 per cent, before rising back above 8 per cent and then dropping below 6 per cent again. Wild swings of this nature in what are regarded as "relatively safe" investments play havoc with the savings philosophy of thousands of international investors planning their long-term financial futures. The increasing instability stems from the massive participation in these bonds by central bankers, institutions and, predominantly, the highly geared American Hedge Funds.

A Batch of Bubbles

Today's international financial market place has no fixed abode. Currencies, commodities, precious metals, derivatives of options and futures, transactions for bonds and shares slosh around the world on an electronic tidal wave of mega-proportions. Each working day, more money changes hands across financial exchanges than is spent on real trading in goods and services by the entire global business community. In such a frenetic environment, it is not surprising to discover that no sooner have we seen the collapse of one unstable bubble, than another has ballooned into being, often from the most unexpected direction. And as this new phenomenon expands to fill the now vacant bubble slot, the investing population becomes blindingly infatuated with whatever it is that has emerged to fill the gap.

We will take a fleeting glance at these nebulous creations as they flash into focus and out again, because the message that they bring rings like a clarion call – **investor beware**. We must be constantly on our guard when we invest in a newly risen star shining brightly on the investment horizon. We may hope it will fulfil its promise of healthy returns, but an exuberant surge can suddenly acquire some of the ugly characteristics of an outright bubble even while we are holding it.

Since the bursting of the global bond bubble, several others have risen to prominence and burst across the scene with bewildering speed, like a shower of shooting stars. Many are simply little local events, so the sequence of eight phases may not readily be discerned as the scenario unfolds. These will probably provoke less damage or have less long-lasting effects than the global examples we discussed in earlier chapters. Only the most significant bubbles will have major repercussions as they attract large-scale international participation, and therefore may have serious and wide-spread implications.

One example of a local bubble occurred in Russia in July 1994. Scores of anxious Muscovites stood in the sweltering heat outside a branch of MMM, a shady investment company that the government had warned was running a giant pyramid scam, a Ponzi scheme, no less, now on the point of collapse. Remember the agitated crowds gathered outside Banque Royale in Paris during the downfall of the Mississippi Bubble in July 1720? And, like the South Sea Company before it, MMM had no real trading facilities. It could only pay dividends to its 10 million existing shareholders from money it acquired from the sales of new shares. Haven't we heard this all before? Towards the end of its brief life the share price fluctuated violently; traders on crowded pavements outside its Moscow headquarters were offering as little as 30,000 roubles ($15) for shares which a few days previously had sold for 110,000 roubles ($55). Sadly, the ending is always the same.

Emerging Markets Emerge

On a more international scale, the switch-back performance of the emerging markets in the mid-1990s illustrates the global dimension of many recent bubbles. The herd instinct of the mighty US mutual fund managers came to the world's attention during the massive exodus of investment dollars that was poured into the emerging markets between 1993 and December 1994. This bubble was borne along on a tidal wave of loose money, searching restlessly for a super-profitable home. A watershed was reached in September 1993 when some Morgan Stanley analysts visited China, with a group of fund managers, who collectively managed $400 billion of clients' funds. After this visit, the positive views of the world-renowned Barton M. Biggs, chief investment strategist at Morgan Stanley and Company at that time sent South East Asian shares soaring. The Hong Kong Hang Seng index rose 20 per cent in five weeks. When Morgan Stanley had a change of heart shortly after this rise, these same markets were sent plunging, as investors *en masse*, rushed to respond to the updated advice. Quixotically, and in market-shaking quantities, they withdrew their cash.

In 1993, almost $40 billion went into stock markets outside the industrialised world. Around $106 billion of emerging market shares were held by foreigners at the end of the year. During December 1993 and January 1994, net new sales of American mutual funds investing overseas totalled $11.5 billion. The proportion of money that found its way into Latin America during the second quarter of 1994 rose to 77 per cent, up from 14 per cent in the first three months of the year. Seven years earlier, the figure was only $2.4 billion. In five years, from 1988 to 1993, emerging market share prices had doubled. In 1992, the average return to investors was 67 per cent, compared to a pedestrian level of around 15 per cent from the funds held in the shares of the major industrial countries.

Most of this money, as much as 90 per cent of the 1993 inflow, was held in open-ended funds. The danger would arise if too many investors suddenly wanted to cash in their profits at the same time. The problem here relates to the gross illiquidity of these newly risen markets. For example, in Indonesia, where average market turnover was $33 million per day in 1993, there would be horrendous problems if thousands of small investors, all wanting to sell their mutual fund holdings at the same time, forced fund managers to liquidate their underlying shares. In such a situation, they might want to unload $50 million of investments per day onto the Indonesian market. Such large transactions could have a savagely adverse impact on prices.

Small, unsophisticated stock markets in the developing countries cannot easily handle massive cash flows, either in or out. When money floods in, however, there is so little available stock to buy, prices can be forced up dramatically. Naturally, investors rarely have a problem with this result, unless they missed out on the rise. In general, they simply relish the prospect of making 67 per cent a year on their investments. The problems of illiquidity are far more unsavoury when the time to sell arrives, however.

In theory, diversification into emerging markets as a shrewd investment-hedging ploy sounded brilliant. In practice, the difficulties of liquidating enormous positions were finally brought home to the great army of small investors in December 1994, when the Mexican economic crisis hit the headlines. A flood of money winged its way back to the markets investors knew best, the mature industrial markets where a humdrum 15 per cent a year return is all one can realistically hope to achieve. This mass exodus signalled the bursting of the emerging market bubble that some commentators had earlier feared would happen.

Yet by definition, as the emerging markets are relatively young, the continuing unfolding of their full potential could well repeat the phenomenal run of ultra-strong growth that accompanied the post-war development of Japan. ING Barings forecast for 1996 was that cash flows of around $50 billion would be targeted at these markets, up from $15 billion in 1995. These flows could receive a significant boost if the new assessment of Wall Street guru, Barton Biggs, Chairman of Morgan Stanley Asset Management, proves correct. In February 1996, he claimed the US stock market was heavily overvalued (the Dow Jones had performed a spectacular bull leap of 45 per cent, rising from 3,850 on 5 January 1995 to 5,600 by 13 February 1996). He foresaw a sharp decline on Wall Street for 1996, but estimated the emerging markets could return 25 per cent. In the view of many analysts, therefore, the emerging markets story has much further to run.

Technology Bubbles – 1995 Style

The astonishing surge in global technology shares during 1995, was spearheaded by the resurgence of high technology shares in America. From January to August 1995, it produced a rise of almost 34 per cent in the Nasdaq composite, which has a 40 per cent weighting of technology shares. The Pacific Coast Stock Exchange technology index, at nearly 400, was 63 per cent up for the year by the end of August. Once again, there was a measure of lax monetary policy by the Federal Reserve Board, which had raised interest rates from 3 per cent to 6 per cent from February 1994 to March 1995, but a rate of 6 per cent was still relatively lenient when associated with a low, competitive dollar and an economy that was continuously restructuring itself to improve profitability. The relatively favourable interest rate regime became the pump, aggravated, no doubt, by a huge inflow of funds coming home early in 1995, as the emerging markets collapsed. However, cautionary warning signals that a top for the technology boom might be appearing were steadily accumulating during the steamy summer months.

Fantasy Land for High Tech New Issues

In his classic work, *The Intelligent Investor*, the legendary American investor, Benjamin Graham warned of the danger of investing in high fashion areas. The relevant example at the time he was writing was the computer craze, then still in its early pioneering stage. Because it was a leading edge sector, and therefore more subject to the vagaries of rapid success and failure, within three years of his warning 23 of the 45 shares he listed as being part of this fashion mania had lost 50 per cent of their value, 12 had completely disappeared and only two had seen an increase in their price. The 1995 equivalent was Wall Street's love affair with everything remotely connected to the Internet. During the early months of 1995, launches of high technology companies in this field give a flavour of the speculative fervour that gripped Wall Street.

One such company was UUNET, an internet access provider. It was floated at $14 in May and was trading at around $43 by mid-August. Another was Netcom On-Line Communications Services; floated at $13 in December 1994, it had reached $34 by mid-August. Spyglass, which makes software to help people surf the Net, was floated at $17 in June 1995 and was trading at $43 two months later. For sheer exuberance, the reception given to the small loss-making company, Netscape Communications, set a record. It began trading on 9 August on the Nasdaq exchange, only 15 months after it was formed. The record of its short performance up to that date illustrates the ferocity of the high technology bug that was mesmerising American investors. Netscape makes software to enable users of the Internet System to browse through its contents, in competition with Spyglass. Its revenues for the first half of its current financial year were only $16.6 million, because it had instituted a policy of giving away its software free in the short term to build up a respectable market presence. On this strategy it had notched up losses of over $4 million in the first half of its current financial year, but it had managed to secure 70 per cent of the market. However, its market share was vulnerable to the 24 August 1995 long-awaited launch of Microsoft's Windows 95. The Microsoft package contained a browser in competition with Spyglass and Netscape. So much hype had surrounded the initial public offering of Netscape that the launch price of $28 shot straight up to $75 on the crush of demand, before falling back to $58.25 at the end of the day, still more than double. At this price it was valued at over $1 billion, and its directors, in true bubble style, had become instant dollar multimillionaires. Later in the year the price reached a high of $174 before the stock was split into two, but it was still trading at $50 a share (equivalent to $100 before the split) in March 1996.

During 1995, many high tech companies received similarly ecstatic receptions on launch. A small maker of computer memory components, Paradigm Technology began trading on 29 June at $14 on a relatively high historic price/earnings ratio (P/E) of 29.6. It closed the first day at $19, and within three days the price had shot up to $24.50 and the P/E was then 51.9. On 16 August, it reached a high of $33.

Ahead of the Microsoft Windows 95 launch, investors, as is their wont, were relishing in advance the monumental returns that might be achieved. Sales of $100 million of the new product were bandied about as a reachable target for its first year on the market. Accordingly, the share price for Microsoft had been storming away right through the early months of 1995. In July it hit a peak of $110, and was still trading at $99.25 a few days prior to the 24 August launch date. At that price, this mega-sized company with a market capitalisation of $57.7 billion (581 million shares at $99.25) was trading on a P/E of 39 (which gives the number of years, 39 in this case, it would take in earnings to recover the cost of buying one share), as if it were a small high-growth company.

Technology shares underwent a couple of sudden wobbles during the summer. Sharp dips in mid-July, and again at the end of August were both followed by a quick recovery. This is a sign that plenty of buyers are waiting on the sidelines, ready to snap up stock on any retreat. They see this as a good chance to buy into the sector, but they may be purchasing the shares of canny insiders selling out after the massive run-up in the first eight months of the year. Unsurprisingly, during this selling the technology indexes stalled. However, by February 1996, these and all the main US indices, were again at new highs.

Spotting the Bubble-Building Signals

We could go on discussing the 1990s crop of bubbles, *ad infinitum*. They show that these are not isolated one-off dramas that may one day find a place in the financial history books. There is obviously no shortage of bubbles; they have reached the ten-a-penny stage. Some bubbles seem to be getting bigger both in size and extent, although this may be an illusion, because in recent years they have increasingly affected global markets. The key question, however, is not whether these unsettling investment dramas are growing more frequent but how is the serious investor to protect himself from the inevitable fallout? This important question certainly deserves to be tackled in a chapter of its own.

CHAPTER FOURTEEN

AN ALPHABET ALERT

In the arena for speculation there are no partial judgements in favour of wealthier investors; all must depend on their financial wits for survival.
J. H. Shennan, *Philippe, Duke of Orléans, Regent of France 1715–1723*

In today's global markets with billions of dollars, yens, pounds and other currencies streaking across the electronic airways like lazer beams, bubbles are constantly forming and exploding. Their appearance is rather like the emerging and disappearing air pockets that erupt on the surface of a hot geyser. Their frequency, global reach and increasingly mega-sized expansion indicate we might expect more of the same, if not worse, as we move towards the new millennium. No one can be quite confident that the much vaunted "crash of crashes" will never occur. And if it does arrive, is there any way we can spot it in good time to take appropriate avoiding action?

Some recently emerging bubbles might ripen into crashes, while others fizzle out rapidly, flopping down exhausted, as quickly as they arose. The distinction between the two states has become more blurred with the growing sophistication of modern global markets. The bubble covers the rapidly growing boom, awaiting an inevitable bust. A crash is altogether more wide-ranging. After a lengthy and vigorous boom, it depicts a dramatic collapse in asset prices perhaps on a global scale, harbouring serious financial repercussions. Unlike the bubbles, which often involve a complete wipeout of the previous rise, a crash may send prices down 15 or 20 per cent in a few days, but rarely sends them spiralling back to their initial pre-boom levels. A crash of crashes would be a mega-event, on a global scale that far outweighed in severity the impacts felt by the Wall Street crash of 1929 and the October crash of 1987.

Whether it is a bubble or a crash, of whatever size, we know everyone will throw up a motley group of similarities, even when the details differ.

So we need to compile a checklist to ensure we can detect these tell-tale similarities as they arrive. Several questions spring to mind. Would you recognise a bubble-building scenario? If you were holding assets in some financial sector that seemed to be developing bubble-like tendencies, would you know what to do? Could you decide what assets to sell and when they should be sold? Could you extricate yourself in good time, before the impending collapse? Where would you put your liberated cash to protect it from disaster if there is a crash of crashes as some doom-mongers predict? The primary objective must be the preservation of capital. Remember the advice meted out to a new immigrant to Israel, dreaming of making his fortune. He was told, if you want to leave Israel with a million, make sure you arrive with two million!

How to Recognise a Coming Collapse

The nightmare scenario for all serious investors is to be caught up in a massive financial crisis which threatens to engulf all one's capital, not knowing why it has happened, how it happened or what to do about it. We are ready now to discuss how to deal with an encroaching collapse by outlining the main signals. These should warn you to prepare for coping with this horror situation if ever it should arise.

As the American financial markets still dominate the world scene, the most important advance indicators will relate to them. Any sudden un-expected moves in either the American stock or bond markets, or in the dollar, are key noteworthy events. If the outlook for the US economy deteriorates markedly, its fate will be reflected in prices there. In addi-tion, the behaviour of the US benchmark 30-year Treasury bond can act as an early warning signal, as bond prices usually peak before equity prices in the economic cycle. The yield of a bond moves in the opposite direction to the price. When the yield on this key bond reaches a low, perhaps somewhere below 6 to 7 per cent, it could be the right time to start taking some precautionary action, even if initially this only means following international events more closely than usual. In the UK, the equivalent yield to watch is on the 10-year Gilt. By early 1994, just before the market turned in February, it had fallen to a low of 6.15 per cent. A more usual level is somewhere between 7.75 and 8.6 per cent.

The Bond Relationships

The three most important indicators to watch are: first, the yield on the benchmark government bonds; secondly, the prevailing rates of inflation; and thirdly, the key interest rates applying in the economy. There is a close link between these three main indicators: bond yields, interest rates and the levels of inflation in the economy, because once a fixed interest bond is issued, its price on the open market will vary with the expected rise or fall in prices of goods and commodities. Changes in these prices are measured by the rate of inflation.

Holders of fixed interest bonds have a manic obsession with future inflation levels, as once they have bought their bonds, they are locked in to a given rate of interest. During a period of rampant inflation, the value of their capital can collapse and the purchasing power of their income will dwindle to virtually nothing. This fate befell the middle classes in Germany during the hyper-inflation years of the mid-1920s. During the post-Second World War years of high US inflation, the value of a Treasury bond bought in 1950 would have fallen by over 50 per cent if it had been held until 1980. From this low point, however, the value of these US bonds has more than doubled, as yields fell to their record post-war lows by October 1993. These gyrations have meant that government bonds have been very poor long-term investments.

The relationship between a bond yield and inflation is often affected by rising or falling commodity prices. In general, commodity prices tend to lead bond yields. The link between commodity prices and bond yields can be traced over many decades, although other factors sometimes intrude, so it does not always follow a consistent pattern. Bond yields and commodity prices collapsed in tandem during the deflation at the end of the last century. They ran in unison until both peaked in 1920 and then subsequently declined in the 1930s. Although bond yields and commodity prices diverged shortly after the Second World War, due mainly to government action to hold bond yields down, after 1960 yields began to track commodities again, when the US administration started progressively to inflate the economy. In the early 1980s, commodity prices were relatively stable but bond prices collapsed because the major international nations were all imposing stringent monetary policies in a united attempt to reduce inflation.

The close relationship between a bond yield and the rate of inflation works through monetary policy and the prevailing level of interest rates. This link provides a good indication of the harsh measures governments occasionally impose to bring inflation back under control. In the early 1980s, governments in the Western democracies raised interest rates to crisis levels to squeeze excess inflation out of their domestic economies. As interest rates rise, the bond yields rise in tandem, to keep them in line with other financial instruments that produce a fixed income. In America during the Volker squeeze which began in 1980, interest rates rose to 17 per cent and stayed there for over a year. It was this prolonged period of high interest rates that drew massive volumes of money into America and helped the dollar to soar to unprecedented levels. In Britain, interest rates similarly rose, reaching 16 per cent, for precisely the same reason.

The Symptoms of Economic Distress

The emergence of crisis levels for the yields on government bonds can indicate that the authorities are taking a firm grip on events to root out excessive inflation, as was the case during the early 1980s. Equally, however, it may indicate that those in command are losing control of the key economic indicators. They will be buffeted by events beyond their control which the crisis level of yields will be reflecting. In either event, the signs of distress are similar. Apart from any special symptoms, unique to every incident, there would invariably be a marked rise in levels of inflation, rising interest rates to 12, 15 or even higher percentage rates, exploding commodity prices and rampant swings in currency exchange rates. There would be a sharply declining rate for the currencies in the most crisis-ridden countries.

Debt levels throughout the economy would rise to exorbitant heights due to punishingly high interest rates. The debt burden would affect all sectors of the community, struggling to repay ever more expensive loans. Individuals, companies, local authorities and central governments would all face sweeping cut-backs to bring their finances back into some semblance of balance. There would additionally be signs of increasing unemployment, social unrest, civilian disobedience, violent demonstrations and possibly even outbreaks of rioting. Many of these symptoms were detectable in the early 1980s, as governments battled to eliminate high inflation. They were also evident again in Britain during the harsh early 1990 recession, when it entered into the European Monetary System Exchange Rate Mechanism at an inappropriately high rate. An increase in the prevalence of many of these elements could indicate a breakdown of society with serious repercussions for financial markets. As we saw in earlier chapters, many of these stress symptoms come to prominence during a period of debt deflation following the collapse of a bubble or a crash, but they might all be early warning signals that a crash of crashes is looming, if corrective measures that governments have put in place do not seem to be working.

Checklist for Emerging Bubbles

If you are becoming suspicious that some of these early warning signals are emerging, you should begin to prepare a checklist. Compiling such a checklist offers a useful starting point, for two reasons: first, it is a systematic way of dealing with your doubts, allowing you to put your thoughts into an orderly framework so you are better prepared for any action that may become necessary. And secondly, it will enable you to judge more clearly how far along the route the chaos scenario has progressed. Not every signal we might expect to find will be present in every bubble event. If it evolves too quickly, some of the eight phases we should be able to identify may blur together.

In addition, there is the awkward problem of unearthing and collating the evidence. It is far easier dealing with historical records that have been written up into books. Ben Bradless of the *Washington Post* described journalism as the first draft of history. And it is to the financial press that we must turn to find our evidence of unfolding bubble events. We may miss some item of vital information at an early stage, unless we are incredibly lucky or the equivalent of a financial Sherlock Holmes, being a genius at ferreting out the important clues. The solution to this handicap is to stay flexible, be alert and keep an open mind.

Primarily, we are looking for a cluster of symptoms that indicate serious financial trouble may be brewing. We are seeking a group of separate incidents that will authenticate the gathering bubble drama. One-off incidents, like the August 1991 coup in the Soviet Union, or the collapse of Barings bank in March 1995, can seem significant at the time, but will readily be brushed off, if there is no true cluster of chaos signals building. Sometimes, the sheer momentum of events, and the serious nature of the developing chain reaction, can serve as a classification of how severe the coming collapse will be. This can be gauged by studying more closely the build-up to the boom, as we have done with the examples in earlier chapters.

Additionally, we may notice the arrival of one, two or more of the extra signs we noted, such as the emergence of an innovative new financial tool, massive participation of the gullible public, rising debt levels, major frauds or a big corporate collapse. What we should begin to find if an over-enthusiastic boom appears to be reaching an unstable peak, is a collection of the known pieces in this jig-saw puzzle of events. When only a few of the remaining pieces appear to be missing, it is clearly time to start preparing for the worst.

Early Nagging Doubts

Accordingly, as soon as your fears are alerted, write down the list of eight bubble phases, and try to pin-point the date when each stage began in the scenario you are examining. I did this for the 1995 technology bubble as I was holding shares in several UK electronic and software companies. I made handsome profits, mainly on paper. So the priority questions soon became, how serious is this over-extended boom? Is this the right time to sell? If so, shall I sell everything or just part of my holdings?

Ideally, to be safe, you would hope to begin writing your list in phase five, the mass participation phase, in the run-up to the peak, although you can never know in advance when the peak will arrive. Even if you are later than phase five when making your assessment, you could hopefully still find yourself in phase six, the first nagging doubts phase. Both phases five and six are excellent jumping off points. They indicate you will be aware and far better prepared to act in good time, ahead of any sudden avalanche of selling. Clearly, if you are really alert, **your** nagging doubts should emerge ahead of the crowd, and certainly before the peak has arrived. Whatever the actual moment when your suspicions are first aroused, the starting point is always the same: visit the local reference library, or the Colindale National Newspaper Library, to read up recent current affairs stories that suggest a boom has reached the over-extended stage or a bubble is building. Try to identify at least the first three to five phases of the crash scenario together with approximate dates when each one began so you can judge how fast the boom is growing. Record the relevant evidence you have found relating to each phase in turn:

Phase One: Onset of the Bubble

Try to date the original trigger event that marked the bubble's onset.

1 Can you identify the actual event?
2 Were there any immediate follow up signs?
3 How long ago did phase one begin?
4 Was it a local, domestic or an international trigger?

Phase Two: Growth in Credit and the Money Supply

1 Are current interest rates very low?
2 Have they reached a low for the cycle or are commentators expecting them to fall lower, say to 4, 3 or even 2 per cent?
3 Is the low rate encouraging banks to lend cheap credit?
4 Are consumers still worrying about repaying debt?
5 Can you detect the emergence of a financial pump with lax interest rates encouraging high consumer and corporate borrowing?

ls the Government planning to spend extra money on public goods and services by borrowing and selling more bonds?

7 Does the central bank seem complaisant about interest rate levels, rates of inflation or mounting public sector debt?

8 Are people borrowing money for house purchases or other major consumer spending?

9 Are consumer stocks booming?

10 Are high street stores enjoying record levels of sales?

11 Are car sales increasing, especially for individuals, rather than corporate fleet car sales?

12 Do banks or building societies report outflows of cash from their depositors accounts, rather than inflows?

13 Is there a global dimension to a loose money stance as discussed in earlier chapters, notably in chapters 10, 11 and 13?

Phase Three: Inflation in Asset Prices

Look for signs that tell you the boom is well-established.

1 Is inflation rising, without the authorities increasing interest rates to damp it down?

2 Is there a general election looming, with politicians handing the electorate more of their own money back in lower taxes or increased welfare spending programmes?

3 Is the bond market rising strongly? If so, keep an eye on the fall in (and level of) the yield on the US 30-year Treasury bond or on a 10-year UK Gilt bond.

4 Are commodity prices rising?

5 Is there a shortage of important commodities, cereals, metals, oil, soft commodities, like sugar, coffee, etc.?

6 Are equity prices moving up robustly, especially in the bubble area?

7 Is the gold price rising? This may indicate investor nervousness.

8 Is there a lot of activity in the futures and traded options markets, or in newly devised derivative instruments?

9 Are luxury objects, fine art, antiques, furniture, old master paintings fetching amazing prices at auctions?

10 Is consumer spending rising?

11 Are property prices rising? This is a tricky indicator in Britain, since the housing market collapsed into a steep deflationary spiral during the early 1990s. It may take many years to recover fully from this deep recession in property values.

12 Are American consumers in the vanguard of the phase three expansion, spending and borrowing across a broad front?
13 Are other areas of the developed or developing world sharing in the new boom?
14 Is the market where the bubble is building anticipating a hugely profitable event some time in the near or more distant future?
15 Have other areas of "conspicuous consumption" recently become hot news?

Phase Four: Pure Speculation and Exaggerated Expectations

1 Are there suddenly some new financial trading ideas with strange names that are making headline news?
2 Are the press highlighting the zany antics of whiz-kid traders?
3 Are some exceptionally successful traders hitting the headlines with reports about their huge profits?
4 Are there press stories which suggest speculators are overtrading?
5 Are the famous hedge funds back in the limelight with stories about the massive profits they are making?
6 Are any of these signs visible in other major markets, especially in America, which is still the premiere market that influences investors world-wide?
7 Are there new issues on offer with exorbitant expectations but no tangible profits in sight right now?
8 On launch, do new issues go to fantastic first day premiums?
9 Has there been a sudden rush of new issues coming to market to take advantage of the strong rise in share prices?
10 Is there a new "leading sector" with marvellous prospects for the next millennium?
11 Are some reliable commentators suggesting the next move in interest rates will be up, not down?

Phase Five: Mass Participation at the Peak

Several vital clues can pop up in phase five.

1 Are small private investors buying huge amounts of shares in collective funds? The statistics for these appear regularly in the press, with comments by the analysts to tell you when private investors are highly active. This is frequently a signal for the onset of phase five, which indicates mass participation.

2 Are small investors from abroad diversifying into UK trusts?

3 Are UK investors diversifying strongly into foreign-based mutual funds, unit and investment trusts?

4 Has there been a lot of recent publicity on the growing numbers of new investment clubs for small investors? These may hit a peak of popularity at the top of the market.

5 Are investment clubs reporting major growth in their portfolios?

6 Are your friends talking about the financial markets at parties, or over the garden fence?

7 Is the press extremely optimistic about prospects for the field where you think the bubble is growing?

8 Is the press reporting silly sayings by famous people?

9 Are analysts confidently predicting further falls in key interest rates?

10 Have there been recent cases of fraud in the sector where you think a bubble may be building?

11 Has a major company in the bubble market recently run into trouble, called in the receivers or stopped trading?

12 Has a big public institution come to the point of collapse?

13 Are the authorities planning to rescue it or allow it to go under? The reaction of the authorities is important because you can gauge from their response how serious the ensuing collapse might be. If they are happy to neglect a crisis in a failing major institution, there could be a serious chain reaction effect for other failures, further down the line. The response of the authorities will indicate their current attitudes towards a major default.

14 Are new issues in the bubble sector coming to market with a fanfare of hype? This might include long queues to obtain prospectuses or hand in last-minute applications for shares. It may surface as phenomenal over-subscriptions for a modest amount of stock on offer, incredible offer prices, or ludicrously high prices during the first few days of trading, as everyone scrambles for a slice of the action.

15 Is the press hugely optimistic about current prospects?

16 Are they talking about a "plateau of prosperity"?

17 Are they forecasting even higher targets for the major indices?

18 Have bids and mergers suddenly become popular, with astonishing prices being offered for the companies being taken over?

19 Are the hostile bidders offering their own shares to investors in the target company, instead of cash? At the peak, the hostile company's shares will have risen strongly with the market, allowing them to buy acquisitions on the strength of their high share prices instead of paying cash.

20 Watch out for official figures that indicate the strength of new records being set, for example in the numbers of bids and mergers. In

February 1996, IFS/Securities Data released statistics showing more than 9,000 American companies, worth $350 billion, were acquired during the great bull market year of 1995. This total topped the 1994 figure by almost 30 per cent and exceeded the level of acquisitions activity reached during the best year in the heady 1980s bull run. In Britain, merger mania was also at full stretch in 1995 with almost 2,000 mergers worth £85 billion, also the highest level of activity since the enthusiastic 1980s. New statistics on record levels of activity are pointers for assessing the run-away nature or not, of any boom. Figures for equity launches also hit new records during 1996. According to Securities Data, total US equity issuance, including secondary and initial public offerings (new flotations), topped $40 bn in the second quarter of 1996, beating the previous quarter by more than half.

21 Is there a flood of rights issues coming to market?
22 Are there stories in the press about the crazy antics of irrational investors?
23 Is the bubble atmosphere attached to a sector or fashion where a wall of money is descending upon a market with limited outlets?
24 Have you spotted any Butterflies? These will be small or modest events that trigger massive responses in dramatic chain reactions of unexpected events.
25 Are global bond and equity markets hitting new highs on a regular basis?
26 Is this a national or an international boom?
27 Can you detect high volatility in prices of assets in the bubble market? This will show itself as wild swings in prices, weekly, daily, or even hourly.
28 Are all the indices rising together or is the advance limited to just a few highly popular sectors? A narrow rise is clearly more dangerous than a wide, broadly-based advance.
29 Check on the charts, to see if the share price or index has spiked up rapidly, leaving all the moving averages behind. Either one of three possible outcomes will follow. First, a gradual consolidation, with the price hovering at its current level, until the main moving averages, 20-day, 50-day and 200-day, have caught up with the price action. The boom may still have further to go in an upward direction once the averages have caught up with the main index of asset prices. Alternatively, the price can fall gradually over the course of a few weeks, to meet the rising moving averages. The third alternative is that the price might drop back as dramatically as it rose. This could mark the onset of an imminent price collapse. If this happens, sell when the price falls decisively below the upward sloping trendline,

or when it cuts down below the 50-day moving average. Always monitor events more closely when you suspect an imminent collapse.

Phase Six: Early Nagging Doubts

Once you have identified some or all of these symptoms in the first five phases of the bubble or crash scenario, you should pay close attention to the progress of events during phase six. The nagging doubt phase is ideally the time you should be selling out of your holdings if you consider that the boom is over-extended and has become extreme. If it is a more modest affair, because the main bubble is occurring in a different market to the one where you are holding investments, you might start reducing your holdings down to a level where you feel comfortable, hoping to stay in for the long-term growth you are expecting.

This is particularly relevant to many markets which suddenly become wildly fashionable, until the bubble bursts, but do have long-term attractions. A five- to 10-year view on the emerging markets or high technology stocks could come into this category. Then you may want to hold on to some shares you own in an area where you expect a knock-on effect of a collapse in another geographical market that has suffered a more intense bubble effect. For example, US high technology shares might have a serious set-back at some stage. Although more reasonably priced technology shares in Europe or Britain could also fall in a copy-cat backlash, if they have lower valuations, they should drop less dramatically. These are important caveats to assess when searching for the onset of phase six.

1 Has the share price or index been hovering around its all-time high for a while?
2 Is it having trouble moving up into higher ground? This reluctance to advance may indicate the wily investors are selling their holdings on to the Johnny-come-lately speculators. This is a damped phase, as knowing insiders sell out to the newcomers, so that buyers and sellers are evenly matched and the prices stay stable around the peak.
3 Does the chart show the index or share price is standing very high above the usual moving averages (20-day, 50-day or 200-day moving averages)? If so, it may be due for a fall.
4 Is the chart beginning to show the formation of a strange attractor shape (a double or triple top, or a head and shoulders pattern)?
5 Has there been a sudden large bout of profit-taking, followed by a strong recovery, when everyone appears to have recovered their poise? This is a very important signal. It is a sure indicator that numerous people are anxious to bank their profits, or are beginning

to have serious doubts. This event happened on several occasions during 1928 and 1929, before the October crash.

6 Is the heavy-weight financial press starting to talk about a bubble?

7 Are a few influential analysts or market commentators sceptical about future prospects?

8 Is there a big worry on the horizon that investors have been ignoring for some time, because the market has been rising strongly?

9 Are people in authority making unhelpful comments which might upset the markets?

10 Are some bid and merger stories coming unstuck and not going through to completion?

11 Are the rights issues receiving a less-than-healthy reception by the market, with large amounts being left with the underwriters?

12 Are some new issues being withdrawn from flotation at the last moment, due to "uncertain market conditions"?

13 Is the market beginning to show signs of high volatility, with days when it rises strongly, followed by days when it plunges down again?

If by some awful oversight you have completely misread the warning signs of phase six, do not panic. You still have another golden opportunity for flight before the onset of the great avalanche of selling.

Phase Seven: The Serious Selling Begins

1 Has there been a major triggering event to mark the onset of serious selling?

2 Can you judge if it will have global implications, or does it represent merely a more modest involvement? This can be gauged by the type of bubble picture you are examining. If it is a serious international boom affecting all the major industrial nations, with massive funds flowing into the main stock markets sending prices surging, the chances must be strong that some important incident with clear international implications, could trigger a collapse which will leap across national barriers to precipitate a global crash.

3 Is the level of inflation becoming a serious international problem?

4 Are some important commodity prices rising, for example, oil, wheat or gold?

5 Has the bond market peaked? Yields on government bonds will start to rise as the bond prices fall. The important US 30-year Treasury bond is the key indicator to watch. Before the selling stampede begins it may have risen above 9 per cent. The 10-year UK Gilt could probably reach 10 or 12 per cent in similar circumstances.

6 Are interest rates threatening to rise, or actually beginning to rise?

7 Is the level of debt among consumers, businesses and public sectors very high or becoming unmanageable?

8 Is the market worrying about an anticipated problem that could come to prominence abruptly?

9 Are the authorities in control, or do they seem to be swept along by the tide of difficult fast-moving events?

10 Do the markets swing about violently, with strong days up followed by heavy profit-taking? Highly volatile markets may indicate the top is near. This volatility can create the double or triple top or the head and shoulders top formation on a chart.

11 Is the flood of rights issues, takeover bids or new issues receiving investor resistance in the market? Large amounts of issues on offer will now be withdrawn or left with the underwriters.

12 Are advisors suddenly withdrawing new issues from the market before the appointed launch date because "market conditions are not favourable".

13 Are bond prices falling more rapidly? The long-dated securities are the best indicators to follow as the yields rise above 8 or 9 or even 10 per cent.

14 Are precious metal prices rising? This is an unreliable indicator now because many more investors use the geared derivatives to protect their portfolios when prices fall.

15 Are there signs that US investors have begun to panic? The all-important US economy and its financial markets cannot be ignored, whatever other areas are doing.

16 Are some market analysts advising clients to take profits?

17 Are the press talking about a crash? In global markets where crashes have now become more accepted as notoriously recurring events, the crash mentality can itself undergo a chaos-induced spurt. It may become self-fulfilling under the force of its own growing momentum if all the appropriate elements are falling into place.

18 Are the bubble sector indices rising while others are falling? This is a sign that the gullible public are buying shares from knowledgeable insiders. There has to be a constant broadly-based advance across all sectors of the market, for the boom to stay intact.

Phase Eight: The Crash, Panic and Stampede into Cash

And finally, if perchance you do get caught out by the collapse of the bubble or the crash that you failed to recognise in good time, don't lose faith. You may still be perceptive enough to recognise the sudden

Butterfly Effect trigger that is about to unleash a selling cascade. If you can identify it, you may have time to sell out half your holdings, followed swiftly by the second half, shortly after your worst fears are confirmed. As we saw, there were at least a few timely selling days prior to the massive sell-off in both the Wall Street crash of October 1929 and in the global October crash of 1987. Financial assets could have been sold during that hiatus period on both occasions without incurring extraordinarily large losses. Again, there was at least one to two months at the start of the Japanese bubble collapse in December 1989, when sales of Japanese equities or unit trust holdings could have been liquidated without large losses as the Nikkei Dow index did not begin its first serious descent until February 1990. Moreover, sales of assets in March 1994 would have prevented further losses as the bond bubble continued to unwind right through the spring and summer months.

No matter how savage the collapse, if you are aware of the progression of events, as we have seen them unfold in each case we have considered, there may still be time to sell some of the shares in your portfolio well before the bottom, to give yourself cash funds ready to reinvest when the dust has finally settled. Arriving at the low point can take a few months, so even if you are a committed long-term investor, it is always a sensible move to raise some cash. You can never be sure how long a market decline will be, especially since some of the most serious examples in the past have lasted two or more years. Depending on your investment attitudes, selling into the fall could present a good opportunity to eliminate some of your holdings which are showing a loss. Alternatively, you can sell shares showing a profit, in the hope of buying them back later, when they have fallen along with everything else.

So what type of phase eight trigger are we now looking for in the final stages of unwinding the boom? Is there a sudden unexpected international shock event? It might take the form of a major international crisis. A major currency collapse, the death of a national leader, a possible war event, a collapse of the banking system in a major industrial nation, a policy dispute between allies; all can trigger a monumentally destructive financial Butterfly Effect. Severe natural disasters might also come into the Butterfly Effect category, acting as a trigger. A world-wide drought, perhaps, or a massive earthquake or volcano eruption, might all have serious international consequences for the financial markets, if other signs of an imminent collapse are present. As one-off incidents with no accompanying market peak, the repercussions would be much more readily containable.

Investors in the know may be able to sell before the major damage occurs. The key areas where international events could destabilise the global economy would include America, Japan, China and the oil-producing regions of the Middle East, or the volatile Latin American region, because it is now so closely linked to American affairs, but if it is unexpected, by definition, it could strike virtually anywhere.

And finally, if all else fails, it is useful to remember that on the really long-term charts, the great October crashes of 1929 and 1987 now look like insignificant blips on the steadily rising indexes. However, we must never forget the old adage that the future may not be like the past, so we should take a brief look now at the concept that haunts many investors as we move towards the twenty-first century – the end of the Golden Age of Western supremacy in the world economy.

The Crash of Crashes Scenario

Earlier we touched on the notion of a crash of crashes, but a few more comments on this important topic seem appropriate here. Because the global economy has become so intermeshed and interdependent, a financial meltdown certainly cannot be entirely dismissed as doom-mongering. If such an event were to occur, I believe it should be preceded by a monumental boom of booms. However, this might not be a precondition if a crash of crashes occurred as the result of a totally unpredictable triggering event. If the conditions are appropriate, a crash of crashes might follow some major discontinuity; it might be a phenomenal natural disaster, or it could be triggered by a national event which has global consequences or adverse repercussions. Many candidates have been suggested for the latter, including the financial collapse of a hugely indebted country, such as America.

Vital Clues From Past Examples

The ragged collapse of the dollar-gold standard in 1971 with its attendant global repercussions gave a foretaste of how a loss of confidence in the mighty greenback could disrupt financial markets on a world-wide scale. The US Treasury had amassed three-quarters of the world's total gold holdings by the late 1950s, when foreign holders of dollars seriously began to convert their money holdings back into metal. This process accelerated in the 1960s when the Kennedy administration began inflating the US economy, creating more money to finance the Vietnam war and introducing deficit-financing policies. The drain on gold reserves finally became an acute crisis, forcing America off the dollar-backed gold standard in August 1971, during President Nixon's period in office.

Although the shock waves of instability were clearly building in the late 1960s, as American officials lost control over the crucial monetary indicators, the aftershock of the collapse of the dollar-gold standard was profound. It ushered in a period of acute international instability. During the early 1970s, a collection of major incidents coincided to create a series of crises that effectively brought the Pax Americana which had prevailed since 1945 to a crushing finale. This is a cluster of signals effect. Having considered the earlier crash scenarios, we should feel we would be able to detect a similar episode in the future. To underline the principles involved, let us take a closer look at the demise of the dollar-based gold standard as discussed in James Dines *The Invisible Crash*.

American-led Crisis – 1970s Style

There was mounting inflation, due to the conjunction of a number of factors. Inflation was exacerbated by the dollar's devaluation; coincidentally, harvests failed and the price of wheat and other cereals soared. The collapse of the dollar brought a decline in the real value of oil being exported by the Middle East producers under OPEC. Low oil prices had deterred other areas of the world from exploiting their oil reserves, so that OPEC had a strong monopoly position in the world market for oil. They used the excuse of the 1973 Yom Kippur War with Israel to raise oil prices four-fold. Western nations had grown dependent on cheap Middle East oil and this price rise was an unexpected blow to their economies. It produced another upwards lurch in the inflationary spiral. These varying elements now conjoined to send inflation roaring up to unprecedented post-war heights. The pieces of the jig-saw were rapidly falling into place.

The consequences were more severe because most Western governments were following a policy of full employment and increasing welfare programmes. These pledges to the electorate had produced large government deficits. The ability to cope with the added shocks of the early 1970s was seriously restricted by the large levels of borrowing to which central governments were already committed. Together with mounting inflation, there were wild swings in interest rates and spiralling commodity prices. Numbers of companies went bankrupt; numerous banks failed. In Britain, there was a severe property collapse and a Bank of England "lifeboat" had to be launched to keep some secondary banks afloat, until their over-stretched balance sheets could recover. Some were too indebted and were allowed to collapse. Currency exchange rates became extremely volatile, once the dollar-gold standard had collapsed. Floating currencies generated additional levels of instability. Commodity prices had to be revised every quarter; index-linking for pay and pensions to take account of rising prices, were only sporadically applied. Government paralysis in coping with the inequalities raised by these *ad-hoc* measures was notable. Severing of index-linking schemes for wages and salaries, pay pauses, dividend controls, and other restrictions were all applied at various stages, but with limited success. There were extensive social unrest and labour strikes, as workers at all levels tried to protect the real value of their pay packets and salaries.

In most of the western democracies, stock markets fell to dismal lows unparalleled in peace time. In Britain, the decline from May 1972 to December 1974 was 73 per cent – its worst ever bear market. However, these massive stock market declines never created a crash. Instead they more closely resembled "the crash that never was", even though many indices sank to record post-Second World War levels. A series of economic shocks were reflected as abrupt falls in short, heavy plunges; each succeeding piece of bad news sent the markets tumbling. There were intermittent rallies within the gathering gloom over a period of nearly two years as the major industrial economies struggled to overcome a capitalist crisis of exceptional intensity.

Is a Repeat Performance Possible?

This scenario of gross instability was unleashed over 25 years ago essentially through a crisis of confidence in America. It could again be set in motion if America's international financial backers decide to withdraw their support and cash in their government bonds *en masse*. The possible occurrence of such an event should not be viewed merely as a scare story, for serious investors need to know as many of the relevant facts as possible if they are to protect their hard-earned capital resources from an unpleasant financial disaster.

Until 1960, around 60 per cent of the Federal Reserve's assets were supported by gold held in Fort Knox. It provided a stable base for the dollar's role as the key reserve currency for international trading and financial transactions. When President Kennedy was elected in 1960 on a programme to expand the domestic economy, the Federal Reserve was encouraged to issue an increasing number of notes without the traditional gold backing. Simultaneously, some gold stocks were sold, undermining the historic levels of gold-backed currency even further. The gradual decline in America's currency indicates the extent of this debasement. Relative to an index of 100 for the purchasing power of the dollar in 1913, its worth had declined to 30 per cent by 1965, and to a mere 8 per cent by 1990. This latter fall represents a drop of over 70 per cent in 25 years. The assets of America's central bank, once 100 per cent gold, are now well over 80 per cent paper government securities bought from the Treasury to finance the growing and persistent deficit. If the Federal Reserve continues to issue notes without the backing of gold, the entire shaky edifice could collapse. This is the shock-horror event that befell the German mark in 1924. Effectively, the currency collapse means everything denominated in it, together with the currency itself, has become worthless. In 1720, John Law's experiment with a paper currency came shuddering to an end, when confidence in his notes totally collapsed.

The extent of America's indebtedness gives a measure of how such a loss of confidence could recur. In 1917 the US Government had only $3 billion of debt when the total national income was $40 billion. This represented 7.5 per cent of national output. By 1994, the ratio of government borrowings exceeded 70 per cent. For years, America has been living beyond its means and increasingly borrowing to maintain spending levels that succeeding administrations have promised to deliver to the electorate. By 1993, America was borrowing at the rate of $1 billion per day, mainly through the central bank issuing government securities, a modern form of printing money. Irwin Stelzer in *The Sunday Times*, 10 November 1996, reported that foreigners owed $1 trillion of US national debt, 20% of the total.

The Oil Wild Card

A collapse of confidence in America could stem from an oil price increase. The recent decline in the value of the dollar has had a major detrimental impact on all the world's oil producers, as oil has been traded in dollars for decades. This loss of purchasing power was a major factor in prompting the Arab oil producers to raise the price of oil in the 1970s. With the growing oil needs of the newly emerging economies, and in particular, China, where oil consumption will dwarf that of America by the turn of the millennium, demands for oil are rapidly expanding. Western dependence on Middle East oil was almost as great by the mid-1990s as it was in the 1970s, and particularly so for America, the largest consumer of the world's energy: 83.88 quadrillion BTUs per year. In the mid-1990s, US oil stockpiles were at a 20-year low, back to the levels which triggered the bold OPEC move in October 1973.

The oil price rises of the 1970s accelerated the loss of American hegemony, exposing its dependence on other nations for vital industrial resources. However, in the 1970s America had tremendous strengths to see it through the crisis: it had vast international currency reserves, the US economy had little debt, US banks and corporations were undoubtedly still the strongest in the world, and its financial position was rock solid. The situation by the 1990s was very different. America had become the world's largest debtor nation. It relied on foreign oil to supply twice as much of its needs as in the 1970s, and most serious of all, its financial markets had become seriously destabilised by a few enormous and over-extended sectors. The mutual funds have become truly gigantic, the hedge funds are equally colossal, and the derivatives markets are astronomic in size. These three sectors so dominate the US domestic financial scene that the entire system can no longer be considered stable.

However, a collapse in America is not the only national candidate to fill the slot of provoking a crash of crashes. A change of leadership in China, hostile to Western democracies, might create a serious disruption to global harmony with its attendant financial stresses and strains. Severe natural disasters could act as a triggering event. Another cause for international concern is a massive drought with a failure of the cereal harvests, as happened in the early 1970s. There are more than another billion mouths to feed since the major grain crises of the 1970s.

The Earthquake Shocker

Another long-threatened candidate is the possibility of vast dislocation in Japan following a formidably debilitating earthquake. There have been major earthquakes in the Tokyo region once every 70 years since the seventeenth century and by 1996, the next one was long overdue. On the last occasion, in 1923, Tokyo was razed and 140,000 people were killed. One estimate by Japan's Tokai Bank suggested damage could amount to Y80,000 billion. The catastrophe would have global implications as Japan repatriated funds from around the world to finance the massive reconstruction. The vast flow of Japanese capital that supports American debt and foreign subsidiaries in Britain, Europe and the South East Asian Tiger economies would rapidly dry up. With this huge cash withdrawal, stock and bond markets around the world might plunge, as happened in the turbulent mid-1970s when a great relocation of wealth was channelled from the oil-consuming nations to the oil-producing OPEC nations.

Silver Lining Possibilities

One source of encouragement to note among this catalogue of gloom is the obvious implication that a crash of crashes would, almost by definition, have to follow a boom of booms. However alarming the unexpected, it does not materialise out of the blue without any advance warning signals. The emergence of a monumental boom around the year 2000 is a central part of the strategic thinking of some key analysts. As far back as 1988, the famous Elliott Wave follower, Glenn Neely forecast the future course of the US stock market with the Dow Jones index exceeding 100,000 by the year 2060. In the UK, Quentin Lumsden, a highly reputed market analyst, running two popular and well-supported newsletters, also predicts a powerful bull market, taking the long-established FT-30 Share index from its March 1996 level of 2,800 to around 10,000 over the next few years.

Another important signal to bear in mind is that the chaos feature of a chain reaction effect is absolutely central to the momentum of major crash scenarios. If there is no chain reaction, even the most horrendous international crisis becomes containable. Look, for example, at the encouraging manner in which the authorities dealt with the aftershock of the October 1987 crash. As we noted in Chapter 11, after a string of blunders, and faced by the stark reality of global stock market collapses, they suddenly came to their collective senses and took the necessary avoiding action precisely to prevent just this emerging horror story that we have been outlining. Hopefully, if they can make the right decisions on one such crucial occasion, this clever trick should be repeatable.

Acting on the Signals

Joseph Schumpeter, the economist, pointed out in his book, *Business Cycles*, "It is easy to make profits when demand exceeds supply. It requires brains to manage in a recession." He was talking about managing a business, but the same philosophy applies just as forcefully to managing your investments. Once you have decided you have identified a possible bubble scenario and know approximately when it has reached phases five or six, you need to decide whether it is a relatively minor event or might herald a really significant global crash. Hopefully, if you have produced a reasonably full checklist of warning signals, the differences between these two eventualities should be obvious. If in doubt, however, always treat the impending collapse with serious respect. J. K. Galbraith had a pithy description of profits in the boom. "Genius," he wrote, "is a short memory in a bull market."

If you think the bubble will be easily contained, sell out a modest proportion of your holdings and put the money on deposit, awaiting the opportunity to return to the market once the débâcle has blown itself out. Alternatively, if you feel confident, you might follow the brilliant example of Richard Cantillon, who during the summer of 1720, went from one bubble to the next, making timely and exceptional profits in each one.

However, if you suspect the boom you are examining might end in a serious crash, it would be wise to sell out of all your holdings. Due to recent investor protection legislation, however, you should spread your cash widely, as a safety precaution. Legislation for investor protection in the banks and building societies only covers a certain modest amount per depositor in each account. If your total cash capital exceeds this level, you might suffer losses in a global crisis of confidence in the banking system, as you will not be fully covered by the compensation levels.

If you are feeling confident about your crash diagnosis, you might take out a suitable futures contract or a put option on the major index of the stock market you know most about. In a serious market collapse, this can produce enormous profits very rapidly. They might serve as a hedge if you are still holding shares in the falling market, hoping to stay in for the long term. What you lose on the value of your long-term portfolio, may be compensated for in good measure by the profits on the put option. As we have seen, the boom can move energetically up to the peak, but for sheer force of action, nothing is so dramatic as the selling cascade in a panic. However, in a crash of crashes scenario, there is no guarantee that brokers will not go bankrupt. In that event, payments may be frozen or never honoured.

Another useful idea is to convert your cash into a strong currency, which can withstand the international meltdown. It may be necessary to avoid the dollar if the cause of the crash is a loss of confidence in America's ability to honour its monumental debts. The appropriate currency will depend on the exact circumstances at the time. It might be the yen, the Deutschmark, the Swiss franc, or none of these. During the hyper-inflation of the 1930s in Germany, several investors, anxious to protect their dwindling capital, borrowed in depreciating German marks to buy dollars, gold or silver. They only changed back again into the German currency when money was needed to buy food and other necessities. Later in the inflationary spiral, however, the strong currency or gold holding would be sold and the loan repaid, at a value far below the borrowing price. This was the final trick that earned Cantillon his currency fortune, using his own capital rather than a loan, when he realised Law's attempts to force a revaluation of the French currency would fail.

Depending on the atmosphere prevailing, when a major crash occurs a holding of gold might be a good hedge although derivative instruments have recently tended to usurp the role that gold formerly played in periods of acute financial distress. However, nothing in the ever changing world of finance can be taken for granted. What happened in the past may be a poor guide to the future. In a crash of crashes, derivative instruments might be just as suspect as any other form of paper financial assets. Indeed, many commentators believe the massive weight of money now tied up in these derivative instruments could be a contributory factor to a future important international crisis.

All paper assets could be exposed to loss if some broking houses were to fail. Areas to avoid are any form of collective investment, unit or investment or mutual funds, in case there should be a massive default. Similarly, do not buy any shares, even if you think gold mines will prosper. You may be unable to sell at a realistic price if you suddenly need the cash. Another source of headache could be insolvency for the stock broker you have used. The proceeds of your sale might get frozen in a bankruptcy situation. Even when compensation is available, your funds could be out of reach for years.

As we have seen in the examples we studied in earlier chapters, some form of reconstruction inevitably follows a huge crash, but it can take months, if not years to agree terms of compensation and receive the payout. All the time you are waiting, there is the stress of uncertainty to overcome and the long delay which is bound to follow before some of your funds are finally restored to you. Compensation arrangements are highly unreliable and often take an inordinate amount of time and energy to effect.

Missing the Warning Signals

Suppose, however that you have the terrible misfortune to miss the critically important signal that is a prelude to disaster; there is still one final golden opportunity to contemplate. Every severe set-back has a silver lining. The crash is a wipeout to clear the decks of existing financial excesses at one gigantic stroke. Previous crash events have clearly shown that investors who stay in to the last can suffer a complete disaster, but then, this calamity is not likely to occur to well-prepared investors. After all, specifically to avoid this ugly fate, you have been reading this book!

And ultimately, we know, the phase transition for investors is a reversible process. During or after the crash, the cruel switch-back from irrational to rational states of investment attitudes takes place. This shift generates an overwhelming shock. It acts as a form of therapy since people awake from their communal madness to confront the nightmare reality of their broken dreams. Investors regain their senses. They might begin to appreciate again the notion of "fair value" but more probably the very idea of investing makes them shudder, as the experiences of Sir Isaac Newton and his South Sea losses relate.

Recovery Will Eventually Begin

Although the sequence of events in a depressing debt deflation will have to unfold before any real recovery can begin, the good news is that people are by nature optimistic. Pessimism has only a limited shelf life for normal human beings. People genuinely want to succeed. At some stage, the majority will start remembering that every set-back can throw up exciting new opportunities. These arise from the debris of the financial devastation when the tides of despondency reach a flood. Eventually, the majority are willing and able to rebuild their shattered lives, but it takes time.

Time is the Great Imponderable

In the lexicon of deterministic chaos events, the most imponderable factor of all is the element of time. One surprising feature of these crash scenarios is the curious behaviour of time. We noted in Chapter 3 that points on a chart might get squeezed together or pulled apart as this is a common feature of chaotic systems. Squeezing and stretching applies most characteristically to time; hence, it becomes the most capricious, unpredictable element we grapple with. The stretching of time will make a nonsense of all our careful calculations about when certain events should happen. Although crashes and bubbles can reach a rubicon stage when they have become deterministic and so will surely occur, their timing can remain hopelessly elusive. As ever, there is a chaos-based explanation for this time drag. In such immensely complex systems, some events can be unpredictably affected by occurences miles away. We saw this effect in the change of direction in the hurricane that was forecast to miss the southern coast of Britain in October 1987. By a chance fluke of timing, the hurricane paused and changed direction very slightly; massive unexpected damage to the southern counties resulted.

Because of this infuriating unpredictability in chaos-based systems, we may completely misread the signals. We might be absolutely right on our diagnosis for the crash, but still get caught out by it, because it sneaks up on us before we have time to act or, worse still, we think we have been mistaken in our analysis and relax our guard right at a crucial moment. We may then stay invested because we have abandoned our correct crash prognosis too soon.

Time is the most untrustworthy element in the chaos equation. You may be convinced that the crash is inevitable. It is, after all, deterministic once all the triggering mechanisms have been put into place. Yet even when the warning signs seem blindingly obvious, knowing the moment when it will unfold can be impossible to guess correctly. And this, as we know, is the essence of chaos. You must therefore be adequately prepared. Analyse all the possible warning signals, as we have reiterated above, and then be patient. Bide your time and wait for the drama to develop, but never forget your top priority is capital preservation. If you lose some of your potential profit but have retained your precious capital intact before the selling avalanche strikes, you will escape unscathed, ready to reinvest all your cherished cash into the next upturn which will surely follow, when the suffering finally abates.

Recognising the Signals

Sometimes, the impact of events can take far longer to unfold than you would imagine was reasonably possible. The momentum is quietly building under the surface, however. So when the activating trigger is accidentally pulled, the explosion is rapid, taking the crisis into its final active phase. Finely judging when this expected moment will arrive will clearly be extremely difficult. You might miss the opportunity to take the avoiding action you were planning if you get beguiled into holding on too long. This is what happened to many bank traders and hedge fund managers during the great bond market boom of 1993. As they discovered, you, in turn, might suddenly be overtaken by the rapidity with which the denouement finally arrives.

It is important, therefore, first to be able to recognise the emergence of a trigger event that might unleash the selling cascade. Perhaps even more important is to follow the advice of countless rational investors, from Nathan Rothschild to Bernard Baruch. Rothschild's famous explanation for how he amassed his wealth was encapsulated in this phrase: "I never buy at the bottom and I always sell too soon." Perhaps this is the best description we can give of the rational investor.

It may be difficult not to let the quixotic behaviour of time get the better of you, but remember, many serious investors, especially the outright doomsters, have warned of an impending crash of crashes for years, holding their money assets in reserve, waiting for this horror story to arrive. Among the most famous is Sir James Goldsmith, the great investor and entrepreneur. He was so convinced a massive bear market was about to overtake all Western civilisation, he put all his enormous wealth into gold bullion and gold mines, not in the least concerned that he had missed out on the enormous 1990s bull market.

Robert Beckman, another great investor, mistimed his forecasts of disaster, but was right in the general trend of events. He predicted a massive housing property bubble in Britain for the mid-1980s in his book, *The Downwave*. He was out by around six years in his timing, however, but his analysis of the looming property bubble, master-minded by mis-calculations by Chancellor of the Exchequer Nigel Lawson in 1987 and 1988, was very prescient in its detail. The poor timing hurt his reputa-tion, but this is a factor of the chaos-induced basis for these events. Judging the timing is the hardest trick of all.

A Summary of Signals: An Alphabet Alert

We have covered a large range of possible events that could produce the cluster of signals we are looking for to indicate a financial crisis is loom-ing. When the cluster is in place, we must look for the missing pieces which will complete the jig-saw puzzle. Looking for a simple mnemonic is one way of coping with the clutter of detail and the title of this chapter suggests a fun method of trying to cope with all the facts we need to remember. We can try an alphabet alert to list the signs were are search-ing for. We begin with a bundle of Bs.

As noted earlier in the chapter, the most important indicator for a coming collapse is the health of the long-dated securities – Treasury or Gilt-edged BONDS. Another vital clue is the BEHAVIOUR of the BULLS and BEARS. When everyone is buying, the moment will come when there is virtually no one left to BUY. Then the bears take command, and savage the market in their search for rampant profits, selling short as prices tumble. We have seen how crucial the BUTTERFLY EFFECT can be for kick-starting a demise into a chaos-induced collapse – a BUBBLE. If you find it complicated to remember all the warning signals listed here, this bundle of Bs alone should help you to scent the true whiff of trouble in good time to take avoiding action.

However, the game of alphabet alert can cover other letters as well, as you may have noticed above when we spoke of searching for signs. Here then is a short list, far from complete, to set you thinking on the alphabet alert road. It should help to remind you of the looming danger signals you should be looking for. My list is a snappy summary of the bubble process, alphabetically speaking:

> Boom build-up
> Butterflies begin
> Bulls beware
> Bonds break
> Bubbles Burst
> Chaos comes
> Crash collapse
> Cash is capital

Credit crunch
Debt deflation
Lengthy liquidation
Recovery renewal
Base-building begins

Understanding Chaos

One fascinating question is what will happen to the unpredictability of financial markets when their underlying chaos basis is better and hence, more widely, understood? Will it then be more difficult to make bumper profits from financial assets? The worry derives from a popular market maxim: when everyone knows something, it isn't worth knowing. We can look at the experience of weather forecasters, grappling with classic symptoms of chaos in the complex, capricious weather patterns that circle the earth. Undisputed mathematical evidence as far back as the 1960s supports the chaos credentials of the atmospheric weather, but even the use of tremendously advanced computing power and satellite station monitoring cannot completely eliminate rough conditions cropping up unannounced as yet.

Unexpected scientific discoveries can revolutionise our views of the world around us. When Lagrange said, "No one can rival Newton, for there is only one world and he discovered it," he hadn't reckoned on quantum mechanics or chaos theory. On the very long time scale, therefore, it is interesting to note the comparatively lengthy periods of time required for new scientific developments to enter the field of public awareness. Newton's masterly grasp of the mathematics underpinning classical science has been known for over 300 years. It forms a large part of the school science curriculum world-wide. We may not be able to give an instant correct definition of an electric dynamo, the force of gravity or the focal length of a lens, but Newtonian science is part of our traditional view of the Universe. By contrast, quantum mechanics, which upgraded that view, came into existence over 70 years ago; apart from a few cliché expressions, like quantum leap and cosmic rays, most people are still completely mystified by the inner workings of quantum theory, despite the fact that all the sophisticated technology of electronics and space travel are products of this remarkable 1920s scientific revolution. On these scientific-awareness timescales, therefore, chaos theory and the science of complexity are complete upstarts. They have only been taken seriously for the last three decades, which means the opportunities for benefiting financially from this new knowledge of behaviour in the financial markets still lies in the gift of a few "insiders", and will probably not become popular knowledge for decades to come.

So what can chaos theory teach us about preserving our precious capital from the disaster of a crash? First, we need to recognise when the unintentional actions of the financial authorities create classic chaos conditions so that we can act accordingly. Secondly, even the most experienced investment sophisticates and cautious long-term investors can sometimes become pure speculators seduced into imagining that increasing profits will continue indefinitely into the future. Are we going to be among them when the music suddenly stops? And thirdly, we need to understand that falling bond prices with rising interest rates sometimes result from the collapse of a chaos financial pump. They are simply the immediate fall-out of the whole process. They will have no rational meaning in terms of the fundamental outlook for the economy, future inflation or the solving of any other short-term problem. None of these fundamental issues is being addressed when a financial pump is raging or powering along towards its ultimate demise. Nor will they begin to play a serious role until the financial pump mechanism has completely unwound itself.

But as a final footnote, perhaps we should stress the key role played by muddle-headed people in authority. Something truly dramatic has to drive normally sober investors and serious-minded professionals from their naturally cautious mental state to become raving short-term speculators. This phase transition needs a suitable triggering event to set it alight. It cannot happen in a vacuum. Once the presiding authorities initiate a financial pump, we mere mortals do not stand a chance of staying aloof. Unless, of course, we know the rules of the game. So as a footnote to the alphabet alert, we need to remember that RULES that underpin events which superficially appear to be RANDOM are precisely what chaos thinking sets out to REVEAL. . . . Which brings us right back to where we began.

BIBLIOGRAPHY

Adams, D. K., *America in the Twentieth Century*, Cambridge University Press, 1967.

Allen, F. L., *Only Yesterday*, London: Harper, 1931.

The Beardstown Ladies Investment Club, *The Beardstown Ladies' Common-Sense Investment Guide*, New York: Hyperion, 1994.

Bak, P., and Chang, T., 'Earthquakes as a Self-Organized Critical Phenomenon', *Journal of Geophysical Research*, 94, B11, November 1989.

Bak, P. and Chen, K., 'Self-Organised Criticality', *Scientific American*, January, 1991.

Bak, P., Chen, K., Scheinkman, J. and Woodford, M., 'Aggragate Fluctuations From Independent Sectoral Shocks: Self-organized Criticality in a Module of Production and Inventory Dynamics', National Bureau of Economic Research, Working Paper No. 4241, 1992.

Beckman, R., *Crashes*, London: Grafton Books, 1990.

Beckman, R., *The Downwave: Surviving the Second Great Depression*, London and Sydney: Pan Books, 1983.

Blakey, G. G., *The Post-War History of the London Stock Exchange 1945 to 1992*, London: Mercury, 1993.

Bootle, R., *The Death of Inflation*, London: Nicholas Brealey, 1996.

Braudel, F., *Civilization & Capitalism: 15th–18th Century*, 3 vols., translated from the French, revised by Sian Reynolds, London: Collins, 1981.

Bruck, C., *The Predators' Ball*, New York: Simon & Schuster, 1989.

Cannon, L., *President Reagan: The Role of a Lifetime*, London & New York: Simon & Schuster, 1991.

Carswell, J., *The South Sea Bubble*, revised edn, London: Alan Sutton, 1993.

Chandler, D., *Marlborough as Military Commander*, 2nd edn, London: Batsford, 1979.

Cohen, B., *The Cultural Science of Man*, London: Codek Publications, 1988.

Cohen, B., 'Why Charts? What Chaos?', 'Market Technician', *The Journal of the STA*, Issue 16, April 1993.

Cook, T. A., *The Curves of Life*, London: Constable & Co., 1914.

Coveney, P. and Highfield, R., *Frontiers of Complexity*, London: Faber & Faber, 1995.

Davidson, J. D. and Rees-Mogg, Sir W., *Blood in the Streets: Investment profits in a world gone mad*, London: Sidgwick & Jackson, 1985.

Davies, P., *Other Worlds*, London: Sphere Books, 1982.

Davis, J. H., *The Kennedy Clan, Dynasty & Disaster*, London: Sidgwick & Jackson, 1985.

Dines, J., *The Invisible Crash*, New York: Random House, 1975.

"When Bears Run Wild", *The Economist*, April 1992.

Viscount Erleigh, *The South Sea Bubble*, New York: Putnam, 1933.

Fallon, I., *Billionaire*, London: Hutchinson, 1991.

Galbraith, J. K., *The Great Crash*, London: Hamish Hamilton, 1955.

Gifford, E., *Money Making Matters*, Cambridge: EBCSL Pubs, 1980.

Gilbert, M., *Winston Churchill, the wilderness years*, London: Macmillan, 1981.

Gleick, J., *Chaos*, New York: Penguin Books, 1987.

Graham, B., *The Intelligent Investor*, 4th edn, New York: Harper & Row, 1973.

Green, D., *Sarah, Duchess of Marlborough*, London: Collins, 1967.

Hall, N., (ed.), *The New Scientist Guide to Chaos*, London: Penguin Books, 1991.

Hillairet, J. *Dictionaire Historique des Rues de Paris*, edition de Minuet, 9th edn., 1985.

Hoover, H., *The Memoirs of Herbert Hoover: The Great Depression 1929 to 1941*, New York: Macmillan, 1952.

Hough, R., *Winston & Clementine: the triumph of the Churchills*, London: Bantam Press, 1990.

Houston, W., *Meltdown*, London: Smith Gryphon, 1993.

Houston, W., *Riding the Business Cycle*, London: Warner Books, 1995.

Hyde, H. M., *John Law*, London: W. H. Allen, 1969.

Johnson, J., *Princely Chandos; James Brydges 1674-1744*, London: Alan Sutton, 1984.

Johnson, J., *Excellent Cassandra: The Life and Times of the Duchess of Chandos*, London: Alan Sutton, 1981.

Joseph, J., *The Japanese; Strange but not Strangers*, London: Penguin Books, 1993.

Kindleberger, C. P., *Manias, Panics and Crashes*, London: Macmillan, 1978.

Lorie, J. H., Dodd, P., and Kimpton, M. H., *The Stock Market, Theories and Evidence*, 2nd edn, New York: Dow Jones-Irwin, 1985.

Lynch, P., *One Up on Wall Street*, New York: Simon and Schuster, 1989.

Mackay, C., *Extraordinary Popular Delusions and the Madness of Crowds*, New York: Harmony Books, 1980.

Malkiel, B. G., *A Random Walk Down Wall Street*, USA: W. W. Norton & Co, 1973.

Mandelbrot, B., "The Variation of Certain Speculative Prices", in Cootner, P. (ed.) *The Random Character of Stock Prices*, MIT Press, 1964.

Mandelbrot, B., *The Fractal Geometry of Nature*, New York: W. H. Freeman, 1982.

Marlow, J., *The Life and Times of George I*, London: Weidenfeld & Nicolson, 1973.

Marsh, P., *The Robot Age*, London: Sphere Books, 1982.

McLeod, H. D., *Theory and Practice of Banking With the Elementary Principles of Currency, Prices, Credit and Exchanges*, 5th edn, London: Longman & Co., 1892–93.

Millard, B. J., *Channel Analysis*, Cheshire: Qudos, 1990.

Millard, B. J., *Profitable Charting Techniques*, Cheshire: Qudos, 1991.

Murphy, A., *Richard Cantillou: Entrepreneur and Economist*, Oxford: Oxford University Press, 1988.

Naisbitt, J., and Aburdene, P., *Megatrends 2000*, London: Sidgwick & Jackson, 1990.

Pagels, H. R., *The Cosmic Code: Quantum physics as the language of nature*. London: Michael Joseph, 1983.

Peters, E. E., *Chaos and Order in the Capital Markets*, New York: John Wiley 1991.

Plumb, J. H., *Sir Robert Walpole: The making of a statesman*, London: Allen Lane The Penguin Press, 1956.

Prechter, Jnr R. R., and Frost, A. J., *Elliott Wave Principle*, 6th edn, New York: New Classics Library, 1990.

Prechter, Jnr R. R. (ed.) *The Major Works of R. N. Elliott*, 2nd edn, New York: New Classics Library, 1990.

Reading, B., *Japan, The Coming Collapse*, London: Weidenfeld & Nicolson, 1992.

Rostow, W. W., *The World Economy: History and Prospect*, Austin & London: Texas Press, 1978.

Schumpeter, J. A., *Business Cycles*, New York: McGraw-Hill, 1939.

Schumpeter, J. A., *The Theory of Economic Development*, Oxford: Oxford University Press, 1961.

Schwager, J. D., *Market Wizards*, New York: Harper & Row, 1990.

Scott Morton, W., *Japan: Its History and Culture*, 3rd edn, New York: McGraw-Hill, 1994.

Shennan, J. H., *Philippe, Duke of Orléans, Regent of France 1715 to 1723*. London: Thames & Hudson, 1979.

Stewart, I., *Does God Play Dice?*, London: Penguin Books, 1990.

Stewart, T. H., *How Charts Can Make You Money*, London: Woodhead-Faulkner, 1989.

Thomas, G., and Morgan-Witts, M., *The Day the Bubble Burst: a social history of the Wall Street Crash*, London: Hamish Hamilton, 1979.

Train, J., *The Midas Touch*, New York: Harper & Row, 1987.

Trump, D., *The Art of the Deal*, London: Century, 1987.

Tvede, L., *The Psychology of Finance*, Oxford: Oxford University Press, 1990.

Vaga, T., *Profiting From Chaos*, New York: McGraw-Hill, 1994.

van Duijn, J. J., *The Long Wave in Economic Life*, London: George Allen and Unwin, 1983.

Wagner, G. S., and Matheny, B. L., *Trading Applications of Japanese Candlestick Charting*. New York: John Wiley & Sons, 1994.

Waldrop, M. Mitchell, *Complexity, The Emerging Science at the Edge of Order and Chaos*, London: Viking, 1993.

White, E. N., (ed.), *Crashes and Panics: The lessons from history*. Illinois: Business One Irwin, 1990.

Wolfram, S., 'Computer Software in Science and Mathematics', *Scientific American*, September 1984.

INDEX

Murphy, Antoin 21, 42, 43, 147, 164, 173, 178, 184

Nakasone 325
Napoleon 157, 168
National Can 298
National City Bank 271, 272
National Recovery Administration 278
National Westminster Bank 285
natural disasters 365, 370
    see also weather
Neely, Glenn 371
negative equity 16
negative feedback 87, 93
Neilson, Robert 163
Netcom On-Line Communications
    Services 350
Netscape Communications 350
New Deal 278
New York Federal Reserve Bank 267
Newton, Sir Isaac 45, 46, 47, 71, 77, 79, 206, 219, 373, 377
Newtonian science, features of 79, 80
Nippon Housing Loan (NHL) 328
Nippon Warrant Fund 324
Niwayama, Mr Keiichiro 328
Nixon, President 366
Noailles, Duke of 160, 161
nonlinearity 64
    in 1929 crash 261-2, 266
    in chaos 81-2
    in gearing 82-3
    in South Sea Company 225-6
non-performing loans 16
Norman, Montagu 257
Northern Rock building society 345
Noyes, Alexander D. 269
NTT 54-7, 90, 308, 309
number drunk investors 60-1, 268

oil 369-70
    prices 282, 285, 289, 367, 369
Olympia & York 342, 343
Onoue, Ms Nui 326
Onslow, 1st Earl of 45
options 13, 180, 339
Orange Nassau, Princess Dowager
    Duchess of 220
order/disorder mixture 85-6

Orléans, Dowager Duchess of 21, 232
Orléans, Philippe, Duke of 20, 151, 154, 161-2
Oslow's insurance 212
Otake, Mrs Nobuko 56-7

Pagels, Heinz 75
panic, definition 4
Paradigm Technology 350
Paramount 50
Paramount-Famous-Lasky 48
Paris brothers 240
Payne, Will 41, 296
Peltz, Nelson 298
Penn Square Bank 285
Pentland, Duke of 244
Percival, Ian 73
Perelman, Ronald 54, 298
Personal Equity Plans (PEPs) 289
Peters, Edgar 108, 136
phase transition 373
    in 1929 crash 267-8
    in chaos 126-7
    for investors 131-2
    for investors at criticality 132-3
    in light 129-31
    in Mississippi Bubble 198
    in sand piles and lasers 127-8
    in South Sea Bubble 228-9
Pickens, T. Boone 298
plateau of prosperity 16
Plumb, J. H. 46, 47
Poincaré, Henry 79
Ponzi, Charles 256
Pope, Alexander 216
portfolio insurance 13, 294, 300
positive feedback 93, 111, 122, 248
    in 1987 crash 88, 290
    in chaos 86-8
    in Japanese Bubble 331-2
    in Mississippi Bubble 194
    in South Sea Bubble 226-7
Prèsses de la Cité, Les 52
Prévost, Abbé 154
Prigogine, Ilya 67, 86
private enterprise 7
privatisation 304-5
programmed trading 13, 300
property prices
    in Britain 291

Index compiled by Annette Musker